TOP 1000 VIDEOS

TO RENT OR BUY

SANDY ROBERTSON

foulsham
LONDON • NEW YORK • TORONTO • SYDNEY

foulsham
The Publishing House, Bennetts Close,
Cippenham, Berkshire, SL1 5AP, England

ISBN 0-572-02557-2

Copyright © 2000 Strathearn Publishing

All Rights Reserved

The Copyright Act prohibits (subject to certain very limited exceptions) the making of copies of any copyright work or of a substantial part of such a work including the making of copies by photocopying or similar process. Written permission to make a copy or copies must therefore normally be obtained from the publisher in advance. It is advisable also to consult the publisher if in any doubt as to the legality of any copying which is to be undertaken.

Printed in Great Britain by St Edmundsbury Press, Bury St Edmunds, Suffolk

To Janine, again!

Thank you to:

Tony at Psychotronic Video; Hollywood Flicks, Askew Road, London; Cathal Tohill; Zwemmers; Cinema Store; Cinema Bookshop; HMV, Oxford Street; Amanda at Aurum Press; Visual Entertainment; BMG Video; BBFC; Dave Lewis at The Associates; Stephi Downs at BFI Films; Brad Stevens; *Uncut?;* Edwin Pouncey; Barry Belasco, Wendy Hobson, Jane Hotson and the editorial team at Foulsham.

Contents

Introduction	7
How to Use This Book	9
Action and Adventure	13
Adult	42
Animation	55
Comedy	65
Drama	95
Epics	139
Family Entertainment	153
Gangsters	163
Hong Kong	181
Horror	188
Musicals	221
Romance	237
Science Fiction	256
Thrillers	279
TV and Special Interest	305
War	315
Westerns	329
World Greats	350
Further Reading	356
Index	358

Introduction

Welcome to our updated and revised second edition, including new titles, a whole new section, and updates and revisions to existing entries. This is not meant to be an encyclopaedia of movies on tape – rather, it's a snapshot of what we believe to be the very best and most popular videos currently available to rent or buy, guaranteeing you a good night's entertainment across a broad range of mainstream categories. So when you are looking for a video for an evening's viewing – or even if you arrive at the shop too late to grab a copy of the latest release – you know how to select the best. It's not a list of my personal favourites (although inevitably there is a degree of subjectivity in any selection and I have let a few of those slip in!), nor is it one of those dubious roll-calls of 'The Greatest Films of all Time' as defined by the critics. But it should ensure that every time you rent a video, you know you're getting one which you will enjoy rather than a disappointing piece of trash which doesn't live up to the blurb on its cover.

Take note that the selection does include Horror and Adult films. Our views on what is acceptable have modified considerably over the years, but you must, of course, use your own judgement when choosing tapes for you and your family. I have included the certificate ratings to help you in making appropriate choices.

I have also indicated where videos have been cut. Some readers informed me that the way to avoid censored videos is to subscribe to the *Film Four* channel, which claims to show films 'uncut ... no compromises', although in fact they admit that the ITC compels them to cut movies to the same level as the BBFC. Perhaps subscribers might like to point out this discrepancy ... with no compromises.

Buying and renting videos is big business these days as the presence of now-familiar big-name stores in our high streets testifies. Paradoxically, they actually present a real threat to viewer choice as we lose our friendly local video shops. You know the sort: the ones who will find that old Western you just *have* to see even though it's been out of print for years, or who will turn a blind eye when a regular customer brings back a tape a day late. Please support your local corner shops – we need them!

May I also suggest you complain if you're not happy with a tape? I see no reason why a tape costing £12.99 or more to buy should be vastly inferior in quality to a film taped off TV, yet that can be the case. You *can* make a difference. My complaint to Columbia TriStar about music left off *Lawrence Of Arabia* prompted an amended reissue (see page 148)!

We hope to continue to produce future editions of this book to expand the choice of videos and keep up to date with the constantly changing selection of video entertainment – so if you spot any errors of fact you can write to me care of the publisher. Similarly, write to me if there are any changes or improvements you wish to suggest – or any superb videos you feel should be considered for inclusion.

Now press 'REWIND' and 'PLAY'!

Sandy Robertson.

How to Use This Book

The reviews in this book are of videos which, as far as we're aware, are currently available to rent and/or buy in the UK. They are presented in categories broadly consistent with the shelf titles in most British stores (Westerns, Horror, Comedy etc.). If a film fits into more than a single genre, however, stores will often shelve copies of the same film in more than one location (*Annie Hall*, for example, might be found in both Romance and Comedy in some shops) – if in doubt, ask the assistants. Though we occasionally note newer formats like laserdisc and DVD, tape is still the dominant vehicle for home viewing in the UK.

Titles are listed alphabetically within each section, though definite/indefinite articles like 'The' and 'A' are ignored unless they are in a foreign language (hence a film beginning with the German 'Das' for 'The' would be listed under 'D'). Titles starting with numerals are placed in ascending numerical order, if they occur, before the As in each segment.

Reviews give the title, director, main stars, year of original production, the country of origin, video label, approximate running time, BBFC certificate and a rating (see overleaf) based on the artistic/ entertainment merit of the film. This is followed by a review, giving an outline of the plot, a short comment on performances, and so on. Where I thought it appropriate, I inserted details of USA Academy Awards (Oscars) gained, source material such as books or plays (unless stated otherwise, the book source normally has the same title as the film), movies related to the one under scrutiny, subtitles and so on. I've tried to include details of any related controversies, cuts, alternative versions and other anecdotal material. Cuts are normally made at the behest of the UK censor (BBFC), though sometimes with older films a choppy or abbreviated print is all that's available to the video labels.

The BBFC certificates below give you a guide on the suitability of the video for the family but you must use your own judgement. (Some tapes now list levels of sex, violence, etc. on the box.)

Uc   Universal: suitable for all, but especially for kids.
U   Universal: suitable for all.
PG   Parental Guidance: some scenes may be unsuitable for children.
12   For persons of 12 or over.
15   For persons of 15 or over.
18   For persons of 18 or over.
R18 Only sold from licensed sex shops to persons 18 or over.

There is no obligation to indicate on the box whether a video is a cut version, though this may change in the future. If you are on the internet, you can look up censor cuts on the BBFC website: http://www.bbfc.co.uk.

Each film is given a 'rating', although this is intended as a guide only as one person may not enjoy a '5' film even though ten others would rate it as the best they have seen in years.

1   Will have some cult appeal or historic merit, but not a 'great' film.
2   Not entirely successful, but worthwhile sequences or performances. Worth a look!
3   Solid entertainment, and certainly worth renting or buying.
4   A really good film, with great acting and visuals.
5   Top-notch stuff. Direction, performances and cinematography of the very highest order. A classic.

Films are assumed to be in colour. If they are in black and white, the indication 'B&W' is given. If a film is a mix of colour and monochrome, this will be shown as 'Col/B&W'.

Running times should be treated as a rough guide only, as they are not always precisely accurate on the video. They will not vary by more than a few minutes. The running times of films on UK VHS-PAL video and TV are about four per cent shorter as they are shown at a faster speed, though sources are often vague as to whether they take account of this when calculating timings. Tapes from France using the SECAM system will only play in black and white, and NTSC tapes from the US will not play at all unless you have a multi-standard VCR. Fortunately, these are now widely available.

The indication 'two-for-one' is used when a film is available on the same tape as (or on a separate tape, packaged with) another film; the two films should be sold at a lower price than one would normally expect to pay if they were bought separately. Some three-for-one tapes are now on sale.

The terms 'letterboxed' and 'widescreen' are interchangeable, and mean that the film is also available in an approximation of the original cinematic aspect ratio, with black areas above and below the picture on normal TV screens (the first term is based on the fact that a widescreen image resembles a letterbox). Most TVs are one-third wider than they are tall, but widescreen films can be well over twice as wide as they are high! Happily, widescreen TVs are now available. Sadly, I use the word 'approximation' because many firms seem to treat widescreen as a gimmick which allows them to charge more than for standard fullscreen 'pan-scan' or 'cropped' tapes which fill the TV screen but lose the extreme ends of the cinema picture. Sometimes the image is not letterboxed fully in order to minimise the black areas on the TV screen; or the film is blown up to make actors' faces closer, then re-cropped to make it look like the proper ratio. All these tricks ignore the fact that punters buy widescreen tapes precisely because they want the full cinema picture – and even firms which show the ratio on the back of the box don't always play the game. Many films are now shot in Super 35, where the black areas can be removed to reveal more picture area instead of pan-scan versions.

Films change label frequently and it's sometimes hard to tell just who owns a movie, so you may find a video has a different labelling on the box, in a catalogue, on the video itself, or on a cut-price version. It makes no difference to the viewing!

I've not noted catalogue numbers: you'll rarely need them to buy or rent a tape, though HMV sell the *Pure Video* catalogues of currently obtainable tapes, with numbers, for a few pounds each. Neither have I noted when a film is in stereo, nor when it is close-captioned for the deaf. Check the boxes for this information, noted by a speech balloon in the shape of a TV. The *Pure Video* catalogue also gives a good listing of tapes captioned for the deaf. (The captions are only revealed when accessed via a special unit.) For information contact the European Captioning Institute, Thurston House, 80 Lincoln Road, Peterborough PE1 2SN (01733 891391).

ACTION AND ADVENTURE

The big-selling cliché of the cinema of the moment is the movie as a 'rollercoaster ride'– as in *Twister* or *Speed* – with huge effects sequences. These are really an update of the terrible disaster-movie genre of the 1970s, albeit a lot more fun. Action and adventure come in many guises, from the James Bond pix to Indiana Jones, Batman and even the old classic Errol Flynn romps, but however you look at them, they are all pure entertainment, ideal for that evening in: sit back, relax, enjoy ...

48 HOURS

EDDIE MURPHY, NICK NOLTE, JAMES REMAR, ANNETTE O'TOOLE
WALTER HILL
USA (CIC) 1982
92m (18)

A cop gets a villain out of prison to help him on a case in this energetic action thriller, made before Nolte was a big star and when Murphy still made an effort to be amusing. There was a cut '15' certificate version around at one time, so check out the box for details. A sequel, *Another 48 Hours*, was a turgid re-run of the same situation.

THE ADVENTURES OF ROBIN HOOD

ERROL FLYNN, OLIVIA DE HAVILLAND, BASIL RATHBONE, CLAUDE RAINS
WILLIAM KEIGHLEY, MICHAEL CURTIZ
USA (WARNER) 1938
102m (U)

The definitive Technicolor version of the myths of the philanthropic bandit of Sherwood Forest and his battles with Prince John and his henchmen. Flynn still cuts a dash and makes the recent Kevin Costner attempt at the part look threadbare, while Rains and Rathbone are deliciously sneering villains. Only whey-faced Olivia de Havilland fails to stir the blood. Three Oscars, including one for Erich Wolfgang Korngold's magnificent score. Also on a two-for-one tape with Flynn's *Captain Blood* (see page 18).

TOP 1000 VIDEOS

THE AFRICAN QUEEN 5

HUMPHREY BOGART, KATHARINE HEPBURN, ROBERT MORLEY, PETER BULL

JOHN HUSTON

USA (FOX) 1951

105m (U)

Based on CS Forester's novel, this unusual film sees an oddball romance emerge when the slovenly captain of a small African steamboat is forced to rescue a prim spinster after her missionary brother dies. Laughs, thrills and heroism abound as they confront the might of the German navy in the days of World War One. Some find Hepburn's performance grating – you may be interested to know she's no less feisty in real life: I once asked her permission to write a poetry cycle based on her career and got a brisk note of refusal for my pains! Bogie won an Oscar for his role as the drunken skipper. Special box available.

AIR FORCE ONE 4

HARRISON FORD, GARY OLDMAN, DEAN STOCKWELL

WOLFGANG PETERSEN

USA (TOUCHSTONE) 1997

120m (15)

When America and her president are seen to be corrupt and ineffectual, the tried and true answer is to turn to the movies for new hope. As in *Independence Day* (see page 268), here we have a pres who can physically kick butt with the best of 'em when under attack. This time we have a nutball (Oldman) taking over the top man's plane in order to force the release of the leader of a small Soviet breakaway state – utter hooey, of course, but Ford (as the feisty pres) and Oldman (nasty in the extreme) do their stuff well and Petersen handles the tense action like a master.

ANACONDA 3

JENNIFER LOPEZ, JON VOIGHT, ICE CUBE, KARI WUHRER

LUIS LLOSA

USA (COLUMBIA TRISTAR) 1997

90m (15)

A TV crew looking to film a lost Amazon tribe pick up a stranger (Voight), whose secret agenda is to trap a legendary 40-foot snake that's worth a fortune. Voight goes over the top as the baddy and there are super CGI (computer-generated imagery) and animatronic snake FX. Terrific stuff if you don't take it seriously, which would be pretty much impossible anyway!

ACTION AND ADVENTURE

BACK TO THE FUTURE ⏱4

MICHAEL J FOX, CHRISTOPHER LLOYD, LEA THOMPSON
ROBERT ZEMECKIS
USA (CIC) 1985
111m (PG)

Wacky time-travel adventure about teenager Marty McFly and his interference in the lives of his parents via a mad professor who turns one of the ill-fated De Lorean sports cars into a temporal racer. Back in the past, the kid invents distorted heavy guitar rock ten years too early. Eat your heart out Jimi Hendrix! Oscar for SFX. Available in widescreen boxed edition with both sequels and a documentary.

BACK TO THE FUTURE PART 2 ⏱2

MICHAEL J FOX, CHRISTOPHER LLOYD, LEA THOMPSON
ROBERT ZEMECKIS
USA (CIC) 1989
103m (PG)

Lacklustre sequel to the first film, shot back-to-back with Part 3 to save cash – it's fun but a slight disappointment after the original.

BACK TO THE FUTURE PART 3 ⏱3

MICHAEL J FOX, CHRISTOPHER LLOYD, MARY STEENBURGEN, LEA THOMPSON
ROBERT ZEMECKIS
USA (CIC) 1989
113m (PG)

Against all expectations, this third part of the saga (shot at the same time as Part 2 for reasons of economy) represented a partial return to form for our heroes: McFly finds himself in the old West, with all the cowpoke-spoofing nonsense one might expect that to entail. A good send-off for the series.

BATMAN 🎬 4

★	MICHAEL KEATON, JACK NICHOLSON, KIM BASINGER, JACK PALANCE, MICHAEL GOUGH
🎬	TIM BURTON
	USA/UK (WARNER) 1989
⏱	121m (15)

Noting recent adult-oriented comics which returned Batman to his dark roots, Hollywood let young director Burton loose with this disturbing, perverse version of the antics of the cowled detective. A million miles from the primary colours of the camp 1960s TV show, with Oscar-winning sets and a hilarious scene-stealing Jack Nicholson as The Joker, this is not a movie for young viewers. Widescreen available. Also boxed with *Batman Returns*.

BATMAN FOREVER 🎬 2

★	VAL KILMER, JIM CARREY, TOMMY LEE JONES, NICOLE KIDMAN
🎬	JOEL SCHUMACHER
	USA (WARNER) 1995
⏱	115m (PG)

Third (and worst) of the current series of big-screen adventures for the Caped Crusader, with Val Kilmer taking over from Michael Keaton in the lead, and a change of director. Carrey does a typically manic Riddler, but the stars and the effects are stronger than the storyline. Widescreen available.

BATMAN RETURNS 🎬 3

★	MICHAEL KEATON, DANNY DeVITO, MICHELLE PFEIFFER, CHRISTOPHER WALKEN
🎬	TIM BURTON
	USA (WARNER) 1992
⏱	126m (15)

If anything, this sequel to the first film is even darker: The Penguin, known to comics fans as a tuxedoed twit, is here shown as a bitter creature with flippers for hands. Sick enough to alienate the studio, their sponsor Burger King and the film's intended audience, but cleverly made. As noted above, *Batman* and *Batman Returns* are available in a boxed set.

BATMAN AND ROBIN 🎬 2

★	GEORGE CLOONEY, ALICIA SILVERSTONE, CHRIS O'DONNELL, UMA THURMAN, ARNOLD SCHWARZENEGGER
🎬	JOEL SCHUMACHER
	USA (WARNER) 1997
⏱	120m (PG)

Fourth Batman flick, and the second under Schumacher's direction, but despite heart-throb Clooney in the lead and the gallery of big-name villains it does not live up to the splendidly macabre first film in the series. Available in a widescreen special boxed edition.

ACTION AND ADVENTURE

BLADE [3]

- WESLEY SNIPES, STEPHEN DORFF, TRACI LORDS, UDO KIER
- STEPHEN NORRINGTON
- USA (ENTERTAINMENT) 1998
- 115m (18)

Occasionaly dazzling, this comic adaptation stars Snipes as a human/vampire hybrid who can roam around in the daylight and who therefore makes a nifty slayer of the undead baddies. He's fighting an attempt by the vampires to take over the world and unleash their god on mankind, so his, er, blade goes snickersnack and computerised blood flies all over the shop. Rather empty stuff, but impressive to look at the first time round. I'm pretty sure the BBFC used their own blades here and there, though I have no specific details.

BLUE THUNDER [4]

- ROY SCHEIDER, WARREN OATES, MALCOLM McDOWELL, CANDY CLARK
- JOHN BADHAM
- USA (SPEARHEAD) 1983
- 105m (15)

Excitingly staged drama about a super helicopter and shenanigans surrounding same. Scheider and smug McDowell are great as the pilot and his old forces adversary (now the big bad boss) respectively. Lots of impressive swooping and crashing. Inspired a TV series of poor quality, but this original is Hollywood craftsmanship at its best.

BOILING POINT [3]

- WESLEY SNIPES, DENNIS HOPPER, LOLITA DAVIDOVICH, VIGGO MORTENSEN
- JAMES B HARRIS
- USA (4-FRONT) 1992
- 89m (15)

Snipes is developing into one of the few reliable black action stars possessed of genuine acting ability and an appeal which crosses racial divides. This revenge thriller was one of his earlier hits and also boasts a fine support turn from movie madman Dennis Hopper.

BROKEN ARROW [4]

- JOHN TRAVOLTA, CHRISTIAN SLATER, SAMANTHA MATHIS, DELROY LINDO
- JOHN WOO
- USA (FOX) 1996
- 86m (15)

Hong Kong action director Woo has had some trouble translating his hyperkinetic style into the more regimented Hollywood way of working, but this is a pretty agreeable compromise. Travolta is a turncoat intent on killing his pal (Slater) and hijacking their plane full of atomic missile warheads. Plenty of nail-biting moments and furious action, even if it doesn't quite match the insane delirium of Woo's best Hong Kong pix such as *The Killer* (see page 185). 'Broken Arrow', incidentally, is allegedly the military term for an aircraft lost while carrying nuclear bombs. Widescreen available.

CAPTAIN BLOOD 🎬4

ERROL FLYNN, OLIVIA DE HAVILLAND, BASIL RATHBONE, LIONEL ATWILL

MICHAEL CURTIZ

USA (WARNER) 1935 B&W

94m (PG)

Spirited version of Raphael Sabatini pirate story, with the same three stars who went on to great success in *The Adventures Of Robin Hood* (see page 13). Duels, ruffled shirts, and many swashes are buckled (or should that be 'buckles are swashed'?). This is apparently a cut print – the original cinema release is listed at 119m. Also on a two-for-one tape with *The Adventures Of Robin Hood* (see page 13).

CLEAR AND PRESENT DANGER 🎬3

HARRISON FORD, WILLEM DAFOE, ANNE ARCHER, JAMES EARL JONES

PHILIP NOYCE

USA (CIC) 1994

136m (12)

Ford returns as Jack Ryan, the CIA character he played in *Patriot Games* (see page 34) – also essayed by Alec Baldwin in *The Hunt For Red October* (see page 26) in another flick based on Tom Clancy's series of novels. Competent rather than masterful, but a reliable cast just about carry it off.

CLIFFHANGER 🎬3

SYLVESTER STALLONE, JOHN LITHGOW, MICHAEL ROOKER

RENNY HARLIN

USA (GUILD) 1993

106m (15)

A breathtaking opening signals what to expect in this action adventure about mountain-rescue daredevil Stallone on the trail of bank heisters. There are some superb stunts and Lithgow is a great slimy villain. An efficient piece of enjoyable nonsense. Cut by BBFC.

CON AIR 🎬4

NICOLAS CAGE, JOHN MALKOVICH, JOHN CUSACK, STEVE BUSCEMI, COLM MEANEY, VING RHAMES, RACHEL TICOTIN

SIMON WEST

USA (TOUCHSTONE) 1997

111m (18)

Spectacular action movie, with Cage as an ex-military hero about to be released from jail after serving time for killing a thug who menaced his wife. Unfortunately he hitches a ride home on a plane carrying psychos like Cyrus the Virus (Malkovich) and serial killer Garland Green (Buscemi), and a hijack ensues. The only dubious element is the ending, hinting that vile but witty Green deserves escape and a chance at freedom because he spares a small girl.

ACTION AND ADVENTURE

CONAN THE BARBARIAN [3]

- ARNOLD SCHWARZENEGGER, SANDAHL BERGMAN, JAMES EARL JONES, MAX VON SYDOW
- JOHN MILIUS
- USA (FOX) 1982
- 121m (15)

Fascist individualism as filtered through the old pulp-mag tales of Robert E Howard's sword 'n' sorcery hero, here incarnate in musclebound Arnie. Spectacularly mounted, but Milius just doesn't have the magical touch needed – compared to the 1960s Italian 'Hercules' films of the likes of Mario Bava and Vittorio Cottafavi starring Arnie's hero Reg Park (see *Hercules Conquers Atlantis*, page 146), there's something lacking. Still well worth watching though. Available in widescreen.

CONAN THE DESTROYER [3]

- ARNOLD SCHWARZENEGGER, GRACE JONES, MAKO, WILT CHAMBERLAIN
- RICHARD FLEISCHER
- USA (ENTERTAINMENT) 1984
- 96m (15)

Fleischer is more adept at this kind of cod-historical effort than Milius but it's a pity he wasn't hired to do the first pic – this is tired stuff, yet still beautiful-looking for all that.

DANTE'S PEAK [3]

- PIERCE BROSNAN, LINDA HAMILTON, CHARLES HALLAHAN
- ROGER DONALDSON
- USA (CIC) 1997
- 104m (12)

Volcano films seem to be a minor Hollywood fetish just now, and this average disaster movie is nothing more than a competent piece of work. It remains to be seen whether or not Pierce Brosnan can parlay his James Bond success into a wider career of megastar dimensions. Issued with some behind-the-scenes footage as a bonus.

DAYLIGHT [3]

- SYLVESTER STALLONE, DAN HEDAYA, VIGGO MORTENSEN, CLAIRE BLOOM
- ROB COHEN
- USA (CIC) 1997
- 110m (12)

Above-average Stallone action film, with the star as a disgraced fellow proving his heroic stature by leading folks trapped in a New York river tunnel to safety. Akin to the formula of the disaster movies of yore, but superior in SFX and execution. The end is ridiculous, but so what?

DELIVERANCE 🎬 5

⭐ JON VOIGHT, BURT REYNOLDS, NED BEATTY, RONNY COX

🎬 JOHN BOORMAN

USA (WARNER) 1972

⏱ 109m (18)

Four city guys take a canoeing trip into backwoods wilderness only to be stalked by degenerate hillbillies. The message (if there is one) appears to be that men who act macho and 'in control' are not always the ones with the will to survive when things get serious. The male rape sequence still packs a punch though very little is actually shown. Now in a new, pristine widescreen version.

DEMOLITION MAN 🎬 3

⭐ SYLVESTER STALLONE, WESLEY SNIPES, SANDRA BULLOCK, NIGEL HAWTHORNE

🎬 MARCO BRAMBILLA

USA (WARNER) 1994

⏱ 111m (15)

Daft but sporadically dazzling action flick set in the future, a peaceful have-a-nice-day world where the only means of coping with a crook freed from suspended animation (Snipes) is to unleash his also-frozen police nemesis (Stallone). Really, this comes into the so-bad-it's-good category, with costumes and story like an old TV *Blake's 7* episode. Very violent. Enjoy! Cut by BBFC.

DICK TRACY 🎬 2

⭐ WARREN BEATTY, AL PACINO, MADONNA, DUSTIN HOFFMAN, PAUL SORVINO

🎬 WARREN BEATTY

USA (TOUCHSTONE) 1990

⏱ 103m (PG)

Oscars for sets, make-up and the Sondheim tune 'Sooner or Later' were well deserved as Pacino mugging away madly under a ton of weird latex make-up and the primary-coloured cityscapes and costumes makes it all very watchable. Unfortunately, Beatty's re-creation of the pulp comic detective hero is wooden in places while Madonna wishes she was Marilyn Monroe.

ACTION AND ADVENTURE

DIE HARD 5

BRUCE WILLIS, BONNIE BEDELIA, WILLIAM ATHERTON, ALAN RICKMAN

JOHN McTIERNAN

USA (FOX) 1988

126m (18)

This was the movie that made TV actor Willis a big-screen star. He's an off-duty cop, visiting his estranged wife's LA offices for Christmas, who stumbles into a robbery-and-hostage situation. Willis is charismatic as the outnumbered, outgunned guy, while Alan Rickman nearly runs away with the film as the wily, callous terrorist robber. A key 80s film which never loses the human element amongst the gunfire and explosions. There have been two sequels: the first, *Die Hard 2* (aka *Die Harder*) came about by accident when the studio noted a story it had bought was too similar to a *Die Hard*-type plot. Solution? Just change the character to that of Willis in the first pic and film it as a sequel! Much better was *Die Hard With A Vengeance*, but the first movie remains the only really classic action picture of the three. Widescreen.

DIRTY HARRY 5

CLINT EASTWOOD, HARRY GUARDINO, JOHN VERNON, RENI SANTONI, ANDY ROBINSON

DON SIEGEL

USA (WARNER) 1971

98m (18)

Originally a vehicle for Frank Sinatra, this super-duper action film has Clint as likeable rogue cop 'Dirty' Harry Callahan, taking on a psycho terrorising San Francisco and its supposedly lame bosses, the police chief and mayor. Condemned as right-wing by some, mainly due to the fact that the psychopath (ably played by Robinson) had a peace symbol on his belt. I think we can assume that was meant as an ironic touch – at least I hope so! I've heard this was much cut by the studio, but there's no mention of this in Don Siegel's autobiography, *A Siegel Film* (Faber). Many sequels, none as entertaining as this tough classic. Now sold in widescreen.

THE DOGS OF WAR 🎬3

CHRISTOPHER WALKEN, TOM BERENGER, COLIN BLAKELY, JO BETH WILLIAMS

JOHN IRVIN

UK (WARNER) 1980

114m (15)

Frederick Forsyth's novel is the basis for this story of double-dealings and mercenaries in contemporary Africa, with Walken a bit too young and clean as the killer-with-a-conscience. He's always an arresting actor, however, and workman-like direction from Irvin and a good support cast make for a flick that hardly deserves its bad reputation.

DR NO 🎬5

SEAN CONNERY, URSULA ANDRESS, BERNARD LEE, JOSEPH WISEMAN

TERENCE YOUNG

UK (MGM/UA) 1962

105m (PG)

The first of the never-ending series based on Ian Fleming's spy hero James Bond was quite a low-budget affair – but with the way the stories later became swamped in gadgetry this may have been a blessing in disguise. Connery is still the only 007 for me, and this tale of a criminal genius in Jamaica remains one of his best. See also *Goldfinger* (page 26), *Thunderball* (page 40) and *You Only Live Twice* (page 278). All the 'Bonds' have been made available recently in digitally remastered versions, and widescreen. In the case of this film, such letterboxing is somewhat superfluous as it wasn't lensed in a true widescreen ratio.

DROP ZONE 🎬3

WESLEY SNIPES, GARY BUSEY, YANCY BUTLER, MICHAEL JETER

JOHN BADHAM

USA (CIC) 1994

97m (15)

Reliable action director Badham does a competent job on this sky-diving effort, released around the same time as *Terminal Velocity* (see page 39), a broadly similar movie. This is marginally the better film, mainly due to Snipes as the good guy and Busey as the twitchy leader of an airborne team of dangerous crooks.

ACTION AND ADVENTURE

THE EDGE

| ANTHONY HOPKINS, ALEC BALDWIN, ELLE MacPHERSON |
| LEE TAMAHORN |
| USA (FOX) 1997 |
| 113m | (15) |

Anthony Hopkins suspects his glammy young wife (supermodel Elle MacPherson) just might be in cahoots with her fashion photographer pal, Alec Baldwin, in a plan to bump him off. She'd then inherit his cash and live happily ever after with the handsome swine. However, just as Hopkins brings up the subject to his nemesis, the light plane the duo are flying in crashes in a wintry forest wilderness. Now they must band together against the elements (and a giant bear intent on eating them), while still keeping an eye on each other for treachery. A fast-moving thriller with plenty of action that'll keep you entertained all the way. Right to the edge, in fact.

THE EIGER SANCTION

| CLINT EASTWOOD, GEORGE KENNEDY, JACK CASSIDY, VONETTA McGEE |
| CLINT EASTWOOD |
| USA (CIC/4-FRONT) 1975 |
| 113m | (15) |

Improbably set-up spy-actioner has Clint as the agent brought out of retirement to spot a traitor on a climbing jaunt. Lots of odd touches, such as Eastwood being paid in artworks, Cassidy as a gay with a poodle that's as camp as he is, and so on. Based on a John Trevanian novel. Seems to be cut, as original running time is noted at 125m.

EMPEROR OF THE NORTH

| LEE MARVIN, ERNEST BORGNINE, KEITH CARRADINE, ELISHA COOK Jnr |
| ROBERT ALDRICH |
| USA (FOX) 1973 |
| 119m | (15) |

Also known as *Emperor Of The North Pole*, this exciting movie by cult director Aldrich concerns the attempt by hobo Marvin to ride vicious rail-guard Borgnine's train in revenge for his brutality against other tramps. Plenty of heart-in-mouth-moments.

ESCAPE FROM LA

KURT RUSSELL, STACY KEACH, STEVE BUSCEMI, PETER FONDA

JOHN CARPENTER

USA (CIC) 1996

96m (15)

Virtually a blow-by-blow remake of the earlier (and superior) *Escape From New York* (see below): Russell is despatched into the city/prison on an important mission. Cynical and lacking in imagination, though it has better stars than it deserves and always looks good.

ESCAPE FROM NEW YORK

KURT RUSSELL, LEE VAN CLEEF, ISAAC HAYES, ERNEST BORGNINE, DONALD PLEASENCE

JOHN CARPENTER

USA (POLYGRAM) 1981

106m (15)

I suppose when this was made, 1997 seemed far off – it predicted that New York would by then be a dumping ground for incorrigibles, given the choice of painless death or fending for themselves in a rancid Big Apple. Russell is promised a third option: freedom if he goes in and rescues the stranded US President, with the added incentive of a timed explosive planted in his neck to make him return as planned. Sprawling, cynical and fun. The recent *Escape From LA* (see above) is virtually a remake.

FACE/OFF

NICOLAS CAGE, JOHN TRAVOLTA, GINA GERSHON, JOAN ALLEN

JOHN WOO

USA (TOUCHSTONE) 1997

133m (18)

After *Broken Arrow* (see page 17) expat Hong Kong action stylist Woo really gets into his stride with this absurd-but-wonderful tale of Cage swapping faces and mannerisms with Travolta in a cat-and-mouse game of secret agents v terrorists. It's a hoot to see the two actors trying to ape each other's tics in this meld of *Eyes Without A Face* (see page 199) and James Bond – insanely inventive entertainment with Woo managing to translate the 'anything goes' Hong Kong feel to the USA. Cut by BBFC.

FIREFOX

CLINT EASTWOOD, FREDDIE JONES, WARREN CLARKE, NIGEL HAWTHORNE

CLINT EASTWOOD

USA (WARNER) 1982

121m (15)

Thrill-a-minute tale which starts out as a complicated espionage story until Clint reaches his destination in the heart of Russia, when it becomes a fine adventure flick as he has to steal a new computer-controlled MIG jet. Great special effects in this adaptation of the Craig Thomas novel. Sadly only available in a pan-scan and cut version, the original running time being 137m.

ACTION AND ADVENTURE

FIRST BLOOD

SYLVESTER STALLONE, RICHARD CRENNA, DAVID CARUSO, BRIAN DENNEHY

TED KOTCHEFF

USA (POLYGRAM) 1982

89m (15)

The initial Rambo movie, based on David Morrell's novel, is a solid action thriller with a downbeat feel quite different from its fantasy-type sequels. Sly is a war hero who objects to being thrown out of a town just for looking a bit dodgy, and minor conflict with the law soon escalates. Has a point to make.

FLESH AND BLOOD

RUTGER HAUER, JENNIFER JASON LEIGH, RONALD LACEY, JACK THOMPSON

PAUL VERHOEVEN

HOLLAND/SPAIN/USA (4-FRONT) 1985

122m (18)

Down-and-dirty epic of sex and violence in medieval times. Realistically nasty stuff with lots of action from the director who went on to major Hollywood success with *RoboCop* (see page 272) and *Total Recall* (see page 277). Hauer is devilish fun and Lacey has a ripe cameo as a grimy priest.

GOLDENEYE

PIERCE BROSNAN, SEAN BEAN, ISABELLA SCORUPCO, JOE DON BAKER

MARTIN CAMPBELL

UK/USA (MGM/UA) 1995

124m (12)

This first Bond movie with Brosnan in the role marks a return to form for the series – it is certainly better than any of the risible Roger Moore vehicles, which treated the series like a 'Carry On' comedy romp. The stunts are genuinely clever rather than simply relying on bigger and bigger explosions, the story is acceptably convoluted, the support more than mere cannon fodder and Brosnan has a hint of Connery's wry glint. Great! Cut by BBFC for film and again for tape, probably so that makers could sell to a broader audience.

GOLDFINGER 5

SEAN CONNERY, HONOR BLACKMAN, GERT FROBE, SHIRLEY EATON, HAROLD SAKATA

GUY HAMILTON

UK (MGM/UA) 1964

105m (PG)

Possibly the best 'Bond' film, where spectacle was on the up but the technology hadn't yet dwarfed the plot. Great scenes: Ms Eaton murdered by being painted in suffocating gold; Bond having a laser aimed at his groin and asking the villain of the piece (who plans to rob Fort Knox) if he expects him to talk: 'No, Mr Bond, I expect you to *die!*'; the fight between Bond and Oddjob (Sakata) with his razor-rimmed bowler; and the crooked golf match. The only thing that might offend modern audiences, even when making allowances for the pic's era, is the idea that the naughtily named Pussy Galore (Blackman) is 'cured' of her implied lesbianism by big, hunky Bond! Letterboxed and digitally remastered. See also *Thunderball* (page 40), *Dr No* (page 22) and *You Only Live Twice,* (page 278). Latest incarnation of James is Pierce Brosnan in *GoldenEye* (see page 25) and *Tomorrow Never Dies* (see page 40).

HIGHLANDER 3

CHRISTOPHER LAMBERT, SEAN CONNERY, CLANCY BROWN, HUGH QUARSHIE

RUSSELL MULCAHY

UK/USA (WARNER) 1986

111m (15)

This moderately entertaining story about duelling immortal warriors has become something of a cult. The UK and USA versions are different, and the director recently combined elements of both for a special laserdisc cut. It inspired sequels and a TV series, which seems strange as it wasn't a mega-blockbuster. Connery and Lambert carry it off, though. Widescreen available.

THE HUNT FOR RED OCTOBER 3

SEAN CONNERY, ALEC BALDWIN, TIM CURRY, SCOTT GLENN

JOHN McTIERNAN

USA (CIC) 1990

129m (PG)

Tom Clancy's novel inspired this tale of a Russian captain who defects and has to convince the West that he wants to hand over his state-of-the-art stealth submarine to them – to some extent it's like an underwater *Firefox* (see page 24). Connery is no Russki ('We shail into hishtory') but he has authority and star magnetism. Baldwin's CIA man character has also been played by Harrison Ford in *Patriot Games* (see page 34) and *Clear And Present Danger* (see page 18). Widescreen available.

ACTION AND ADVENTURE

INDIANA JONES & THE LAST CRUSADE [3]

- HARRISON FORD, SEAN CONNERY, DENHOLM ELLIOTT, JULIAN GLOVER
- STEVEN SPIELBERG
- USA (CIC) 1989
- 127m (PG)

Third 'Indie' epic returns to the Nazi period of his début as our hero searches for the Holy Grail. Some stunning sequences and gnarly support from Connery as Jones's dad. Boxed set of all three films available in widescreen. (Note: the late River Phoenix plays adolescent Indie in an opening segment that provided the impetus for the *Young Indiana Jones* TV series.)

INDIANA JONES & THE TEMPLE OF DOOM [2]

- HARRISON FORD, KATE CAPSHAW, KE HUY QUAN
- STEVEN SPIELBERG
- USA (CIC) 1984
- 118m (PG)

The rogue archaeologist goes to India. Not a patch on the first film, *Raiders Of The Lost Ark* (see page 36), due to horrific imagery that may put kids off. Cut by BBFC. Boxed set of all three 'Indie' pix available, also in widescreen.

THE ITALIAN JOB [3]

- MICHAEL CAINE, NOEL COWARD, BENNY HILL, RAF VALLONE
- PETER COLLINSON
- UK (CIC/4-FRONT) 1969
- 96m (PG)

Cult adventure about Brit villains pulling off a robbery in Italy with a fleet of Mini Minors. The stunts are delightful and amazing, while Coward camps up his cameo as a jailed crime lord. Dated.

THE JACKAL [4]

- BRUCE WILLIS, RICHARD GERE, SIDNEY POITIER, DIANE VENORA
- MICHAEL CATON-JONES
- USA (CIC) 1998
- 119m (18)

Loose updating of *The Day Of The Jackal* (see page 287), now turned into an action romp full of loud bangs and sensationalism (Willis's first screen kiss *with a man*.) Mercilessly panned by the critics on its release, this is actually good, solid, entertaining fun.

27

JAWS

ROY SCHEIDER, ROBERT SHAW, RICHARD DREYFUSS, MURRAY HAMILTON

STEVEN SPIELBERG

USA (CIC) 1975

118m (PG)

Peter Benchley's novel about small-town politics and relationships affected by a killer shark is here presented as a gripping thrill-machine that is tense and startling by turns. Spielberg is allegedly planning a *Jaws* remake or special edition. Oscars include one for the haunting John Williams score. Widescreen. Cut for film by BBFC.

THE JEWEL OF THE NILE

MICHAEL DOUGLAS, KATHLEEN TURNER, DANNY DeVITO, SPIROS FOCAS

LEWIS TEAGUE

USA (FOX) 1985

101m (PG)

Sequel to *Romancing The Stone* (see page 37), same great cast, but not a patch on the original. Typical Hollywood logic: a film is a success, so they make it all over again and hope it'll be another hit. Very light, but nonetheless enjoyable.

JOURNEY TO THE CENTER OF THE EARTH

JAMES MASON, PAT BOONE, ARLENE DAHL, DIANE BAKER

HENRY LEVIN

USA (FOX) 1959

126m (U)

Energetic rendering of the Jules Verne classic about an expedition to the earth's core, which is depicted as a world of marvels. The art direction, Bernard Herrmann's score and Mason's acting make it perfect for kids of all ages from nine to 90, but using real lizards instead of animation for the dinosaur sequences was a mistake. It's a shame that this is released as an 'All-time Great', but not in its original CinemaScope framing.

ACTION AND ADVENTURE

JURASSIC PARK 🎬4

⭐ SAM NEILL, LAURA DERN, JEFF GOLDBLUM, RICHARD ATTENBOROUGH

🎬 STEVEN SPIELBERG

USA (CIC) 1993

⏱ 126m — PG

A Michael Crichton story of a theme park on an island off Costa Rica, run by geneticists and featuring live dinosaurs created from ancient DNA (extracted from prehistoric blood samples obtained via the guts of mosquitoes trapped in amber). Mad idea, but you'll believe it when you see the mix of animatronics and computer images used to create the dinos – which run wild just as the park is being road-tested. There are holes in the plot: at least one strand about a sick saurian is simply dropped and never returned to, but with all the excitement you'll hardly notice. Sequel, *The Lost World* (Sir Arthur Conan Doyle will turn in his grave), is out now (see page 31). Widescreen available – though I believe the image has possibly been blown up within the frame to make it more readable on small TVs. This was certainly the case with the USA tape and disc release. Though the film has a PG cert, there's an added note that some scenes may be too intense for some young viewers.

THE KILLER ELITE 🎬4

⭐ JAMES CAAN, ROBERT DUVALL, BURT YOUNG, BO HOPKINS, GIG YOUNG

🎬 SAM PECKINPAH

USA (MGM/UA) 1975

⏱ 122m — 18

P eckinpah's bizarre version of Robert Rostand's novel about conflict between renegade spies and their ex-employers is a mad, violent tale. The director's preferred ending, which wasn't used, had a dead character coming back to life as if to indicate that the whole movie was a joke! In my book, even minor Sam Peckinpah is great Sam Peckinpah.

LEGEND 🎬3

⭐ TOM CRUISE, TIM CURRY, MIA SARA, DAVID BENNENT

🎬 RIDLEY SCOTT

UK (WARNER) 1985

⏱ 90m — PG

S cott's attempt to film an original myth rather than an extant fable is enchanting to look at, not least due to devilish Curry in his outsize red horns as he stalks the last unicorn in order to bring on an age of darkness. There are two versions with two entirely different music scores. BBC TV often shows the US version.

LETHAL WEAPON

MEL GIBSON, DANNY GLOVER, GARY BUSEY, TOM ATKINS
RICHARD DONNER
USA (WARNER) 1987
105m (18)

Action-packed story of unhinged policeman and the effects of his demented, near-suicidal ways on his partner. Lots of mayhem, bangs and whizzes made for a smash hit, propelled by Gibson's star power and his interaction with Glover. Ongoing sequels (see below). Available in widescreen.

LETHAL WEAPON 2

MEL GIBSON, DANNY GLOVER, JOE PESCI, PATSY KENSIT
RICHARD DONNER
USA (WARNER) 1989
109m (18)

Formulaic sequel to the first film. Our dynamic duo are up against drug-dealing diplomats, while Gibson finds time for romance with Kensit. Humour is added to the mix by Pesci. Widescreen available.

LETHAL WEAPON 3

MEL GIBSON, DANNY GLOVER, JOE PESCI, RENE RUSSO
RICHARD DONNER
USA (WARNER) 1992
118m (15)

Tired sequel to the earlier pix. Rene Russo appears as a martial-arts expert copper in this escapist tale, which finds our boys chasing cop-killers. Widescreen available.

LETHAL WEAPON 4

MEL GIBSON, DANNY GLOVER, JOE PESCI, RENE RUSSO, CHRIS ROCK, JET LI
RICHARD DONNER
USA (WARNER) 1998
121m (15)

The nadir of this action series, with the two leads continually telling us that they're 'too old for this' – but we can see that for ourselves. The return of Russo and Pesci and the addition of comedian Rock and Hong Kong martial-arts movie star Li can't compensate for a franchise at the end of its tether, but it'll suffice if you're a diehard fan of the series. Lots of action, at least. Cut at cinema release. (Note: the cuts – over a minute's worth – meant the director's commentary had to be scrapped from the DVD as it was out of synch!)

ACTION AND ADVENTURE

THE LOST WORLD: JURASSIC PARK ▶3

JEFF GOLDBLUM, RICHARD ATTENBOROUGH, PETER POSTLETHWAITE, JULIANNE MOORE, ARLISS HOWARD

STEVEN SPIELBERG

USA (CIC) 1997

123m (PG)

By-the-numbers sequel to *Jurassic Park* (see page 29): turns out there are even more saurians to be dealt with, stashed on a secret island near the one in the original flick. Edgy maths genius Goldblum is along for the ride, this time with a big-game hunter (Postlethwaite) intent on bagging a male Tyrannosaurus Rex, and another couple of pesky kids (just like the first film) for the young audience to identify with. Great FX, though the jaw-dropping factor is diminished the second time out.

THE LONG KISS GOODNIGHT ▶3

GEENA DAVIS, SAMUEL L JACKSON

RENNY HARLIN

USA (NEW LINE) 1996

115m (18)

There's a touch of self-parody about this deliberately over-the-top actioner with its crazy stunts, big bangs and flamboyant heavy-weapon wielding. Directed by Davis's then-husband Harlin, with a nicely judged performance from Samuel L Jackson of *Pulp Fiction* (see page 177) fame. A good evening's entertainment.

LOST IN SPACE ▶2

MATT LE BLANC, GARY OLDMAN, WILLIAM HURT, MIMI ROGERS, HEATHER GRAHAM

STEPHEN HOPKINS

USA (ENTERTAINMENT) 1998

130m (PG)

A sci-fi Swiss Family Robinson, this Robinson family are the Earth's survivors' last hope as they set off from a declining Earth to colonise the only other habitable planet. Teenage audiences will enjoy the action and the effects. Also on DVD.

MAD MAX ▶4

MEL GIBSON, TIM BURNS, STEVE BISLEY, JOANNE SAMUEL

GEORGE MILLER

AUSTRALIA (WARNER) 1979

100m (18)

The film which made Gibson a star. The USA actor, who'd lived in Australia since boyhood, stars in this story about a near future world where petrol is short and cops spend their time chasing bikers on the highways. The original picture opened on the bottom of a double bill in London's Leicester Square, where it soon emerged that punters were paying to see the little Aussie flick and not the big picture. *Mad Max* became a world-wide hit. Widescreen.

MAD MAX 2: THE ROAD WARRIOR ⑤

MEL GIBSON, BRUCE SPENCE, VERNON WELLS, EMIL MINTY

GEORGE MILLER

AUSTRALIA (WARNER) 1981

91m   (18)

The best of the 'Mad Max' pix. Director Miller had a bigger budget and put it to good use in a display of stunts and pyrotechnics to shame the largest Hollywood studio. Our hero, devastated by the loss of his wife in the first film, roams the wastelands until he encounters a settlement threatened by a crew of punk bikers. Released as *The Road Warrior* in the USA, as the original film was not so well known there.

MAD MAX: BEYOND THUNDERDOME ③

MEL GIBSON, TINA TURNER, FRANK THRING, ANGELO ROSSITTO

GEORGE MILLER, GEORGE OGILVIE

USA (WARNER) 1985

102m   (15)

The third 'Mad Max' movie sees another increase in budget though the story quality dips. The plot seems to be in two parts: first Max stumbles into a community run by Aunty Entity (Turner) and has to fight for his life in a bizarre gladiator arena. Then, thrown into the desert to die, he comes upon a tribe of lithe, lost kids who see him as a messiah. The mythic overtones of religiosity take the edge off some of the action, though there are still some great moments.

THE MARK OF ZORRO ④

TYRONE POWER, LINDA DARNELL, BASIL RATHBONE, GALE SONDERGAARD

ROUBEN MAMOULIAN

USA (FOX) 1940 B&W

93m   (U)

Swashbuckling classic from one of the great American directors. Power poses as a fop in old Mexico, while in reality he's the righter-of-wrongs, the masked hero Zorro. Rathbone is at his slimy best. Magnificent swordfight at the climax.

ACTION AND ADVENTURE

THE MASK OF ZORRO [3]

ANTHONY HOPKINS, CATHERINE ZETA-JONES, ANTONIO BANDERAS, STUART WILSON, MATT LETSCHER, L.Q. JONES

MARTIN CAMPBELL

USA (COLUMBIA TRISTAR) 1998

132m (PG)

Spirited revamp of Johnston McCulley's man-in-the-mask creation that (more or less) follows the formula of the Tyrone Power 40s incarnation: our hero poses as languid fop by day, emerging as camp swashbuckler by night. Here we get two Zorros for the price of one: after years in clink, Hopkins is too old for the game; but when the adversary who left his wife dead and stole his child returns, he trains Banderas (who has a grudge of his own) to be the new Zorro. Zeta-Jones is the grown-up daughter who is loved by both heroes in different ways. Director Campbell, who revived Bond with *GoldenEye* (see page 25), fares less well here: one minute Banderas and rising superstarlet Zeta-Jones are sexily undressing each other with rapiers in a fencing match, the next we get Hopkins emoting and laying on the pathos. The pic could comfortably lose 20 minutes if someone would just shave a few seconds off each of those scenes of men and horses running back and forth … It *was* a hit, though, and in the right mood you'll find it a hard film to dislike. Sequels are hinted at in the climactic dialogue.

MERCURY RISING [2]

BRUCE WILLIS, ALEC BALDWIN

HAROLD BECKER

USA (CIC) 1998

107m (15)

A young autistic boy has cracked the US's most advanced encryption code, 'Mercury', and thus becomes a threat to the government, who order his elimination. Renegade federal agent Willis sets out to protect him and uses the child's uncanny abilities to bring his adversaries to justice. Action-packed thriller which tries to show a caring side to the traditional tough-guy. Also on DVD.

MISSION: IMPOSSIBLE [4]

TOM CRUISE, JON VOIGHT, EMMANUELLE BEART, HENRY CZERNY

BRIAN DE PALMA

USA (CIC) 1996

106m (PG)

One of De Palma's less personal films, this is an adaptation of an old TV series (like his earlier film *The Untouchables*, see page 180). Little remains of the original, except the basic format of agents doing improbable things to a background of that noodling theme tune. The plot is far-fetched, but the action is pure celluloid-packaged adrenalin: look out for the scene where Cruise dangles above a burglar-proof room in a harness. A great night's entertainment.

NEVER SAY NEVER AGAIN [3]

SEAN CONNERY, EDWARD FOX, MAX VON SYDOW, KLAUS MARIA BRANDAUER

IRVIN KERSHNER

UK (WARNER) 1983

128m (PG)

Connery outraged his ex-employers by starring in this unofficial remake of *Thunderball* (see page 40), the rights being owned by Irish entrepreneur Kevin McClory. It's not quite as good as the original, but worth seeing all the same.

OUTBREAK [3]

DUSTIN HOFFMAN, RENE RUSSO, MORGAN FREEMAN, DONALD SUTHERLAND

WOLFGANG PETERSEN

USA (WARNER) 1995

113m (15)

All-too-plausible tale of a killer virus plague carried to the USA by an escaped monkey. The aura of controlled panic is well maintained throughout, and, while it may not be in the league of *Midnight Cowboy* (see page 124), the part of the army doctor on the trail of the disease makes a welcome return to form for Hoffman after an arid spell of many years.

PAPILLON [4]

STEVE McQUEEN, DUSTIN HOFFMAN, VICTOR JORY, DON GORDON, ANTHONY ZERBE, GEORGE COLOURIS, WOODROW PARFREY

FRANKLIN J SCHAFFNER

USA (CINEMA CLUB) 1973

144m (18)

Lengthy and detailed version of the book by Henri Charrière, telling of his numerous attempts to escape from his confinement in the hellish French Guyana penal colony of Devil's Island. McQueen strips away all his movie-star glamour as he shows us a man undergoing physical and mental torture, and Hoffman is amusing and tragic by turns as his forger pal who stubbornly refuses to believe his wife has deserted him.

PATRIOT GAMES [3]

HARRISON FORD, ANNE ARCHER, PATRICK BERGIN, SEAN BEAN

PHILIP NOYCE

USA (CIC) 1992

117m (15)

Ford's first outing as Tom Clancy's novel-series hero, CIA man Jack Ryan – see also *Clear And Present Danger* (page 18) and *The Hunt For Red October* (page 26) for more on this character. On holiday in the UK he thwarts an IRA attack, is knighted (!) and then becomes a target. Plenty of action and excitement, but a bit overlong.

ACTION AND ADVENTURE

THE PEACEMAKER 3

⭐ GEORGE CLOONEY, NICOLE KIDMAN, ARMIN MUELLER-STAHL

🎬 MIMI LEDER

USA (DREAMWORKS) 1997

⏱ 120m (15)

TV hunk Clooney teams up with Kidman to thwart mad, bad folk threatening the UN building with stolen Russian nuclear hardware. Predictable explosive melodrama which has proved a big hit in the video rental market in the UK. It's good to look at, at least.

THE POSEIDON ADVENTURE 3

⭐ GENE HACKMAN, ERNEST BORGNINE, SHELLEY WINTERS, RODDY McDOWALL

🎬 RONALD NEAME

USA (FOX) 1972

⏱ 112m (PG)

This adaptation of a Paul Gallico novel makes for perhaps the best of the 1970s disaster movies – but that's not saying much! The usual formula: a group of people in a bad situation (this time an upturned ocean liner) reveal their personal problems as they battle to get free. And of course they're all played by stars. Oscars for SFX and for song ('The Morning After').

PREDATOR 3

⭐ ARNOLD SCHWARZENEGGER, CARL WEATHERS, BILL DUKE, JESSE VENTURA

🎬 JOHN McTIERNAN

USA (FOX) 1987

⏱ 102m (18)

Top troops on a rescue up the jungle find themselves battling a shape-shifting alien in this effective, gory, shoot-'em-up. Not a classic, but it has its moments.

THE PRISONER OF ZENDA 3

⭐ STEWART GRANGER, DEBORAH KERR, JAMES MASON, ROBERT COOTE

🎬 RICHARD THORPE

USA (WARNER) 1952

⏱ 97m (U)

This remake of the 1937 Ronald Colman version of Anthony Hope's novel is often derided, but it's actually a nifty fairytale picture. Granger plays two parts: the lazy royal of a small country and the distantly-related Englishman who has to take his place to prevent political disaster. Rich colour and a typically vile villain (Mason) make for unimpeachable and jolly entertainment.

RAIDERS OF THE LOST ARK 🎬 5

HARRISON FORD, KAREN ALLEN, PAUL FREEMAN, JOHN RHYS-DAVIES

STEVEN SPIELBERG

USA (CIC) 1981

112m (PG)

First and undoubtedly the best of the three 'Indiana Jones' pix, with Ford as the raffish archaeologist on the track of the lost Ark of the Covenant – also sought by the Nazis for its mysterious powers. Closely modelled on serials of the World War Two era, but with a much improved budget, this is full of whip-cracking, snake-pits and rotting skeletons. The edge-of-your-seat pre-credits sequence sets the tone brilliantly. The two sequels just don't have the same magic, though they were hugely successful. Oscars include one for SFX.

RAMBO: FIRST BLOOD PART 2 🎬 3

SYLVESTER STALLONE, STEVEN BERKOFF, RICHARD CRENNA, CHARLES NAPIER

GEORGE P COSMATOS

USA (POLYGRAM) 1985

92m (15)

Sequel to the superior *First Blood* (see page 25). Army boss Crenna is aiming to harness alienated veteran Rambo's deadly talents, offering him a mission to rescue long-forgotten USA POW's from the Vietnam conflict who're being held in Cambodia. Lots of explosions and shots of Sly's oiled chest.

RAMBO 3 🎬 2

SYLVESTER STALLONE, RICHARD CRENNA, MARC DE JONGE

PETER McDONALD

USA (POLYGRAM) 1988

94m (18)

Rambo goes to Afghanistan to fight the Reds and rescue bossman Crenna. The most expensive (and least effective) of the three Rambo pix, and cut heavily by the UK censor for violence.

ROB ROY 🎬 4

LIAM NEESON, TIM ROTH, JESSICA LANGE, JOHN HURT, BRIAN COX

MICHAEL CATON-JONES

USA/UK (MGM/UA) 1995

113m (15)

Issued at the same time as *Braveheart* (see page 141), this is another tale of a Scots hero battling against both the English and enemies closer to home. Neeson makes a dashing lead, but the picture is nearly stolen by Roth as a foppish, evil cad who violates our hero's woman. Great action and top scenery. Cut by 24 seconds.

ACTION AND ADVENTURE

THE ROCK 🎬4

⭐ SEAN CONNERY, NICOLAS CAGE, ED HARRIS, MICHAEL BIEHN

🎬 MICHAEL BAY

USA (HOLLYWOOD) 1996

⏱ 131m (15)

Blockbuster thriller about a political prisoner (Connery) let out of clink by nasty USA authorities to help agent Cage battle an aggrieved military man (Harris) who has taken over the prison on the island of Alcatraz. The pace never lets up, and it has become increasingly apparent that any pic like this which takes Connery on board is doing itself a big, big favour. Totally ludicrous but a decided hoot. Cut by BBFC. Widescreen.

ROMANCING THE STONE 🎬3

⭐ MICHAEL DOUGLAS, KATHLEEN TURNER, DANNY DeVITO, ZACK NORMAN

🎬 ROBERT ZEMECKIS

USA (FOX) 1984

⏱ 101m (PG)

Soldier-of-fortune and woman-in-peril form uneasy alliance in this comic upstart partially inspired by the success of *Raiders Of The Lost Ark* (see page 36). Lame sequel: *The Jewel Of The Nile* (see page 29).

THE RUNNING MAN 🎬3

⭐ ARNOLD SCHWARZENEGGER, MARIA CONCHITA ALONSO, YAPHET KOTTO, JIM BROWN

🎬 PAUL MICHAEL GLASER

USA (ENTERTAINMENT) 1987

⏱ 97m (18)

Based on a novel by Stephen King (penned under the pseudonym Richard Bachman) and helmed by TV's *Starsky and Hutch* star Glaser, this is one of many thrillers with the theme of modern sports taken to a logically deadly extreme. Has a reputation among Arnie's fans, but looks a tad cheap.

RUSH HOUR 🎬2

⭐ JACKIE CHAN, CHRIS TUCKER

🎬 BRETT RATNER

USA (ENTERTAINMENT) 1998

⏱ 98m (12)

This is one for the martial arts fans – it is filled with stunts and action as two cops from different cultures have to find a way beyond their differences in order to battle the common enemy. Not a new storyline but you don't watch it for the originality of the plot. Also on DVD.

THE SEA HAWK 🎬3

⭐ ERROL FLYNN, FLORA ROBSON, CLAUDE RAINS, DONALD CRISP

🎬 MICHAEL CURTIZ

USA (WARNER) 1940 B&W

⏱ 122m (U)

A Rafael Sabatini novel again provides the basis for a Flynn swashbuckler, as in *Captain Blood* (see page 18). Sir Francis Drake hassles the piratical Spaniards – or is that the other way around? Flynn at his handsome, strutting best. Show it to your kids to let them know there was life before Tom Cruise.

THE SIEGE 🎬3

⭐ DENZEL WASHINGTON, BRUCE WILLIS, ANNETTE BENING

🎬 EDWARD ZURICK

USA (FOX PATHE) 1998

⏱ 111m (15)

The dilemmas faced by an FBI agent, played by Washington, and an army general (Willis) when they pool resources to put an end to the escalating violence perpetrated by a terrorist group in New York. In the midst of action-packed drama, it offers a considered insight into the terrorist mind.

SIX DAYS, SEVEN NIGHTS 🎬2

⭐ HARRISON FORD, ANNE HECHE

🎬 IVAN REITMAN

USA (BUENA VISTA) 1998

⏱ 98m (12)

When their plane crashes in a storm, a dream vacation turns into a nightmare as two people who would very much rather not be together find they have to get together to overcome the obstacles ahead of them – and behind and on both sides! Predictable, but a sound action movie for fans of Ford.

SPEED 🎬4

⭐ KEANU REEVES, SANDRA BULLOCK, DENNIS HOPPER

🎬 JAN DE BONT

USA (FOX) 1994

⏱ 111m (15)

A movie for which the term 'rollercoaster' was made. Our heroes are aboard a bus with a bomb planted by madman Hopper, the catch being that it will go off if the vehicle drops below a certain speed. A massive hit and rightly so. Widescreen available.

ACTION AND ADVENTURE

SPEED 2 – CRUISE CONTROL

JASON PATRIC, SANDRA BULLOCK, WILLEM DAFOE

JAN DE BONT

USA (FOX) 1997

120m (PG)

By-the-numbers retread of the previous *Speed* movie by director De Bont. With only Sandra Bullock and lacking his hero (Keanu Reeves) and villain (Dennis Hopper) from the debut flick (see above), the director isn't quite able to match the first movie, though there is still plenty of action.

SUPERMAN – THE MOVIE

CHRISTOPHER REEVE, MARLON BRANDO, MARGOT KIDDER, GENE HACKMAN

RICHARD DONNER

USA/UK (WARNER) 1978

137m (PG)

Epic, star-studded version, recounting comic hero's origins, suffers slightly from the difficulty of uniting the backstory and a final resolution. Numerous sequels, offshoots, TV shows, etc. The part seems jinxed: early Superman George Reeves killed himself, while Christopher Reeve has since been paralysed in a tragic riding accident. Oscars for SFX. (Note: apparently, there's a cheapo, unauthorised Indian rip-off of this film that makes for weird viewing!) Widescreen available.

TERMINAL VELOCITY

CHARLIE SHEEN, NASTASSJA KINSKI, JAMES GANOLFINI, CHRISTOPHER McDONALD

DERAN SARAFIAN

USA (HOLLYWOOD) 1994

98m (15)

Convoluted spy film revolving around sky-diving and hijacked Russian gold. There are some breathtaking stunt sequences, but the cast and plot are strictly routine by comparison. Still, a sure-fire lager-and-curry midnight movie.

THE TERMINATOR

ARNOLD SCHWARZENEGGER, LINDA HAMILTON, MICHAEL BIEHN, LANCE HENRIKSEN

JAMES CAMERON

USA (VISION) 1984

102m (18)

Inventive, low-budget story about an android (Arnie) who comes back in time to kill the woman who will give birth to a revolutionary hero of the future. Rekindled Arnie's career and put director Cameron into the major league. See sequel on page 40.

TERMINATOR 2: JUDGMENT DAY 🎬4

ARNOLD SCHWARZENEGGER, LINDA HAMILTON, ROBERT PATRICK, EDWARD FURLONG

JAMES CAMERON

USA (GUILD) 1991

130m (15)

This sequel to the first pic had a mega-budget and was one of the first films to use computer 'morphing' in a big way. Arnie returns, this time as a 'good' android bent on protecting the kid who is the future saviour of the world, at the same time getting the boy's mum out of the asylum where she's been placed because of her ravings about time-jumping machine-men. Unfortunately for them all, a far superior android is on their trail. Astounding effects that can hardly be put into words – a perfect wedding of tricks and plot. Don't miss it. Longer version for TV.

THUNDERBALL 🎬4

SEAN CONNERY, ADOLFO CELI, CLAUDINE AUGER, LUCIANA PALUZZI

TERENCE YOUNG

UK (MGM/UA) 1965

125m (PG)

Great 'Bond' film about hijacked bomb-carrying plane, rather similar to the recent *Broken Arrow* (see page 17). Soaring John Barry score and thrilling undersea fights. Remade as *Never Say Never Again* (see page 34). Now available in widescreen, digitally remastered version. See also *Dr No* (page 22), *Goldfinger* (page 26) and *You Only Live Twice* (page 278). Celi, the baddie here, made a rip-off Italian flick called *Operation Kid Brother* – with Connery's sibling Neil!

TOMORROW NEVER DIES 🎬3

PIERCE BROSNAN, JOE DON BAKER, TERI HATCHER, JONATHAN PRYCE, MICHELLE YEOH

ROGER SPOTTISWOODE

UK/USA (WARNER) 1997

114m (12)

Brosnan's second stab at the 007 mantle is something of a let-down after the refreshing heights of *GoldenEye* (see page 25), despite the presence of Pryce, TV *Superman*-babe Hatcher and Hong Kong starlet Yeoh. Spottiswoode directs in reliable manner and it will please die-hard fans of the series, though it neither shakes nor stirs! Cut by BBFC. Available in widescreen.

ACTION AND ADVENTURE

TOP GUN

TOM CRUISE, KELLY McGILLIS, VAL KILMER, TOM SKERRITT

TONY SCOTT

USA (CIC) 1986

110m (15)

Flash-bang-wallop action/ romance about USA Navy fliers competing to be 'top gun' in their F-14 squadron. I rate it three for the undeniably fine action sequences. The song 'Take My Breath Away' won an Oscar. Widescreen available. Note: director Scott is the less-talented sibling of Ridley Scott, who directed classics like *Alien* (see page 259) and *Blade Runner* (see page 262). The film got a memorable come-uppance in a recent movie called *Sleep With Me,* in which motormouth film director Quentin Tarantino does a cameo as a party guest with a theory that *Top Gun* has a homosexual subtext which involves the other fliers urging Tom Cruise to ditch Kelly McGillis and 'go the gay way'; in defence of this notion he draws dark inferences from alleged dialogue about fliers 'riding each other's tails'. Cruise won a libel case in 1998 against a paper which falsely claimed he was gay in real life.

TRUE LIES

ARNOLD SCHWARZENEGGER, JAMIE LEE CURTIS, ART MALIK, TIA CARRERE

JAMES CAMERON

USA (CIC) 1994

135m (15)

The director of *Aliens* (see page 259) and *The Abyss* (see page 258) helms above-par spy action for big Arnie, with some great stunts – especially the helicopter-dangling one re-enacted by Ms Curtis at the Oscars. Art Malik makes a nicely evil villain, too. Available in widescreen, though some sources state that the image has been blown up/cropped. Cut for film and video.

TWISTER

BILL PAXTON, JAMI GERTZ, HELEN HUNT, CARY ELWES

JAN DE BONT

USA (CIC) 1996

108m (PG)

Another spectacle from De Bont, maker of *Speed* (see page 38). The tornado SFX, though obviously more impressive on the big screen, are still worth a look on video. The script isn't hot on characterisation, but the film is entertaining nevertheless. Slight BBFC cut.

ADULT

Video provides an ideal medium for 'adult' entertainment. After all, most of us, I think it would be fair to say, would rather indulge in such pursuits in the privacy of our own home. However, if you are hoping that your local video store will provide you with an ever-changing supply of porn, you will be sadly disappointed.

In the USA and most of Europe, adults are allowed free access to hard-core movies – by which term I mean films where the stars indulge in real sexual acts on-screen under the unflinching gaze of the camera. In the UK the situation is very different: only soft-core (simulated) sex is normally permitted, and the few hard-core movies which do get a release are censored. I'm not being pedantic here or saying that a movie is worthless if the BBFC removes a few seconds, but the fact is that nobody watches sex films for the plot – and even some of the more artistically ambitious flicks (like those of cult figure Michael Ninn) lost their flavour when shorn of minutes of sex content before being deemed fit to be viewed by British adults.

Things may be changing, however. In recent years the censor has passed hard sex scenes in so-called 'educational' videos, and some hard core was controversially passed in an attempt to 'test the waters' with the public. Also significant was the *Evening Standard* story about a Soho video dealer charged with selling uncertificated pornography. As his lawyer had anticipated, the case against him collapsed when the judge advised the police to reconsider the charge, on the basis that the average 1997 jury just wouldn't find heterosexual sex obscene. Big studios have begun making films about the porn business – *Boogie Nights*, *8mm*, etc. – and porn stars like Traci Lords and Jenna Jameson have appeared in mainstream fare.

My own favourite sex film is *Baby Face*, an old classic by US director Alex De Renzy, although the film was issued here only in bowdlerised form, and it may be years yet before your average high-street dealer (or even licensed sex stores where R18 material is sold) will freely offer such pix. In the meantime, what follows is a trawl through what you can currently rent or buy on tape in the Adult section.

ADULT

9½ WEEKS

MICKEY ROURKE, KIM BASINGER, DAVID MARGULIES, MARGARET WHITTON

ADRIAN LYNE

USA (FOX) 1986

112m (18)

Often over-valued, pseudo-sadomasochistic bonkfest. The title derives from the duration of the lust-fuelled collision of the two leads, and inspired many similarly-titled movies. Rather a patina of arty pretension to my mind, although to be fair, you get to see Basinger before she began to fade – though she's made a comeback of sorts with *LA Confidential* (see page 120) – ditto Mickey Rourke, a fine actor who is under-used. Based on Elizabeth McNeill's novel of the same name. Available in widescreen.

AI NO BOREI

TATSUYA FUJI, KAZUKO YOSHIYUKI, TAKAHIRO TAMURA

NAGISA OSHIMA

JAPAN/FRANCE (CONNOISSEUR) 1978

100m (18)

Companion film to the infamous *Ai No Corrida* (1976) – still banned on tape, due, no doubt, to the gruelling penis-severing scene – this is another tale of doomed love, with a man and woman embarking on an affair and bumping off the girl's inconvenient husband, only to find themselves plagued by his ghost. Luminescent photography and impassioned playing make this a classic of its kind. Widescreen. Subtitled.

THE ART OF LOVE

MARINA PIERRO, MICHELLE PLACIDO, MASSIMO GIROTTI

WALERIAN BOROWCZYK

ITALY/FRANCE (JEZEBEL) 1984

93m (18)

Arthouse director who edged his way into classy eroticism, Borowczyk may have now been abandoned by the serious critics, but that doesn't mean he has ditched genuine commitment to his work. He fetishises objects and images, and this visualisation of a series of sex lectures for lechers given by Ovid to an audience of ancient Romans gives ample rein to his propensity for ripe and passionate action. Subtitled and widescreen.

BEYOND THE VALLEY OF THE DOLLS ▐4▌

DOLLY READ, CYNTHIA MYERS, EDY WILLIAMS, JOHN LAZAR

RUSS MEYER

USA (FOX) 1970

102m (18)

Rare big-studio outing for breast-fetishist Meyer is a witty lampoon of the Hollyweird milieu of the original *Valley Of The Dolls* (1967), though not an actual sequel. Busty all-girl rock group move to California and become involved in many ups 'n' downs (and ins 'n' outs) when they join the entourage of crazed manager Z-Man, who throws pervy parties that drive him to exclaim things like, 'This is my happening and it freaks me out!' (a line recently reprised in comedy hit *Austin Powers – International Man Of Mystery* – see page 70). Energetically photographed in psychedelic Hieronymous Bosch tones by Fred J Koenekamp with a climactic massacre inspired by the Manson murders – but you wouldn't know it from this faded, cut, non-widescreen tape. Available as a letterboxed import laserdisc, and has been shown semi-widescreen (and uncut) by Channel 4 TV.

BLANCHE ▐3▌

MICHEL SIMON, GEORGES WILSON, LIGIA BRANICE

WALERIAN BOROWCZYK

FRANCE (CONNOISSEUR) 1971

90m (PG)

Early Borowczyk film about the young bride of a nasty aristocrat who finds herself at the mercy of powerful men who lust after her beauty. Typically opulent costumes and authentic historical feel, though lacking the explicit sex that became the director's trademark in later pix.

BOOGIE NIGHTS ▐3▌

MARK WAHLBERG, HEATHER GRAHAM, BURT REYNOLDS, JULIANNE MOORE

PAUL THOMAS ANDERSON

USA (ENTERTAINMENT) 1997

148m (18)

A 70s-era epic about a dumb lad who finds fame and fortune when sleazemaster Reynolds points out that he has a great asset between his legs. Hence he's reborn as porn star Dirk Diggler, envy of men everywhere. Wahlberg is amusing as our young innocent (complete with prosthetic penis), while Graham is Roller Girl, whose speciality is bonking on skates. A timely satire on the sex film industry, but with a dark, depressing message.

ADULT

COMMON-LAW CABIN

ALAINA CAPRI, BABETTE BARDOT, ADELE REIN

RUSS MEYER

USA (TROMA/RM) 1967

69m (18)

Meyer has been called the 'rural Fellini' on account of an early run of pix like this, cod morality tales full of earthy sex in backwoods surroundings. Take a man and a couple of girls running a shabby tourist lodge miles from anywhere, then more guys 'n' babes turn up and the fireworks begin. Crisply transferred from the original negative, but was it worth the effort? Strangely, there is virtually no bare flesh on show despite the 18 certificate.

CRIMES OF PASSION

KATHLEEN TURNER, ANTHONY PERKINS, BRUCE DAVIDSON, ANNIE POTTS

KEN RUSSELL

USA (VISION) 1984

102m (18)

Classy professional girl has an alternative identity as China Blue, call-girl catering to the lubricious fantasies of all and sundry while freeing her own wild side. Bizarre performance from Perkins as a pseudo-priest wielding a killer dildo. Heavily censored before being issued.

CRASH

JAMES SPADER, DEBORAH UNGER, ROSANNA ARQUETTE, ELIAS KOTEAS, HOLLY HUNTER

DAVID CRONENBERG

CANADA (COLUMBIA TRISTAR) 1996

96m (18)

Controversial screen version of JG Ballard's futuristic novel which gave the BBFC and the tabloids apoplexy is here released (finally) on tape in its uncut cinema form. Set among a group of people who get their kicks re-enacting celebrity car accidents and sexualising the resultant wounds and scar tissue, it shows how a rather numb young couple (Spader and Unger) are drawn into the weird circle in an attempt to revive their feelings. Filmed with the cold glamour of sleek car ads, it's sick, stylish and brilliant. There is no explicit sex, in case you're interested, at least not in the traditional sense of the phrase.

45

DARK HABITS

CARMEN MAURA, LAURA CEPEDA, CRISTINA S PASCUAL

PEDRO ALMODOVAR

SPAIN (TARTAN) 1983

111m (18)

*S*panish cult sleazemaster Almodovar spins a sick story about a singer on the run who enters a convent. But this is no jaunt in the manner of Whoopi Goldberg's 'Sister Act' films – these nuns are lesbians, junkies, sex novelists, acid casualists and all-round weirdos. Sure to offend, especially in a Catholic land such as Spain. Subtitled and widescreen.

THE DARK SIDE OF LOVE

MONICA GUERRITORE, LORENZO LENA, GILLA NOVAK

SALVATORE SAMPERI

ITALY (JEZEBEL) 1985

88m (18)

Disabled teenage boy living with his aunt gets involved in her naughty sex life, amid bouts of oddball attempts at philosophising. Plenty of atmosphere. Widescreen.

DIRTY WEEKEND

LIA WILLIAMS, DAVID McCALLUM, RUFUS SEWELL, SYLVIA SYMS, IAN RICHARDSON

MICHAEL WINNER

UK (POLYGRAM) 1993

96m (18)

The bad press Michael Winner gets is just journalistic laziness as he has actually done some fine work – and this, I'd say, is one of his best. Like Abel Ferrara's *Angel Of Vengeance*, aka *Ms 45* (1980) (see page 280), it's about a woman who tires of constant male abuse – from rape to stalking and straightforward everyday yobbery – and decides to take violent punitive action. The grimy, drab Britain shown is not shabby film-making (as some critics said) but is in fact entirely apt for the mood the picture tries to convey. Anyone who has seen Winner's USA pix with Charles Bronson will know that he can turn out slickly glossy work with the best of them. Even as they panned *Dirty Weekend*, the hacks had to give credit to Lia Williams' gutsy-yet-fragile lead performance, which makes this a must-see lost classic.

EGON SCHIELE EXCESSES

MATHIEU CARRIERE, JANE BIRKIN, CHRISTINE KAUFMAN

HERBERT VESELY

W GERMANY (REDEMPTION) 1980

83m (18)

Story of the end of the Austrian artist's life and the trouble he got himself into by painting a teenage girl – she accused him of making advances and his nude drawings of her were used as evidence that he was a child pornographer. A serious and adult work about the effect of moral hysteria on art. How apt.

THE EROTIC DREAMS OF CLEOPATRA

MARCELLA PETRELLI, RITA SILVA, ANDREA COPPOLA

CESAR TODD

ITALY/FRANCE (JEZEBEL) 1983

85m (18)

More stylishly set up than most of these porn efforts in the style of *Caligula* (see page 141), *The Erotic Dreams Of Cleopatra* may not, in terms of spectacle, be a patch on Liz Taylor's *Cleopatra* (see page 142), but it presents the sexual frolics in imaginative and lush settings. Surprisingly, considering the scene of horse-masturbation (similar to that in *Caligula II – The Untold Story*, which is banned in the UK) the censor has apparently resisted the urge to snip away at the action. This may be because the animal sex in this case is shown in shadow only – how artistic! Letterboxed at near fullscreen ratio.

EROTIKA

SAMANTHA STRONG, PORSCHE LYNN, NIKKI SINN

ROBERT McCALLUM

USA (PURGATORY) 1995

83m (18)

Glossy, stylised hard core shot under a pseudonym by indie director Gary Graver. Small-town American gal moves to Los Angeles and sleeps with lots of people, with some fake feel-good feminist philosophising thrown in. Way better that the average USA porno, but (of course) the hard-core footage has been brutally excised. Many scenes of the star being orally pleasured by both sexes, for those who are looking for that sort of thing.

ESCAPE FROM BROTHEL 🎬3

PAULINE CHEN, ALEN FONG, RENA MURAKAMI
WONG LUNG WEI
HONG KONG (EASTERN HEROES) 1991
97m (18)

This is one of the films from Hong Kong classified as 'Category III' – their censor rating for movies with lots of sex and violence, usually featuring permutations of both. This sort of thing doesn't sit well with the BBFC and this print has been totally butchered by them, which is a shame as a lot of effort seems to have been put in by the video company – the tape is in widescreen, subtitles are in the black area under the picture, and there's an original trailer. The opening line ('Suzie, I can't wait much longer, my aphrodisiac has already worn off!') will give you some idea of what to expect.

ESKIMO NELL 🎬3

MICHAEL ARMSTRONG, KATY MANNING, ROY KINNEAR, ANNA QUAYLE, CHRISTOPHER BIGGINS
MARTIN CAMPBELL
UK (MEDUSA) 1974
81m (18)

Better-than-usual cheesy Brit sex farce directed by the man who went on to helm the hit James Bond pic *GoldenEye* (see page 25). Real-life movie-maker Michael Armstrong stars as a director asked to film the erotic ditty of the title. According to exploitation veteran David McGillivray in the excellent *Sexadelic* magazine, this is what actually happened in real life! Bored by the idea, he made up the film as we have it here: director has to make the pic in four different versions for various backers (family film/hard core/gay Western/martial arts musical) and mayhem results. Pals were cast and the characters are allegedly spoofs of certain film-industry folk, with Armstrong's psychedelic clothes supposedly based on the garb of Michael Winner. Lots of odd cameos – note the appearance of one-time British TV's *Dr Who* girl Katy Manning.

EVIL SENSES 🎬2

MONICA GUERRITORE, GABRIELLE LAVIA, MIMSY FARMER
GABRIELE LAVIA
ITALY (ART HOUSE/ANGEL) 1986
90m (18)

Gorgeously filmed erotic thriller from husband-and-wife team Lavia and Guerritore, with the former as a killer-for-hire, hiding out in a whorehouse. Soft sex and some nasty violence, though the censor has inflicted cuts (on the latter especially).

FASTER, PUSSYCAT! KILL ... KILL!

- TURA SATANA, HAJI, LORI WILLIAMS, SUSAN BERNARD, STUART LANCASTER
- RUSS MEYER
- USA (TROMA/RM) 1966 B&W
- 83m (18)

Kitsch domination fantasy from breast-lover Meyer, with rough, tough girls dishing out butch violence in the American desert. A cult pic with no real nudity or overt sex, just fast cars and faster women.

FLESH GORDON

- JASON WILLIAMS, SUZANNE FIELDS, JOHN HOYT
- HOWARD ZIEHM, MICHAEL BENVENISTE
- USA (ENTERTAINMENT) 1974
- 84m (18)

*S*pot-on parody of the original *Flash Gordon* serial. Planet Mongo becomes Planet Porno, Dr Zarkov is now Dr Jerkoff, etc. Apparently began life as a hard-core effort but, when the makers saw how good the film was looking, they decided to go for a more mainstream approach. SFX are wonderful, including a stop-motion animated 'Penisaurus'! Very, very funny. A poor sequel, *Flesh Gordon 2* aka *Flesh Gordon Meets The Cosmic Cheerleaders*, was made some years later and is also available on tape.

IMMORAL TALES

- LISE DANVERS, FABRICE LUCHINI, PALOMA PICASSO
- WALERIAN BOROWCZYK
- FRANCE (CONNOISSEUR) 1974
- 99m (18)

Four-tale compendium of Borowczyk's typically luscious, overheated fetishisation of the female sex in historical mode. One story is about legendary vampire Countess Bathory, another about Lucrezia Borgia and so on. Widescreen and subtitled print of a movie that was obviously a labour of lust.

MIRANDA

- SERENA GRANDI, ANDREA OCCHIPINTI, MALISA LONGO
- TINTO BRASS
- ITALY (ART HOUSE/ANGEL) 1985
- 95m (18)

Village barmaid just can't help driving the lads wild. Weak story, but Tinto Brass, director of *Caligula* (see page 141), brings a down-to-earth horniness to the proceedings – indeed, sex movie expert David Flint has described the film (in *Flesh & Blood* magazine) as 'a knicker-lover's delight'! Need I say more. Widescreen.

MONDO TOPLESS [2]

BABETTE BARDOT, DIANE YOUNG, PAT BARRINGER

RUSS MEYER

USA (TROMA/RM) 1966

60m (18)

Cheap mockumentary about the alleged topless craze of the 60s, lensed by breast-crazed Meyer in the wake of *Faster, Pussycat! Kill ... Kill!* (see page 49). Lots of outsize jiggling mammaries.

NAKED – AS NATURE INTENDED [2]

PAMELA GREEN, BRIDGET LEONARD, ANGELA JONES

GEORGE HARRISON MARKS

UK (JEZEBEL) 1961

58m (15)

Legendary 'tits 'n' ass' pic from photographer Harrison Marks, starring his muse Pamela Green, who also appears in *Peeping Tom* (see page 211). No real sex – the BBFC made sure of that even before the production began – but it's an amusing relic of what was once thought risqué.

ORGY OF THE DEAD [2]

CRISWELL, FAWN SILVER, PAT BARRINGER

STEPHEN C APOSTOLOFF

USA (WARNER) 1965

91m (18)

Produced by famed 'bad' moviemaker Ed Wood and starring his pal, gleefully mad Hollywood 'psychic' Criswell, this is a fitfully fun piece about a couple who get stranded in a graveyard only to have our ghoulish hero totally torture them by having the naked dead folk dance for his delectation. The plot is lacking and the film is over-long, but it has to be seen for its camp novelty value.

SCANDALOUS GILDA [3]

MONICA GUERRITORE, GABRIELLE LAVIA, PINA CEI

GABRIELE LAVIA

ITALY (JEZEBEL) 1985

88m (18)

More from the Lavia/Guerritore team. Demented philosophical tale, with nasty rapes, cartoon penises and casual sex. So off-handedly odd that it does succeed in holding the interest for much of the running time.

ADULT

THE SEXUAL LIFE OF THE BELGIANS

JEAN-HENRI COMPERE, NOE FRANCQ, SOPHIE SCHNEIDER

JEAN BUCQUOY

BELGIUM (TARTAN) 1994

81m (18)

Autobiographical story of the director's sex life as a young man: scenes of him getting seduced by a randy schoolgirl when he saves her from fellow pupils, nipping his dick on some dentures, penning porn and sleeping with an inflatable bedmate. And this apparently is only the first part of a trilogy! Slightly letterboxed. Subtitled.

SHATTER DEAD

STARK RAVEN, FLORA FAUNA, MARINA DEL REY

SCOOTER McCRAE

USA (SCREEN EDGE) 1994

84m (18)

Screen Edge specialise in releasing cutting-edge low-budget (this was shot on tape) indie films, and this is probably their best release so far. Set in a future world where death is defunct and people must choose whether to 'die' young and keep their looks forever or to sink into an eternity of decrepitude, this is more imaginative than most big studio sex/violence fare. Scene of a girl being sexually penetrated with a gun has been cut by the BBFC.

SHOWGIRLS

ELIZABETH BERKELY, GINA GERSHON, KYLE MacLACHLAN, ROBERT DAVI

PAUL VERHOEVEN

USA (FOX) 1995

126m (18)

Derided on cinema release, Verhoeven's exposé of tacky sex-opera goings-on among Las Vegas strip dancers ought to achieve cult status on tape: lots of breasts and unintentional hilarity. Available in widescreen. Cut by the censor.

SPANKING THE MONKEY

JEREMY DAVIES, ALBERTA WATSON, CARLA GALLO

DAVID O RUSSELL

USA (TARTAN) 1996

98m (18)

Unwholesome sexual frustrations beset the hero of this witty look at small-town USA life as he endlessly attempts to find solace in the act of the title (masturbation) while locked in the loo. Occasionally hilarious and subversive in the extreme.

STRANGE DAYS

RALPH FIENNES, JULIETTE LEWIS, ANGELA BASSETT

KATHRYN BIGELOW

USA (CIC) 1995

141m (18)

Future *noir* about a hustler who sells illicit video clips that the buyer can play back mentally in order to experience directly the originator's own thrills. When a 'snuff' tape of a real killing falls into his hands trouble isn't far behind ... It's a very long movie but a great performance from Fiennes as the video dealer will keep you glued to the screen. The BBFC have cut 13 seconds of sexual violence. Ironic, given the plot.

SUPERVIXENS

SHARI EUBANK; CHARLES NAPIER, USCHI DIGARD, HAJI

RUSS MEYER

USA (TROMA/RM) 1975

104m (18)

One of Meyer's best films, *Supervixens* is like a live-action, sexed-up 'Road Runner' cartoon. A man goes on the run after being falsely accused of killing his wife and gets involved in several sexy encounters of the bra-busting kind. One violent scene has apparently been cut by the BBFC, losing 47 seconds of footage; this is odd, as Meyer recently stated that he would not allow any of the films he owns (of which this is one) to come out in a cut form. The cut doesn't spoil the pic however. Some of the Meyer tapes have now been re-issued on Polygram, allegedly in more complete forms.

TANDEM

KINO MAHITO, ISHIWARA YURI, HAZUKI HOTARU
TOSHIKI SATO
JAPAN (PINK JAPAN) 1994
57m (18)

Pink films are Japan's porn, and, though hard sex acts and even pubic hair are usually digitally masked, the makers substitute lots of S&M, masturbating, piddling – you name it, they do it. In this short entry, a biker and an office worker make friends and fall out and in between the two events we see their sexual dreams. Part art, part porno, very Japanese. Subtitled and widescreen. Cut by BBFC.

UP!

RAVEN DE LA CROIX, KITTEN NATIVIDAD, CANDY SAMPLES
RUSS MEYER
USA (TROMA/RM) 1976
80m (18)

A 'Who-killed-the-Nazi?' plot (Meyer is always including Martin Bormann references in his pix) is intermingled with the usual japes and cantilevered bosoms in what is undoubtedly one of Meyer's best nudie efforts. Typically over the top. Another cut (1m 29s) Meyer pic, despite his vow not to allow censored versions.

VAMPYROS LESBOS

SOLEDAD MIRANDA, DENNIS PRICE, EWA STROEMBURG
JESS FRANCO
W GERMANY/SPAIN (REDEMPTION) 1970
86m (18)

The prolific Franco helms a dreamy 70s sex-vampire saga starring his then favourite muse, the late Soledad Miranda. A mix of the director's speciality nightclub strip stuff and arty sex where kites stand in for bats, sunlight for darkness and the camera lingers on scorpions, mannequins and blood. There are two versions available: one packaged to resemble the recent hit soundtrack CD (which includes the promo music video clip), the other in normal Redemption packaging (which includes a trailer). Subtitled and widescreen.

VENUS IN FURS 🎬 3

ANNE VAN DER VEN, RAYMOND THIRY, MEREDITH CHAN-A-HUNG

MAARTJE SEYFERTH, VICTOR E NIEUWENHUIJS

NETHERLANDS (VISIONARY) 1994 B&W

70m (18)

One of several stabs at the Sacher-Masoch story (there is also one by Jess Franco), this was put together on a minuscule budget by two documentary-makers and follows the novel faithfully. The author gave his name to masochism, so you won't be surprised to learn this is a tale of a man who is a slave to his whip-swishing mistress. Dazzling, considering the budget; this is worthy of investigation.

VIXEN 🎬 3

ERICA GAVIN, HARRISON PAGE, VINCENTE WALLACE

RUSS MEYER

USA (TROMA/RM) 1968

70m (18)

One of Meyer's better 'domestics': yet another tale of a rural babe tired of husband and on the lookout for randy tourists. The success of *Vixen* gave Meyer his shot at the major leagues with *Beyond The Valley Of The Dolls* (see page 44) for Fox.

WHORE 🎬 4

THERESA RUSSELL, ANTONIO FARGAS, SANJAY

KEN RUSSELL

USA (POLYGRAM) 1991

81m (18)

Russell transposes cabbie David Hines' play *Bondage* (about Kings Cross prostitutes) from London to the USA with some success. Ms Russell (no relation) talks to the camera as she goes through the highs and lows of her day as a not-so-happy hooker. Eventful, sad, funny and superbly acted by the small cast. The only flaw I can see is that Theresa Russell is just *too* damn good-looking for a cheap streetwalker!

WR MYSTERIES OF THE ORGANISM 🎬 3

MILENA DRAVIC, IVICA VIDOVIC, JACKIE CURTIS

DUSAN MAKAVEJEV

YUGOSLAVIA/WEST GERMANY (CONNOISSEUR) 1971

80m (18)

Legendary movie based on the works of sex-guru Wilhelm Reich. This is the version the director prepared for British TV's Channel 4 in which the scene of Jim Buckley having his penis plaster-casted is optically obscured, but it really makes little difference. Impenetrable (!) but never boring.

ANIMATION

There's no doubt about it: you can't beat a good cartoon video for keeping the kids quiet. But there's far more animation on video nowadays than just good ol' *Tom And Jerry*.

With the advent of increasingly sophisticated computer technology, animation now turns up alongside other special effects tools in all kinds of movies: it not only conjured up many of the dinosaurs for *Jurassic Park*, but furnished some of the wilder lion footage for the recent *The Ghost And The Darkness*. It's funny to think that when Disney first used computer animation 'shortcuts', they were heavily criticised by purists – although techniques such as 'rotoscoping' (where scenes are drawn using live footage as a basis) had been in use for years. Of course, the first computer animations were relatively simple: a sequence for the 1982 Disney live-action film *Something Wicked This Way Comes*, of a train magically turning into a carnival site, was scrapped because it simply didn't look real.

There are many types of animation and if you're into this, your video store should have plenty to offer you. The new computerised genre culminated in *Toy Story*, where the imagery looks three-dimensional rather than having the 'flat' appearance of cartoons – but for years experts like Ray Harryhausen have been lensing models a frame at a time to make monsters that can even be made to interact with live footage. The UK's own Nick Park has won Oscars with his *Wallace and Gromit* shorts (which are available to buy on video), using similar techniques. For some, though, the classic cartoons like *Tom And Jerry* and the numerous Warners shorts by Chuck Jones (*Bugs Bunny, Road Runner, et al*) are the ones to see. Again, there are many collections of these shorts available to buy on tape. Recently there have been releases of Japanese adult cartoons *(anime)* with an emphasis on sex and gore. Some extend over several tapes but they are often cut by the BBFC.

For the purpose of this book, I've decided simply to present a short selection of feature-length movies, classics where animation is the main (in most cases, the sole) film technique used. A note on the Disney films I've featured: the studio continues to make feature-length cartoons, with *The Hunchback Of Notre Dame* and *Hercules* recently on release in cinemas.

While they do release their cartoons to video, they have a policy of making only a few titles available to buy for a limited period. This is very frustrating, I know, but you should be able to rent classic titles from your local tape library.

THE 7TH VOYAGE OF SINBAD [5]

KERWIN MATTHEWS, TORIN THATCHER, KATHRYN GRANT, RICHARD EYER

NATHAN JURAN

USA (CINEMA CLUB V) 1958

89m (U)

Everyone has a film which made an impact on them when they were very young – this is mine. I'll never forget the moment when Ray Harryhausen's animated giant Cyclops emerges roaring from his lair – mind-boggling stuff. And this 'Arabian Nights' fantasy has more wonders to dwarf the sketchy human characters: a sword-fighting skeleton, a snake-woman, a fire-breathing dragon, two-headed birds. There's also an imposing score by Bernard Herrmann. Harryhausen made two further 'Sinbad' movies many years later, but they lack the naive passion of this first classic.

101 DALMATIANS [4]

Voices of:
ROD TAYLOR, BETTY LOU GERSON, J PAT O'MALLEY and others

WOLFGANG REITHERMAN, HAMILTON S LUSKE, CLYDE GERONIMI

USA (DISNEY) 1961

79m (U)

A better bet than the recent live-action version, this telling of Dodie Smith's classic tale is one of the best Disney cartoon features. Nasty Cruella de Vil is hoarding dalmatian puppies to make herself a spotted fur coat, but when she steals the brood of feisty Pongo and Perdita she's messed with the wrong pooches! Atmospheric recreation of the 'twilight barking', where dogs across the land howl messages in relay, and stylish artwork make it great for adults as well as kids.

ANIMATION

ALADDIN [4]

Voices of:
ROBIN WILLIAMS and others

RON CLEMENTE, JOHN MUSKER

USA (DISNEY) 1992

91m (U)

The highlight of this magic carpet ride is Robin Williams as the voice of the genie – his improvisational skills seem to have driven the animators to new heights of inspiration as the character transforms himself and the world around him to match his array of voices – dazzling. The lead characters pale a little by comparison in my view, but it's still excellent entertainment. Oscars for best score and song ('A Whole New World').

AN AMERICAN TAIL [3]

Voices of:
DOM DELUISE, NEHEMIAH PERSOFF, CHRISTOPHER PLUMMER and others

DON BLUTH

USA (CIC) 1986

78m (U)

Delightful and moving cartoon about a family of poor mice who flee the pogroms of mother Russia and leave their *shtetl* for a new life in America. Bluth is an escapee himself – from the Disney studios. His picture is as well animated as any Disney effort, but one doubts whether they would have made this story. A smashing little cartoon.

ANASTASIA [3]

Voices of:
MEG RYAN, KIRSTEN DUNST, KELSEY GRAMMER, CHRISTOPHER LLOYD, ANGELA LANSBURY, JOHN CUSACK

DON BLUTH/GARY GOLDMAN

USA (FOX) 1997

91m (U)

From Don *(An American Tail)* Bluth comes this immaculately rendered cartoon, which proves that animators don't need to be harnessed to Disney to create great work. A young girl teams up with a confidence trickster in the wake of the Russian revolution and flees to Paris to seek out the last of the royal Romanovs. Is she (or isn't she) the escaped Princess Anastasia, that's the question. Amnesia and the mad monk Rasputin complicate matters. The songs are just about okay, but it is the animation and the celebrity voices that make this a glittering romp. In reality, the old lady who all her life claimed to be Anastasia, escaped from the massacre of the royals by Bolsheviks, was recently shown, via DNA tests, to have been an impostor. How sad. Another beautiful mystery bites the dust of history, and bitter it tastes, too. Stick to the movie.

ANTZ

Voices of:
WOODY ALLEN, SYLVESTER STALLONE, SHARON STONE, CHRISTOPHER WALKEN, GENE HACKMAN

ERIC DARNELL/TIM JOHNSON

USA (CIC) 1999

79m (PG)

Neat computer animation about the trials and tribulations of life in an ant hill. Allen provides the voice of the nerdy hero, with Stone as the love interest. A toss-up for the best insect cartoon between this and the almost simultaneously released *A Bug's Life* (see page 59).

BASIL, THE GREAT MOUSE DETECTIVE

Voices of:
VINCENT PRICE, BARRIE INGHAM, MELISSA MANCHESTER and others

JOHN MUSKER, RON CLEMENTE, DAVE MICHENER, BURNY MATTISON

USA (DISNEY) 1986

80m (U)

Fab confection about a mouse version of Sherlock Holmes dubbed Basil as a tribute to the screen's great player of the part, Basil Rathbone. Our little hero fights not Moriarty but the evil Professor Rattigan, voiced to fruity perfection by the late Vincent Price. This was the first Disney cartoon to use computer animation, thus enraging the purists. Shame on 'em: it's a smashing film.

BEAUTY AND THE BEAST

Voices of:
PAIGE O'HARA, ROBBY BENSON, ANGELA LANSBURY and others

GARY TROUSDALE, KIRK WISE

USA (DISNEY) 1992

85m (U)

Sumptuous version from Disney of the classic fairy tale. Embellishments include the amusing walking/talking household objects. Oscars for the Menken/Ashman score. Definitely the best of the studio's more recent pix.

THE BFG

Voices of:
DAVID JASON, AMANDA ROOT, ANGELA THORNE

BRIAN COSGROVE

USA (VCI) 1990

88m (U)

Classic animation based on Roald Dahl's famous tale about the Big Friendly Giant who snatches little Sophie from her bed at the orphanage when she spots him handing out dreams during the night. She joins him on his task of collecting and distributing dreams, and they hatch a plan to rid the world of the child-eating giants – among them the Trogglehumper and the Bloodbottler – with the help of the Queen of England. Delightful story for the young and not-so-young which combines a magical innocence with Dahl's rasping humour.

ANIMATION

A BUG'S LIFE 🎬4

Voices of:
DAVE FOLEY, KEVIN SPACEY, JULIA LOUIS-DREYFUS

JOHN LASSETER

USA (DISNEY) 1998

93m (15)

Brilliant state-of-the-art offering from the Disney team behind *Toy Story* (see page 64). A renegade ant hires an out-of-work flea circus to help him fight a battalion of wicked grasshoppers. Also on DVD.

FANTASIA 🎬5

Voices of:
DEEMS TAYLOR (Narrator),
LEOPOLD STOKOWSKI AND THE PHILADEPHIA ORCHESTRA,
MICKEY MOUSE

BEN SHARPSTEEN

USA (DISNEY) 1940

120m (U)

Ambitious undertaking for Disney in which pieces of classical music are wedded to cartoon imagery with varying degrees of success. High points include Mickey Mouse as the Sorcerer's Apprentice (where you could almost believe the music was written for the film rather than the reverse) and the demonic 'Night on Bare Mountain' sequence. The film has lost a few snippets, including a 'racist' clip of a black centaur polishing its hooves like a shoeshine boy. I'm not sure I approve – one can't condone racism but how will we ever know where it existed if we keep going back and rewriting history by erasing 'offensive' images? The film won a special Oscar for Stokowski and the orchestra.

JAMES AND THE GIANT PEACH 🎬4

Voices of:
SIMON CALLOW, RICHARD DREYFUSS, JANE LEEVES, SUSAN SARANDON, DAVID THEWLIS, MIRIAM MARGOLYES

HENRY SELICK

USA (GUILD) 1996

76m (U)

Weird screen retelling of Roald Dahl's popular children's fantasy from the director of *Tim Burton's The Nightmare Before Christmas* (see page 64) using computer animation to crazed effect. Demented fun for all ages, which works just as well on the small screen as it did in cinemas.

JASON AND THE ARGONAUTS 4

TODD ARMSTRONG, NIALL MacGINNIS, HONOR BLACKMAN, NIGEL GREEN
DON CHAFFEY
UK (CINEMA CLUB V) 1963
104m (U)

Only marginally less satisfying than *The 7th Voyage Of Sinbad* (see page 56) – though some prefer it – this is animator Ray Harryhausen tackling Greek mythology via a horde of stop-motion animation creatures, including bat-winged harpies and the seven-headed hydra. Todd Armstrong makes a handsome Jason in search of the golden fleece (though his voice was dubbed by another actor) and Bernard Herrmann comes up with another imaginative score. A nice touch is the notion of the gods looking down and toying with the lives of mortals. Harryhausen tried to repeat the formula many years later with *Clash Of The Titans*, but it was a pale imitation of this glorious epic.

KING KONG 5

FAY WRAY, ROBERT ARMSTRONG, BRUCE CABOT, FRANK REICHER
MERIAN C COOPER, ERNEST SCHOEDSACK
USA (4-FRONT) 1933 B&W
100m (PG)

Based on an idea by Edgar Wallace, this is the classic (for once the word is completely justified) story of a huge ape brought back to civilisation from a prehistoric island. In New York he escapes and climbs the Empire State Building with Fay Wray in his hairy hand – one of the most instantly recognisable images in movie history. Animator Willis O'Brien (the man who inspired Ray Harryhausen) had already created the monsters for the silent version of Conan Doyle's *The Lost World*, and his Kong looked so real that at least one reviewer at the time of release thought it was a man in a suit. The fingerprints of the animator positioning the model between frames made the fur appear to move on film – a fault he passed off as intentional, saying it was the ape bristling with anger! For years only prints shorn of some of the more violent footage were in circulation, but happily this video is from an uncut archive copy.

ANIMATION

LADY AND THE TRAMP

Voices of:
PEGGY LEE, STAN FREBERG, BARBARA LUDDY and others

HAMILTON S LUSKE, CLYDE GERONIMI, WILFRED JACKSON

USA (DISNEY) 1955

77m (U)

Lesser fare from Disney, about a romance between two dogs, though many have a soft spot for it. Highlight is Peggy Lee's voicing of the sexy Peggy in the dogs' home. This was Disney's first CinemaScope cartoon feature, but it's pan-scan on tape, I'm afraid.

THE LION KING

Voices of:
JEREMY IRONS, JAMES EARL JONES and others

ROGER ALLERS, ROB MINKOFF

USA (DISNEY) 1994

84m (U)

Founded on the notion that there's a lotta mileage in the old good-v-evil family sagas, this predictable but fun cartoon tells of a cute young lion due to inherit the throne from his King of Beasts pop. But nasty uncle Scar (a wonderfully slimy voicing by Jeremy Irons) has other plans. Grrreat pack of gangsterish hyenas. Oscar-winning musical score from Tim Rice and Elton John may or may not be to your taste.

THE LION KING II – SIMBA'S PRIDE

Voices of:
MATTHEW BRODERICK, NATHAN LANE, ERNIE SABELLA, ROBERT GUILLAUME

ROB LADUCA, DARRELL ROONEY

USA (DISNEY) 1998

78m (U)

It may not have the power of the original, but this made-for-video film is still good family entertainment as the story tracks the adult Simba and his wayward daughter Kiara. Comedy duo Pumbaa and Timon feature.

THE LITTLE MERMAID

Voices of:
BUDDY HACKETT, KENNETH MARS, JODI BENSON and others

JOHN MUSKER, RON CLEMENTE

USA (DISNEY) 1989

82m (U)

Slight confection from Disney about cute li'l undersea gal. Apparently she was originally topless, but the moralists got cold feet and gave her a seashell bra! Oscars for best score and song ('Under the Sea').

MYSTERIOUS ISLAND [3]

HERBERT LOM, MICHAEL CRAIG, JOAN GREENWOOD, GARY MERRILL

CY ENDFIELD

UK (CINEMA CLUB V) 1961

101m (U)

Jules Verne story about escapees in a prison break via balloon during the American Civil War who end up on a weird isle populated by Captain Nemo (Lom) and oodles of outsize Ray Harryhausen creatures. Rather than construct a crab model, he improvised with a dead one bought from MacFisheries! Another fine Bernard Herrmann score.

ONE MILLION YEARS BC [4]

JOHN RICHARDSON, RAQUEL WELCH, MARTINE BESWICK

DON CHAFFEY

UK (WARNER) 1966

100m (PG)

Hammer's foray into (relatively) big-budget films, a remake of a Victor Mature caveman romp, bolstered by Ray Harryhausen's animated saurians and starlet Raquel Welch in that itsy-bitsy, teeny-weeny, furry little rabbit bikini. What a combination! The monsters may not be as smoothly rendered as the beasts in *Jurassic Park* (see page 29), but they have character which comes from having one man at the helm. Thunderous, percussive score from Mario Nascimbene.

PINOCCHIO [4]

Voices of:
DICKIE JONES, DON BRODIE, CLIFF EDWARDS and others

BEN SHARPSTEEN, HAMILTON S LUSKE

USA (DISNEY) 1940

88m (U)

Oft-filmed story of a puppet boy who comes to life. The scenes of him being abducted on his way to school and spirited to an evil place full of bad lads may scare some younger children. Oscars for best score and song ('When You Wish Upon a Star').

POCAHONTAS [3]

Voices of:
MEL GIBSON, BILLY CONNOLLY, LINDA HUNT and others

MIKE GABRIEL, ERIC GOLDBERG

USA (DISNEY) 1995

81m (U)

Bears very little relation to the true story of Native American girl Pocahontas. In spite of the rumbustious presence of Billy Connolly as the voice of one amiable rascal, it's a little bit twee, though worth watching.

ANIMATION

SLEEPING BEAUTY 🎬 4

Voices of:
MARY COSTA, BILL SHIRLEY,
BARBARA LUDDY and others

CLYDE GERONIMI

USA (DISNEY) 1958

75m (U)

Lovingly drawn fairy story from Disney, with a splendidly evil witch casting her spell over the innocent heroine. The 70mm widescreen grandeur will be lost here, though: Disney really ought to consider issuing their widescreen material in letterbox format.

SMALL SOLDIERS 🎬 3

GREGORY SMITH, KIRSTEN DUNST;
Voices of: TOMMY LEE JONES,
FRANK LANGELLA

JOE DANTE

USA (CIC) 1998

105m (PG)

Boy and girl find that a new lot of toys delivered to a shop owned by the lad's dad have been contaminated by military computer chips, making them wage war against each other. Worse, the Commando Elite (led by Major Chip Hazard) don't just hate the opposing side (the Gorgonites), they want to kill humans, too! Echoes of director Dante's *Gremlins* (see page 81) here, but with the realistic computer animation of *Toy Story* (see page 64) – great fun.

THE SWORD IN THE STONE 🎬 3

Voices of:
RICKY SORENSON, ALAN NAPIER,
GINNY TAYLOR and others

WOLFGANG REITHERMAN

USA (DISNEY) 1963

80m (U)

Arthurian legend gets the Disney treatment in this adaptation of TH White's *The Once And Future King*. Not considered one of the studio's high points, but I've always had a soft spot for it: the battle of magic between Merlin and the witch is a belter of a sequence, at least.

TIM BURTON'S THE NIGHTMARE BEFORE CHRISTMAS [4]

Voices of:
DANNY ELFMAN, CHRIS SARANDON and others

HENRY SELICK

USA (DISNEY) 1993

76m (PG)

Many assume that this was directed by Burton: in fact, it is based on an idea he had for a story while he was an animator at Disney. When people leave Disney (like Don Bluth, of the 'American Tail' films), they are often seen as rivals and rarely have any further dealings with the studio – but the old firm have definitely done themselves a favour by agreeing to make this project. Using computer animation, it conjures up a world eerily similar to that of Burton's *Beetlejuice* (see page 71). Bad boy Jack Skellington, who 'runs' Hallowe'en, decides to do the dirty on Santa and usurp the Christmas hols for his own evil ends. The dark imagery may frighten some youngsters, but it is a beautifully made film. Very Charles Addams-like, which is a compliment.

TOY STORY [4]

Voices of:
TOM HANKS, TIM ALLEN and others

JOHN LASSETER

USA (DISNEY) 1995

77m (PG)

The first full-length computer animation film is a hilarious bit of fluff about toy cowboy Woody (voiced by Tom Hanks) being jettisoned by his owner in favour of dumb spaceman Buzz Lightyear (voiced by Tim Allen), and has proved a hit with adults and kids alike. Although created by computer, the images have none of the 'flatness' of cartoons: they look like real toys walking and talking.

WHO FRAMED ROGER RABBIT [4]

BOB HOSKINS, CHRISTOPHER LLOYD, STUBBY KAYE, JOANNA CASSIDY

ROBERT ZEMECKIS

USA (TOUCHSTONE) 1988

99m (PG)

Bravura mix of real actors and cartoon characters, based on Gary K Wolf's novel *Who Censored Roger Rabbit?* about a private eye who enters 'Toontown' – a film studio where animated characters supposedly exist for real. If you enter into the silly spirit of the thing you'll enjoy yourself no end, as the makers overcame initial reluctance by different franchise-holders and managed to include famous 'toon characters from various studios. Opens with a clever example of star Roger's own work to get us in the mood. His sensual wife, Jessica Rabbit, even became a *Playboy* centrefold in real life! Amazingly, there has never been a sequel to this massive hit. Oscars for editing and audio/visual effects work.

COMEDY

If it's home entertainment for all the family you're after, then where better to start than in the comedy section? However, making a selection of good comedy videos is no easy task: what is funny to one person may be excruciatingly dull to another; so all I can do here is play safe by including the massively popular giants of the genre (Woody Allen, The Marx Brothers, Mel Brooks, Robin Williams, etc.), the latest finds (Jim Carrey, for example), and a few personal favourites. Due to the vast output of some screen comics and the restriction that choices must be currently on tape, I've only been able to include the smallest sampling of the work of Peter Sellers and Bob Hope. 'Carry On' movies are also virtually a genre in themselves, so rather than review one or two, I've reviewed the series as an entity in a separate note.

At the moment, Hollywood appears to be treating comedy like all other movies: a hit must be copied or spawn sequels. Hence *Driving Miss Daisy* (about a driver and his tetchy old charge) was virtually reincarnated as *Guarding Tess* (about a bodyguard and his tetchy old charge) – and can anyone tell the difference between headbanging comic duos Bill and Ted, Wayne and Garth *(Wayne's World)* and Beavis and Butthead? Party on, dudes!

10

DUDLEY MOORE, JULIE ANDREWS, BO DEREK, ROBERT WEBBER

BLAKE EDWARDS

USA (WARNER) 1979

118m (18)

Married songsmith pursues a young woman he sees and rates as a perfect '10' on the hit parade of beauty in this sporadically funny sex romp. The message that beauty has more to do with what's inside a person than superficial looks will be lost on most male members of the audience, who will be content to drool over Ms Derek's justly famed body.

1941

JOHN BELUSHI, TIM MATHESON, NANCY ALLEN, DAN AYKROYD, CHRISTOPHER LEE

STEVEN SPIELBERG

USA (CIC) 1979

112m (PG)

A major flop for Spielberg, but now something of a hip cult, this is a big spectacle based on the supposed invasion of California by the Japanese in World War Two. It's his attempt to do an epic laff-riot like *It's A Mad, Mad, Mad, Mad World* (see page 83) but it really needs a huge screen to pull it off.

ACE VENTURA: PET DETECTIVE

JIM CARREY, COURTENEY COX, SEAN YOUNG, TONE LOC

TOM SHADYAC

USA (WARNER) 1994

87m (PG)

Carrey is not my favourite type of actor – to me he seems to be a rubber-faced, rubber-stamp of Jerry Lewis circa the early 60s – but he does have a popular following so he is certainly doing something right. This is the best of his works, and is agreeably silly enough. On a two-for-one tape with the sequel.

THE ACID HOUSE

EWEN BREMNER, KEVIN McKIDD, MARTIN CLUNES, STEPHEN McCOLE, JEMMA REDGRAVE

PAUL McGUIGAN

SCOTLAND (FILM FOUR) 1998

106m (18)

Three tales from the pen of Irvine *Trainspotting* Welsh, and involving a couple of the stars of that pic. *The Granton Star Cause* is about an unfortunate who is turned into a fly by God – shades of Kafka! *A Soft Touch* is about a lad abused by all and sundry. The title story concerns an LSD-mad raver who swaps minds with a baby. All in all, not a patch on the marvellous *Trainspotting* (see page 136) but inventively bizzare all the same.

COMEDY

THE ADDAMS FAMILY [4]

ANJELICA HUSTON, RAUL JULIA, CHRISTOPHER LLOYD, DAN HEDAYA

BARRY SONNENFELD

USA (CINEMA CLUB V) 1991

96m (PG)

Lovingly crafted update of the old TV show adapted from Charles Addams' drawings of a ghoulish cartoon family. Some of the acid commentary on American society may be gone, but the sets and acting are a delight throughout. See sequel below.

ADDAMS FAMILY VALUES [4]

ANJELICA HUSTON, RAUL JULIA, CHRISTOPHER LLOYD, JOAN CUSACK

BARRY SONNENFELD

USA (CIC) 1993

94m (PG)

A sequel that's every bit as much fun as the first film, with a particularly mischievous showing from little Christina Ricci as the coolly calculating daughter of the family. Sadly, with star Raul Julia deceased, the series seems to be stalled for good, although a new TV show with a new cast has begun.

AIRPLANE [5]

ROBERT HAYS, JULIE HAGERTY, ROBERT STACK, LLOYD BRIDGES

JIM ABRAHAMS, DAVID ZUCKER, JERRY ZUCKER

USA (CIC) 1980

84m (PG)

Madcap, risqué spoof of the stupid 'Airport' series of disaster flicks, with several reliable players sending themselves up something rotten. Ideally suited to video: the jokes come so rapidly that the ability to rewind for a second glance is essential. A hoot.

AMERICAN GRAFFITI [4]

RICHARD DREYFUSS, HARRISON FORD, RON HOWARD, CHARLES MARTIN SMITH

GEORGE LUCAS

USA (CIC) 1973

108m (PG)

Wacky, slapstick comedy about the coming-of-age of small-town American buddies as they leave school and prepare for the wide world. Lucas became a top film-maker with the *Star Wars* movies (see Science Fiction chapter), Howard switched to directing, and Ford is now a megastar legend. This pic was much copied but never improved upon.

AND NOW FOR SOMETHING COMPLETELY DIFFERENT

★ JOHN CLEESE, ERIC IDLE, GRAHAM CHAPMAN, MICHAEL PALIN, TERRY JONES, TERRY GILLIAM

IAN McNAUGHTON

UK (CINEMA CLUB V) 1972

85m (PG)

Many of the *Monty Python's Flying Circus* TV sketches are here, re-shot on film stock, making a nice time-capsule for those who weren't around for the original BBC broadcasts. Personally, though I loved the Python style in my schoolboy days, I now find that the increased sophistication of today's comedy (which has taken on board the anarchic social criticism of the team and expanded upon it) makes some of the material look very dated indeed. The same could be said of the Goons, of course: the price of innovation? Note: all the Python TV shows are now available in a huge boxed set, released as we went to press (see page 310).

ANIMAL CRACKERS

★ THE MARX BROTHERS, MARGARET DUMONT, LILLIAN ROTH

VICTOR HEERMAN

USA (CIC) 1930 B&W

98m (U)

'This morning I shot an elephant in my pyjamas – how he got in my pyjamas I'll never know!' So says Groucho Marx in this adaptation of the comic team's hit Broadway show. Groucho, Harpo, Chico and Zeppo are all here in a classic piece of wisecracking, slapstick mayhem.

ANIMAL HOUSE

★ JOHN BELUSHI, TIM MATHESON, TOM HULCE, JOHN VERNON

JOHN LANDIS

USA (CIC) 1978

104m (15)

First and funniest of the *National Lampoon* gagfests, brimming with rude slapstick, set in and around college fraternities and featuring the late Belushi at his gross best. Hulce went on to star in hit drama *Amadeus*. Also known as *National Lampoon's Animal House*.

COMEDY

ANNIE HALL

DIANE KEATON, WOODY ALLEN, TONY ROBERTS, CAROL KANE, PAUL SIMON

WOODY ALLEN

USA (WARNER) 1977

89m (15)

One of Allen's best, a touching, funny romantic comedy about a wacky girl and a nerdish comedian, with typically Allen-ish observations on life: 'a relationship is like a shark – if it doesn't keep moving forward it dies. I think what we've got here is a dead shark'. Keaton's mismatched, Oxfam-style clothes became a fashion trend. Oscars: best film, actress (Keaton), direction, screenplay (Allen and Marshall Brickman).

ARSENIC AND OLD LACE

CARY GRANT, PRISCILLA LANE, PETER LORRE, RAYMOND MASSEY

FRANK CAPRA

USA (WARNER) 1941 B&W

113m (PG)

Near-screwball film of the old chestnut about crazed murdering grannies, with sharp direction from Capra and a wonderful cast of top players. Sick and sardonic – perhaps that's why release was held back until 1944 though the pic was filmed three years earlier. A camp classic.

ARTHUR

DUDLEY MOORE, LIZA MINELLI, JOHN GIELGUD, TED ROSS

STEVE GORDON

USA (WARNER) 1981

93m (15)

This easy-going comedy about a layabout millionaire who spends his days in an agreeable haze of booze and casual sex until true love strikes was a surprise hit. Both Moore as the loveable lush and Minelli as his gal acquit themselves well, but Gielgud steals the show (and won an Oscar) in the support part of the droll, filthy-mouthed butler who has to clear up the empties and dismiss last night's hookers after his master's excesses. The theme tune also won an Oscar. There was a sequel, *Arthur 2: On The Rocks*, but it failed to match the louche charm of its predecessor.

AUSTIN POWERS – INTERNATIONAL MAN OF MYSTERY 🎬 4

MIKE MYERS, ELIZABETH HURLEY, MIMI ROGERS

JAY ROACH

USA (FOX) 1997

91m (15)

Deliciously camp homage to 60s spy spoofs like *Our Man Flint* and *Dr Goldfoot And The Girl Bombs*. How do you spoof a spoof? I dunno, but *Wayne's World* honcho Myers manages it in this pic, lensed in authentically garish psychedelic colour, in the twin roles of shag-mad Powers and his nemesis Dr Evil, a groovy secret agent and a Blofeld-like baddy both released from the suspended animation they've been frozen in since those fabulous 60s. On hand to update Powers on the advances in civilisation is modern babe Vanessa Kensington (a surprisingly able Hurley). Great fun if you like that sort of thing. Sequel: *The Spy Who Shagged Me*.

BAD TASTE 🎬 4

PETER O'HERNE, PETER JACKSON, MIKE MINETT, TERRY POTTER

PETER JACKSON

NEW ZEALAND (4-FRONT) 1988

90m (18)

First film from highly-rated director Jackson is a ghastly, gory, sick, hilarious horror piece about idiotic secret agents fighting cannibal aliens. Minuscule-budget 'shock' flicks like this are apt to get a hammering from the censor, but the BBFC realised what the director was trying to do, saw the joke and let the film through unscathed. Don't see it on a full stomach!

BEDAZZLED 🎬 3

PETER COOK, DUDLEY MOORE, ELEANOR BRON, RAQUEL WELCH

STANLEY DONEN

UK (FOX) 1967

101m (PG)

Update of *Faust*, with Devil Cook tempting his then-partner Moore with the seven deadly sins: naturally, in the swinging 60s Raquel Welch was trotted out as Lust. Not as nimble as it wants to be, but it's great to see the late Cook in his prime. A faded relic. Rumours of a remake.

COMEDY

BEETHOVEN

CHARLES GRODIN, BONNIE HUNT, DEAN JONES, STANLEY TUCCI

BRIAN LEVANT

USA (CIC) 1992

87m (U)

Knockabout funny concerning the havoc wrought by a rescued St Bernard on the family who saved it from a nasty geezer. A sure bet for children, with a nice appearance by Tucci (who played Richard Cross in TV hit *Murder One*). Has already spawned one sequel so far: *Beethoven's 2nd* (1993).

BEETLEJUICE

MICHAEL KEATON, GEENA DAVIS, ALEC BALDWIN, WINONA RYDER

TIM BURTON

USA (WARNER) 1988

88m (15)

Showcase for director Burton's insane ideas and the pic which first matched him with Keaton, with whom he worked on *Batman* and its first sequel, *Batman Returns* (both on page 16). Mad story involves a couple who come to realise they're dead after a car smash, and who hire freelance ghoul Keaton to rid their beloved home of new tenants. In the process, they form a bond with the new family's morbid daughter because she's the only human who seems able to tune in to what's going on! The imagery is unique, skewed and unsettling: like a Charles Addams aiming for the 90s and beyond. Amazing. (Also on a two-for-one tape with *The Witches Of Eastwick* – see page 93, the devilish Jack Nicholson comedy.)

BEVERLY HILLS COP

EDDIE MURPHY, JUDGE REINHOLD, STEVEN BERKOFF, RONNY COX

MARTIN BREST

USA (CIC) 1984

101m (15)

Motormouth Murphy in first of the action/comedy films about a black street cop, Axel Foley, and his adventures in the refined purlieus of California. His wisecracks are undeniably amusing first time around, and this is definitely the best of his pix. Diehard Eddie fans will love it!

BILL AND TED'S BOGUS JOURNEY

KEANU REEVES, ALEX WINTER, GEORGE CARLIN, JOSS ACKLAND

PETER HEWITT

USA (ENTERTAINMENT) 1991

98m (PG)

Originally to be called *Bill And Ted Go To Hell*, this second story of the dumb-but-cool rock dudes sees them murdered by robot doubles before they meet the grim reaper and ... you don't really want to hear this, do you? Sort of live-action *Beavis And Butthead* and immense fun, the only worrying thing being the apparent message that it is okay to be stupid as long as you are pure in spirit and love rock 'n' roll, because then you can beat the baddies who want to control the world. Sadly, that's just what the real bad guys would love you to believe! Wake up, the reaper's coming! Two-for-one tape with *Bill And Ted's Excellent Adventure* (see below) available.

BILL AND TED'S EXCELLENT ADVENTURE

KEANU REEVES, ALEX WINTER, GEORGE CARLIN, BERNIE CASEY

STEPHEN HEREK

USA (ENTERTAINMENT) 1989

90m (PG)

Low-budget time-travel comedy about two rock-loving California nerds who discover that they're the future of mankind – but only if they pass their exams! Stupid-yet-funny: became a 'sleeper' hit through word-of-mouth and propelled Reeves towards stardom. Spawned sequel and TV cartoons. I'll leave it to you to decide whether it is better/worse than similar *Wayne's World* (see page 93) and *Beavis And Butthead* (see page 308). Two-for-one tape with sequel (see above) also available.

BILLY LIAR

TOM COURTENAY, JULIE CHRISTIE, MONA WASHBOURNE, WILFRED PICKLES

JOHN SCHLESINGER

UK (WARNER) 1963 B&W

98m (PG)

Overpraised, sad, dour story about a dreamer who finally is unable to take the steps to freedom urged on him by his girlfriend. You come away angry at him for being such a loser, despite the many hilarious touches. I mean, what guy wouldn't scoot away to London with a young Julie Christie along for the run?

COMEDY

BLAZING SADDLES

- CLEAVON LITTLE, GENE WILDER, MADELINE KAHN, DOM DE LUISE
- MEL BROOKS
- USA (WARNER) 1970
- 94m (15)

A mega-hit at the time of first release, this cowboy spoof is still full of healthy vulgarity but to me feels slightly smug and dated. Unfortunately, it led Mel Brooks to embark on a series of progressively less amusing parodies of other genres, of which the best was 1974's *Young Frankenstein* (see page 94). He is an immensely astute and talented producer, but he still continues with these 'spoofs' to the present day, even though they all seem to play for only a week or so in cinemas and get a critical drubbing. One can only suppose they make money somehow, somewhere. This remains his best work, along with cult film *The Producers* (see page 89).

THE BLUES BROTHERS

- JOHN BELUSHI, DAN AYKROYD, CAB CALLOWAY, CARRIE FISHER
- JOHN LANDIS
- USA (CIC) 1980
- 127m (15)

This wildly successful cult flick about two cool dudes trying to save an orphanage is really just an excuse for the late Belushi to goof off amid superb action stunts and guest spots for many music legends. At the time of release, the duo recorded a live album of old soul songs which was a Number One hit in the USA record charts, and there has recently been a successful *Tribute To The Blues Brothers* stage show in the UK. A new 'Blues Brothers' film has recently emerged, to bad reviews.

BOB ROBERTS

- TIM ROBBINS, ALAN RICKMAN, GORE VIDAL, GIANCARLO ESPOSITO
- TIM ROBBINS
- USA (CINEMA CLUB V) 1992
- 104m (15)

Shrewd pseudo-documentary about the rise of a right-wing USA political candidate who cleverly uses the weapons of the counterculture in a 'straight' context: he sings folk songs deriding alleged welfare scroungers and his album covers ape the designs of old Dylan hits. Sinister and possibly prophetic despite the humour. Unbelievably, one major UK film critic opined that the joke was on the director because the ideas put forward by the conniving politician in the movie were jolly good and made perfect sense to him! Now that's even more disturbing than the film. As Oscar Wilde said, life imitates art ...

THE BREAKFAST CLUB ★4

EMILIO ESTEVEZ, JUDD NELSON, MOLLY RINGWALD, ALLY SHEEDY

JOHN HUGHES

USA (CIC) 1984

93m (15)

Touching, funny, believable story about a group of misfits stuck in a detention class for high-school troublemakers. As we listen to them talk, they gradually reveal, not without barbed wit, their personal problems. Judd Nelson appears to have got lost in the wake of his 'Brat Pack' fame, but this movie shows just what a fine actor he really is. And whatever happened to Ringwald and Sheedy, so affecting and effective here? A little lost classic ensemble job. Sheedy has since won praise for 1998's *High Art*.

BRITANNIA HOSPITAL ★3

LEONARD ROSSITER, JILL BENNETT, FULTON MACKAY, GRAHAM CROWDEN

LINDSAY ANDERSON

UK (WARNER/LUMIERE) 1982

111m (15)

Typically grim humour from Anderson, with a chaotic, demented NHS hospital standing for the collapse of the Britain of Thatcher and big business. You'll laugh until you're sick to your stomach, that is if you manage to raise a chuckle at all. Not much fun, but I hardly suppose it was intended to be.

BROADCAST NEWS ★5

WILLIAM HURT, HOLLY HUNTER, ALBERT BROOKS, JACK NICHOLSON

JAMES L BROOKS

USA (FOX) 1987

127m (15)

Romantic comedy about a TV producer torn between her smitten, clever best friend and the handsome-but-dumb newscaster who gets all the breaks simply because of his looks. A witty, incisive examination of the way news on the box is sold as mere entertainment for the brain-dead, with a great cast. Do see it!

THE BURBS ★3

TOM HANKS, COREY FELDMAN, CARRIE FISHER, BRUCE DERN

JOE DANTE

USA (CIC) 1989

97m (PG)

Dante's oddball fantasy about the corruption lurking beneath suburbia for those who pry too much into their neighbours' affairs. Not a hit, but now has a following. The BBFC made slight cuts because film clips seen on TV during the pic are from films not legally available in the UK(!).

COMEDY

THE CABLE GUY

JIM CARREY, MATTHEW BRODERICK

BEN STILLER

USA (COLUMBIA TRISTAR) 1996

92m (12)

Bizarre hybrid comedy-thriller about a depressed young man (Broderick) whose life is invaded by the deranged cable TV installer (Carrey) whom he bribes to provide him with free access to movie channels. Carrey is his usual crazed self, but the fact that we are never sure if we're watching comedy or tragedy takes some of the enjoyment out of what might have been a great story.

'CARRY ON ...' A SPECIAL NOTE!

Instead of reviewing individual entries in the 'Carry On' series, I think it is best simply to insert this note looking at the films as a whole. The series is virtually a genre in itself, vulgar Brit humour of the panto and seaside postcard transferred to film. Cast members came and went, but a core group of Kenneth Connor, Charles Hawtrey, Sid James and the marvellous Kenneth Williams were around for most of the pix – though the posthumous release of Williams' diaries reveal that he felt (rightly) that not enough effort went into the writing or acting by many of those involved. From *Carry On Sergeant* (1959) to *Carry On Columbus* (1992), there were 30 films plus compilations and offshoots. The movie known as *Carry On Don't Lose Your Head* (1966) was initially issued as simply *Don't Lose Your Head*, because the makers wrongly thought the series had had its day. *Carry On Columbus* was a belated attempt to revive the series for the 90s with new stars to cash in on the serious (eh?) 'Columbus' movies being made at the time – an old trick they'd pulled off at the time of Liz Taylor's *Cleopatra* (see page 142) with *Carry On Cleo* (1965). Gerald Thomas directed most of the films and many are still around on video, but I think most pundits agree that it's definitely now time to call a halt to all this carry on! (Most of the available films are on Warner, Cinema Club Video and 4-Front.) Boxed set: *The Complete Carry-On* at £99.99!

CASANOVA'S BIG NIGHT

BOB HOPE, JOAN FONTAINE, BASIL RATHBONE, VINCENT PRICE

NORMAN Z McLEOD

USA (CIC) 1954

82m (U)

Hope takes a break from the never-ending 'Road' pictures with Bing Crosby to appear in this handsomely mounted piece of tosh about the great lover and his troubles. Throwaway nonsense, but Hope is as amusing as ever and Rathbone and Price beef up the cast no end. Only the most churlish will fail to smile.

CITY SLICKERS

BILLY CRYSTAL, HELEN SLATER, JACK PALANCE, BRUNO KIRBY

RON UNDERWOOD

USA (CINEMA CLUB V) 1990

109m (15)

Chucklesome adventure of city boys learning to be cowboys under the unforgiving tutelage of leathery old hand Palance, who won an Oscar for his efforts. The film was successful enough to spawn a sequel and to be parodied in a jeans advert. Harmless and very funny in places: definitely worth renting, if not owning.

CRIMES AND MISDEMEANORS

MARTIN LANDAU, WOODY ALLEN, ALAN ALDA, CLAIRE BLOOM, MIA FARROW

WOODY ALLEN

USA (VISION) 1989

100m (15)

One of Woody's better serious/comic hybrids, a musing on murder and infidelity with a sterling turn from Landau, an actor who has only recently been recognised as the fine performer he is. Allen plays his usual glum worrywart, providing comic relief just when things look to be getting too dramatic for comfort. A lovely bit of film-making.

CROCODILE DUNDEE

PAUL HOGAN, LINDA KOZLOWSKI, DAVID GULPILIL, MARK BLUM

PETER FAIMAN

AUSTRALIA (POLYGRAM) 1986

93m (15)

Screen debut for comic Hogan, in which he plays a rough bushman lured from the Aussie outback to the concrete jungle of New York – which he takes on with a mixture of charm and a Very Big Knife Indeed. An amusing romantic comedy which certainly changed Hogan's life – he ditched his wife for his co-star, blonde bombshell Kozlowski. He has never quite equalled its success, even with the 1988 sequel *Crocodile Dundee 2*.

A DAY AT THE RACES

THE MARX BROTHERS, MAUREEN O'SULLIVAN

SAM WOOD

USA (WARNER) 1937 B&W

109m (U)

Another Marx Brothers classic slice of tomfoolery. Also on a two-for-one tape with *A Night At The Opera* (1935), yet another Marx Brothers effort and also helmed by Sam Wood.

COMEDY

DEAD MEN DON'T WEAR PLAID

STEVE MARTIN, RACHEL WARD, CARL REINER, RENI SANTONI

CARL REINER

USA (CIC/4-FRONT) 1982 B&W

88m (PG)

One-note spoof of the classic monochrome private eye movies of yore. Clips from many favourites are skilfully woven into the story, with Martin on form as he responds to the dialogue with amusing quips. If it was being put together nowadays, of course, new technology would enable the comic to be placed in the old footage for a much funnier and smoother effect. Although the joke wears a little thin before the finale, the film still offers a fair share of laughs.

DEATH BECOMES HER

MERYL STREEP, BRUCE WILLIS, GOLDIE HAWN, ISABELLA ROSSELLINI

ROBERT ZEMECKIS

USA (CIC) 1992

104m (PG)

Fast-and-furious comic roller-coaster from Zemeckis who made the *Back to the Future* films (see page 15). Oscar-winning computer effects – which show the stars twisting and rubbernecking all over the shop – are astonishing the first time around.

DIRTY ROTTEN SCOUNDRELS

STEVE MARTIN, MICHAEL CAINE, BARBARA HARRIS, DANA IVEY, GLENNE HEADLY

FRANK OZ

USA (4-FRONT) 1988

110m (PG)

Remake of the 1964 Brando film *Bedtime Story*. Two rival con-artists on the French Riviera take a bet to see who can swindle a glamorous TV star first. Quite well written, but really it's the silly japes of Martin and Caine which make it a reasonably engaging story.

DIVORCING JACK

DAVID THEWLIS, RACHEL GRIFFITHS, JASON ISAACS, ROBERT LINDSAY

DAVID CAFFREY

UK (MOSAIC) 1998

110m (15)

A cynical Irish newspaper columnist with a fondness for the booze wakes up to find that the woman he has just made love to is dead. His only ally in his fight to find his way through the ensuing chaotic events is a nun. Fun comedy thriller.

DR DOLITTLE [2]

- EDDIE MURPHY
- BETTY THOMAS
- USA (FOX PATHE) 1998
- 105m (PG)

Successful doctor and family man Dolittle's life is turned upside down when he rediscovers his latent talent. An updated version of the classic tale of the man who can talk to the animals, laced with Eddie Murphy's zany style of humour.

DR STRANGELOVE, OR HOW I LEARNED TO STOP WORRYING AND LOVE THE BOMB [4]

- PETER SELLERS, STERLING HAYDEN, SLIM PICKENS, GEORGE C SCOTT
- STANLEY KUBRICK
- UK (ENCORE) 1963 B&W
- 91m (PG)

Based on Peter George's novel *Red Alert* (aka *Two Hours To Dream*), this classic cold war comedy has Sellers in three parts: the USA President trying to recall bombers sent to nuke Russia, a demented ex-Nazi and a stiff-upper-lip Brit. Like its non-comedy equivalent *Fail Safe* (see page 113), it is very much of its time but remains a sour commentary on atomic stalemate. A typically icy Kubrick picture, with Sellers, Hayden and Scott acting manically. Characters with names like Buck Turgidson clue you in that this is high farce. Unique.

DRIVING MISS DAISY [4]

- JESSICA TANDY, MORGAN FREEMAN, DAN AYKROYD, PATTI LUPONE
- BRUCE BERESFORD
- USA (WARNER) 1989
- 94m (U)

Slushy yet genuinely warm and amusing story of the quarter-century relationship between a tetchy white woman and her black chauffeur in America's deep south. Based on Alfred Uhry's play, it won Oscars for best film, actress (Tandy), adapted screenplay and make-up. The recent movie *Guarding Tess* was an obvious attempt at replicating the formula.

DUMB AND DUMBER [3]

- JIM CARREY, JEFF DANIELS, LAUREN HOLLY
- PETER FARRELLY
- USA (FIRST INDEPENDENT) 1994
- 102m (12)

Carrey and Daniels are two slapstick fools in this amusing but thoroughly inconsequential piece of nonsense. Though hardly a classic comedy, this was a box-office hit, and offers some entertaining moments.

COMEDY

EDUCATING RITA [4]

MICHAEL CAINE, JULIE WALTERS, MAUREEN LIPMAN, MICHAEL WILLIAMS

LEWIS GILBERT

UK (RANK) 1983

110m (15)

Willy Russell's mega-hit play transfers smoothly to the screen, with Walters as a working-class girl anxious to better herself by studying for a university degree, and Caine as the alcoholic lecturer who urges her to go for it. Bittersweet romance which garnered Oscar nominations for Caine and Walters.

ENTERTAINING MR SLOANE [3]

BERYL REID, HARRY ANDREWS, PETER McENERY, ALAN WEBB

DOUGLAS HICKOX

UK (WARNER/LUMIERE) 1969

90m (15)

Half-arsed (ooh-er!) attempt to film the late Joe Orton's bisexual comedy of manners, with Reid and Andrews as the old duffers lusting after McEnery's leather-clad houseboy. Orton's work is notoriously hard to bring off (double ooh-er!) in that the farcical elements have to be played dead straight (*triple* ooh-er!) for the humour to bite. Though not a complete success, the film is worth watching as it offers a record of the play.

FEAR AND LOATHING IN LAS VEGAS [2]

JOHNNY DEPP, BENICIO DEL TORO, TOBEY MAGUIRE

TERRY GILLIAM

USA (CIC) 1998

118m (18)

Fitfully amusing but finally enervating movie of gonzo hack Hunter S Thompson's book about his drug-fuelled trip to gambling hell. What was hilarious on the printed page tends to tire the eyes when transposed with leaden exactitude to the screen, reminding the viewer that to meet a loud egomaniac on drugs in real life would, in all probability, be no fun at all.

FIRST WIVES CLUB [3]

BETTE MIDLER, GOLDIE HAWN, DIANE KEATON

HUGH WILSON

USA (CIC) 1996

98m (PG)

Revenge fantasy for the Hormone Replacement Therapy generation, with trio of glamorous and successful women uniting to take a swipe at the hubbies who ditched them. Fairly witty script and glossy smirking from the three stars. Some great one-liners from Bette Midler but suffers slightly from trying to get a message across instead of concentrating on the comedy.

A FISH CALLED WANDA 🎬4

JOHN CLEESE, KEVIN KLINE, JAMIE LEE CURTIS, MICHAEL PALIN

CHARLES CRICHTON

UK (WARNER) 1988

103m (15)

Veteran director Crichton came out of retirement to direct this hit farce about missing loot being chased by a misfit gang of jewel robbers. Curtis is sexy and Kline won the Oscar for best supporting actor, but the result doesn't quite live up to its inflated reputation as the craziest comedy of the 80s.

THE FULL MONTY 🎬4

ROBERT CARLYLE, PAUL BARBER, MARK ADDY, TOM WILKINSON

PETER CATTANEO

UK (FOX) 1997

88m (15)

Surprise Brit hit about unemployed men escaping the horrors of the dole by forming a male strip troupe, with great performances all round (in the film, not the troupe!). The story isn't *that* original (a similar tale had appeared as a TV play) but the exuberant execution made it a success in America, a market normally resistant to parochial Brit stories. A real measure of the film's impact is that when the title phrase is used these days people immediately think of the movie, rather than the subject under discussion. Funny, and quite touching in places.

GHOSTBUSTERS 🎬3

DAN AYKROYD, BILL MURRAY, SIGOURNEY WEAVER, RICK MORANIS

IVAN REITMAN

USA (CINEMA CLUB V) 1984

101m (PG)

Like a comedy version of TV's *X-Files*, with a bunch of loony parapsychologists using hi-tech to combat the supernatural infestations of the modern world. Startling SFX and some good jokes. Sequel: *Ghostbusters 2* (1988).

GOOD MORNING, VIETNAM 🎬4

ROBIN WILLIAMS, FOREST WHITAKER, ROBERT WUHL, TUNG TUANH TRAN

BARRY LEVINSON

USA (TOUCHSTONE) 1988

116m (15)

Based on real-life American forces disc jockey Adrian Cronauer, this showcases Williams' ad-libbing style to perfection. He plays a DJ broadcasting to US troops in Vietnam who comes into conflict with his superiors when he refuses to toe the line with staid music and chat – but, predictably, the ordinary soldiers love his anarchic style. Hilarious moments, though the storyline is a little weak – the problem lies in the fact that there is no way you can make the Vietnam conflagration seem like fun.

COMEDY

THE GRADUATE ▦4

DUSTIN HOFFMAN, KATHERINE ROSS, ANNE BANCROFT

MIKE NICHOLS

USA (BMG) 1967

106m (15)

Coming-of-age story, based on the Charles Webb novel, about a young man who is seduced by an older woman but then falls for her daughter. Very much of-its-time, but fresh performances and the score by Simon and Garfunkel ('Mrs Robinson', *et al*) made the pic a smash and Hoffman a star. Oscar for director Nichols. The social satire on American mores is dated, but it's still quite funny in places. If you can locate a copy, *Goodbye Columbus*, a similar movie from the same era is, I think, far better.

GREMLINS ▦4

ZACH GALLIGAN, PHOEBE CATES, HOYT AXTON, JUDGE REINHOLD

JOE DANTE

USA (WARNER) 1984

102m (15)

Demented and cartoonish riot about some odd little creatures which multiply and get nasty if you don't follow the pet care rules, with typically dark subtext from director Dante. Fab scenes of the evil little devils running amok and creating havoc in a Spielbergian small American town. Available in widescreen. Sequel: *Gremlins 2: The New Batch* (1990).

GROUNDHOG DAY ▦3

BILL MURRAY, ANDIE MacDOWELL, CHRIS ELLIOTT, MARITA GERAGHTY

HAROLD RAMIS

USA (COLUMBIA TRISTAR) 1993

101m (PG)

Daft premise about a TV man sent to a small town to cover the witless annual festival, only to find that he must constantly relive the same day over and over again. Some romance, some laughs and a romantic ending. Don't look too deeply for meaning, just enjoy at a light-hearted level. Widescreen available.

HANNAH AND HER SISTERS ▦4

WOODY ALLEN, MICHAEL CAINE, MIA FARROW, BARBARA HERSHEY, DIANNE WIEST, CARRIE FISHER, MAX VON SYDOW

WOODY ALLEN

USA (VISION) 1986

102m (15)

Typically classy romantic comedy from Allen centred around the complex love lives of a group of sisters and their suitors, husbands and friends. Won deserved supporting performance Oscars for Caine and Wiest.

HARVEY 🎬 5

⭐ JAMES STEWART, JOSEPHINE HULL, VICTORIA HORNE, PEGGY DOW

🎬 HENRY KOSTER

USA (CIC) 1950 B&W

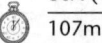

⏱ 107m (U)

Splendid version of the Mary Chase play about attempts to lock a dipsomaniac in an asylum because he holds conversations with the giant white rabbit of the title, which is invisible to all but himself. Non-stop screwball confusion and a nice message about the sanctity of the individual, driven by a wonderful performance from Stewart. He revived the play in the 1970s on the London stage to deserved acclaim. The play won a Pulitzer Prize and the movie won Hull a best supporting actress Oscar.

HEAR MY SONG 🎬 4

⭐ NED BEATTY, ADRIAN DUNBAR, SHIRLEY ANN FIELD, DAVID McCALLUM

🎬 PETER CHELSOM

UK (CIC) 1991

⏱ 104m (15)

Entertaining tale about a plan to stage a concert starring legendary Irish tenor Josef Locke. Ned Beatty, usually confined to secondary character parts, gives an outstanding performance in this great little film.

HEATHERS 🎬 4

⭐ WINONA RYDER, CHRISTIAN SLATER, SHANNEN DOHERTY, KIM WALKER

🎬 MICHAEL LEHMANN

USA (CINEMA CLUB V) 1989

⏱ 98m (18)

Slyly nasty tale of a girl who tires of her membership of a snobby group of high school girls, only to be prompted by her new weirdo beau into bumping them off (along with other sundry twerps). Goes a bit cock-eyed towards the end, but still an original debut for the director, with nifty work from the two lead stars. Humour at its blackest.

HOT SHOTS 🎬 3

⭐ CHARLIE SHEEN, LLOYD BRIDGES, CARY ELWES, EFREM ZIMBALIST Jnr

🎬 JIM ABRAHAMS

USA (FOX) 1991

⏱ 81m (PG)

From the makers of *Airplane* (see page 67) and *Naked Gun* (see page 86) comes this madcap send-up of *Top Gun*, with lots of visual puns and foolishness. Tries a tad too hard, but not bad. Sequel: *Hot Shots Part Deux*.

COMEDY

THE HUDSUCKER PROXY [4]

TIM ROBBINS, PAUL NEWMAN, JENNIFER JASON LEIGH, CHARLES DURNING

JOEL COEN

USA (COLUMBIA TRISTAR) 1994

107m (PG)

Homage of sorts to the screwball comedies of Frank Capra from the brothers Coen. Robbins is the eager-to-please nerd, plucked from obscurity to the top of the tree by scheming boss Paul Newman in an attempt to grab big bucks. Hilarious, and the 30s-style sets amaze.

THE IMPORTANCE OF BEING EARNEST [4]

MICHAEL REDGRAVE, MICHAEL DENNISON, EDITH EVANS, JOAN GREENWOOD

ANTHONY ASQUITH

UK (RANK) 1952

91m (U)

Classic screen version of Oscar Wilde's sparkling comedy of manners, with Evans making the perfect Lady Bracknell. She's supported by a glittering cast of top British thespians, including Margaret Rutherford and Miles Malleson as well as the big stars. Witty, wonderful, marvellous. May seem dated to younger audiences, but that's their loss. Recent cinema restoration.

IT'S A MAD, MAD, MAD, MAD WORLD [3]

SPENCER TRACY, PHIL SILVERS, JERRY LEWIS, TERRY-THOMAS, JACK BENNY

STANLEY KRAMER

USA (WARNER) 1963

148m (U)

The idea of making an epic, widescreen, spectacular comedy is an odd one, but that's what Kramer attempted in this multi-star pic about a bunch of disparate folk in search of buried loot. It doesn't quite come off, but the star cameos and Oscar-winning SFX carry the thing along. Not available in widescreen. The original running time was 192m, but the last copy I saw had the above-listed 148m timing. Worth checking before you buy or rent to ascertain if you're getting the full movie.

JERRY MAGUIRE [3]

TOM CRUISE, KELLY PRESTON, CUBA GOODING Jnr, RENEE ZELLWEGER

CAMERON CROWE

USA (COLUMBIA TRISTAR) 1996

133m (15)

Described by *Sight & Sound* as 'Comedy, romance and satire on American football', this is an unbelievable story about a sports agent who tells his bosses that they should have less clients and really, er, *care* for them. Naturally, he's fired. How he fights back takes up the rest of the story. If only life was like that. Well reviewed but overrated.

83

KIND HEARTS AND CORONETS 🎬 5

⭐ DENNIS PRICE, ALEC GUINNESS, JOAN GREENWOOD, MILES MALLESON

🎬 ROBERT HAMER

UK (WARNER/LUMIERE) 1949 B&W

⏱ 101m (U)

Roy Horniman's novel *Noblesse Oblige* ably transferred to screen, with Price as murderer bumping off eight aristocrats (all played by Guinness) on his way to a title. Smooth as a perfect sherry and a British comedy classic.

KING OF COMEDY 🎬 3

⭐ ROBERT DE NIRO, JERRY LEWIS, SANDRA BERNHARD, TONY RANDALL

🎬 MARTIN SCORSESE

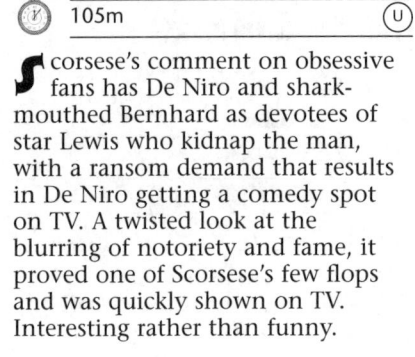

USA (WARNER) 1981

⏱ 105m (U)

Scorsese's comment on obsessive fans has De Niro and shark-mouthed Bernhard as devotees of star Lewis who kidnap the man, with a ransom demand that results in De Niro getting a comedy spot on TV. A twisted look at the blurring of notoriety and fame, it proved one of Scorsese's few flops and was quickly shown on TV. Interesting rather than funny.

THE LAVENDER HILL MOB 🎬 4

⭐ ALEC GUINNESS, STANLEY HOLLOWAY, SIDNEY JAMES, ALFIE BASS

🎬 CHARLES CRICHTON

UK (WARNER/LUMIERE) 1951 B&W

⏱ 77m (U)

Oscar-winning screenplay about bank employee (Guinness) and his pals robbing a gold shipment. Delightful Ealing classic which still packs a load of laughs. Unforgettable cast of old hands and famous faces. See it at least once.

LITTLE VOICE 🎬 5

⭐ JANE HORROCKS, MICHAEL CAINE, BRENDA BLETHYN, JIM BROADBENT, EWAN McGREGOR

🎬 MARK HERMAN

UK (BUENA VISTA) 1998

⏱ 93m (15)

Brilliant British comedy about a painfully shy young girl who has the gift of being able to sing like all the finest stars. Superb performances by all the cast, including the sleazy agent played by Caine and the over-the-top Northern woman played by Brenda Blethyn. Also on DVD.

COMEDY

LOST IN AMERICA 🎬4
JULIE HAGERTY, ALBERT BROOKS, MICHAEL GREEN, GARY MARSHALL
ALBERT BROOKS
USA (WARNER) 1985
88m — (15)

An executive drops out after missing a promotion and takes to the road with his wife in a camper van, only to lose all their savings at Las Vegas when the lady gets gambling fever. Hilarious, but the ending in which our hero goes back and grovels for a job at his old firm is misjudged and depressing, albeit true to life. Not a hit, but a cult film.

LOVE AT FIRST BITE 🎬3
GEORGE HAMILTON, SUSAN ST JAMES, RICHARD BENJAMIN, DICK SHAWN
STAN DRAGOTI
USA (MIA) 1979
96m — (15)

Dracula spoof with old smoothie Hamilton romancing the girl he meets when he emigrates to the USA. Horror comedies are notoriously difficult to pull off, but this has a deserved reputation as a daft slice of lightweight foolishness.

THE MEANING OF LIFE 🎬3
JOHN CLEESE, GRAHAM CHAPMAN, ERIC IDLE, TERRY GILLIAM, MICHAEL PALIN
TERRY JONES
UK (CIC) 1983
107m — (15)

The third Python movie, with the usual *mélange* of bizarre and sick sketches – including a musical number about sperm and the exploding gut of greedy Mr Creosote! Aka *Monty Python's The Meaning Of Life*. Note: the running time given is for the original, but some references claim that video editions exist which run for as little as 86m. As always, check the box!

MONTY PYTHON AND THE HOLY GRAIL 🎬3
JOHN CLEESE, MICHAEL PALIN, TERRY JONES, GRAHAM CHAPMAN, ERIC IDLE
TERRY GILLIAM, TERRY JONES
UK (FOX) 1975
90m — (15)

Medieval madness from the Python team, with severed limbs and silly jokes. Classed as their best effort by some fans, but I find it wears thin after one screening.

MONTY PYTHON'S LIFE OF BRIAN 🎬 4

JOHN CLEESE, GRAHAM CHAPMAN, MICHAEL PALIN, TERRY JONES

TERRY JONES

UK (CIC) 1979

93m (15)

Very controversial in its time, Python's spoof of a false biblical messiah lampoons the life of Jesus with such delights as the famed sequence of crucified men singing 'Always Look on the Bright Side of Life'. Guaranteed to offend someone, somewhere, even today.

MY COUSIN VINNY 🎬 4

JOE PESCI, RALPH MACCHIO, MARISA TOMEI, FRED GWYNNE

JONATHAN LYNN

USA (FOX) 1992

119m (15)

The normally scary Pesci brings his comedic talents to the fore here as an inept lawyer called down south to help his young relative and his friend, who've been wrongly accused of violent crime. The culture clash is dryly presented, and the sultry Tomei rightly won a Best Supporting Actress Oscar as Vinny's smart but long-suffering babe.

NAKED GUN 🎬 3

LESLIE NIELSEN, PRISCILLA PRESLEY, O.J. SIMPSON, GEORGE KENNEDY

DAVID ZUCKER

USA (CIC) 1988

81m (15)

Subtitled *From The Files Of Police Squad*, this movie was inspired by the cult TV gagfest of that name. From the same team as *Airplane* (see page 67), with much the same quickfire style of idiotic humour. It's amazing to see how Nielsen has changed course in late career from being a straight actor to become a droll funnyman. Other noticeable cast members include Priscilla Presley and the now-notorious OJ Simpson. Two sequels so far.

COMEDY

NATIONAL LAMPOON'S VACATION [4]

CHEVY CHASE, RANDY QUAID, BEVERLY D'ANGELO, JOHN CANDY

HAROLD RAMIS

USA (WARNER) 1983

98m (15)

National Lampoon began as a college humour mag, went to news-stands, branched into records parodying the foibles of the rock world, and finally moved on to the silver screen. This is one of many National Lampoon flicks (see also Animal House, page 68), featuring typically earthy, stupid jokes as a middle-American family undergo a nightmare journey when they decide to visit a naff theme park for their holidays. It was popular enough to spawn a series of vacation-themed 'Lampoon' pix.

THE NUTTY PROFESSOR [3]

EDDIE MURPHY, JAMES COBURN, JADA PINKETT

TOM SHADYAC

USA (CIC) 1996

91m (12)

This remake of a Jerry Lewis comedy from the 60s is basically the Jekyll and Hyde story played for laughs. Murphy goes from nerdy fatty to smooth lothario via the (superbly executed) SFX and, as in his patchy Coming To America, much fun comes via the star being rendered unrecognisable under a series of clever make-ups.

THE ODD COUPLE [4]

JACK LEMMON, WALTER MATTHAU, JON FIEDLER, HERB ELEMAN

GENE SAKS

USA (CIC) 1968

106m (PG)

Neil Simon's stage hit about two mismatched flatmates (one obsessively neat, the other a slob) makes for one of Lemmon and Matthau's spirited, superb pairings. Not to be missed. Spawned a hit TV series with Tony Randall and Jack Klugman taking over the parts. Delightful stuff. 1998 sequel: The Odd Couple II.

THE OPPOSITE SEX [2]

CHRISTINA RICCI, LISA KUDROW, MARTIN DONOVAN, LYLE LOVETT

DON ROSS

USA (COLUMBIA TRISTAR) 1998

97m (18)

Addams Family star Ricci has grown up in this film into a foul-mouthed and rebellious teenager who escapes from her lousy life in Louisiana by stealing $10,000 and setting off on a frenetic cross-country chase to LA.

PATCH ADAMS

ROBIN WILLIAMS

TOM SHADYAC

USA (UNIVERSAL) 1998

113m (12)

Based on the life of a real doctor who used zany humour to improve the well-being of his patients and fell foul of authority for his pains. High feel-good factor. Also on DVD.

PRIMARY COLORS

JOHN TRAVOLTA, EMMA THOMPSON, BILLY BOB THORNTON, LARRY HAGMAN   KATHY BATES

MIKE NICHOLS

USA (CIC) 1998

137m (15)

Good film version of the controversial novel (anonymously published, but later credited to a journalist) inspired by the sexual shenanigans of the man who made it to the White House. Travolta is an uncanny facsimile of Bill Clinton, but I'm afraid I just couldn't swallow Emma Thompson as the feisty wife. Amusing script, though, and the picture is smoothly directed by old hand Mike Nichols.

PRIVATE BENJAMIN

GOLDIE HAWN, ARMAND ASSANTE, ROBERT WEBBER, EILEEN BRENNAN

HOWARD ZIEFF

USA (WARNER) 1980

110m (15)

Wry, sprightly comedy with Hawn as a spoiled rich girl who joins the army thinking she's going to a special version where the recruits bed down in luxury condominiums and get breakfast in bed. Soon waking up to the fact that she's been duped, she buckles down and makes a real career for herself. Though the tale gets bogged down in turgid romance, it's fun all the same. Inspired a lame TV series.

PRIVATE PARTS

HOWARD STERN, ROBIN QUIVERS, JENNA JAMESON, MARY McCORMACK

BETTY THOMAS

USA (ENTERTAINMENT) 1997

105m (18)

Ribald biopic of outspoken USA radio host Howard Stern, directed in breezy style by Betty Thomas (who starred as Lucy Bates on TV's *Hill Street Blues*) and with long-haired foulmouth Stern playing himself. He was the first of the shock-jocks and was never equalled, spewing forth obscenities while battling with phone-in listeners, sponsors and bosses alike. Very funny if you're broad-minded.

COMEDY

THE PRODUCERS [5]

⭐ ZERO MOSTEL, GENE WILDER, DICK SHAWN, KENNETH MARS

🎬 MEL BROOKS

USA (4-FRONT) 1967

⏱ 84m (PG)

The first and best Mel Brooks comedy romp is a characteristically oddball tale about two conmen who plan to make a killing by finding a play that is bound to fail and then selling the shares in the production several times over, thus ensuring that no one will expect to see a payday. They choose a musical about Hitler penned by a mad Nazi – but their plans go awry. A gallery of weirdos and some hilarious set pieces make this a comedy that stands up to repeated viewings. Oscar: screenplay (Brooks).

A SHOT IN THE DARK [4]

⭐ PETER SELLERS, ELKE SOMMER, GEORGE SANDERS, HERBERT LOM

🎬 BLAKE EDWARDS

USA (WARNER) 1964

⏱ 101m (PG)

First sequel to *The Pink Panther*, charting the further adventures of bumbling Inspector Clouseau (Sellers). The series went downhill from here, ending in dire efforts issued after Sellers's death, but this still cuts the mustard. The Henry Mancini music was used in a series of cartoons starring the Pink Panther character familiar from the credit sequences of many of the films.

SIR HENRY AT RAWLINSON END [4]

⭐ TREVOR HOWARD, PATRICK MAGEE, VIVIAN STANSHALL, HARRY FOWLER

🎬 STEVE ROBERTS

UK (TARTAN) 1980

⏱ 75m (15)

Poetic and surreal Brit whimsy about a crusty aristo in his crumbling pile. Based on records and radio readings by the late Vivian Stanshall of anarchic UK rock/trad jazz abusers The Bonzo Dog Band. Stanshall was a man who trod a fine line between madness and genius, not always carefully, and it's great to have this filmic record of one of his finest conceits.

SLUMS OF BEVERLY HILLS [3]

⭐ NATASHA LYONNE, ALAN ARKIN, MARISA TOMEI

🎬 TAMARA JENKINS

USA (FOX PATHE) 1999

⏱ 88m (15)

Story about coming of age in the 70s with emphasis on the trials and tribulations of teenage girls. A low-budget film from Robert Redford's Sundance Institute that makes up for lack of dollars with humour and a great turn by Marisa Tomei. She won an Oscar for *My Cousin Vinny* (see page 86), but where has she been since? She easily steals this movie.

STILL CRAZY 🎬 2

BILLY CONNOLLY, JIMMY NAIL, STEPHEN REA, TIMOTHY SPALL, BILL NIGHY, JULIET AUBREY, BRUCE ROBINSON

BRIAN GIBSON

UK (COLUMBIA TRISTAR) 1999

91m (15)

An off-the-wall British comedy which charts the progress of a group of guys who try desperately to recapture the magic of their former success in a rock band, 20 years after a bitter split.

STRIKE! 🎬 3

KIRSTEN DUNST, GABY HOFFMAN, LYNN REDGRAVE, HEATHER MATARAZZO

SARAH KERNOCHAN

USA (ALLIANCE) 1998

93m (15)

Feminist comedy set in American gal's school, circa 1963, with a strong cast and believable characters. Veers quite deftly between flimsiness and poignancy, but in spite of all its manifest virtues I fear this is not one for the lager-swilling laddish audience. A ladies'-night-in treat, I guess.

THERE'S SOMETHING ABOUT MARY 🎬 3

CAMERON DIAZ, MATT DILLON, BEN STILLER

BOBBY AND PETER FARRELLY

USA (FOX) 1998

114m (15)

Much-lauded, vulgar romantic comedy, which has as its main claim to fame a scene where our irresistably sexy heroine mistakes some – how shall we say? – male human genetic material for a dollop of hair gel. A smash hit in UK cinemas and the performances are, one has to say, well-judged and genuinely hilarious in places. Too long, though. Peter Farrelly gave us *Dumb and Dumber* (see page 78), if that's an encouragement to you.

THIS IS SPINAL TAP 🎬 4

MICHAEL McKEAN, ROB REINER, CHRISTOPHER GUEST, HARRY SHEARER

ROB REINER

USA (POLYGRAM) 1984

82m (15)

On-the-money spoof rockumentary charting the supposed excesses of an imaginary band, all the way from teen psychedelia to heavy metaldom and exploding drummers. Anyone who has served time in the pop biz will find it even more amusing than the ordinary viewer, what with complaints about backstage sandwiches and albums with titles like 'Smell the Glove'. A much-needed jab in the beergut for an over-inflated business.

COMEDY

THIS YEAR'S LOVE

KATHY BURKE, JENNIFER EHLE, IAN HART, DOUGLAS HENSHALL, CATHERINE McCORMACK, DOUGRAY SCOTT, EMILY WOOF

DAVID KANE

UK (ENTERTAINMENT) 1999

104m (18)

A rather sardonic romantic comedy about the lives and loves – as they say – of a group of Londoners. Great soundtrack and a strong British cast.

TIN CUP

KEVIN COSTNER, RENE RUSSO, DON JOHNSON, CHEECH MARIN

RON SHELTON

USA (WARNER) 1996

130m (15)

Sort of a *Rocky* for golf fans; an amusing, well-acted and scripted piece about the struggles of a golf professional and his girlfriend. Much fun is to be had from this nicely observed movie.

TO DIE FOR

NICOLE KIDMAN, JOAQUIN PHOENIX, MATT DILLON, DAVID CRONENBERG

GUS VAN SANT

USA (POLYGRAM) 1995

102m (15)

The normally freckle-faced Kidman is transformed here as a steely-thighed, ambitious blonde determined to make it big as a TV reporter at any cost. Using sex and seduction, she stops at nothing to get her way, but her amorality recoils on her in this hilarious, murderous black comedy. A sweetly sardonic indictment of the cult of the cathode personality. Movie director Cronenberg cameos as a hitman.

TOOTSIE

DUSTIN HOFFMAN, TERI GARR, JESSICA LANGE, BILL MURRAY, GEENA DAVIS, ELLEN FOLEY, CHARLES DURNING

SYDNEY POLLACK

USA (CINEMA CLUB V) 1982

112m (15)

Engagingly silly farce about a desperate actor who dresses as a woman to get a role in a popular soap opera, only to find himself with a dilemma when he falls in love with a girl star of the show. Immensely successful, and Lange won an Oscar for best supporting actress. Also available in a widescreen edition from Columbia TriStar.

TRADING PLACES 🎬 4

🌟 EDDIE MURPHY, DAN AYKROYD, JAMIE LEE CURTIS, DON AMECHE, RALPH BELLAMY

🎬 JOHN LANDIS

USA (CIC) 1983

⏱ 111m (15)

A couple of jaded old millionaires bet on whether a homeless bum can do as well as a rich man if they are simply forced to swap lives. Very funny picture with a hint of the style of the old Frank Capra screwball comedies from Hollywood of yore. Curtis is *très* sexy and Murphy was still a new star who felt compelled to make an effort when he made this, but the film is nearly stolen by Ameche and Bellamy as the old rogues.

TWINS 🎬 3

🌟 DANNY DeVITO, ARNOLD SCHWARZENEGGER, CHLOE WEBB, KELLY PRESTON

🎬 IVAN REITMAN

USA (CIC) 1988

⏱ 102m (PG)

Two men meet and realise that, in spite of appearances, they are twins. Unbelievable, but the stars hurry it along and there are enough laughs along the way to make it worth renting. Schwarzenegger shows a previously unsuspected flair for comedic playing.

UNCLE BUCK 🎬 3

🌟 JOHN CANDY, MACAULAY CULKIN, AMY MADIGAN, LAURIE METCALF

🎬 JOHN HUGHES

USA (CIC) 1989

⏱ 96m (15)

A kind, but slovenly, uncle babysits some recently bereaved kids with unexpectedly hilarious results. A good performance by the late John Candy in this competent, well-executed, if sentimental, domestic comedy.

THE WAR OF THE ROSES 🎬 3

🌟 MICHAEL DOUGLAS, KATHLEEN TURNER, DANNY DeVITO, SEAN ASTIN

🎬 DANNY DE VITO

USA (FOX) 1989

⏱ 111m (15)

Bitter, black farce about a battling married couple who engage in a war of attrition that destroys all around them. The fun gradually wears out, but the stars do their best. Based on a novel by Warren Adler.

COMEDY

WAYNE'S WORLD [4]

MIKE MYERS, DANA CARVEY, ROB LOWE, TIA CARRERE

PENELOPE SPHEERIS

USA (CIC) 1992

95m (PG)

Expanded from characters first seen in TV snippets, this is about two heavy-metal nerds who run a public access TV show from home. Comparisons with *Bill And Ted/ Beavis And Butthead* notwithstanding, it laughs at itself while staying hip enough to get the youth vote – though the plot is predictable. Rob Lowe sends up his sex-god image and Carrere makes a believable rock babe, but Myers and Carvey carry the show. Sequel: *Wayne's World 2* (1993).

WHAT'S NEW PUSSYCAT? [3]

PETER O'TOOLE, PETER SELLERS, WOODY ALLEN, URSULA ANDRESS

CLIVE DONNER

USA/FRANCE (MGM/UA) 1965

108m (15)

Dated Woody Allen script, delivered in very flashy swinging 60s style by Donner. Now a cultish curio, with the neurotic sex-therapy theme a hint of the concerns Allen would return to in a more sophisticated mode. Tom Jones had a smash hit with the Hal David/Burt Bacharach theme song.

WHITE MEN CAN'T JUMP [3]

WESLEY SNIPES, WOODY HARRELSON, ROSIE PEREZ

RON SHELTON

USA (FOX) 1992

111m (15)

A miable comedy about two basketball hustlers – one black, one white – who form a partnership rooking the gullible punters they meet on street corner courts. Harrelson and Snipes make a likeable double act.

THE WITCHES OF EASTWICK [2]

JACK NICHOLSON, CHER, MICHELLE PFEIFFER, SUSAN SARANDON

GEORGE MILLER

USA (WARNER) 1987

114m (18)

Based on the John Updike novel, this tells the story of three randy ladies who conjure the Devil (a typecast Nicholson) to satisfy their needs but find him a little more trouble than they bargained for. Quite funny, but never seems sure whether it means to be a comedy or a scare ride. Also on a two-for-one tape with horror/comedy *Beetlejuice* (see page 71).

TOP 1000 VIDEOS

WITHNAIL AND I ⑤

RICHARD E GRANT, PAUL McGANN, RICHARD GRIFFITHS, MICHAEL ELPHICK

BRUCE ROBINSON

UK (CIC) 1986

103m ⑮

Hilarious and irreverent 60s story of a couple of failing actors who plan a holiday in the country cottage of a flamboyantly homosexual relative. Recently reissued on the tenth anniversary of first release, this has a cult reputation due, mainly, to the fruity, eye-rolling performance of Grant. Brilliant. Widescreen available.

WORKING GIRL ④

SIGOURNEY WEAVER, MELANIE GRIFFITH, HARRISON FORD, ALEC BALDWIN

MIKE NICHOLS

USA (FOX) 1988

109m ⑮

Dumped-on secretary Griffith uses her boss Weaver's absence to take over her job, designer wardrobe *and* boyfriend – but what'll happen when the bitch queen gets back? A morality tale with a bite and plenty of laughs, not to mention Carly Simon's Oscar-winning song 'Let the River Run'. A deserved smash hit.

YOUNG FRANKENSTEIN ③

GENE WILDER, MARTY FELDMAN, TERI GARR, PETER BOYLE, GENE HACKMAN, MADELINE KAHN

MEL BROOKS

USA (FOX) 1974 B&W

106m ⑮

One of Brooks's best gagfests is an uncannily accurate and loving spoof/tribute to the early Universal horror films, notably Rowland V Lee's *Son Of Frankenstein*. Shot in authentic monochrome and utilising Kenneth Strickfaden's spectacular lab FX from the originals, this is a treat for kids of all ages.

DRAMA

While there are movies in this section which could arguably have made interesting and acceptable appearances in other categories (*Se7en*, say, on page 132), the main purpose here is to ensure the inclusion of films that are worthy of note but which don't easily lend themselves to pigeon-holing: *Quiz Show*, for instance, which is not a romance, a comedy, a thriller or an adventure, yet remains a deftly made, brilliantly acted, thought-provoking piece of cinema. Skip this section at your peril, for if you do, you'll miss some of the best pictures in the book – and some of the best additions to your tape collection.

ABSENCE OF MALICE

PAUL NEWMAN, SALLY FIELD, BOB BALABAN, WILFORD BRIMLEY

SYDNEY POLLACK

USA (VIDEO COLLECTION) 1980

111m (PG)

This tale of a news reporter who runs a story which has dire consequences for a blameless man is eternally topical with the on-going debate about balance between press rights and the need for a privacy law. Solid acting from the two stars.

THE ACCUSED

JODIE FOSTER, KELLY McGILLIS, BERNIE COULSON, LEO ROSSI

JONATHAN KAPLAN

USA (CIC/4-FRONT) 1988

116m (18)

Harrowing drama about a girl who gets gang-raped in a bar after drunkenly flirting with the customers. Her lawyer (McGillis) infuriates her by letting the perpetrators off with lesser charges, but makes amends by bringing to book the men who cheered as the rape took place. Grim rumination on the question of whether doing a bit of reckless carousing should ever be allowed to render a woman open to the accusation of 'asking for it' – and whether doing nothing to stop a crime is a crime in itself. Foster won an Oscar for her performance as the victim.

ALL THE PRESIDENT'S MEN [3]

ROBERT REDFORD, DUSTIN HOFFMAN, MARTIN BALSAM, HAL HOLBROOK, JASON ROBARDS, JACK WARDEN

ALAN J PAKULA

USA (WARNER) 1976

132m (15)

Talky but well-acted story of Woodward and Bernstein, the two *Washington Post* reporters who exposed the political espionage and financial corruption behind the Watergate burglary and ultimately brought about the downfall of Presdent Nixon. Oscars: supporting actor (Robards), screenplay (William Goldman, from book by Woodward and Bernstein), sets and sound. Director Pakula sadly died in a freak car accident in 1998.

AMERICAN BUFFALO [4]

DENNIS FRANZ, DUSTIN HOFFMAN, SEAN NELSON

MICHAEL CORRENTE

USA (FILMFOUR) 1997

83m (15)

David Mamet's play provides the basis for this character study of three crooks involved in a plot to steal a rare coin. Set in a crummy pawn shop, the downbeat essay in duplicitousness is carried along by fine acting from Dennis Franz (of TV's *NYPD Blue*) and a nasty Hoffman. The less-than-cinematic setting betrays its stage origins, but this is another compelling story from a master yarn-spinner.

AMERICAN GIGOLO [3]

RICHARD GERE, LAUREN HUTTON, NINA VAN PALLANDT, HECTOR ELIZONDO

PAUL SCHRADER

USA (CIC) 1980

112m (18)

Sexual athlete for hire is accused of murder and only one of his women clients can get him off – but she doesn't want him to use her name. Calvinist rebel Schrader concocts a typically jaundiced look at LA sleaze, with a nice performance from Gere as the male tart with a noble heart.

AMISTAD [3]

ANTHONY HOPKINS, MORGAN FREEMAN, NIGEL HAWTHORNE, PETER POLSTLETHWAITE, MATTHEW McCONAUGHEY

STEVEN SPIELBERG

USA (DREAMWORKS) 1997

148m (15)

Deliberately worthy story of early American courtroom battle over whether slaves had the right to attack the ship's crew delivering them into bondage – was it mutiny or justified revolt? Good performances, particularly from Hopkins as the advocate who became an American leader, but it does go on a bit.

APOLLO 13 [4]

TOM HANKS, KEVIN BACON, BILL PAXTON, GARY SINISE, ED HARRIS

RON HOWARD

USA (CIC) 1995

134m (PG)

Even though the historically-minded will know the outcome, this is a thoroughly engrossing real-life adventure set aboard the malfunctioning USA space-capsule of the title. Tom Hanks gives a believable, measured performance as astronaut Jim Lovell, battling against all the odds to get his crew back to earth alive.

THE APOSTLE [3]

ROBERT DUVALL, FARRAH FAWCETT, TODD ALLEN

ROBERT DUVALL

USA (CIC) 1998

128m (12)

Duvall writes, directs and stars in this fine little drama about a minister in the south of the USA who finds his sins coming back to haunt him. Obviously a labour of love, and Duvall's performance is one to cherish. Worth a look.

AWAKENINGS [3]

ROBIN WILLIAMS, ROBERT DE NIRO, JOHN HEARD, PENELOPE ANN MILLER

PENNY MARSHALL

USA (CINEMA CLUB V) 1990

115m (15)

Based on the career of Dr Oliver Sacks, this moving film tells of an unorthodox medic (Williams) who discovers that a group of patients thought to be mindless vegetables have, in fact, been aware of their condition despite being immobile for decades. If the realisation is horrifying, the scenes of the 'awakenings' under experimental drug treatment are both moving and funny. Contains the simple message that every moment of life is precious and not to be wasted. Much good acting, including a touching performance by De Niro as one of the patients.

BACKDRAFT [3]

ROBERT DE NIRO, KURT RUSSELL, WILLIAM BALDWIN, DONALD SUTHERLAND

RON HOWARD

USA (CIC) 1991

131m (15)

Tale of sibling rivalry between two Chicago firemen. A little long, though the SFX are great, and the film is saved by De Niro as a shrewd arson detective on the track of pyromaniac Sutherland.

THE BAD AND THE BEAUTIFUL 〔4〕

KIRK DOUGLAS, LANA TURNER, WALTER PIDGEON, DICK POWELL, BARRY SULLIVAN, GLORIA GRAHAME, GILBERT ROLAND

VINCENTE MINELLI

USA (WARNER) 1952 B&W

118m (PG)

To its credit, Hollywood is always pretty vicious when it turns its critical gaze on itself: this prime piece of navel-contemplation is a flamboyant tale of the ups-and-downs of a megalomaniac producer and the effect he has on those around him, with a confident central performance from Douglas and nice work from those in his orbit. Several Oscars, including best supporting actress for Grahame as a southern belle.

BAD DAY AT BLACK ROCK 〔3〕

SPENCER TRACY, ROBERT RYAN, LEE MARVIN, ANNE FRANCIS

JOHN STURGES

USA (WARNER) 1954

81m (PG)

Sadly available only in pan-scan, this tense tale involves a one-armed man arriving in an unfriendly desert town to investigate what happened to a Japanese-American pal. Although the film is rather worthy and over-regarded by critics, and probably best seen on a large screen, the cast make the most of the suspense.

BARTON FINK 〔3〕

JOHN GOODMAN, JOHN TURTURRO, JUDY DAVIS, STEVE BUSCEMI

JOEL COEN

USA (COLUMBIA TRISTAR) 1991

112m (15)

Murder and mystery assail a young writer new to Hollywood in this slab of weirdness from the acclaimed Coen brothers writer/director team. Despite its cult reputation, this is a tad over-ambitious and isn't quite up to the dazzling standard of their best pix, such as *Fargo* (see page 113) and *Blood Simple* (see page 281).

BASQUIAT 〔4〕

JEFFREY WRIGHT, DAVID BOWIE, DENNIS HOPPER, CHRISTOPHER WALKEN

JULIAN SCHNABEL

USA (GUILD) 1996

102m (15)

Biopic of street artist who was taken up by the New York cognoscenti, worked with Warhol and died of drug abuse, leaving behind paintings that are now worth a bundle. Rock star Bowie plays Warhol quite effectively here and the film is a fascinating glimpse into the hip art world of the time.

DRAMA

BEACHES 🎬3

BETTE MIDLER, BARBARA HERSHEY, SPALDING GRAY, JOHN HEARD

GARY MARSHALL

USA (TOUCHSTONE) 1988

118m (15)

Based on Iris Rainer Dart's novel, this is a mildly engaging story of the enduring friendship of two women from disparate backgrounds – a rich girl and a would-be singer. Maudlin ending, but the occasional laughs and the two stars will keep you watching.

THE BEDFORD INCIDENT 🎬3

RICHARD WIDMARK, SIDNEY POITIER, JAMES MacARTHUR, MARTIN BALSAM

JAMES B HARRIS

USA (ENCORE) 1965 B&W

98m (PG)

One of the better cold war 'brink of nuclear insanity' pix of the 60s with USA warship captain Widmark playing cat and mouse with a Russian sub in icy waters. Real sweaty-palms stuff, with some fine acting.

THE BIG BLUE 🎬4

JEAN RENO, ROSANNA ARQUETTE, JEAN-MARC BARR, PAUL SHENAR

LUC BESSON

FRANCE (FOX) 1988

114m (15)

Unusual movie of friendship, love and competition set against the strange sport of 'free diving' – the divers have no breathing gear, but test their endurance by holding on to a rope at incredible depths for amazing lengths of time. Beautiful photography and an astonishing dream sequence make up for some lukewarm acting. The film was cut for international release, but the full 174m version is available in a special boxed set.

BIG WEDNESDAY 🎬3

JAN-MICHAEL VINCENT, WILLIAM KATT, GARY BUSEY, ROBERT ENGLUND

JOHN MILIUS

USA (BLACK DIAMOND) 1978

119m (PG)

Hymn to the glories of male bonding in the Californian surfing culture of the 60s. The young pals gradually see their idyllic existence eroded by age, responsibilities and the Vietnam War. The most personal of Milius's pix. Available in widescreen.

TOP 1000 VIDEOS

BILLIONAIRE BOYS CLUB [4]

JUDD NELSON, RON SILVER, FREDRIC LEHNE, BRIAN McNAMARA

MARVIN J CHOMSKY

USA (VIDEO COLLECTION) 1987

175m (15)

The most underrated of the 'Brat Pack' actors of the 80s, Nelson excels in this made-for-TV story based on the true tale of a charismatic young wheeler-dealer whose schemes led to murder. This appears to be a slightly edited version.

THE BIRDMAN OF ALCATRAZ [5]

BURT LANCASTER, KARL MALDEN, THELMA RITTER, NEVILLE BRAND

JOHN FRANKENHEIMER

USA (WARNER) 1961 B&W

148m (PG)

Classic account of Robert Stroud, a 'lifer' who became an expert on avian diseases while imprisoned. Lancaster gives a towering performance, and there's no attempt to whitewash Stroud's murderous nature. Able support from Ritter as his supportive but jealous mother, and from Malden and Brand as his jailers. A genuine masterpiece.

THE BLACKBOARD JUNGLE [3]

GLENN FORD, ANNE FRANCIS, SIDNEY POITIER, VIC MORROW

RICHARD BROOKS

USA (MGM/UA) 1955 B&W

101m (12)

Dated but well-made version of Evan Hunter's novel of classroom violence. The 'kids' look to be in their thirties, and the rock 'n' roll of Bill Haley hardly seems likely to inspire mayhem – but the story still carries us along.

BODY HEAT [4]

WILLIAM HURT, KATHLEEN TURNER, TED DANSON, MICKEY ROURKE, RICHARD CRENNA

LAWRENCE KASDAN

USA (WARNER) 1981

108m (18)

Rich bitch uses sex to draw her lawyer beau into a plot to slay her husband. Considered wildly naughty at time of release, but with passage of time its virtues as a worthwhile steamy thriller are more likely to impress.

DRAMA

THE BOUNTY [4]

ANTHONY HOPKINS, MEL GIBSON, LIAM NEESON, LAURENCE OLIVIER, EDWARD FOX, DANIEL DAY-LEWIS

ROGER DONALDSON

UK (FOX) 1984

128m (15)

Based on Roger Hough's book *Captain Bligh and Mr Christian*, this Robert Bolt script was intended as a vehicle for the late, great David Lean – but director Donaldson does an excellent job of attempting to convey a more rounded portrait of the main protagonists involved in the 'Mutiny on the Bounty' tragedy than seen in previous films on the tale. Hopkins is a brilliant but irascible and aloof Bligh, with Gibson as a brattish Christian seduced by sun and sex. Well worth seeing.

BOYZ 'N' THE HOOD [3]

ICE CUBE, CUBA GOODING Jnr, LARRY FISHBURNE, ANGELA BASSETT

JOHN SINGLETON

USA (COLUMBIA TRISTAR) 1991

107m (15)

Interesting first film from director Singleton about efforts of a lone black father to keep his kids out of gang trouble in their poor Los Angeles ghetto home. Sprawls and drifts a bit but is highly rated by many critics.

BREAKING THE WAVES [3]

EMILY WATSON, UDO KIER, JEAN-MARC BARR

LARS VON TRIER

DENMARK/SWEDEN/NORWAY/ FRANCE/NETHERLANDS (GUILD) 1996

152m (18)

Cult hit about the tortured mind of a girl married to a European oil-rig worker and her dire life in a dreary coastal dump in Scotland. Rave reviews all round, apparently, but I'm mystified. Looks good, I'll say that! Widescreen.

BREAST MEN [3]

DAVID SCHWIMMER, CHRIS COOPER, LOUISE FLETCHER, EMILY PROCTER

LAWRENCE O'NEIL

USA (HIGH FLIERS) 1997

91m (18)

Satire based on the true story of two Texas plastic surgeons who invented breast implants. Ranging from the 60s to the 80s, it shows, with a mix of humour and horror, how the idea of helping women was corrupted by avarice. Schwimmer (from TV's *Friends*) is ideal as the man who dreams of being the 'breast' in the world but sees his aspirations turn to ashes. Made for USA cable channel HBO.

THE CAINE MUTINY [3]

HUMPHREY BOGART, FRED MacMURRAY, VAN JOHNSON, LEE MARVIN

EDWARD DMYTRYK

USA (CINEMA CLUB V) 1954 B&W

119m (U)

A crew rebel against their disturbed captain and then have to justify their actions in a court-martial. Bogart excels as Captain Queeg in this taut version of Herman Wouk's Pulitzer Prize-winning novel. Charlton Heston took the part in the London stage version, *The Caine Mutiny Court Martial*, many years later – though the play was more concerned than the movie with exploring the dubious motives of some of the crew (and the heroic actions which led to Queeg's mental problems). The play was later remade as a TV movie with a different cast.

CASABLANCA [5]

HUMPHREY BOGART, INGRID BERGMAN, CLAUDE RAINS, PAUL HENREID, PETER LORRE, SYDNEY GREENSTREET, DOOLEY WILSON

MICHAEL CURTIZ

USA (WARNER) 1943 B&W

102m (U)

One of those films to which the label 'classic' truly does apply. Based on a play (only finally seen on the stage in the 90s!) called *Everybody Comes To Rick's* by Murray Burnett and Joan Alison, it concerns Bogie's disillusioned club owner in World War Two Casablanca. Will he help the girl who dumped him years ago? More importantly, will he help her husband flee the Nazis, too? On this slender thread hangs a masterwork of ensemble playing. But you don't need me to tell you that, I hope. Oscars for best pic, director and script. Special edition with documentary. As time goes by (sorry), it only seems to improve – if that were possible.

DRAMA

CAT ON A HOT TIN ROOF [3]

ELIZABETH TAYLOR, PAUL NEWMAN, BURL IVES, JACK CARSON

RICHARD BROOKS

USA (WARNER) 1958

103m (15)

Steamy Tennessee Williams play provides the basis for this epic about a southern family dripping with neurotic sexuality, avarice and mendacity. Lusty tosh with much gloriously bad acting, especially from Ives as the bulky Big Daddy, patriarch of the clan. Remade for TV in 1984.

THE CHAMBER [3]

GENE HACKMAN, FAYE DUNAWAY, CHRIS O'DONNELL

JAMES FOLEY

USA (CIC) 1996

108m (15)

Young lawyer meets his estranged grandad to defend him on a last-ditch death-row attempt to escape execution for a racist bombing murder. In the process he tries to discover why the old man took the rap for others. Though John Grisham's story doesn't transfer particularly well to the screen, the film is worth watching for the grizzled, nasty Hackman.

CHARIOTS OF FIRE [4]

BEN CROSS, IAN CHARLESON, NIGEL HAVERS, IAN HOLM, JOHN GIELGUD

HUGH HUDSON

UK (FOX) 1981

118m (U)

Rather plodding and overrated, yet still a quality piece of entertainment, this fact-based story tells of two students (one Christian, one a Jew) who compete in races at the 1924 Olympics. Skilful depiction of the prejudices and mores of the era in Colin Welland's Oscar-winning script, and a nicely judged performance by the late Ian Charleson. Other Oscars: best picture/score (Vangelis)/costumes.

CHINATOWN [4]

JACK NICHOLSON, FAYE DUNAWAY, JOHN HUSTON, BURT YOUNG

ROMAN POLANSKI

USA (CIC) 1974

131m (15)

Classic private eye adventure of corruption and incest set in Los Angeles of the 30s with Nicholson as Jake Gittes, the bewildered 'tec at the heart of the case. Great period feel, and Robert Towne's literate screenplay won an Oscar. Director Polanski turns up in a cameo as the thug who slits Jake's nose open. An underrated sequel, *The Two Jakes*, appeared in 1990. Widescreen available.

THE CINCINNATI KID

STEVE McQUEEN, EDWARD G ROBINSON, KARL MALDEN, ANN-MARGRET, TUESDAY WELD, RIP TORN

NORMAN JEWISON

USA (WARNER) 1965

101m (15)

Card-sharp tale that is an attempt to ape the hot-youngster-against-old-pro story of the Paul Newman film *The Hustler*. Would have worked better in black-and-white, and the proceedings cannot have been helped by director Sam Peckinpah being replaced by Norman Jewison shortly after shooting began on the spurious charge that Peckinpah wanted to make a 'dirty' movie. Worth seeing however for old hands like Robinson and the wonderfully-named Rip Torn.

CITIZEN KANE

ORSON WELLES, JOSEPH COTTEN, EVERETT SLOANE, AGNES MOORHEAD, DOROTHY COMINGORE, GEORGE COLOURIS

ORSON WELLES

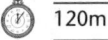

USA (4-FRONT) 1941 B&W

120m (U)

Oft-cited as the best film of all time, this drama of a ruthless press baron was highly controversial in its day. Young Welles, fresh-faced and already famed for scaring the USA with his radio broadcast of HG Wells' *War of the Worlds* (presented as a news bulletin spoofing a real Martian attack), was given an unprecedented total-control deal and used every cinematic trick in the book (and some that weren't) to dazzle his audience. News boss WR Hearst assumed the pic was based on him and tried to have the negative bought and destroyed, but it was released and won an Oscar for best screenplay for Welles and Herman J Mankiewicz. Gregg Toland's cinematography and the acting by Welles' Mercury Players make this a film largely deserving of its inflated reputation. Welles was never again granted this kind of control or budget, and spent the rest of his life making movies with flashes of brilliance and taking cameo parts to scare up cash for his projects. It is indeed sad to think what films he could have created with the budget of just one of today's trashy blockbusters.

THE COLOR OF MONEY

PAUL NEWMAN, TOM CRUISE, MARY ELIZABETH MASTRANTONIO, JOHN TURTURRO

MARTIN SCORSESE

USA (TOUCHSTONE) 1986

115m (15)

One of Scorsese's least successful movies and a follow-up to Newman's 60s classic *The Hustler*. This time his pool-shark character is older and wiser and takes on young Cruise as an apprentice, but it drifts toward the end and has less impact than the earlier film. Newman won the Best Actor Oscar. Based on the novel by Walter Tevis.

DRAMA

THE COLOR PURPLE ▶3

WHOOPI GOLDBERG, DANNY GLOVER, RAE DAWN CHONG, OPRAH WINFREY

STEVEN SPIELBERG

USA (WARNER) 1985

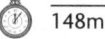

148m (15)

Epic attempt at a serious, sentimental story by Spielberg, based on the novel by Alice Walker about the ups and downs of a black woman in America's Deep South. Over-long and rather maudlin but nicely shot and directed. Available in a widescreen version.

COOL HAND LUKE ▶4

PAUL NEWMAN, GEORGE KENNEDY, DENNIS HOPPER, STROTHER MARTIN

STUART ROSENBERG

USA (WARNER) 1967

121m (15)

Based on Donn Pearce's novel, this is the effective story of a young rebel without a cause who, jailed for drunkenly lopping the heads off parking meters, inspires fellow inmates in a brutal southern chain-gang. It boasts an outstanding showing from Newman in the lead and an Oscar-winning performance from Kennedy as his buddy. The tragic ending and an unusually (for him) understated score from Lalo Schifrin make this a picture well worth seeking out. Now in widescreen.

COURAGE UNDER FIRE ▶4

MEG RYAN, DENZEL WASHINGTON, LOU DIAMOND PHILLIPS, SCOTT GLENN

EDWARD ZWICK

USA (FOX) 1996

111m (15)

Investigation into the death of a female military hero fuels a great and gruelling drama dealing with battlefield ethics, machismo and truth. The question is: does Ryan deserve her posthumous decoration and glory, or condemnation as a bad leader? Duplicity abounds, but will the facts come out? Plenty of nervous tension, guilt and fine acting here.

A CRY IN THE DARK ▶3

MERYL STREEP, SAM NEILL, CHARLES TINGWELL, BRUCE MYLES

FRED SCHEPISI

USA/AUSTRALIA (MGM/UA) 1988

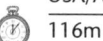

116m (15)

True story of Lindy Chamberlain, who claimed her baby was carried off by a wild dingo during a camping trip in the Australian outback. She was jailed for murder but subsequently exonerated and released. Streep is convincing, but her usual facility with accents deserts her here and led to people coming out of cinemas squawking 'A ding-go's gawt mawyee *bay-bee*'.

CRY FREEDOM 🎬 4

KEVIN KLINE, DENZEL WASHINGTON, PENELOPE WILTON, ALEC McCOWEN, JOHN THAW

RICHARD ATTENBOROUGH

UK (CIC) 1987

158m (PG)

Worthy true-life story of how writer Donald Woods escaped with his family from South Africa in order to tell the world how the authorities had murdered his friend, black activist Steve Biko. Like many films of its type, it was criticised for concentrating on the white characters, but it does get an important message across while holding the attention. Washington was nominated for an Oscar. The American TV version is somewhat longer.

THE CRYING GAME 🎬 3

STEPHEN REA, FOREST WHITAKER, JAYE DAVIDSON, MIRANDA RICHARDSON

NEIL JORDAN

UK (POLYGRAM) 1992

108m (18)

Cult hit involving the IRA and matters of sexual identity. Even if the final revelation is known to most people these days, whether they've seen the movie or not, the acting and direction carry it along. Still Jordan's best effort – in the eyes of most punters at least.

DANGEROUS GAME 🎬 3

HARVEY KEITEL, JAMES RUSSO, MADONNA

ABEL FERRARA

USA (POLYGRAM) 1995

108m (18)

Originally released in the USA as *Snake Eyes*, this typically weird (and autobiographical?) film from the director of *Bad Lieutenant* (see page 164) is about a manipulative moviemaker and his effect on the lives of his actors, both on and off the set. Not one of Madonna's best films, but still worth seeing.

DANGEROUS LIAISONS 🎬 4

GLENN CLOSE, JOHN MALKOVICH, MICHELLE PFEIFFER, KEANU REEVES, UMA THURMAN, PETER CAPALDI

STEPHEN FREARS

USA (WARNER) 1988

115m (15)

Classic French novel by Choderlos de Laclos (and the play based on it by Christopher Hampton) inspired this wickedly amusing story of an eighteenth-century lady who passes her time in scheming with the love lives of friends and enemies. Close and Malkovich are excellent, and it's nice to see Peter Capaldi in a big movie – a marvellous actor. Oscars: art, costumes, script.

DRAMA

DEAD MAN WALKING 🎬5

⭐ SUSAN SARANDON, SEAN PENN, SCOTT WILSON, ROBERT PROSKY

🎬 TIM ROBBINS

USA (POLYGRAM) 1995

⏱ 122m (15)

Oscar-winning story based on the life of Sister Helen Prejean, an American nun who gives spiritual comfort to both death row prisoners and the victims of their crimes, urging the former to realise their offences and the latter to attempt forgiveness. The film never flinches from showing the righteous anger of bereaved families, and also makes the obscenity of capital punishment the subject of a more honest protest by contrasting the execution of one man (Sean Penn, outstanding in a part based on a composite of real-life cases handled by Prejean) with flashbacks to his hideous crime. Penn moves from arrogance to self-realisation, gradually making the audience sympathise with his initially repulsive character, and Sarandon is never sanctimonious. A must-see, whatever your thoughts on the death penalty.

DEAD POETS SOCIETY 🎬4

⭐ ROBIN WILLIAMS, ROBERT SEAN LEONARD, ETHAN HAWKE, JOSH CHARLES

🎬 PETER WEIR

USA (TOUCHSTONE) 1989

⏱ 123m (PG)

Best of the 'inspirational teacher' genre which flourished in the 80s (and far superior to the later, racially patronising *Dangerous Minds*), this pic gives Robin Williams one of his best non-comic roles as a young master at an expensive boys' school whose pupils admire him so much that they resurrect the secret club he once belonged to – with tragic consequences. Oscar: screenplay.

THE DEFIANT ONES 🎬4

⭐ TONY CURTIS, SIDNEY POITIER, THEODORE BIKEL, LON CHANEY Jnr

🎬 STANLEY KRAMER

USA (WARNER) 1958 B&W

⏱ 96m (U)

Chase story of two prisoners – one black, one white – who escape while chained together and have to learn to understand each other. Fine work from the two leads. Inferior TV remake appeared circa 1985.

DETOUR

TOM NEAL, ANN SAVAGE, CLAUDIA DRAKE, EDMUND MacDONALD

EDGAR G ULMER

USA (VISIONARY) 1945 B&W

65m (15)

Classic from a 'poverty row' studio by cult director Ulmer involves a hitch-hiker who accidentally becomes enmeshed in murder. A legendary *film noir* and a textbook example of no-resource genius. Based on the Martin Goldsmith novel.

THE DEVILS

OLIVER REED, VANESSA REDGRAVE, DUDLEY SUTTON, GEMMA JONES, GEORGINA HALE, MAX ADRIAN, MURRAY MELVIN, MICHAEL GOTHARD

KEN RUSSELL

UK (WARNER) 1971

103m (18)

Russell's film, still controversial today, explores how one woman's sexual obsession became the vehicle for political and ecclesiastical corruption in seventeenth-century France. Based on John Whiting's play and on Aldous Huxley's book *The Devils of Loudun*, Russell's movie embellishes the facts with all manner of gore and naked nuns. Reed gives his best-ever performance as the worldly priest who, accused of satanism by Redgrave, finds faith in martyrdom. There are great sets by Derek Jarman and a weird score from Peter Maxwell Davies. The picture was slightly cut by the BBFC. BBC TV showed the UK print in semi-widescreen some time ago, though an NFT attempt to find the BBFC-cut footage was unsuccessful. Warner have now issued that master to replace the previously available pan-scan of the heavily censored US version. The letter-boxing remains cropped as on television. Warners say this is due to the film being unavailable for remastering, it having been 'disassembled for long-term restoration'!

DEVIL'S ADVOCATE

AL PACINO, CRAIG T NELSON, CHARLIZE THERON, KEANU REEVES

TAYLOR HACKFORD

USA (WARNER) 1997

135m (18)

After a young defence lawyer gets a child molester off, the suggestively named John Milton (Pacino) hires him to look after his chums, who include a homicidal politico (Nelson). Pacino is, of course, the Devil, there to tempt folks down the left-hand path. Although the film reminds me of an old *film noir* (*Alias Nick Beal*, with Ray Milland) to which it can't come close, the story does pull the viewer in, and Pacino is great.

DRAMA

DISCLOSURE [4]

MICHAEL DOUGLAS, DEMI MOORE, DONALD SUTHERLAND, DENNIS MILLER

BARRY LEVINSON

USA (WARNER) 1994

123m (18)

Typical blend of intrigue and hi-tech from the pen of Michael Crichton, with Douglas wrongly accused of sex abuse by an ambitious colleague, high-flier Demi Moore. A tight script, clever use of computer FX and superb acting make this a film which grips right up until the final frames. Highly topical, in both the aspects of sexual politics in the workplace and the explosion of electronic storage of secrets.

DO THE RIGHT THING [3]

DANNY AIELLO, OSSIE DAVIS, JOHN TURTURRO, SPIKE LEE

SPIKE LEE

USA (CIC) 1989

114m (18)

A brave attempt to blend laughs and sociology, with black customers rioting after the boss of the local pizza joint refuses to put pictures of black stars on the wall alongside snaps of Italian-Americans such as Sinatra and Co. Starts off amusing but finally leaves a sour taste in the mouth as one contemplates the follies and pettiness of humanity.

DOG DAY AFTERNOON [3]

AL PACINO, JOHN CAZALE, CHARLES DURNING, LANCE HENRIKSEN

SIDNEY LUMET

USA (WARNER) 1975

119m (15)

Pacino scored an early hit in this story, based on true facts, of an inept bank robber who gets involved in a siege with a vault full of hostages while attempting to steal cash for his gay lover's sex-change operation! Oscar for screenplay. Widescreen.

THE DOORS [4]

VAL KILMER, MEG RYAN, KYLE MacLACHLAN, KEVIN DILLON, FRANK WHALEY, MICHAEL MADSEN, MIMI ROGERS

OLIVER STONE

USA (GUILD) 1991

134m (18)

Not a musical, though the soundtrack is greatly enhanced by the music of the group of the title, but a warts 'n' all biopic of Doors singer Jim Morrison, played with uncanny verisimilitude by Kilmer, as he progresses from rising young sex god of 60s LA to dying alcoholic blues poet in 70s Paris. The pop milieu of the period is dazzlingly recreated by Stone. The film needs a widescreen showing, but as far as I'm aware the only time it has been made available on video in this format was via a short-lived special edition sold only by WH Smith.

DRUGSTORE COWBOY 4

MATT DILLON, KELLY LYNCH, JAMES REMAR, JAMES LE GROS, WILLIAM S BURROUGHS

GUS VAN SANT

USA (VISION) 1989

97m (18)

Based on an unpublished novel by James Fogle, this was a bizarrely compelling and successful film about a gang of junkies who rob chemists to sustain their habits, detailing their hit-and-miss escapades and run-ins with the law. Leader Dillon decides to come off drugs after one of his gang dies of an overdose, but his past catches up with him. Strange visual effects and convincing acting made this an oddly moving salute to lost youth. Lovely cameo appearance by one of your humble scribe's acquaintances, famed addict and author, the late William S Burroughs (playing a junkie priest, of all things).

EAST OF EDEN 3

JAMES DEAN, RAYMOND MASSEY, JO VAN FLEET, JULIE HARRIS

ELIA KAZAN

USA (WARNER) 1955

115m (PG)

Dean died with only three pix under his belt and became a legend, the first American teenager of real note. This version of the John Steinbeck novel about two sons battling for the love of a stiff-necked father shows him at his tortured best. Van Fleet got an Oscar for best supporting actress. Available in a widescreen edition. Remade as a TV mini-series many years later. For the economy minded, there's a two-for-one package with Dean's *Rebel Without A Cause*.

DRAMA

EASY RIDER 🎬[4]

⭐ PETER FONDA, DENNIS HOPPER, JACK NICHOLSON, PHIL SPECTOR

🎬 DENNIS HOPPER

USA (COLUMBIA TRISTAR) 1969

⏱ 94m (18)

Quintessential low-budget road movie, which made Hollywood realise that the youth market wanted their own stories and their own music, and that it did not take multi-million-dollar profligacy to provide them. Hopper and Fonda play two hippy bikers on a drug-dealing trip across America which ends in death. Nicholson's cameo as a soused southern wastrel began his inexorable rise to stardom. Soundtrack by then-hot groups such as Steppenwolf, the Jimi Hendrix Experience, the Byrds and others more obscure. Available in widescreen.

ED WOOD 🎬[4]

⭐ JOHNNY DEPP, MARTIN LANDAU, SARAH JESSICA PARKER, BILL MURRAY

🎬 TIM BURTON

USA (TOUCHSTONE) 1994 B&W

⏱ 121m (15)

Odd to think that a biopic of Wood, often sneered at as the most inept Hollywood director ever (though his films have a bizarre mood all their own), should garner two Oscars: one for make-up, the other for Martin Landau's wonderful performance as faded, morphine-addicted star Bela Lugosi. Director Burton obviously empathises with Wood's weird vision, but even in monochrome the film looks too glossy to be authentic, and Depp too young for a transvestite war hero. See it anyhow. Based on Rudolph Grey's book *Visions of Ecstasy* (Faber).

THE ELEPHANT MAN 🎬[4]

⭐ JOHN HURT, ANTHONY HOPKINS, JOHN GIELGUD, FREDDIE JONES, ANNE BANCROFT

🎬 DAVID LYNCH

USA/UK (WARNER) 1980 B&W

⏱ 118m (PG)

Hurt is unrecognisable as Victorian sideshow freak John (in real life Joseph) Merrick, whose face and body were hideously distorted by tumours – possibly resulting from the disease neurofibromatosis or perhaps Proteus syndrome – and who was rescued by surgeon Sir Frederick Treves (played here by Hopkins in the days before he too became a 'Sir'). The direction is rather tear-jerking for the normally unflinching Lynch, but the pic is lensed in luminous monochrome by Freddie Francis. It's based on the memoirs of Treves, though the film hints at the parallels between the surgeon's use of the Elephant Man and those who showed him as a freak. Widescreen available. Nominated for seven Oscars and won best film and actor (Hurt) at the BAFTAs.

ELIZABETH 🎬4

☆ CATE BLANCHETT, GEOFFREY RUSH, KATHY BURKE, CHRISTOPHER ECCLESTON, RICHARD ATTENBOROUGH, ERIC CANTONA

🎬 SHEKHAR KAPUR

UK (POLYGRAM) 1998

⏱ 119m (15)

The makers of this film about the early life of the first Queen Liz were anxious to avoid a standard 'frock flick', and in hiring the Oscar-nominated Australian Blanchett as star, and veteran Indian director Kapur (best known here for the controversial *Bandit Queen*), they've succeeded. A Tudor tale of love and conspiracy, it dazzles the eyes and brain.

ELMER GANTRY 🎬4

☆ BURT LANCASTER, JEAN SIMMONS, DEAN JAGGER, SHIRLEY JONES

🎬 RICHARD BROOKS

USA (WARNER) 1960

⏱ 142m (PG)

Lancaster exploits his acrobatic athleticism in this story of a phoney evangelist in 20s America, running, jumping and ranting about God and the Devil to rake in the donations. Well-written by the director from the Sinclair Lewis novel. Oscars: best actor (Lancaster), best supporting actress (Jones), screenplay.

EMPIRE OF THE SUN 🎬3

☆ CHRISTIAN BALE, JOHN MALKOVICH, NIGEL HAVERS, MIRANDA RICHARDSON

🎬 STEVEN SPIELBERG

USA (WARNER) 1987

⏱ 146m (PG)

Based on JG Ballard's autobiographical novel, this tells the story of a boy in a Japanese prison camp after he's separated from his parents in World War Two China. A largely overblown mix of Brit stiff-upper-lips and large explosions, but it does have its moments.

THE ENGLISH PATIENT 🎬3

☆ RALPH FIENNES, KRISTIN SCOTT THOMAS, JULIETTE BINOCHE, WILLEM DAFOE

🎬 ANTHONY MINGHELLA

USA (BUENA VISTA) 1996

⏱ 155m (15)

A badly burned pilot in 1943 North Africa tells his story of love, espionage and betrayal to his nurse amid desert scenery and his Italian hospital bed. Judge for yourself whether this version of Michael Ondaatje's post-colonial novel deserved to win a staggering nine Oscars, including best pic. Available in widescreen.

DRAMA

FAIL SAFE [3]

HENRY FONDA, DAN O'HERLIHY, WALTER MATTHAU, LARRY HAGMAN

SIDNEY LUMET

USA (ENCORE) 1963 B&W

108m (PG)

Nuclear disaster movie. When an American weapons system goes wrong and bombs the USSR, the President's only hope of averting a world war is to offer to destroy one of his own cities in order to prove to the enemy that he's told the truth. Suspenseful stuff, based on the novel by Harvey Wheeler and Eugene Burdick.

FALLING DOWN [4]

MICHAEL DOUGLAS, ROBERT DUVALL, FREDERIC FORREST, BARBARA HERSHEY

JOEL SCHUMACHER

USA (WARNER) 1992

108m (18)

Anyone who has ever lost their temper under stress will sympathise with this story of a redundant man, estranged from his family, who simply walks away from his car in an LA traffic jam and gets involved in a series of violent confrontations. After he defeats muggers and then uses their gun to deal with a snotty shop assistant, a weary cop, Duvall, is sent on his trail. Both Duvall and Douglas (as the protagonist) give thoroughly realistic performances – though I fear many will find it hard to identify with the cop's admonition that Douglas has no right to act on the anger he feels towards those in power who made false promises of job security for those who obey society's rules. Still, our anti-hero's fate may make you lie down and count to ten next time you feel yourself about to explode.

FARGO [5]

FRANCES McDORMAND, STEVE BUSCEMI, HARVE PRESNELL, PETER STORMARE, WILLIAM H MACY

JOEL COEN

USA (POLYGRAM) 1995

98m (18)

Off-beat tale of heavily pregnant police chief (McDormand, who deservedly bagged an Oscar for her work here) investigating a car dealer who has arranged for two inept kidnappers to fake the abduction of his wife. Whimsical, funny, bloody and engrossing, with the Scandinavian accents of the small US town of the title adding to the air of other-worldliness. Also won an Oscar for best screenplay for director Coen (husband of McDormand) and his brother Ethan. Please do see it.

TOP 1000 VIDEOS

FATAL ATTRACTION 🎬 4

⭐	MICHAEL DOUGLAS, GLENN CLOSE, ANNE ARCHER, ELLEN FOLEY
🎬	ADRIAN LYNE
	USA (CIC) 1987
⏱	114m (18)

The dangers of illicit romantic entanglements are pointed up in this story of a married man who has a fling only to find that the object of his lust has become psychotically fixated on him. Based on the short *Diversion*, to which the makers bought the rights in order to make sure it will never be seen again – so much for studio dedication to film history and preservation! Available in a widescreen version, with a bonus of the original ending which was dumped after previews. Pity they didn't include *Diversion* as well.

A FEW GOOD MEN 🎬 4

⭐	TOM CRUISE, JACK NICHOLSON, DEMI MOORE, KIEFER SUTHERLAND
🎬	ROB REINER
	USA (COLUMBIA TRISTAR) 1992
⏱	138m (15)

Military courtroom drama about an investigation into the circumstances surrounding the death of a young US Marine at the hands of his buddies. Agreeable work from Cruise and Moore as the lawyers on the case, but the star is undoubtedly Nicholson. Though he only has a handful of scenes, his performance as a mad-eyed commander who demands complete loyalty from his boys, dominates the movie. The final confrontation between Nicholson and Cruise is an absolute corker. Widescreen available.

THE FIELD 🎬 3

⭐	RICHARD HARRIS, JOHN HURT, SEAN BEAN, BRENDA FRICKER, FRANCES TOMELTY, TOM BERENGER
🎬	JIM SHERIDAN
	UK (CINEMA CLUB V) 1990
⏱	109m (15)

Harris is outstanding as the tenant of an Irish peat field who has long coveted ownership of the land and is outraged when a visiting American dares to bid against him for it. Although this tragic tale sags a little towards the end, the film is worth seeing for its fine acting from the supporting cast, especially Hurt as a wily yokel. Based on the play by John B Keane.

DRAMA

FIELD OF DREAMS 🎬4

KEVIN COSTNER, RAY LIOTTA, JAMES EARL JONES, BURT LANCASTER, AMY MADIGAN

PHIL ALDEN ROBINSON

USA (ENTERTAINMENT) 1988

101m (PG)

Delightful fantasy about a farmer who, having felt compelled to raze his crops to build a baseball field, then sees it filled with members of a (real-life) disgraced team who threw the World Series years before – except that they're ghosts. He ends by bringing a famous writer out of retirement and manages a reconciliation with his own late father. If it all sounds mad and twee on paper, on screen it works as a message about never giving up on your most personal dreams. Based on the novel *Shoeless Joe*, by WP Kinsella, in which the writer character was named as real author JD Salinger, creator of *The Catcher in the Rye*.

FRIED GREEN TOMATOES AT THE WHISTLE STOP CAFE 🎬3

JESSICA TANDY, MARY STUART MASTERSON, MARY LOUISE PARKER, KATHY BATES

JON AVNET

USA (CINEMA CLUB V) 1991

130m (PG)

Old woman tells young woman about restaurant run by her two pals in 30s USA. A funny, touching fable of female empowerment in the face of male boorishness. A bit long, but worth the effort. Based on Fannie Flagg's novel.

FROM HERE TO ETERNITY 🎬4

BURT LANCASTER, DEBORAH KERR, MONTGOMERY CLIFT, FRANK SINATRA, DONNA REED

FRED ZINNEMANN

USA (COLUMBIA TRISTAR) 1953 B&W

114m (PG)

Classic film version of the James Jones novel of the lives and loves of those in and around a rough US army camp in Hawaii just before the attack on Pearl Harbor. Magnificent acting by Clift as the man who irritates his superiors by refusing to box due to the death of a previous opponent, and there's that famous love scene between Burt and Deborah in the foaming surf. Eight Oscars, including best picture, director, supporting actor and actress (Sinatra and Reed), cinematography and screenplay.

GI JANE 🎬3

DEMI MOORE, VIGGO MORTENSEN, ANNE BANCROFT

RIDLEY SCOTT

USA (FIRST INDEPENDENT) 1996

125m (15)

A 'serious' version of *Private Benjamin* (see page 88): a woman's battle to get respect in the army. Panned mercilessly, but the antics of shaven-headed Demi hit it big with the girl-power constituency and the pic has apparently been a rental video hit in the UK.

GOOD WILL HUNTING [4]

MATT DAMON, BEN AFFLECK, ROBIN WILLIAMS, MINNIE DRIVER

GUS VAN SANT

USA (MIRAMAX) 1997

121m (15)

Stars Damon and Affleck scripted this hit movie, about a campus tearaway who is cleverer than the college professors, as a vehicle for themselves. The gamble paid off with a rash of award nominations and a couple of Oscars. Can Damon's gal (Driver) and mentor (Williams) save him from himself and nudge him in the right direction? You can't argue with success, but I think it takes too long to tell the tale.

GORILLAS IN THE MIST [3]

SIGOURNEY WEAVER, BRYAN BROWN, JULIE HARRIS, IAIN CUTHBERTSON

MICHAEL APTED

USA (WARNER) 1988

124m (15)

Biopic of Dian Fossey, who was murdered in 1985 while studying and attempting to save the endangered mountain gorillas of Rwanda. The story hardly needed the love interest emphasised to such a degree, as her life and work were clearly interesting enough without it. Weaver seems to realise this and acts throughout as if to make her character as unfanciable as possible. Not to be sniffed at – and that's not a gorilla joke!

THE GRAPES OF WRATH [3]

HENRY FONDA, JOHN CARRADINE, CHARLEY GRAPEWIN, JANE DARWELL

JOHN FORD

USA (FOX) 1940 B&W

129m (PG)

Ford's version of John Steinbeck's novel of the dustbowl depression embodies much the same pioneer spirit as his Westerns, albeit in a less mythical context. Over-reverent, perhaps, but well-made. Oscar: best supporting actress (Darwell).

GRIDLOCK'D [4]

TIM ROTH, TUPAC SHAKUR, THANDIE NEWTON

VONDIE CURTIS-HALL

USA/UK (4-FRONT) 1996

87m (18)

Roth and the late Shakur are two hapless junkies who decide to quit drugs and get themselves into rehab, and this grimly hilarious little picture charts their battles with the form-filling, wait-in-line machinery that thwarts them at every turn. The next time someone tells you that addicts who decide to stop are lavished with care, run this movie for them. Roth is always good, while Shakur is useful enough to make one speculate that the rapper might have become a star in pix had he not been brutally slain.

DRAMA

HENRY – PORTRAIT OF A SERIAL KILLER 🎬 5

- MICHAEL ROOKER, TOM TOWLES, TRACY ARNOLD
- JOHN McNAUGHTON
- USA (ELECTRIC) 1990
- 83m (18)

One of the most important independent pix of recent years. Based on the (possibly dubious) confessions of real serial killer Henry Lee Lucas, this is a gruesome near-documentary presentation of Henry and his buddy planning and executing various sex murders. The UK censor was upset by the director's refusal to insert implicit criticism of the actions of the protagonists, so there are cuts and at least one sequence has been re-edited in the version on sale here. McNaughton has not lived up to the promise of this film with his later mainstream movies, though Rooker (see *JFK*, page 119) and Towles have become regular Hollywood support players of some ability. A sequel has recently emerged (see below) with a new cast and director.

HENRY – PORTRAIT OF A SERIAL KILLER 2 🎬 3

- NEIL GUINTOLI, RICH KOMENICH, KATE WALSH
- CHUCK PARELLO
- USA (MOSAIC) 1996
- 84m (18)

A new actor appears in the title role for this finally released sequel to the notorious movie, which has a new director too. Slicker and not as troubling as the earlier film, this one sees Henry continuing his amoral adventures in slaughter. Well-made and you can't look away – rather like a road accident. Subtitle: *Mask Of Sanity*.

HILARY AND JACKIE 🎬 2

- EMILY WATSON, RACHEL GRIFFITHS, CHARLES DANCE
- ANAND TUCKER
- UK (FILM FOUR) 1998
- 117m (15)

Controversial but ultimately rather tawdry examination of the life and death of musician Jacqueline du Pré, her crippling illness and her relationship with her sibling (not to mention the sibling's hubby). Watson does a good job as the artist, but the film has been much lambasted for its prurience and juggling with the truth. (Note: some of the controversy seems to have been manufactured. A young musician who played at a protest outside a cinema where the film was showing has recently stated that she was hired to do so, and that her fee arrived in an envelope bearing the name of the movie's PR firm. Said firm refused to comment beyond saying that the person who handled the film has since left.)

TOP 1000 VIDEOS

HOPE FLOATS

SANDRA BULLOCK, HARRY CONNICK Jnr, GENA ROWLANDS

FOREST WHITTAKER

USA (FOX PATHE) 1998

110m (PG)

When a woman watching her husband on a TV talk show discovers that he is cheating on her with a younger woman, she returns to her Texas home town with her daughter to try to rebuild her life. Touching story of a woman's attempt to find the strength to trust after her trust has been betrayed. Two-hanky entertainment.

THE HORSE WHISPERER

ROBERT REDFORD, KRISTIN SCOTT THOMAS, SAM NEILL, DIANNE WIEST

ROBERT REDFORD

USA (BUENA VISTA) 1998

162m (PG)

Based on the novel inspired by the true-life story of a man who learned to 'talk' to wild horses (incidentally, some of the man's claims about his family life have recently been challenged by those who know him). Could have been an interesting film, but it winds up being an excessively long hymn to Redford the movie star. Lots of people love it, though, so don't let me stop you.

HOW GREEN WAS MY VALLEY

WALTER PIDGEON, MAUREEN O'HARA, RODDY McDOWALL, DONALD CRISP, ANNA LEE

JOHN FORD

USA (FOX) 1941 B&W

118m (U)

Sentimental but enjoyable film version of Richard Llewellyn's novel about life in a Welsh village. Coal mining was never this cosy in real life, but fine actors and sharp script carry it along. Oscars: best picture, director, cinematography, art direction and supporting actor (Crisp).

IN THE NAME OF THE FATHER

DANIEL DAY-LEWIS, PETER POSTLETHWAITE, EMMA THOMPSON

JIM SHERIDAN

UK (CIC) 1993

127m (15)

Critics moaned over some factual errors, but this true story of the people wrongly imprisoned for many years for the IRA bombs in Guildford remains a shocking, sobering experience that will shatter your faith in British justice. Police are shown as both brutal and cynical. Day-Lewis is fine as Gerry Conlon, but Postlethwaite steals the film as his bewildered father.

DRAMA

JFK 🎬 3

⭐ KEVIN COSTNER, TOMMY LEE JONES, GARY OLDMAN, SISSY SPACEK, JOE PESCI, WALTER MATTHAU, JACK LEMMON, DONALD SUTHERLAND, JOHN CANDY, MICHAEL ROOKER

🎬 OLIVER STONE

USA (WARNER) 1991

⏱ 189m ⓵⓹

Over-long, star-laden account of lawman Jim Garrison's attempt to unveil the conspiracy that led to the 1963 assassination of President Kennedy. Deftly uses flashbacks and monochrome inserts to explore the various possibilities, but unless you pay rigid attention you are liable to get lost trying to work out what is established fact and what is mere supposition. Costner tries hard as an upright Henry Fonda-type, but looks too boyish for the role. The real Garrison appears as Judge Warren, whose commission whitewashed the murder as the act of lone nut Lee Harvey Oswald. A terrible crime against democracy was committed, but the benefit of hindsight has changed our hitherto rose-tinted view of the victim. Available in pan-scan, in widescreen and even in a widescreen director's cut, packaged with a documentary tape on the case. Take your choice – at least it's better than Stone's execrable *Nixon*, his companion biopic of Kennedy's nemesis.

KILLER 🎬 4

⭐ JAMES WOODS, ROBERT SEAN LEONARD, ELLEN GREENE

🎬 TIM METCALFE

USA (FIRST INDEPENDENT) 1997

⏱ 87m ⓵⓼

Produced by Oliver Stone and with a typically fine central performance by James Woods, this pic (subtitled *A Journal Of Murder*) tells the true story of Carl Panzram. Imprisoned on minor charges in the USA earlier this century, he killed while in jail and spent the time before his hanging penning a shocking autobiography in which he confessed to numerous sex-crimes and murders. While Panzram was obviously a product of a brutal youth, the movie tries a bit *too* hard to make us feel sorry for him: he's shown killing a vicious guard, whereas in reality his victim was an innocent civilian jail worker, and we're never told that many of his confessed rapes and slayings involved young boys. It's a tad like trying to make a sulky anti-hero out of Moors Murderer Ian Brady. Still, Woods is fabulously watchable and there's able support, especially from Robert Sean Leonard as a prison guard who befriends the killer. Got a scant cinema release – don't overlook it now.

THE KILLING FIELDS 🎬4

SAM WATERSTON, HAING S NGOR, JOHN MALKOVICH, JULIAN SANDS

ROLAND JOFFE

UK (WARNER) 1984

⏱ 136m (15)

True story of a US reporter's attempt to regain contact with his Cambodian guide, left behind when the Khmer Rouge took over the country. Superbly authentic work from Ngor as the guide – hardly surprising as he was a victim of the terror himself. Dr Ngor, who was, sadly, murdered recently, won a richly deserved best supporting actor Oscar. Other Oscars: editing and cinematography.

KISS OF THE SPIDER WOMAN 🎬4

WILLIAM HURT, RAUL JULIA, SONIA BRAGA, MILTON GONCALVES

HECTOR BABENCO

BRAZIL/USA (ELECTRIC) 1985 COL/B&W

⏱ 120m (15)

Unusual story of a political prisoner whose spirits are kept up by the recounting of a tacky film plot by his drag-queen cellmate. The late Julia is good as the politico, but the star is Hurt as the homosexual who initially infuriates his friend but who finally inspires him by the resilience he finds through fantasy. The inserts from the imaginary movie, which is loosely based on a character in a couple of real Hollywood movies, are shown in black and white. Oscar: best actor (Hurt).

LA CONFIDENTIAL 🎬4

KEVIN SPACEY, KIM BASINGER, DANNY DeVITO, RUSSELL CROWE

CURTIS HANSON

USA (WARNER) 1997

⏱ 132m (18)

Streamlined version of one of James Ellroy's complex Los Angeles novels, telling the story of cops, junkies, police brutality, etc., etc., in early 50s Hollywood. Despite the simplification and the ditching of some characters, the story is still somewhat hard to follow but is redeemed by nicely-judged performances all round. Justifiably lauded at the Oscars (Basinger won best supporting actress) and well worth seeing.

LAST EXIT TO BROOKLYN 🎬4

JENNIFER JASON LEIGH, STEPHEN LANG, BURT YOUNG, STEPHEN BALDWIN

ULI EDEL

WEST GERMANY (POLYGRAM) 1989

⏱ 98m (18)

Darkly compelling movie of Hubert Selby Jnr's controversial novel about 50s hookers, dopers and sundry other sleazy folk. Jason Leigh gives the outstanding performance here, but not a film to watch if you're looking for a pick-me-up!

LEGENDS OF THE FALL 🎬3

BRAD PITT, ANTHONY HOPKINS, AIDAN QUINN, JULIA ORMOND

EDWARD ZWICK

USA (COLUMBIA TRISTAR) 1994

129m (15)

Ins-and-outs of brothers in love and war as they move between their wilderness home and civilisation, between romance and hate-fuelled rage. The full plot is too complex to detail here, but director Zwick (of *Glory* fame, see page 322) keeps the action ticking over as the picture moves in an ever more tragic direction. Savagely superior soap-opera. Widescreen and boxed set available.

LENNY 🎬4

DUSTIN HOFFMAN, VALERIE PERRINE, GARY MORTON, JAN MINER

BOB FOSSE

USA (WARNER) 1974 B&W

111m (18)

Biography of Lenny Bruce, the first alternative standup comic and a man whose numerous brushes with the law over drugs and obscenity led to his downfall. Hoffman's performance was criticised at the time, but it's hard to see how it could have been bettered. It may be a truism that funny men don't have funny lives, but this movie illustrates the fact all too harrowingly.

LONE STAR 🎬4

KRIS KRISTOFFERSON, FRANCES McDORMAND, MATTHEW McCONAUGHEY, RON CANADA

JOHN SAYLES

USA (COLUMBIA TRISTAR) 1996

130m (15)

Deep mystery as modern-day sheriff Kristofferson investigates events in the past. Support from the marvellous McDormand and the up-and-coming McConaughey make this an intriguing drama that's worth a look. Available in widescreen.

LOOKING FOR RICHARD 🎬3

AL PACINO, KEVIN SPACEY, ALEC BALDWIN, WINONA RYDER

AL PACINO

USA (GUILD) 1996

112m (12)

Thought-provoking piece by Pacino, as he records his efforts to stage Shakespeare's *Richard III* and tries to fathom the fascination of the play with the help of actors, friends and passers-by. A brave and entertaining piece of documentary genius. Widescreen.

LOVE IS THE DEVIL [4]

DEREK JACOBI, TILDA SWINTON, DANIEL CRAIG, ADRIAN SCARBOROUGH

JOHN MAYBURY

UK/FRANCE/JAPAN (ARTIFICIAL EYE) 1998

90m (18)

Jacobi looks amazingly like the real Francis Bacon in this portrait of the controversial painter's life in the decadent milieu of London's Colony Club and his sexual relationship with an unstable young crook. The latter character perhaps takes up too much of the film, but for the most part this is an inventive and seductive piece of cinematic biography.

THE MADNESS OF KING GEORGE [4]

NIGEL HAWTHORNE, HELEN MIRREN, IAN HOLM, RUPERT EVERETT, AMANDA DONOHOE

NICHOLAS HYTNER

UK (COLUMBIA TRISTAR) 1995

106m (PG)

Based on Alan Bennett's play *The Madness of George III* (allegedly renamed in case Americans wondered if they'd missed the first two films!), this has wonderfully affecting performances all round, especially from Hawthorne as a man who realises his sanity is in danger yet is unable, for once in his life, to control events. Bennett slyly draws parallels with the current British Royal Family: 'To be the Prince of Wales is not a position, it is a predicament.' Available in a letterboxed de luxe package, this is a film which rightly garnered many awards. Intelligence and entertainment need not be incompatible.

THE MAN WITH THE GOLDEN ARM [3]

FRANK SINATRA, KIM NOVAK, DARREN McGAVIN, ELEANOR PARKER

OTTO PREMINGER

USA (VISIONARY) 1955 B&W

120m (PG)

Controversial in its day, this film of Nelson Algren's book stars Sinatra as Frankie Machine, whose 'golden arm' refers to both his card-dealing skills and his heroin addiction. This was probably the first movie to play out the highs and lows of junkiedom with any truth. Sinatra scores (ahem) brilliantly in the lead. Worth catching.

DRAMA

MEET JOE BLACK [3]

BRAD PITT, ANTHONY HOPKINS, CLARE FORLANI

MARTIN BREST

USA (UNIVERSAL) 1998

173m (12)

Death takes on the body of a tragic-accident victim, Pitt, to find out what being alive is really like. In return for being his earthly guide, media tycoon Hopkins is given a few extra days to put his life in order before he dies. Pitt displays an intriguing and engaging innocence as he tries to figure out what life is all about, while those around him try to work out who he is and where he has come from. But the problems really start when Hopkins' daughter begins to fall in love with him ...

MICHAEL COLLINS [4]

LIAM NEESON, ALAN RICKMAN, JULIA ROBERTS, STEPHEN REA

NEIL JORDAN

UK (WARNER) 1996

127m (15)

A massive fuss was expected by the distributors of this biopic of the original IRA godfather, but there were few protests, except from those who questioned the accuracy of some scenes. Collins, who negotiated the ill-fated treaty that led to the division of Ireland and is the cause of the 'troubles' today, ended up wearing an army uniform and was killed by his own ex-comrades. He seems to have been aware of his own fall-guy status, compounding the air of tragedy in this well-made picture. Neeson gives a fine performance in the lead and is shaping up to be one of the major stars of the future.

MIDNIGHT COWBOY 4

JON VOIGHT, DUSTIN HOFFMAN, BRENDA VACCARO, SYLVIA MILES, VIVA

JOHN SCHLESINGER

USA (WARNER) 1969

108m (18)

Dated version of James Leo Herlihy novel about a non-sexual love affair between two hustlers in 60s New York, Voight as a naive cowboy stud and Hoffman as the tramp 'Ratso' Rizzo. Influenced by Warhol flicks of the time and featuring members of his 'Factory' entourage, it's a clever subverting of underground image into overground substance, a tragicomic paean to not-so-beautiful losers. Singer Harry Nilsson is often erroneously credited with the score; in fact he merely sang Fred Neil's song 'Everybody's Talkin'': the score is by John Barry. Oscars: picture, director, screenplay.

MIDNIGHT EXPRESS 4

BRAD DAVIS, JOHN HURT, RANDY QUAID, BO HOPKINS

ALAN PARKER

UK (COLUMBIA TRISTAR) 1978

121m (18)

Oscar-winning script by Oliver Stone is an exaggerated version of the true story of a young American's imprisonment in a Turkish jail for attempting to smuggle cannabis out of the country – interesting in the light of the accusations of untruths levelled at later Stone projects such as *JFK* (see page 119). Good performances from Hurt and Quaid as the jailed misfits who adopt the scared kid in the corrupt prison, but the ending seems a bit too pat. Some grim violence, including a man having his tongue bitten off. Widescreen available.

MIDNIGHT IN THE GARDEN OF GOOD AND EVIL 3

KEVIN SPACEY, JUDE LAW, JOHN CUSACK, JACK THOMPSON

CLINT EASTWOOD

USA (WARNER) 1997

155m (15)

John Berendt's book, about a real-life murder mystery involving a gay antiques dealer and his street-hustler beau down in Savannah, Georgia, is transformed at the hands of director Clint into 155 minutes of efficient but sadly draggy celuloid. Spacey is always a class act, but the old cliché applies here: the book was better. Okay, however, if you're in the mood to lay back and succumb to its limited charms.

DRAMA

MRS BROWN 🎬3

JUDI DENCH, BILLY CONNOLLY, ANTONY SHER, GEOFFREY PALMER

JOHN MADDEN

USA/UK/IRELAND (BUENA VISTA) 1997

99m (15)

Well-made story of the irreverent relationship between Queen Victoria (Dench) and her highland ghillie John Brown (Connolly), as he attempts to assuage her prolonged mourning over the death of her husband Prince Albert. The subtext of continuing Scottish servility to the English has been criticised, but nothing can detract from the accomplished acting and production values. Although the title of the film is *Mrs Brown*, the video box has the legend *Her Majesty Mrs Brown*, just in case audiences are in any doubt of what the film is about.

MY BEAUTIFUL LAUNDRETTE 🎬3

DANIEL DAY-LEWIS, SAEED JAFFREY, ROSHAN SETH, SHIRLEY ANN FIELD

STEPHEN FREARS

UK (PVG) 1985

97m (15)

Cult movie about a young British Asian and the luxury washeteria he runs with his gay lover. Maybe not the most exciting film ever, though it's a touching story, with moments of violence.

MY LEFT FOOT 🎬4

DANIEL DAY-LEWIS, RAY McANALLY, BRENDA FRICKER, FIONA SHAW

JIM SHERIDAN

UK (ELECTRIC) 1989

103m (15)

The story of Christy Brown, the Irish writer, who fought against cerebral palsy to become an author by using the one part of his body he could control – the eponymous foot – to tap out words on a keyboard. Oscars for Day-Lewis and Brenda Fricker, who plays his mother. An inspiring movie about the power of the human will to overcome seemingly insurmountable odds.

NAKED LUNCH 🎬 4

⭐ PETER WELLER, JUDY DAVIS, IAN HOLM, ROY SCHEIDER, JULIAN SANDS

🎬 DAVID CRONENBERG

UK/CANADA (FIRST INDEPENDENT) 1991

⏱ 111m   (18)

A synthesis of the 'unfilmable' literary sex/dope fantasy by the late William S Burroughs and his experiences in trying to write the book, including his accidental shooting of his wife. Hallucinatory imagery and talking insect typewriters, not to mention bug killers hooked on their own exterminating powder. The mad alien world of lifelong gay junkie Burroughs fits in with director Cronenberg's body-loathing world view just fine, but the result only proves the impossibility of translating the book's scattergun ideas into narrative cinema. A marvellous try, though! Available in widescreen.

THE NAME OF THE ROSE 🎬 4

⭐ SEAN CONNERY, F MURRAY ABRAHAM, CHRISTIAN SLATER, RON PERLMAN

🎬 JEAN-JACQUES ANNAUD

FRANCE/ITALY/WEST GERMANY (POLYGRAM) 1986

⏱ 124m   (18)

Billed as a 'palimpsest' (look it up) of Umberto Eco's fat intellectual novel, this tells of a Sherlock Holmes-style monk investigating murder and mystery in an ancient monastery with the help of his Watsonish young assistant. The grubby fourteenth-century atmosphere is well handled, and Connery is at his best.

NIL BY MOUTH 🎬 3

⭐ RAY WINSTONE, KATHY BURKE, CHARLES CREED-MILES

🎬 GARY OLDMAN

UK/USA (FOX) 1997

⏱ 123m   (18)

Actor Oldman's directional debut is a grim but compelling view of a South London family beset by drugs, booze and violence. Much-praised but inevitably depressing, it is saved by brutally honest acting from Winstone and Burke. Widescreen. Won several awards, including two BAFTAS.

DRAMA

OF MICE AND MEN [3]

JOHN MALKOVICH, GARY SINISE, SHERILYN FENN, CASEY SIEMASZKO

GARY SINISE

USA (MGM/UA) 1992

111m (PG)

Decent, if a little too subdued, version of John Steinbeck's story of two poor men in depression America: the childlike Lennie (John Malkovich) and his minder George (Sinise). Doesn't stand comparison with the 1939 version which featured Lon Chaney Jnr's classic turn as Lennie, but still worth renting if you're a fan of the story.

ON GOLDEN POND [3]

HENRY FONDA, KATHARINE HEPBURN, JANE FONDA, DABNEY COLEMAN

MARK RYDELL

USA (4-FRONT) 1981

109m (PG)

Henry Fonda's final movie sees him paired with daughter Jane in a story about a grump coming to terms with the onset of old age and the need to settle up emotional accounts with his wife and child. Oscars for Henry Fonda and Katharine Hepburn, and for Ernest Thompson for the screenplay based on his own play. Slush, but quality slush.

ON THE WATERFRONT [4]

MARLON BRANDO, LEE J COBB, ROD STEIGER, EVA MARIE SAINT, KARL MALDEN

ELIA KAZAN

USA (COLUMBIA TRISTAR) 1954 B&W

103m (PG)

Classic version of Budd Schulberg's novel of corruption among dockers and union officials. Brando is fabulous as the ex-fighter who finally decides to take a stand in the face of opposition from his brother (Steiger) and the boss (Cobb), both of whom give larger-than-life performances. Oscars: best picture, director, actor (Brando), supporting actress (Saint) and cinematography.

ONE FLEW OVER THE CUCKOO'S NEST

JACK NICHOLSON, LOUISE FLETCHER, DANNY DeVITO, WILL SAMPSON, CHRISTOPHER LLOYD, BRAD DOURIF

MILOS FORMAN

USA (POLYGRAM) 1975

134m (18)

Marvellous film adaptation of Ken Kesey's novel about a rebel who elects to go to a mental hospital thinking it'll be a softer option than jail, with tragic consequences when his free-spirit nature squares up to a sadistic nurse. Nicholson and Fletcher are stunning as the rebel and the nurse, and the cast includes several actors who would go on to bigger things. Oscars: best actor (Nicholson), best actress (Fletcher), best picture, director and screenplay. Available on a two-for-one tape with the Nicholson vehicle *Carnal Knowledge*.

PACIFIC HEIGHTS

MICHAEL KEATON, MELANIE GRIFFITH, MATTHEW MODINE, MAKO

JOHN SCHLESINGER

USA (FOX) 1990

98m (15)

Another of the early 90s splurge of thrillers where ordinary life choices prove deadly, like *The Hand That Rocks The Cradle* (see page 290) or *Single White Female* (see page 301). Respected Brit Schlesinger tries to make something of this one, which is about a couple who take a tenant to make ends meet and (just about) live to regret it. Soon he's stopping the rent, gutting the place and (amazingly) getting the law on his side. It's all too plausible (at least until the main climax), with Keaton as the charming, loony scam artist, and liable to put you off being a landlord for life.

A PASSAGE TO INDIA

ALEC GUINNESS, JUDY DAVIS, VICTOR BANERJEE, PEGGY ASHCROFT, NIGEL HAVERS

DAVID LEAN

UK (WARNER) 1984

163m (PG)

Ashcroft is superb as the adventurous old lady who goes on a trip with her son's future wife to India, where they befriend a local doctor, only for him to end up being accused of a sex attack. This version of the EM Forster novel is on the slow side, and is not one of Lean's best films. Compare it to *Lawrence Of Arabia* (see page 148) and you'll agree. However, it's lovingly shot, and won Oscars for best actress (Ashcroft) and best score (Maurice Jarre).

DRAMA

THE PEOPLE vs LARRY FLYNT

WOODY HARRELSON, COURTNEY LOVE

MILOS FORMAN

USA (COLUMBIA TRISTAR) 1996

124m (18)

Biopic of the publisher of politically-incorrect US porn mag *Hustler*, showing his battles with the courts, drugs and the aftermath of an assassination attempt that left him confined to a wheelchair and flirting with Christianity. If it wasn't true, the story would be deemed too far-fetched to film! Harrelson makes a likeable monster who says all he's guilty of is bad taste. The message is that free speech is for everybody, not just those we think are worthwhile.

PERFORMANCE

JAMES FOX, MICK JAGGER, ANITA PALLENBERG, MICHELE BRETON, ANTHONY VALENTINE

NICOLAS ROEG, DONALD CAMMELL

UK (WARNER) 1970

102m (18)

Classic hallucinatory comment on 60s decadence, with Fox as gangster on the run seeking refuge with fading rock star Jagger in his weird, *ménage-à-trois* household. Directed by two cult moviemakers and full of great music and jarring editorial flourishes, this is a much-pondered and acclaimed piece. Pristine print, plus trailer. Widescreen.

PHILADELPHIA

TOM HANKS, DENZEL WASHINGTON, JASON ROBARDS, MARY STEENBURGEN, ANTONIO BANDERAS

JONATHAN DEMME

USA (COLUMBIA TRISTAR) 1994

125m (12)

Demme made this movie as a sop to activists who had been outraged by his portrayal of a gay killer in *The Silence Of The Lambs* (see page 301). The story is maudlin yet curiously effective and moving (largely due to Hanks), revolving around a gay lawyer who enlists homophobe Washington to sue the firm that fired him because he had AIDS. While his staunchly supportive parents don't ring true, Hanks carries the picture and won an Oscar for his performance.

POSTCARDS FROM THE EDGE

MERYL STREEP, SHIRLEY MacLAINE, DENNIS QUAID, GENE HACKMAN, RICHARD DREYFUSS

MIKE NICHOLS

USA (COLUMBIA TRISTAR) 1990

97m (15)

Funny drama about fraught relations beetween a movie star and her daughter, well acted by Oscar-nominated Streep with a fine support cast. Based on Carrie Fisher's autobiographical novel, inspired by her relationship with her own Hollywood parents, Debbie Reynolds and Eddie Fisher.

PRESUMED INNOCENT 🎬 3

- HARRISON FORD, GRETA SCACCHI, RAUL JULIA, BRIAN DENNEHY
- ALAN J PAKULA
- USA (WARNER) 1990
- 121m (18)

Based on Scott Turow's hit novel, this is a competent and fairly engrossing drama about a respected lawyer (Ford) suspected of murdering an attractive female colleague. There are enough twists to sustain interest to the surprise ending. Quality formula.

PRICK UP YOUR EARS 🎬 4

- GARY OLDMAN, ALFRED MOLINA, VANESSA REDGRAVE, JULIE WALTERS, WALLACE SHAWN
- STEPHEN FREARS
- UK (VISION) 1987
- 111m (18)

John Lahr's biography of gay playwright Joe Orton – murdered by his lover who then took his own life – is brought hilariously and lovingly to the screen via a scintillating script by Alan Bennett and stellar acting from Oldman and Molina as the doomed literary jesters. Great stuff.

QUIZ SHOW 🎬 5

- RALPH FIENNES, PAUL SCOFIELD, JOHN TURTURRO
- ROBERT REDFORD
- USA (HOLLYWOOD) 1994
- 128m (15)

True story of an academic who fell from grace when it was discovered he was being 'fed' the answers on a TV quiz of the 50s in order to keep the public tuning in to root for a popular winner. Fiennes is a revelation as the tempted innocent and Scofield nearly steals the pic as his deeply disappointed intellectual dad. May not sound much on paper but you'll be doing yourself a grievous wrong if you pass this one by. One of the best films of the 90s.

RAGING BULL 🎬 4

- ROBERT DE NIRO, CATHY MORIARTY, JOE PESCI, THERESA SALDANA
- MARTIN SCORSESE
- USA (WARNER) 1980 B&W
- 124m (18)

Scorsese's tribute to the great boxing pix of yesteryear is based on the life of Jake La Motta, who crashed from ring hitter to nightclub owner. De Niro gained weight for the later stages of the film to show the angry man's decline, and rightly won an Oscar for his effort. Slow-motion vision and sound (plus colour effects) are employed in the gruelling fight scenes. The film also won an Oscar for editing.

DRAMA

RAIN MAN

DUSTIN HOFFMAN, TOM CRUISE, VALERIA GOLINO, JACK MURDOCK

BARRY LEVINSON

USA (WARNER) 1988

128m (15)

Attending his dad's funeral, Cruise finds out he has an autistic sibling who has been left everything in his father's will. He hopes to get the estate made over to him but soon finds that his irritating brother is in many ways a brilliant man. Oscars: best film, director and screenplay and best actor (Hoffman). Note: according to some sources, the original print was 140m (136m on video), so check the box if this matters to you.

REMAINS OF THE DAY

EMMA THOMPSON, ANTHONY HOPKINS, JAMES FOX, CHRISTOPHER REEVE

JAMES IVORY

UK/USA (COLUMBIA TRISTAR) 1993

130m (U)

This elegant film of Kazuo Ishiguro's novel tells the story of a repressed English servant and his love. It was nominated for several Oscars – Emma Thompson won for best actress. Widescreen available.

REVERSAL OF FORTUNE

JEREMY IRONS, GLENN CLOSE, RON SILVER, ANNABELLA SCIORRA

BARBET SCHROEDER

USA (CINEMA CLUB V) 1990

106m (15)

Oscar-winning role for Irons as Claus von Bulow, the real-life aristocrat accused of attempting to kill his wife (and consigning her to a coma) with an injection of insulin. Von Bulow was freed by master lawyer Alan Dershowitz, on whose book the film is based (he also worked on the OJ Simpson case), but the movie manages to avoid libel while still leaving doubt in the viewer's mind about his guilt or innocence. Extremely entertaining even when you know the outcome.

ROCKY 🎬 5

SYLVESTER STALLONE, TALIA SHIRE, BURT YOUNG, BURGESS MEREDITH

JOHN G AVILDSEN

USA (WARNER) 1976

114m (PG)

Those who snigger at Stallone as if he was some incurably thick hunk are having to eat their words due to his impressive part in the recent *Copland* (see page 285) – but more mature observers never forgot that his leap to the big time began with his writing and starring in this moving little pic about a broken-down fighter's last chance at romance and fame. All the dreadful sequels notwithstanding, *Rocky* still stands up as a model of what Stallone can do on a good day. Oscars: best pic/ director/editing.

SCHINDLER'S LIST 🎬 4

LIAM NEESON, RALPH FIENNES, BEN KINGSLEY, CAROLINE GOODALL

STEPHEN SPIELBERG

USA (CIC) 1994 COL/B&W

197m (15)

Spielberg was finally accepted as a serious film director with this true story of Oskar Schindler, a Nazi speculator in Poland during World War Two who felt the tug of conscience and ended up using his money to save the Jewish slave workers in his employ. Neeson is smooth as Schindler and Fiennes is unnerving as a concentration camp boss who likes nothing better than shooting a few inmates during pre-breakfast target practice. Though in monochrome, the film has some colour effects and a final colour coda which shows the actors who played the Jews accompanying their real-life models to Schindler's grave. Nominated for ten Oscars, it won only one, for best picture. Available in widescreen.

SE7EN 🎬 4

BRAD PITT, MORGAN FREEMAN, KEVIN SPACEY, GWYNETH PALTROW

DAVID FINCHER

USA (ENTERTAINMENT) 1994

126m (18)

Icy tale of a serial killer working his way through murders based on the seven deadly sins. Though many found it dark and disgusting, the acting is undoubtably superb. Some prints, including the one used for video mastering, were struck using a special recovered-silver process called CCE which makes even the dimmest scenes tolerable to the viewer. Widescreen.

DRAMA

SEVEN YEARS IN TIBET [2]

BRAD PITT, DAVID THEWLIS, MAKO

JEAN-JACQUES ANNAUD

USA (ENTERTAINMENT) 1997

129m (18)

Moody Pitt vehicle, extolling the life-changing qualities of Tibet. Designed mainly for Brad fans as others may find it slow-moving. Tibet is a big thing with Hollywood liberals outraged by China's human rights abuses and fascinated by Buddhism and the exiled Dalai Lama, the subject of Scorsese's recent *Kundun*.

SHADRACH [3]

HARVEY KEITEL, ANDIE MacDOWELL, MARTIN SHEEN

SUSANNA STYRON

USA (NU IMAGE) 1999

85m (12)

A compassionate and moving story seen through the eyes of Martin Sheen, looking back at the summer of his tenth year when he was living with the proud and explosive Vernon Dabney and his sassy wife. Dabney's life is set in turmoil when an old slave comes to claim the right to be buried in the plantation he now owns. Humour and compassion combine in this drama which will interest those who like to examine character as much as action.

SHAWSHANK REDEMPTION [4]

TIM ROBBINS, MORGAN FREEMAN, JAMES WHITMORE

FRANK DARABONT

USA (GUILD) 1994

131m (15)

Lengthy but always engaging version of a Stephen King novelette *(Rita Hayworth and the Shawshank Redemption)* about a wrongly imprisoned man who overcomes a brutal regime to change his own life and those of the men around him. It may not be a believable or serious prison picture, but it makes for a truly pleasurable and uplifting couple of hours. Nominated for a gallery of Oscars.

SHINE [4]

GEOFFREY RUSH, ARMIN MUELLER-STAHL, LYNN REDGRAVE, JOHN GIELGUD

SCOTT HICKS

AUSTRALIA (BUENA VISTA) 1996

101m (15)

Moving story of disturbed, brilliant pianist, David Helfgott, from sad childhood to the success and relative happiness of today. Excellent central performance by Rush as the adult Helfgott. Some critics carp about the pianist's odd style of playing, which often also involves singing or humming along to the music, but audiences have taken him (and the film) to their hearts. Oscar: best actor for Geoffrey Rush.

SID AND NANCY 🎬3

★ GARY OLDMAN, CHLOE WEBB, DAVID HAYMAN, EDWARD TUDOR-POLE

🎬 ALEX COX

UK (BMG) 1986

⏱ 109m (18)

Oldman is a reasonable facsimile of that most self-destructive member of the Sex Pistols, Sid Vicious, in this biopic about his doomed, heroin-fuelled romance with the disturbed American groupie Nancy Spungen. He was charged with murder when she was found stabbed to death beside him in their New York hotel room, but died of an overdose before he could be tried. Many who knew them doubt his guilt and there were rumours of a frame-up by unpaid drug dealers, but the film doesn't solve the mystery.

SMOKE 🎬3

★ HARVEY KEITEL, WILLIAM HURT, STOCKARD CHANNING, FOREST WHITAKER

🎬 WAYNE WANG

USA (HOLLYWOOD) 1995

⏱ 108m (15)

Intricate tale of cigar-seller and pals scripted by Paul Auster. Harvey Keitel's cigar store is the focal point for various characters to meet, talk, interact and philosophise. Note: there is a companion piece of sorts, *Blue In The Face*, with Keitel, Lou Reed and others delivering monologues and stories direct to camera. Interesting.

STEPMOM 🎬3

★ JULIA ROBERTS, SUSAN SARANDON, ED HARRIS

🎬 CHRIS COLUMBUS

USA (COLUMBIA TRISTAR) 1998

⏱ 120m (12)

A mother has a running battle with her ex-husband's younger partner for the control and affections of her children. When she finds she is terminally ill, however, she decides that they both have to find a way to make the best of the time she has remaining. Plenty of Kleenex required for this one.

THE SWEET SMELL OF SUCCESS 🎬4

★ BURT LANCASTER, TONY CURTIS, MARTIN MILNER, SUSAN HARRISON

🎬 ALEXANDER MacKENDRICK

USA (WARNER) 1957 B&W

⏱ 96m (PG)

Brit MacKendrick helmed this sewer-level study of a pompous USA gossip columnist (Lancaster) and the PR who runs at his gilded heels (Curtis). Their grimy pact goes horribly awry when Curtis bungles his assignment to snuff the romance between Lancaster's sister and a young jazz musician. Sparklingly vicious script by Clifford Odets.

DRAMA

A TIME TO KILL [3]

MATTHEW McCONAUGHEY, SAMUEL L JACKSON, SANDRA BULLOCK, KEVIN SPACEY, DONALD SUTHERLAND, KIEFER SUTHERLAND, BRENDA FRICKER, PATRICK McGOOHAN, M EMMET WALSH

JOEL SCHUMACHER

USA (WARNER) 1996

143m (15)

Author John Grisham criticised *Natural Born Killers* for inciting violence – strange, then, that this faithful retelling of his novel suggests that it's okay to spray bullets around if your child is raped, and that even if you cripple an innocent bystander, heck, he'll forgive you. And then you'll be let off anyway. We all might, of course, do what the 'hero' does here – but that's why trials are conducted by impartial juries. Manipulative but well made. Grisham really has a cheek.

TITANIC [4]

LEONARDO DiCAPRIO, KATE WINSLET, BILLY ZANE, GLORIA STUART, DAVID WARNER, BERNARD HILL, FRANCES FISHER, KATHY BATES, BILL PAXTON

JAMES CAMERON

USA (FOX) 1998

189m (12)

After his gruelling experience with *The Abyss* (see page 258), director James Cameron goes for another watery epic – but for this, the umpteenth take on the true story of the sinking by an iceberg of the great liner on her maiden voyage, he relies on a dockside replica and mucho CGI (computer-generated imagery) FX. Actually, for once the FX don't swamp the plot: they are often quite seamlessly integrated to give shots impossible with a real camera, such as a swoop that glides the length of the ship before homing in on the two romantic leads at the prow. And there we have the pic's flaw: it deals *too* much with the love between poor boy and rich girl being menaced by her nasty hubby-to-be (Zane), whereas I'd have liked more spectacle. Awash with Oscar nominations and successes, though sadly veteran thesp Gloria Stuart (who starred in the original *The Invisible Man,* among others) didn't win after being nominated for best supporting actress. The scale of the movie will be lost on TV but at least if you're not a fan, you can turn down the volume on *that* Celine Dion song. Available in widescreen.

THE TOWERING INFERNO 🎬 3

STEVE McQUEEN, PAUL NEWMAN, WILLIAM HOLDEN, FAYE DUNAWAY

JOHN GUILLERMIN, IRWIN ALLEN

USA (WARNER) 1974

158m (15)

Hacked together from a couple of forgettable pulp stories, this tale of a burning skyscraper set the style for disaster movies to come: endanger a lot of famous faces with big bangs while they bicker about love and survival. Quite entertaining.

TRAINSPOTTING 🎬 4

EWAN McGREGOR, EWEN BREMNER, JONNY LEE MILLER, ROBERT CARLYLE

DANNY BOYLE

SCOTLAND (POLYGRAM) 1995

93m (18)

This serio-comic version of Irvine Welsh's acclaimed novel of episodes in the lives of a group of Edinburgh heroin addicts may disgust some, but, bolstered by fantasy sequences (such as a headlong dive into 'the worst toilet in Scotland' in search of lost morphine suppositories) and a great music soundtrack, there's no denying its ingenuity and raw power. The title derives from drug deals being made in an old railway station, though this isn't made clear in the film version. 14-second censor cut for video.

TREES LOUNGE 🎬 4

STEVE BUSCEMI, ANTHONY LAPAGLIA, CHLOE SEVIGNY

STEVE BUSCEMI

USA (BMG) 1996

91m (15)

Directorial stint for actor Buscemi, revolving around the clientèle of the cruddy bar of the title. No great story, just the pleasure of watching some fine thespians doing their stuff and making it all look deceptively easy. Catch it – it's worth watching.

THE TRUMAN SHOW 🎬 3

JIM CARREY, ED HARRIS, NATASCHA McELHONE, LAURA LINNEY

PETER WEIR

USA (CIC) 1998

99m (PG)

Attack on the intrusion of the media into real life by Aussie director Weir takes the form of a tale of a young man (Carrey) whose whole existence is broadcast as a TV show. Ed Harris is the criminally all-powerful producer who steals Carrey's life for ratings. Not as serious (or original) a movie as it thinks it is, but lovely to look at.

DRAMA

THE USUAL SUSPECTS 📽️4

⭐ GABRIEL BYRNE, STEPHEN BALDWIN, CHAZZ PALMINTERI, PETER POSTLETHWAITE, KEVIN SPACEY

🎬 BRYAN SINGER

USA (POLYGRAM) 1995

⏱️ 101m   (18)

Byzantine complexity abounds in this story of crooks in search of the criminal mastermind who appears to be controlling their lives and dogging their steps. Subtle acting from a brilliant cast. Oscars: Best Screenplay, Best Supporting Actor for Spacey. Available in widescreen, also in pan-scan on a two-for-one tape with *Mulholland Falls*.

WALL STREET 📽️4

⭐ MICHAEL DOUGLAS, CHARLIE SHEEN, DARYL HANNAH, TERENCE STAMP, SEAN YOUNG

🎬 OLIVER STONE

USA (FOX) 1987

⏱️ 120m   (15)

One of Stone's more commercial efforts, this look at big-business corruption won an Oscar for Douglas as the devilish Gekko: a boss wearing loud braces who spouts sayings like, 'Greed is good' and 'Lunch is for wimps' as he seduces eager young Sheen into his wicked ways. See this before you get carried away by free windfall shares from your building society!

WHO'S AFRAID OF VIRGINIA WOOLF? 📽️3

⭐ ELIZABETH TAYLOR, RICHARD BURTON, SANDY DENNIS, GEORGE SEGAL

🎬 MIKE NICHOLS

USA (WARNER) 1966

⏱️ 124m   (15)

Edward Albee's classic American play is presented here as a soused slanging match between sour, middle-aged college prof and his missus, conducted in front of an embarrassed younger couple. A bit of a downer, but both ladies won Oscars, as did Haskell Wexler's camera work, the sets and costumes. A Liz 'n' Dick *tour de force*, with the famous couple firing on all cylinders from start to finish.

WILDE

STEPHEN FRY, JUDE LAW, VANESSA REDGRAVE, JENNIFER EHLE

BRIAN GILBERT

UK (POLYGRAM) 1997

112m (15)

Somewhat overpraised biopic on *fin de siècle* Irish writer Oscar Wilde and his fatal attraction for the handsome but petulant Lord Alfred Douglas, which led to his ruin and imprisonment for then-illegal sodomy. It has been said that the multi-talented Fry was born to play the role of Wilde but, though he looks the part, his delivery is altogether too languid when it should be vigorous and sharp. A lovely film to look at, with an imaginative opening set during Wilde's trip to the Wild West, it doesn't match up to the 60s pic *The Trials Of Oscar Wilde*, starring Peter Finch.

WITNESS

HARRISON FORD, KELLY McGILLIS, LUKAS HAAS, DANNY GLOVER

PETER WEIR

USA (CIC) 1985

108m (15)

Detective Ford hides out in Amish religious town to protect the small boy who witnessed a murder while on a trip to the city. He also finds time to attempt a doomed romance with the lad's mother. An excellent blend of thoughtful drama and shoot-'em-up. Oscars for script and editing.

EPICS

Epics are notoriously hard to define: to some, an epic is any 70mm movie which is long enough to merit an intermission or a trip to the lavatory. *How The West Was Won* would probably, on that basis, qualify – if it wasn't already in the Westerns section. Ditto *2001*, which is in the Science Fiction chapter. To many, the only true epics were made in the USA and invariably set in ancient Rome. Others favour the old Italian sword-and-sandal pix (or 'peplums', from the short skirts worn by the male gladiator-types therein). I've tried to be fair to all these notions, but I accept that some may baulk at my inclusion of Shakespearean and other historical films. I've only included those works which seem to me to have a genuine epic quality to them. Sadly, however, the day of the real epic seems to have gone. The odd anomaly nothwithstanding (such as *Braveheart*), the classics of the genre were all produced in the 50s and 60s, when producers were showmen and budgets were for true spectacle, not just special effects explosions.

THE 10 COMMANDMENTS 4

CHARLTON HESTON, YUL BRYNNER, EDWARD G ROBINSON, ANNE BAXTER

CECIL B DeMILLE

USA (CIC) 1956

219m U

DeMille's remake of his 1923 silent on the life of Moses made Heston's name synonymous with epic biblical kitsch for years after. Nice performances, though rather theatrical in places. Oscar for effects. Widescreen tape.

55 DAYS AT PEKING 4

CHARLTON HESTON, DAVID NIVEN, AVA GARDNER, FLORA ROBSON

NICHOLAS RAY

USA/SPAIN (VIDEO COLLECTION) 1962

147m U

One of a series of epics made in the 60s in Europe by USA showman Sam Bronston, this is set in the period of the Chinese Boxer Rebellion of 1900. Gardner as a Russki Countess is stiff, but the rest of the cast are on top form, especially Robson as the wily Dowager Empress. Ray quit through ill health and the film was finished by Guy Green and Andrew Marton.

BARABBAS ★4

ANTHONY QUINN, JACK PALANCE, SILVANO MANGANO, ARTHUR KENNEDY

RICHARD FLEISCHER

ITALY/USA (MIA) 1962

128m (PG)

'**B**egins where the other big ones leave off' – so ran the ads. True enough, as this is the story of the bandit the mob chose to free instead of Jesus – and an engrossing tale it is too, aided by a top-notch bit of overacting from Quinn. Rather diminished in this pan-scan version.

BECKET ★4

RICHARD BURTON, PETER O'TOOLE, DONALD WOLFIT, MARTITA HUNT

PETER GLENVILLE

UK (ODYSSEY) 1964

142m (PG)

Tale of the martyred archbishop (Burton) from his early days as chum-in-ribaldry of Henry II (O'Toole, a role he reprised in *The Lion In Winter*) to later life as a genuinely pious priest. Fab cast of UK thesps. The sets were re-used for the horror film classic *The Masque of the Red Death*. The screenplay, based on Jean Anouilh's play, won an Oscar.

BEN-HUR ★5

CHARLTON HESTON, STEPHEN BOYD, JACK HAWKINS, HUGH GRIFFITHS

WILLIAM WYLER

USA (MGM/UA) 1959

209m (PG)

This is *the* epic, for many. Woven around the story of Christ, it is a remake of the silent classic based on Lew Wallace's novel about a Jewish lord betrayed by his Roman friend – he survives slavery to return for vengeance via a stunningly lensed chariot race (shot by Sergio Leone and others on the second unit). Widescreen and boxed-set available. Won a staggering 11 Oscars, including best picture, direction, actor (Heston) and music.

EPICS

BRAVEHEART 🎬 5

⭐ MEL GIBSON, PATRICK McGOOHAN

🎬 MEL GIBSON

USA/SCOTLAND (FOX) 1995

⏱ 170m ⑮

This Oscar-winning story of Scots patriot William Wallace's fight against English tyrant Edward Longshanks is a wonderful piece of film-making by star/director Gibson. Pity that foolish 'love interest' was added, but he doesn't shirk the hero's sad end – even if history is twisted to add glory. Although I'm a Scot, I'm no fan of the 'Scotia Nostra' of expats who revel in all things tartan – but this is such bravura stuff I'll make an exception. The Scottish baring behinds at the English army is a historical truth, as anyone who has been to a Scotland-England football match at Wembley can attest.

CALIGULA 🎬 4

⭐ MALCOLM McDOWELL, TERESA ANN SAVOY, PETER O'TOOLE, JOHN GIELGUD, HELEN MIRREN, LORI WAGNER

🎬 TINTO BRASS, BOB GUCCIONE

ITALY/USA (ELECTRIC) 1979

⏱ 90/156m ⑱

Much-maligned epic penned by Gore Vidal, about a mad, perverted Roman emperor. Financed by *Penthouse* magazine with no expense spared, and featuring amazing sets, the film was remarkable for being the first hard-core sex movie to star respected actors. The magazine's boss, Bob Guccione, shot more sex footage himself and added it to the director's work. The times given are for the shortest and longest versions available worldwide. The UK 90m tape is unlikely to include the incredible scenes of cruelty and orgies present in the print I saw in America on first release. There is rumoured to be a German cut with even more barbarous stuff, but I can't say if this is true. An experience, to say the least. Inspired several fake sequels, rip-offs, etc., including *Caligula II – The Untold Story*, in which a woman has sex with a horse!

THE CHARGE OF THE LIGHT BRIGADE 🎬 4

DAVID HEMMINGS, TREVOR HOWARD, HARRY ANDREWS, JOHN GIELGUD

TONY RICHARDSON

UK (CONNOISSEUR) 1968

⏱ 141m (PG)

Revisionist look at the legendary British heroic disaster. A political antidote to the Errol Flynn version, brimming with great UK acting talent. This tape is slightly cut by the censor due to alleged cruelty to horses – but not in the manner of *Caligula II* (see *Caligula*, page 141)!

CLEOPATRA 🎬 4

ELIZABETH TAYLOR, RICHARD BURTON, REX HARRISON, GEORGE COLE, MARTIN LANDAU, RODDY McDOWALL

JOSEPH L MANKIEWICZ

USA (FOX) 1963

⏱ 248m (PG)

The film which ruined two marriages, got executives sacked and nearly destroyed a studio. Various stars and directors were on and off at various times, but it has to be said that in spite of the length, this is a literate and engaging film and one can't imagine anyone being better than Taylor and Burton. Incredibly, the present four-hours-plus version is missing some two hours of original footage! The director intended to issue two films, but was overruled though there is a project underway with the aim of convincing the studio to restore the missing footage. Widescreen tape available. Oscars for cinematography, effects, art/sets, costumes. (And yes, that *is* George Cole who starred in TV's *Minder*!)

CROMWELL 🎬 4

RICHARD HARRIS, ALEC GUINNESS, ROBERT MORLEY, DOROTHY TUTIN

KEN HUGHES

UK (VIDEO COLLECTION) 1970

⏱ 134m (PG)

Somewhat wordy tale of Cromwell and his politicking with King Charles, but it has the virtue of a solid lead performance by Harris to commend it. This is a cut version, apparently, also now in widescreen at full price from Columbia TriStar.

EPICS

DEMETRIUS AND THE GLADIATORS [3]

★ VICTOR MATURE, SUSAN HAYWARD, MICHAEL RENNIE

🎬 DELMER DAVES

USA (FOX) 1954

⏱ 97m   (PG)

Western ace Daves was perhaps not the man to helm this sequel to *The Robe* (see page 150), with crazed Caligula going spare in search of Christ's garment which he thinks is magically endowed. Widescreen tape available.

DOCTOR ZHIVAGO [4]

★ OMAR SHARIF, JULIE CHRISTIE, ROD STEIGER, ALEC GUINNESS

🎬 DAVID LEAN

UK (MGM/UA) 1965

⏱ 185m   (15)

Epic of romance and Russian revolution based on Boris Pasternak's novel. A love story with an end that would wrench the heart – if only one felt anything for the characters. Several Oscars, including the hit music score. Widescreen and boxed edition.

EL CID [4]

★ CHARLTON HESTON, SOPHIA LOREN, HERBERT LOM, HURD HATFIELD, JOHN FRASER

🎬 ANTHONY MANN

SPAIN/USA (VIDEO COLLECTION) 1961

⏱ 172m   (U)

This was one of several classic epics made in Spain in the 60s by Samuel Bronston, an American producer who used Europe as a base. Mann was equally adept at Westerns and epics, and he handles with style the story of the eleventh-century Spanish patriot's battles with the Moors. The love angle is laboured in the extreme, but the cast disport themselves well and the spectacle is tops. The newly restored print has not yet emerged on video.

EXCALIBUR [4]

★ NICOL WILLIAMSON, NIGEL TERRY, HELEN MIRREN, CHERIE LUNGHI

🎬 JOHN BOORMAN

UK/USA (WARNER) 1981

⏱ 140m   (15)

Boorman's dream of a definitive version of the Arthurian legends is realised here in a glowing, golden vision. Williamson is remarkable as a slightly seedy Merlin with an impenetrable accent. Lots of armour and blood and sunsets. Widescreen.

THE FALL OF THE ROMAN EMPIRE [4]

STEPHEN BOYD, SOPHIA LOREN, JAMES MASON, ALEC GUINNESS, CHRISTOPHER PLUMMER

ANTHONY MANN

SPAIN/USA (4-FRONT) 1964

172m (U)

Another Mann–Bronston film, severely underrated critically – perhaps due to the lack of a Heston for the lead. Some awesomely beautifully scenes of snowy landscapes and huge armies, but these will be diminished here due to a) incorrectly letterboxed print, and b) only cut versions being available. A sad fate for an interesting movie. Restoration, anyone?

A FISTFUL OF DYNAMITE [4]

JAMES COBURN, ROD STEIGER, ROMOLO VALLI

SERGIO LEONE

ITALY (WARNER) 1971

132m (18)

Original title in Italy was *Giu La Testa* (*Duck, You Sucker*), but in France it was *Once Upon A Time ... The Revolution* – a more pleasing notion, as the film is the centrepiece of a sort of trilogy with *Once Upon A Time In The West* (see page 340) and *... In America* (see page 176). This was a problematic film: the stars went to Italy thinking they were to make a film with Leone, as original director Peter Bogdanovich's contract had fallen through. They arrived to find they were expected to work with an Italian protégé of the great man – and refused. Leone finally reluctantly helmed this tale of an IRA man (Coburn) and a bandit (Steiger) confronting political realities in the Mexican revolution, but the complete 158m widescreen cut is tragically rare. Worth seeing, however, even in this mutilated format. (Full print now on USA laserdisc.)

FLAVIA THE HERETIC [4]

FLORINDA BALKAN, MARIA CASARES, CLAUDIO CASSINELLI

GIANFRANCO MINGOZZI

ITALY/FRANCE (REDEMPTION) 1974

86m (18)

Naughty-nun flicks are a popular subgenre in Italy. This tells the story of an oppressed girl who sides with the invading infidels to take revenge on her Christian abusers – but in the end they prove treacherous, too. Widescreen. Shocking imagery, cut by the BBFC.

EPICS

GANDHI [4]

BEN KINGSLEY, CANDICE BERGEN, JOHN MILLS, MARTIN SHEEN, JOHN GIELGUD

RICHARD ATTENBOROUGH

UK/INDIA (CINEMA CLUB V) 1982

188m (PG)

Eight Oscars for this epic account of Gandhi's life, including best actor for Kingsley and best picture. We follow Gandhi as he quits his life in the legal profession to fight for peace, becomes a world statesman and is finally martyred for his beliefs. There were complaints that only someone of pure Indian blood ought to have played the role, but one can't imagine Kingsley's work being bettered and this is surely the sort of racial pedantry which Gandhi himself would have deplored. Other Oscars include best director, screenplay, cinematography and costumes. Also in widescreen on Columbia TriStar at a higher price.

GENGHIS KHAN [3]

OMAR SHARIF, STEPHEN BOYD, JAMES MASON, ELI WALLACH

HENRY LEVIN

UK/USA/WEST GERMANY (VIDEO COLLECTION) 1965

119m (PG)

Sprightly and spectacular story of a very bad barbarian who is painted as not-quite-so-bad in this version of his life. Mason has a bizarre cameo role as a Chinese diplomat. Boyd snarls superbly as evil Jamuga, GK's arch-enemy.

GONE WITH THE WIND [5]

CLARK GABLE, VIVIEN LEIGH, OLIVIA DE HAVILLAND, LESLIE HOWARD

VICTOR FLEMING

USA (MGM/UA) 1939

240m (PG)

One of the most popular movies of all time, based on Margaret Mitchell's blockbuster novel of the old South and the American Civil War. Leigh was signed only after a massive search to find the right actress to play the heroine – and she won an Academy Award. The film has undergone negative-cleaning and other restoration techniques and looks great. Won eight Oscars, including best picture.

GREYSTOKE [4]

CHRISTOPHER LAMBERT, IAN HOLM, RALPH RICHARDSON, ANDIE MacDOWELL

HUGH HUDSON

UK (WARNER) 1984

129m (PG)

This attempt at a literate version of the 'Tarzan' story is only partly a success. Some of the scenes of the return to England, notably when Tarzan meets an ape in a cage and calls it 'Daddy' (!), aim for pathos but only provoke laughter. McDowell (as Jane) was dubbed by Glenn Close. A laudable, beautifully shot try at doing something different with the Edgar Rice Burroughs hero. The print shown on TV is longer than the one released to UK cinemas.

HAMLET

MEL GIBSON, GLENN CLOSE, ALAN BATES, PAUL SCOFIELD

FRANCO ZEFIRELLI

USA (COLUMBIA TRISTAR) 1990

129m (PG)

Don't laugh – Mel holds his own as the troubled Dane in this epic version of Shakespeare's tragedy. At least, unlike so many other attempts, it doesn't come over as just a filmed stage play. Full of sparks.

HENRY V

KENNETH BRANAGH, EMMA THOMPSON, DEREK JACOBI, PAUL SCOFIELD

KENNETH BRANAGH

UK (COLUMBIA TRISTAR) 1989

137m (PG)

Branagh does the impossible and outdoes Olivier's version of the Bard's play; curiously, both films are exactly the same length. If the previous film was taken as wartime patriotism, this one shows the horrors and muddy exhaustion of war. Every Brit actor of merit seems to be here. The definitive version – for now. Oscar for costumes.

HENRY VIII AND HIS SIX WIVES

KEITH MICHELL, CHARLOTTE RAMPLING, DONALD PLEASENCE

WARIS HUSSEIN

UK (WARNER) 1972

120m (PG)

Film remake of the TV show, which also starred Michell. Entertaining, but inevitably taken at a clip compared to the more leisurely BBC series.

HERCULES CONQUERS ATLANTIS

REG PARK, FAY SPAIN, ETTORE MANNI

VITTORIO COTTAFAVI

FRANCE/ITALY (PARAGON) 1961

80m (PG)

Classic peplum by master of the genre Cottafavi, starring Brit muscleman Park, the man who inspired Arnold Schwarzenegger to pump iron. Widescreen, though not indicated on box, as the ratio is somewhat cropped. It's possible this title may be (technically) deleted, but I've seen enough copies around in stores to indicate you should be able to find it if you look. Sadly, the same cannot be said of Mario Bava's companion piece, *Hercules In The Centre Of The Earth*, starring Park and Christopher Lee, which was available on the same label. If any reader knows where I can find a copy, I'll be eternally grateful!

EPICS

IVAN THE TERRIBLE 🎬 4

NIKOLAI CHERKASSOV, SERAFIMA BIRMAN, ERIC PYRIEV

SERGEI EISENSTEIN

USSR (TARTAN) 1944/6 B&W/COL

185m (PG)

Although the third section was never finished, the two completed parts of this Russian epic tell the story of the great tyrant's life from childhood to encroaching old age. A marvellous piece of cinema by any standard. Parts 1 and 2 are available separately. The third section was never completed due to Stalin's interference.

JUDGMENT AT NUREMBERG 🎬 4

SPENCER TRACY, JUDY GARLAND, BURT LANCASTER, MONTGOMERY CLIFT

STANLEY KRAMER

USA (WARNER) 1961

178m (PG)

Movingly acted story of the trials of Nazis at the end of World War Two. Lancaster is powerful as a man who realises the enormity of his crimes, while Clift as a witness gives a performance that is searing and painful to watch. The sad fact, though, is that at the same time as the Allies were trying big-name Nazis, they were protecting others (scientists and so forth) who they felt were 'useful'. Never again? Don't you believe it. Two Oscars, one for Abby Mann's screenplay (based on his TV play), the other for Maximilian Schell as a lawyer.

KHARTOUM 🎬 4

CHARLTON HESTON, LAURENCE OLIVIER, RICHARD JOHNSON, RALPH RICHARDSON

BASIL DEARDEN

UK (WARNER) 1966

127m (PG)

Heston is magisterial as General Gordon, as is Olivier as the Mahdi. The two enemies never met, but for dramatic purposes such a scene is absolutely essential. Olivier is as over-the-top as Heston is restrained. Excellent. Pan-scan only.

THE LAST EMPEROR 🎬 3

JOHN LONE, JOAN CHEN, PETER O'TOOLE, VICTOR WONG

BERNARDO BERTOLUCCI

ITALY/CHINA/UK (2ND SIGHT) 1987

156m (15)

Winner of nine Oscars (including best picture), this is the epic account of Pu Yi, final emperor of China. We see him develop from child to playboy wastrel to just another face in the communist crowd. Though glacial and probably overlong, it does have atmosphere. Judge for yourself whether it deserved all those awards. Director's cut now available at 210m. Both versions in widescreen.

THE LAST OF THE MOHICANS [4]

DANIEL DAY-LEWIS, MADELEINE STOWE, MAURICE RÖEVES, WES STUDI

MICHAEL MANN

USA (WARNER) 1992

122m (PG)

A rousing version by Mann, one of the best action directors working today, of James Fenimore Cooper's 'Hawkeye' novel. Day-Lewis makes a good square-jawed hero, battling his arch-enemy (Studi) to save Stowe. An amazing-looking pic, with thrilling battle sequences. Widescreen tape available.

THE LAST TEMPTATION OF CHRIST [3]

WILLEM DAFOE, HARVEY KEITEL, HARRY DEAN STANTON, DAVID BOWIE

MARTIN SCORSESE

USA (CIC) 1988

156m (18)

Ignore the ridiculous and unjustified controversy about this film of Nikos Kazantzakis's novel on the life of Jesus – there is little to shock here. Sadly, there's little to entertain, either. It's a worthy enough project, but stars and director seem just too 'modern' to be at home with this genre. Worth seeing, though, just to check out a good cast and to see what all the fuss was about.

LAWRENCE OF ARABIA [5]

PETER O'TOOLE, OMAR SHARIF, ALEC GUINNESS, ANTHONY QUINN, JACK HAWKINS, CLAUDE RAINS, DONALD WOLFIT, ARTHUR KENNEDY, ANTHONY QUAYLE

DAVID LEAN

UK (COLUMBIA TRISTAR) 1962

217m (PG)

Winner of seven Oscars, and perhaps the best epic of all, Lean's 70mm story of TE Lawrence and the First World War desert campaign was nibbled away over the years. In 1989, restorer Robert Harris completed the near-impossible task of putting back the cuts, re-doing lost soundtrack, etc., and then allowed Lean to fine-tune the material. This version was issued on tape with musical overture and intermission music, properly letterboxed. Now Columbia have put out a '35th Anniversary' tape: the widescreen image is altered (though I'm assured this is the correct 70mm ratio), the music has been cut, over two minutes of footage discovered by Harris are still not included, and Michael Wilson is denied his co-writing credit with Robert Bolt as per the Academy ruling. Try to find the earlier widescreen tape – it has a full-length drawing of O'Toole on the box. NB: After I alerted them, the company found the overture had been omitted in error. All praise to them for recalling the master tapes and fixing the problem. New copies are stickered 'Includes the overture' and the company *will* swap your old copies on request!

EPICS

LORD JIM 🎬 4

⭐ PETER O'TOOLE, JAMES MASON, CURT JURGENS, ELI WALLACH, JACK HAWKINS

🎬 RICHARD BROOKS

UK (ENCORE) 1964

⏱ 148m (PG)

Undervalued film version of Conrad tale. After *Lawrence*, O'Toole found himself temporarily typecast as an enigmatic, flawed anti-hero – but he makes a great job of it in this outing. You can almost smell the jungle rot, the indecision and the fear before our boy redeems himself.

MACBETH 🎬 4

⭐ JON FINCH, FRANCESCA ANNIS, MARTIN SHAW, JOHN STRIDE

🎬 ROMAN POLANSKI

UK (COLUMBIA TRISTAR) 1971

⏱ 134m (15)

Gory, epic version of Shakespeare's tale of witchery and dark ambition. Plenty of weird scenes and outdoor footage, with not a whiff of theatrical boards, make this a better bet than most other movie versions. Sadly not out in widescreen.

A MAN FOR ALL SEASONS 🎬 4

⭐ PAUL SCOFIELD, WENDY HILLER, ROBERT SHAW, LEO McKERN

🎬 FRED ZINNEMANN

UK (COLUMBIA TRISTAR) 1966

⏱ 116m (U)

Beautifully acted version of Robert Bolt's play about the trial of Sir Thomas More, who would not swear an oath that the divorce and new marriage of Henry VIII was legal. Pretty unimpeachable, but I will now commit heresy and say that I find Charlton Heston's cable TV remake a far, far better thing. So throw me in the Tower!

MUTINY ON THE BOUNTY 🎬 4

⭐ MARLON BRANDO, TREVOR HOWARD, TARITA, RICHARD HARRIS

🎬 LEWIS MILESTONE

USA (MGM/UA) 1962

⏱ 177m (15)

One of several versions of the classic tale of the shipboard revolt. Brando's accent is a hoot, but Trevor Howard is suitably vile. The trouble is that this reading of the events has since been shown to be rather skewed – apparently Cap'n Bligh was not as nasty as we've been led to believe. This is the most epic and visual version, for sure. Widescreen.

QUO VADIS [3]

ROBERT TAYLOR, DEBORAH KERR, PETER USTINOV, LEO GENN

MERVYN LEROY

USA (MGM/UA-WARNER) 1951

162m (PG)

Feisty, randy Roman (Taylor) gets converted to Christianity by his girlfriend (Kerr). Slow tosh, saved by the wonderfully camp capering of Ustinov as Nero. What a crooner!

THE RIGHT STUFF [4]

SAM SHEPARD, DENNIS QUAID, SCOTT GLENN, ED HARRIS

PHILIP KAUFMAN

USA (WARNER) 1983

185m (15)

Epic recounting of the American space race and the astronauts involved, warts and all. Based on the book by Tom Wolfe. Gripping for the whole ride. Won Oscars for SFX, sound and others. Widescreen.

THE ROBE [3]

VICTOR MATURE, RICHARD BURTON, JEAN SIMMONS, MICHAEL RENNIE

HENRY KOSTER

USA (FOX) 1953

129m (U)

Christians and Romans fight over the robe of Jesus. A bit slow, but worth seeing, as it did win Oscars. See *Demetrius And The Gladiators* (page 143). Shot in widescreen and TV-shaped versions simultaneously.

SAMSON AND DELILAH [4]

VICTOR MATURE, HEDY LAMARR, ANGELA LANSBURY, GEORGE SANDERS

CECIL B DeMILLE

USA (CIC) 1949

122m (U)

Biblical tale of the man who needed no more than the jawbone of an ass to slay his enemies. He offends Delilah by preferring her sister, and so she contrives to chop off his strength-giving locks and have him enslaved by the ruling race to which she belongs. You know the rest. Recently remade for TV with Liz Hurley as Big D.

EPICS

SOLOMON AND SHEBA [3]

YUL BRYNNER, GINA LOLLOBRIGIDA, GEORGE SANDERS

KING VIDOR

USA (MGM/UA-WARNER) 1959

139m (PG)

Filming on this biblical love story had to be scrapped when star Tyrone Power suddenly died of a heart attack, and the movie was begun again with Brynner replacing him. Was it worth it? Well, despite being on the melodramatic side, it looks pretty good.

SPARTACUS [5]

KIRK DOUGLAS, LAURENCE OLIVIER, TONY CURTIS, JEAN SIMMONS, CHARLES LAUGHTON, PETER USTINOV, HERBERT LOM

STANLEY KUBRICK

USA (CIC) 1960

188m (PG)

Producer Douglas fired director Anthony Mann and brought in Kubrick to helm this film, based on Howard Fast's self-published novel about the illiterate slave who led a failed revolt against the might of ancient Rome. It won four Oscars (including a supporting actor award for Ustinov) but was cut by the censors. The full version, with some mild sex and violence restored, is now available on widescreen tape, with the overture music included. (For one scene the sound has been lost, so Tony Curtis had to re-do his dialogue with Sir Anthony Hopkins standing in for the late Laurence Olivier. The scene had been cut due to implied homosexual desire for Curtis's character by Olivier's.) A sombre epic – no happy endings here, but plenty of great performances.

THRONE OF BLOOD [5]

TOSHIRO MIFUNE, ISUZU YAMADA, MINORU CHIAKI

AKIRA KUROSAWA

JAPAN (CONNOISSEUR) 1957 B&W

105m (PG)

Macbeth transposed to ancient Japan. More visual than literary, with eerie atmospherics and spirits calling for much blood. A bit of a masterwork, really.

THE VIKINGS [5]

KIRK DOUGLAS, TONY CURTIS, JANET LEIGH, ERNEST BORGNINE

RICHARD FLEISCHER

USA (WARNER/ELITE) 1958

116m (PG)

Cruel story of two half-brothers who don't know they're related. One loses an eye, the other a hand, one's a Viking, the other a slave, but both are in love with the same girl. Lots of raping and pillaging and a real swashbuckling showdown. Produced by Douglas, this was a big hit and much imitated. Often shown on afternoon TV, with the brutality snipped out. Uncut on tape, and in widescreen.

WAR AND PEACE 🎬 3

⭐ HENRY FONDA, AUDREY HEPBURN, HERBERT LOM, MEL FERRER

🎬 KING VIDOR

ITALY/USA (CIC/4-FRONT) 1956

⏱ 211m   (U)

Even at this length, this is a condensed version of Tolstoy's tale of war between France and Russia. The epic story doesn't quite come together, though the stars do their best.

WAR AND PEACE 🎬 4

⭐ LUDMILA SAVELYEVA, SERGEI BONDARCHUK, VASILY LANOVOI

🎬 SERGEI BONDARCHUK

USSR (TARTAN) 1967

⏱ 403m   (PG)

Now, if you're truly a glutton for the real thing, try this! This three-tape boxed set is the longest version of this epic so far issued in the UK, costing more than the $40 million of *Cleopatra* (see page 142) and taking five years to film. S-l-o-w, but worthy, well-made and spectacular, it won the Oscar for best foreign picture – but that may have been an award for sheer tenacity of spirit. Seriously, this has got to be the ultimate version of Tolstoy's classic.

WATERLOO 🎬 3

⭐ ROD STEIGER, CHRISTOPHER PLUMMER, ORSON WELLES, JACK HAWKINS

🎬 SERGEI BONDARCHUK

ITALY/USSR (COLUMBIA TRISTAR) 1971

⏱ 128m   (U)

Seriously confused (as you'd expect, with the film being cut to half the length of the original 240m Russian print) movie version of Napoleon's big defeat at the hands of the Brits. Based on part of Tolstoy's novel *War and Peace* – does Bondarchuk never get tired of adapting this? Worth seeing for comparisons with his version of the whole book (see above).

ZULU 🎬 5

⭐ STANLEY BAKER, MICHAEL CAINE, JACK HAWKINS, NIGEL GREEN

🎬 CY ENDFIELD

UK (CIC) 1963

⏱ 135m   (PG)

Baker produced this story of a Brit regiment's fight against an overwhelming force of Zulu warriors at Rorke's Drift, a tiny outpost in Natal in 1879. The small band of men won several Victoria Crosses between them, and the tale has passed into legend. For all its imperialist, gung-ho gloss, the film tells a neat story. Well worth seeing. Available at last in a widescreen tape.

Family Entertainment

Films that young kids and parents can watch comfortably together are not as rare as moral campaigners would have us believe. Despite the howlings of American politicians about sex and violence on-screen, Hollywood knows that a solid family movie will always do good business in the multiplexes and on video. So here's a selection of the best, ranging from Disney classics right up to modern smashes such as *Free Willy* and *Home Alone*.

13 GHOSTS

CHARLES HERBERT, JO MORROW, MARTIN MILNER, MARGARET HAMILTON

WILLIAM CASTLE

USA (ENCORE) 1960 B&W

79m (PG)

Who'd-a-thunk-it? A horror film for kids! When I saw this back in 1960 in the cinema, viewing aids were handed out (a typical William Castle gimmick) so that when the ghosts appeared you could choose to see them or not, depending on which bit you looked through. Sadly, this trick has not been included on the video release, making the ghosts pretty hard to see and depriving the movie of its selling point. Still, it's fun – and it won't scare the toddlers.

THE ADVENTURES OF PINOCCHIO

MARTIN LANDAU, JONATHAN TAYLOR THOMAS, GENEVIÈVE BUJOLD, UDO KIER, DAWN FRENCH

STEVE BARRON

UK/FRANCE/GERMANY/CZECH REPUBLIC/USA (POLYGRAM) 1996

94m (U)

Imaginative version of the classic tale of the puppet who comes to life. Brilliant cast and visuals make it worthy of comparison with the Disney cartoon (see page 62). Kids will love it and adults can enjoy the top cast hamming it up gloriously.

TOP 1000 VIDEOS

BABE 🎬5
⭐ JAMES CROMWELL (AND LOTS OF TALKING ANIMALS!)
🎬 CHRIS NOONAN
USA (CIC) 1995
⏱ 89m Ⓤ

Charming fable about a runty piglet saved from the chopping block when it reveals an unprecedented talent for herding sheep. The mix of FX and real animals is wonderful, and the personalities given the various farmyard creatures all seem believable and never twee, in spite of the mid-Atlantic accent of the star piglet. The way the sheep huddle and bleat 'Wooo-ooolllf!' whenever the grumpy sheepdog hoves into view is especially sharp. A sardonic edge undercuts any tendency to sickliness, but kids'll still love it. Flop sequel: *Babe: Pig In The City*.

BIG 🎬3
⭐ TOM HANKS, ELIZABETH PERKINS, ROBERT LOGGIA, JOHN HEARD
🎬 PENNY MARSHALL
USA (FOX) 1988
⏱ 100m Ⓟ🅶

Another variation on the common-or-garden body-swap theme, in which a kid achieves his wish of overnight adulthood. Works due to a typically smooth performance from Hanks. A good fun film.

BORN FREE 🎬3
⭐ VIRGINIA McKENNA, BILL TRAVERS, GEOFFREY KEEN, PETER LUKOYE
🎬 JAMES HILL
UK (CINEMA CLUB V) 1966
⏱ 91m Ⓤ

Joy Adamson's book about rearing and releasing lion cub Elsa back into the wild is the basis for this lovely hit movie, sure to please kids who care for animals. Oscars: score and song. Sequel: *Living Free*.

CHITTY CHITTY BANG BANG 🎬3
⭐ DICK VAN DYKE, LIONEL JEFFRIES, SALLY ANN HOWES, BENNY HILL
🎬 KEN HUGHES
UK (WARNER) 1968
⏱ 145m Ⓤ

Based on Ian (James Bond) Fleming's fantasy about a flying car. Fun and a good cast will help keep the little ones amused for a time, but the excessive length defeats all the efforts in the end. The beauty of video is that at least you can watch it in segments!

FAMILY ENTERTAINMENT

DALEKS – INVASION EARTH 2150 AD

PETER CUSHING, JILL CURZON, RAY BROOKS, ANDREW KEIR

GORDON FLEMYNG

UK (WARNER/BEYONDVISION) 1966

84m (U)

When the roll of actors who've played Dr Who is called, people always forget the best of them: Peter Cushing. He never took the part on TV, but appeared in two spin-off movies made to cash in on the popularity of the villains of the series, the Daleks. This is the second and best of those films, and despite the cheap 'n' cheerful effects work it benefits from lush colour and a widescreen transfer to tape. Brats raised on digital animation may need reminding that this is an old film: please treat it gently!

DANNY THE CHAMPION OF THE WORLD

JEREMY IRONS, SAMUEL IRONS, ROBBIE COLTRANE, CYRIL CUSACK, MICHAEL HORDERN

GAVIN MILLAR

UK (BMG) 1989

99m (U)

Feisty Roald Dahl tale about a lad who fights off property developers intent on taking over the land where his caravan is parked. Kids never fail to respond to Dahl's stories of vile adults and resourceful sprogs. Try it.

DRAGONHEART

SEAN CONNERY (voice of Draco), DENNIS QUAID, DAVID THEWLIS

ROB COHEN

USA (CIC) 1996

103m (PG)

Massively entertaining fantasy film featuring an animated dragon named Draco, with the droll voice of Sean Connery. It forms a relationship with Quaid in a movie which rather lampoons the notion of the heroic days of yore. The effects are marvellous in the extreme, but never overwhelm the plot. Cut by BBFC.

THE EDUCATION OF LITTLE TREE

JAMES CROMWELL, JOSEPH ASHTON, GRAHAM GREENE

RICHARD FRIEDENBERG

USA/UK/FRANCE (CIC) 1997

111m (PG)

Enjoyable and wholesome family movie, about the raising of a half-Cherokee kid by his grandparents in America's Smokey Mountains. Never gets too sickly, and both acting and direction are fab. Based on the book by Forrest Carter, the rather odd, right-wing political character who also penned the source material for Clint Eastwood's *The Outlaw Josey Wales* (see page 341).

EDWARD SCISSORHANDS 🎬4

JOHNNY DEPP, VINCENT PRICE, WINONA RYDER, DIANNE WIEST

TIM BURTON

USA (FOX) 1990

98m (PG)

Typically dark modern myth from Burton. An elderly inventor dies before finishing work on his creation and as a result, the bizarre punk-like boy is left with scissors for hands. Rescued from the inventor's expressionist mansion by a kindly housewife and transplanted to suburbia, USA, the lad tries to make use of his mechanical mitts, but has trouble fitting in. Might be seen as a parable on how society treats those who are 'different' – the disabled, etc. – but all but the youngest kids ought to enjoy it even if they miss the message. Widescreen available. Cut by the BBFC.

FLY AWAY HOME 🎬4

ANNA PAQUIN, JEFF DANIELS, DANA DELANEY

CARROLL BALLARD

USA (COLUMBIA TRISTAR) 1996

103m (U)

Based on a true story, this is about a little girl who adopts a family of baby geese and helps them fly home. Manages to avoid ickyness, and the Canada geese (so hated by London park keepers) prove themselves natural actors. Cut by the BBFC.

FREE WILLY 🎬3

JASON JAMES RICHTER, LORI PETTY, MICHAEL MADSEN, JAYNE ATKINSON

SIMON WINCER

USA (WARNER) 1993

112m (U)

While cleaning up his graffiti from a crappy seaquarium, a troubled lad makes pals with a (supposedly) untrainable Orca. Realising that the killer whale is miserable in captivity, the kid plots to arrange its freedom. As a movie it works – and after widespread outrage that the whale was actually still living in crummy quarters, 'Willy' has been moved to a sea-pen, with release in mind. Two sequels so far.

THE GOONIES 🎬3

COREY FELDMAN, JOSH BROLIN, SEAN AUSTIN, ROBERT DAVI

RICHARD DONNER

USA (WARNER) 1985

109m (PG)

Noisy movie about kids who find pirate treasure and do some community good at the same time. From the Steven Spielberg stable. A perennial hit with yobby lads of a certain age.

FAMILY ENTERTAINMENT

HOME ALONE

MACAULAY CULKIN, JOE PESCI, DANIEL STERN, JOHN HEARD, JOHN CANDY

CHRIS COLUMBUS

USA (FOX) 1990

98m (PG)

Virtually a live action cartoon, with brattish Culkin using increasingly violent methods to repel the sleazy burglars trying to invade his house. Charmless, but fast-and-furious and a massive hit all over the globe.

HOME ALONE 2

MACAULAY CULKIN, JOE PESCI, DANIEL STERN, JOHN HEARD, CATHERINE O'HARA

CHRIS COLUMBUS

USA (FOX) 1992

120m (PG)

This time Culkin is left in the big city by his forgetful parents only to be menaced once more by the same thugs as in the first film, of which this is a virtual retread. Critics were concerned by the escalation of violence, which is never shown to have consequences. You'd be better off ignoring BBFC certifications and running *The Wild Bunch* (see page 348) for your children – at least it has the message that violent acts hurt people.

HOME ALONE 3

ALEX D LINZ, HAVILAND MORRIS

RAJA GOSNELL

USA (FOX) 1997

98m (PG)

Third in the brat-in-peril series. Macaulay Culkin was too old and his Dad too obnoxious for the studio execs to deal with, so Linz takes over. There's a new director too, but the package is not a patch on the first film, though it passes the time.

HONEY, I BLEW UP THE KID

RICK MORANIS, LLOYD BRIDGES, MARCIA STRASSMAN, AMY O'NEILL

RANDAL KLEISER

USA (DISNEY) 1992

89m (U)

Sequel to *Honey, I Shrunk The Kids* (see page 158): this time Moranis enlarges his two-year-old son via a raygun and has mucho SFX fun trying to corral him and get him back to scale.

HONEY, I SHRUNK THE KIDS [4]

RICK MORANIS, MATT FREWER, MARCIA STRASSMAN

JOE JOHNSTON

USA (DISNEY) 1989

101m (U)

Classic family entertainment in the Disney style of old: scientist Moranis reduces offspring and they face myriad dangers in their garden, which now seems like a jungle filled with most upsetting creatures! Huge hit. See page 157 for the sequel – another has since emerged. Superb FX.

IN SEARCH OF THE CASTAWAYS [5]

HAYLEY MILLS, MAURICE CHEVALIER, WILFRED HYDE-WHITE, GEORGE SANDERS

ROBERT STEVENSON

UK/USA (DISNEY) 1961

94m (U)

This mesmerisingly spectacular film will be undoubtedly diminished on the small screen, but it remains a rollercoaster ride of hugely enjoyable proportions. The title pretty much gives away the plot which is based on the Jules Verne story *Captain Grant's Children*. Must-see: even the most sophisticated toddler will not remain unmoved.

INNERSPACE [3]

DENNIS QUAID, MEG RYAN, MARTIN SHORT, KEVIN McCARTHY

JOE DANTE

USA (WARNER) 1987

116m (PG)

Spoof on the theme of *Fantastic Voyage* (see page 266), with a scientist accidentally injected into the bloodstream of someone after being miniaturised. Won a deserved Oscar for special effects. Available in widescreen.

JUMANJI [4]

ROBIN WILLIAMS, JONATHAN HYDE, KIRSTEN DUNST, BRADLEY PIERCE

JOE JOHNSON

USA (COLUMBIA TRISTAR) 1995

104m (PG)

Demented story concerning a malevolent boardgame that conjures up all manner of traps and dangerous wildlife each time the dice are thrown. Williams is fine as a previous victim, unlocked from his purgatory when someone else continues his interrupted game of years before, but his normally ebullient style is swamped by the amazing FX work. Children will love it, though it might be too scary for little 'uns.

FAMILY ENTERTAINMENT

THE KARATE KID 🎬3

	RALPH MACCHIO, NORIYUKI 'PAT' MORITA, MARTIN KOVE, ELISABETH SHUE
	JOHN G AVILDSEN
	USA (COLUMBIA TRISTAR) 1984
	122m (15)

The old theme of wimpy kid learning self-defence at the hands of a master and settling scores with his new skills. The '15' certificate seems harsh – the sequels (the first of which is available on a two-for-one tape with this film) were rated 'PG' which seems more apt.

MARY POPPINS 🎬3

	JULIE ANDREWS, DICK VAN DYKE, GLYNIS JOHNS, DAVID TOMLINSON
	ROBERT STEVENSON
	USA (DISNEY) 1964
	133m (U)

Twee but amusing adaptation of PL Travers's novel about a magical nanny: Van Dyke has the worst cock-er-nee accent in movie history, but the film is lovely to look at and quite rightly won Oscars for Andrews (best actress), music, special effects, etc. Best suited to younger kids.

MATILDA 🎬5

	MARA WILSON, DANNY DeVITO, RHEA PERLMAN, PAM FERRIS
	DANNY DeVITO
	USA (COLUMBIA TRISTAR) 1996
	98m (PG)

A ka *Roald Dahl's Matilda*, this is the usual wonderful Dahl mix of swinish adults and smart kids: our heroine is a bright gal with dumb folks and a dastardly headmistress to contend with, and naturally she trashes the lot of 'em. DeVito handles the direction with aplomb as well as appearing as Matilda's awful dad. Grrrrreat stuff!

MIGHTY JOE YOUNG 🎬2

	BILL PAXTON, CHARLIZE THERON
	RON UNDERWOOD
	USA (BUENA VISTA) 1999
	110m (PG)

Extraordinary special effects move seamlessly from computer-generated images to 'live' action and this will enthral family audiences. After poachers have shattered his family life, Joe has lived in remote mountains with his best friend, played by Theron. When he is once again threatened by determined poachers, it is decided to move him to an animal conservancy in California. This is a remake, with several nods to the original (such as a cameo by classic animator Ray Harryhausen).

THE NEVERENDING STORY [4]

NOAH HATHAWAY, BARRETT OLIVER, PATRICIA HAYES, MOSES GUNN

WOLFGANG PETERSEN

UK/WEST GERMANY (WARNER) 1984

90m (U)

Michael Ende's novel is the source of this fable about a boy who runs from bullies into an old bookshop, where he finds a magic tome that catapults him into a delightful world so different from the one he knows. There is a sequel, and both are available together on a two-for-one tape if you prefer. Younger kids should love this movie.

THE PARENT TRAP [2]

DENNIS QUAID, LINDSAY LOHAN, NATASHA RICHARDSON

NANCY MYERS

USA (BUENA VISTA) 1998

123m (PG)

Remake of the Disney classic, which starred a youthful Hayley Mills, in which twin sisters – brought up in London and California each longing for a family – meet up at summer camp and exchange places in a bid to reunite their parents. Lighthearted family entertainment.

THE PRINCESS BRIDE [5]

CARY ELWES, PETER FALK, MANDY PATINKIN, BILLY CRYSTAL

ROB REINER

USA (CINEMA CLUB V) 1987

94m (PG)

Lovely movie for adults and children alike, based on William Goldman's novel. Grouchy kid doesn't fancy having Gramps read him a soppy book about princesses and brides, but as the tale gets under way he (and we) soon warm to it. A knowing and delicious revamp of the swashbuckler genre, with some smashing cameos from fine performers. If you've never heard of this movie, let alone seen it, you are in for a treat.

THE RAILWAY CHILDREN [3]

JENNY AGUTTER, DINAH SHERIDAN, WILLIAM MERVYN, IAIN CUTHBERTSON

LIONEL JEFFRIES

UK (WARNER) 1970

104m (U)

E Nesbit novel provides the basis for a simple story of children's lives beside a railway as they wait to hear if their father is to be found guilty of spying. It's a pity Lionel Jeffries only directed a few films, especially on this showing.

FAMILY ENTERTAINMENT

RING OF BRIGHT WATER

BILL TRAVERS, VIRGINIA McKENNA, PETER JEFFREY, RODDY McMILLAN

JACK COUFFER

UK (ODYSSEY) 1969

102m (U)

Making *Born Free* (see page 154) seems to have been a turning point in the lives of husband-and-wife Travers and McKenna – even when they weren't making films about wildlife, like this one, they were campaigning to help endangered species. This is an enjoyable, simple story about friendship between man and otter, based on Gavin Maxwell's book.

SWISS FAMILY ROBINSON

JOHN MILLS, DOROTHY McGUIRE, JAMES MacARTHUR, TOMMY KIRK

KEN ANNAKIN

USA (DISNEY) 1960

126m (U)

Second of three filmed versions of the Johann Wyss novel about a shipwrecked family, and definitely the best. Not really in the same class as *In Search Of The Castaways* (see page 158) but guaranteed to appease the younger thrill-seekers amongst you.

TEENAGE MUTANT NINJA TURTLES

ELIAS KOTEAS, JUDITH HOAG, JAMES SAITO, MICHAEL TURNEY

STEVE BARRON

USA (4-FRONT) 1990

87m (PG)

First of the films based on the cult comics about the martial arts amphibians. The fan mania seems to have died away, so kids may turn up their noses at this these days. Plus the BBFC are still obsessed with the supposed danger of martial arts weapons, and even though the turtle here was using a string of sausages instead of real rice-flails in a fight they insisted on cuts! Aren't you glad your kids are being protected from frankfurter brutality?

THIEF OF BAGDAD

CONRAD VEIDT, SABU, REX INGRAM

MICHAEL POWELL, LUDWIG BERGER, TIM WHELAN, ZOLTAN KORDA, WILLIAM CAMERON MENZIES, ALEXANDER KORDA

UK (CARLTON) 1940

102m (U)

A riot of colour and imagination, this fairy tale for all ages has a magic eye stolen from a temple, a genie escaping from a bottle and FX that still seem great today. Amazingly coherent for a film assembled by a multiplicity of directors here and in the US during World War Two. Script by the lovely character actor Miles Malleson.

THOSE MAGNIFICENT MEN IN THEIR FLYING MACHINES (Or How I Flew From London To Paris In 25 Hours And 11 Minutes)

ROBERT MORLEY, SARAH MILES, TERRY-THOMAS, STUART WHITMAN

KEN ANNAKIN

UK (FOX) 1965

138m (U)

Spiffingly silly-ass stuff about the early days of manned flight. The late Terry-Thomas all but steals the show as an out-and-out bounder up to all manner of dastardly deeds. In July 1998, director Annakin was given a retrospective at the NFT.

THE WIND IN THE WILLOWS

STEVE COOGAN, TERRY JONES, ERIC IDLE, STEPHEN FRY, JOHN CLEESE

TERRY JONES

UK (GUILD) 1996

87m (U)

Excellent version of the Kenneth Grahame classic about the adventures of Toad, Ratty, Mole and their neighbours. The only thing missing, as usual, is the yearning, mystical quality of the book – but that would (sadly) be lost on most kids anyway. It's certainly super to look at, at any rate.

GANGSTERS

Gangsters first became a staple of movies with the prohibition-inspired 1930s classics from Warner Brothers, starring the likes of Humphrey Bogart and James Cagney and there was a spate of late 60s efforts after the style of *Bonnie And Clyde*. They enjoyed something of a rebirth with the 1970s success of Francis Ford Coppola's *The Godfather*, and the genre is taking off once again as young writers and directors follow the lead of Quentin Tarantino's violent classics *Reservoir Dogs* and *Pulp Fiction* with films such as the UK hit *Lock, Stock And Two Smoking Barrels*. While all of these forms, as well as offshoots such as black 'gangsta' movies and the dark, often literary-inspired *film noir* genre, are well covered on video, there is one area that remains in need of rediscovery: in the wake of the 'Godfather' films, Italian directors made a series of ultra-violent Mafia thrillers, often with middle-ranking American players in the lead. Few of these are available, yet a considerable cult has built up around them. To name just one, Damiano Damiani's *Confessions Of A Police Captain*, starring Martin Balsam, thoroughly deserves to be seen again. And Tarantino, always on the ball, has *his* baddies watch a video of one of these (which I recognise as once having been on a UK tape as *Street Killers*) in his film *Jackie Brown*. Re-issue anyone?

AL CAPONE [4]

ROD STEIGER, FAY SPAIN, NEHEMIAH PERSOFF, MARTIN BALSAM

RICHARD WILSON

USA (FOX) 1959 B&W

104m (15)

Violent, flashy account of the rise and fall of the legendary Chicago hoodlum. Steiger gives a showy, mesmerising performance in the lead, ably supported by a cast which includes Martin Balsam as a corrupt journalist in the gang lord's employ. Lensed by Lucien Ballard in sharp-edged, gritty monochrome. Remains one of the best Capone movies in spite of many later big-budget versions of the story.

THE ASPHALT JUNGLE [4]

STERLING HAYDEN, SAM JAFFE, JAMES WHITMORE, MARILYN MONROE

JOHN HUSTON

USA (MGM/UA) 1950 B&W

108m (PG)

Classic heist picture elevated by Huston's unsentimental direction and fine ensemble playing by a superb cast. Hayden is suitably tough, and Jaffe excels as the old-timer finally brought down through lingering too long over the suggestive dancing of a sexy teenager in a bar. A landmark film. There have been three remakes, none of which remotely approaches the intelligence and quality of the original.

BAD LIEUTENANT [5]

HARVEY KEITEL, ZOE LUND, FRANKIE THORN, ANTHONY RUGGIERO

ABEL FERRARA

USA (GUILD) 1992

96m (18)

Cult director Ferrara (who started out as the maker of previously banned horror flick *The Driller Killer*, see page 197) relies on Keitel to carry this picture, which has little plot and is mainly a character study of a crooked, drugged-up cop as bad as the gangsters he chases. Keitel gives a stunning performance as the cop, investigating the rape of a nun and being so moved by her forgiveness of the rapists that he releases them, sealing his own fate at the same time. The UK video was heavily cut by the censor, and the music is not that on the cinema version due to legal problems. Nevertheless, worth watching in any form.

BILLY BATHGATE 🎬3

🌟 DUSTIN HOFFMAN, NICOLE KIDMAN, BRUCE WILLIS, LOREN DEAN

🎬 ROBERT BENTON

USA (TOUCHSTONE) 1991

⏱ 102m (15)

Based on a novel by EL Doctorow and scripted by Tom Stoppard, this is the story of an ambitious youngster who gets involved with gang-leader Dutch Schultz (Hoffman, on good form) and falls in love with his girlfriend. A fair story, with Willis excellent as a hit man, but at the end one is left feeling that the title character is one whom things simply happen around rather than to.

BLACK RAIN 🎬3

🌟 MICHAEL DOUGLAS, ANDY GARCIA, KATE CAPSHAW, KEN TAKAKURA

🎬 RIDLEY SCOTT

USA (CIC) 1989

⏱ 120m (18)

Two cops deliver a Japanese hoodlum back to his homeland from the USA, but lose him at the last moment. Determined to make good, they stay on and get involved in more murky matters than they can handle. The mood of cultural dislocation between the Yanks and the Japs is well handled, and Douglas is believable as the mildly corrupt cop who returns to the straight-and-narrow after his partner is killed. Not one of Scott's best, but it looks nice and rattles along at a cracking pace. Oscar: sound.

BONNIE AND CLYDE 🎬5

🌟 WARREN BEATTY, FAYE DUNAWAY, GENE HACKMAN, MICHAEL J POLLARD, ESTELLE PARSONS

🎬 ARTHUR PENN

USA (WARNER) 1967

⏱ 106m (18)

Hugely influential film about two real-life 30s American rural thugs and their gang. In spite of the gory finale it tends to make violence seem exciting and fun at times, though it's worth watching for the fine acting and excitement value. Oscars: best supporting actress (Parsons) and cinematography. Available in boxed set with book. Now in widescreen.

BRING ME THE HEAD OF ALFREDO GARCIA 🎬4

🌟 WARREN OATES, ISELA VEGA, GIG YOUNG, KRIS KRISTOFFERSON

🎬 SAM PECKINPAH

USA (WARNER) 1974

⏱ 108m (18)

A sleazy piano player in a Mexican bar learns that a local gang lord wants the head of the man who impregnated his daughter. Knowing the man is already dead, he accepts the contract and plans simply to dig up the grave and claim his prize. Things are not that simple, however. This nihilistic classic was initially seen as a decline for Peckinpah, and has only lately been given its critical due. The title has become a byword for nastiness in film and has been much parodied: *Bring Me The Head Of Dobie Gillis*, etc.

TOP 1000 VIDEOS

BRONX WARRIORS 4

VIC MORROW, MARK GREGORY, FRED WILLIAMSON, CHRISTOPHER CONNOLLY

ENZO G CASTELLARI

ITALY/USA (UNIQUE) 1982

82m (18)

Futuristic tosh set in a Manhattan which has become little more than territory fought over by rival garishly clad youth gangs. A box-office hit and a major title in the early days of home video, it inspired sequels and rip-offs. Cut, but in widescreen format.

BUGSY 3

WARREN BEATTY, ANNETTE BENING, HARVEY KEITEL, BEN KINGSLEY, JOE MANTEGNA

BARRY LEVINSON

USA (20/20) 1991

131m (18)

Star-studded story of the gangster who built Las Vagas into a gambling paradise. The actors are all fine but it seems too polished and glitzy for a mob story. Bugsy Siegel was a nasty piece of work, but he rates a better pic than this. Penned by James Toback, who has made some interesting films in his time. This isn't comparable with his low-budget Harvey Keitel vehicle *Fingers*, an amazing gangster pic about a pianist who doubles as a thug. Now *that* should be on tape.

CAPONE 3

BEN GAZZARA, HARRY GUARDINO, JOHN CASSAVETES, SYLVESTER STALLONE

STEVE CARVER

USA (FOX) 1975

97m (18)

A gutsy Roger Corman production utilising stock footage from his own Capone effort *The St Valentine's Day Massacre*. Surprisingly top-notch cast for a cheapjack movie. Gazzara can't dispel memories of Rod Steiger's interpretation of Capone, however.

CARLITO'S WAY 5

AL PACINO, SEAN PENN, PENELOPE ANN MILLER, VIGGO MORTENSEN

BRIAN DE PALMA

USA (CIC) 1993

145m (18)

De Palma's best gangland epic, on a par with his *Scarface* (also with Pacino, see page 178) and miles better than the over-polished *The Untouchables*, (see page 180). Pacino is a heroin dealer who, released via a technicality found by his lawyer, resolves to go straight and wed the girl of his dreams – but the old life will not allow him to let go. Penn is marvellous as the crooked lawyer who both saves our anti-hero from jail and then seals his fate. It's truly remarkable, in the middle of today's war on drugs to see a mainstream Hollywood picture that accepts that someone who once dealt heroin is not necessarily a demon. Available in a perfect widescreen format.

GANGSTERS

CASINO 🎬4

⭐ ROBERT DE NIRO, SHARON STONE, JOE PESCI, JAMES WOODS

🎬 MARTIN SCORSESE

USA (CIC) 1995

⏱ 178m (18)

Scorsese used to seem incapable of making a mediocre movie, but this tale of a mob-controlled gambling house feels rather like a re-run of the director's superior *Goodfellas* (see page 170). The film is worth seeing for the gleaming credits sequence by the late Saul Bass, the stellar cast, and Sharon Stone's costumes! Widescreen available.

COLORS 🎬5

⭐ SEAN PENN, ROBERT DUVALL, MARIA CONCHITA ALONSO, RANDY BROOKS

🎬 DENNIS HOPPER

USA (4-FRONT) 1988

⏱ 121m (18)

As Hopper is one of my heroes, my proudest moment during my tenure as *Penthouse* film critic was seeing the walls of Leicester Square tube station plastered with posters for this flick – all bearing my name and the quote, 'A must-see film'. And so it is. The story is of an old cop (Duvall) and his young sidekick (Penn) patrolling the no-go areas of Los Angeles where gun-toting youth gangs rule the streets. The actors are entirely believable, and Hopper directed the film in real tough areas with real gangster extras. Fabulous. This version has some footage not in the original cinema release.

THE CRIMINAL 🎬4

⭐ STANLEY BAKER, SAM WANAMAKER, MARGIT SAAD, PATRICK MAGEE

🎬 JOSEPH LOSEY

UK (LUMIERE) 1960 B&W

⏱ 97m (PG)

Made in England by then-blacklisted American director Losey, this tough portrait of a career criminal who accepts jail as an occupational hazard is exciting yet grim, with a downbeat ending. Baker is all too real as the villain (in real life he was a pal of the Krays) and Magee is chilling as a cruel prison officer. A Brit crime classic.

DONNIE BRASCO 🎬4

⭐ AL PACINO, JOHNNY DEPP, MICHAEL MADSEN, ANNE HECHE

🎬 MIKE NEWELL

USA (ENTERTAINMENT) 1997

⏱ 126m (18)

True story of an undercover cop who infiltrates a Mafia crew by befriending a lower-echelon hoodlum. An engrossing but somewhat downbeat tale from British director Newell, which nevertheless rated highly with critics. Depp seems a bit too young and pretty to be a top-rank copper, but Pacino is excellent as the betrayed crook. Give it a whirl.

167

FORCE OF EVIL

JOHN GARFIELD, THOMAS GOMEZ, BEATRICE PARSON

ABRAHAM POLONSKY

USA (2ND SIGHT) 1948 B&W

78m (PG)

Moody piece about two brothers involved in the numbers racket, the illegal lottery run by the Mob. Lots of symbolism and allegorical flourishes don't overwhelm Garfield's powerful performance. A key film of the 1940s, its doomy feel no doubt influenced by the director's persecution in the McCarthy anti-communist witch-hunts.

THE GENERAL

JON VOIGHT, BRENDAN GLEESON, ADRIAN DUNBAR, ANGELINE BALL

JOHN BOORMAN

UK/IRELAND (WARNER) 1998 B&W

119m (15)

Boorman scored an award at Cannes for his direction of this biopic of notorious Irish criminal godfather Martin Cahill (Gleeson), with Voight as the RUC man on his tail. The movie fared badly at the box office, possibly due to the contemporaneous TV film on Cahill stealing the potential audience. It'd be a crime to miss it now. Widescreen box with book on Cahill available.

GET SHORTY

JOHN TRAVOLTA, GENE HACKMAN, RENE RUSSO, DANNY DE VITO

BARRY SONNENFELD

USA (MGM/UA) 1995

105m (15)

Based on Elmore Leonard's novel inspired by a real-life debt collector, this was Travolta's first big hit subsequent to his rediscovery at the hands of Quentin Tarantino in *Pulp Fiction* (see page 177). Travelling to Hollywood to get debts owed by director Hackman, Travolta gets involved in film-producing and other less salubrious pastimes. (Then again, film-producing ain't all that salubrious when you come to think of it.) Witty, sharp, and the cast look like they're having a ball. You will too.

THE GETAWAY

STEVE McQUEEN, ALI MacGRAW, BEN JOHNSON, SLIM PICKENS

SAM PECKINPAH

USA (WARNER) 1972

117m (18)

Scripted by Walter Hill from Jim Thompson's novel, this was a star vehicle with Peckinpah under no illusions but that he was simply a hired hand. Nevertheless, he still managed to inject his trademark concerns about loyalty and violence into the story about an ex-con and his wife. Even MacGraw, who couldn't act if a gun was put to her head, can't slow the pace. Available in widescreen. Avoid the remake.

THE GODFATHER 🎬 [5]

⭐ MARLON BRANDO, AL PACINO, DIANE KEATON, JAMES CAAN, ROBERT DUVALL

🎬 FRANCIS FORD COPPOLA

USA (CIC) 1971

⏱ 167m [18]

Classic Mafia dynastic epic based on the Mario Puzo novel, with Brando as the old boss under attack and Pacino as the 'clean' son forced to helm the family business. Oozes quality from every frame. Oscars for best picture, best actor (Brando) and best screenplay. Essential viewing.

THE GODFATHER PART II 🎬 [5]

⭐ AL PACINO, ROBERT DE NIRO, ROBERT DUVALL, DIANE KEATON

🎬 FRANCIS FORD COPPOLA

USA (CIC) 1974

⏱ 190m [18]

That rarity, a sequel that improves on the original. The story is split between the early adventures of the Brando character (played here as a young man by Robert De Niro) and the further trials of Pacino as the new Don. Coppola has reworked the two films several times, adding extra footage, for video packages and TV airings. This film won Oscars for best picture, director, supporting actor (De Niro) and more.

THE GODFATHER PART III 🎬 [3]

⭐ AL PACINO, DIANE KEATON, ANDY GARCIA, ELI WALLACH, SOFIA COPPOLA

🎬 FRANCIS FORD COPPOLA

USA (CIC) 1990

⏱ 163m [15]

This third part of the saga sees Pacino as an old guy trying to hold on to his empire. Most critics praised it, but to me it has a false feel, as if Coppola has lost the thread. Pacino is unconvincing as an aged man, Coppola's nepotism in casting his own daughter comes adrift as she simply cannot act, and the plot involving corrupt Vatican officials seems forced rather than an organic follow-on from previous events. Worth watching as a follow-on to the other two films (see above). The video apparently is a director's cut which includes nine minutes of scenes which were cut from the cinema release.

GOODFELLAS 🎬 5

RAY LIOTTA, ROBERT DE NIRO, JOE PESCI, LORRAINE BRACCO, PAUL SORVINO

MARTIN SCORSESE

USA (WARNER) 1990

139m (18)

Brutal true story of Henry Hill, a kid who joined the local Mob as a teenager, progressed to bigger things and ended up informing on his chums when caught dealing drugs. Scorsese dazzles with every cinematic trick in the book (including having the protagonist descend from the witness stand in court and directly address the cinema audience), and sets scenes of the most awful cruelty against a background of nostalgic rock songs. It's really an actors' film, though, with sterling work from all concerned, especially Liotta as Hill, De Niro as his thieving mentor and Pesci (who won an Oscar) as a cheerful psychopath.

GOTTI 🎬 4

ARMAND ASSANTE, ANTHONY QUINN, WILLIAM FORSYTHE

ROBERT HARMON

USA (HIGH FLIERS) 1996

117m (18)

Superior made-for-TV film about the downfall of John Gotti, USA Mafia boss once dubbed 'the teflon don' because no charge could stick to him. Award-winning star role for Assante, with top support from Quinn and Forsythe. Engrossing.

THE GRIFTERS 🎬 3

JOHN CUSACK, ANGELICA HUSTON, ANNETTE BENING, PAT HINGLE

STEPHEN FREARS

USA (POLYGRAM) 1990

105m (18)

Brit Frears attempts to interpret a Jim Thompson story of related professional criminals, but though widely praised I'm afraid it feels rather cold and empty to me. See it for the fine performances.

HEAT 🎬 5

ROBERT DE NIRO, AL PACINO, VAL KILMER, JON VOIGHT

MICHAEL MANN

USA (WARNER) 1995

171m (15)

This story of a top cop and head gangster stalking each other is unique for being the first time De Niro and Pacino acted together – the scene where they meet and discuss their lives is a tour de force of eyeball-to-eyeball acting genius. Mann is a master of the action film, and this is one of his best. The film is, interestingly enough, a large-scale reworking of a movie he made for TV, known variously as *LA Takedown* (see page 172), *LA Crimewave* and *Made In LA*, with lesser-known stars. Widescreen available.

GANGSTERS

JACKIE BROWN 🎬 4

⭐ ROBERT DE NIRO, PAM GRIER, SAMUEL L JACKSON, BRIDGET FONDA, ROBERT FORSTER, MICHAEL KEATON

🎬 QUENTIN TARANTINO

USA (BUENA VISTA) 1998

⏱ 148m (15)

Not really up to the standard of Tarantino's earlier efforts, this frisky adaptation of Elmore Leonard's book *Rum Punch* has at least given the director the opportunity to employ some of his exploitation-movie favourites alongside the big names. Air stewardess Grier gets caught with cash and drugs destined for her gun-runner boss Jackson and his dumb moll Fonda, and how she extricates herself by juggling the authorities, the baddies and helpful bail-bondsman Forster (Oscar-nominated) forms the rest of the pic. It's all slickly handled and the 2½-hour running time flies by. There's not a duff performer here, but Jackson as the cocky crook and De Niro as his sullen chum are outstanding. As with all Tarantino films, it is full of cultural allusions and there's a hot soundtrack. It may not be *Reservoir Dogs* (see page 178) or *Pulp Fiction* (see page 177), but Tarantino obviously wants to show he can work with other people's material. Widescreen available.

KEY LARGO 🎬 4

⭐ HUMPHREY BOGART, EDWARD G ROBINSON, LAUREN BACALL, LIONEL BARRYMORE, CLAIRE TREVOR

🎬 JOHN HUSTON

USA (WARNER) 1948 B&W

⏱ 97m (??)

Thriller about a gangster hiding out during a storm in the Florida Keys and making life tough for the occupants of the sleazy hotel he picks as a bolthole. A bona fide legendary flick. Trevor won an Oscar for best supporting actress as a drunken gangster's moll.

THE KILLING OF A CHINESE BOOKIE 🎬 3

⭐ BEN GAZZARA, TIM CAREY, SEYMOUR CASSEL, ALICE FRIEDLAND

🎬 JOHN CASSAVETES

USA (ELECTRIC) 1976

⏱ 113m (15)

As well as being a respected actor, Cassavetes was also a highly regarded independent director. This is a long, character-led story about a nightclub owner told the only way out of his big debt to the Mob is to shoot an aged Chinese bookmaker for them. It has an improvised feel and a seedy reality about it that make it a compelling experience. Apparently there are two different versions of the film in existence as the director re-edited the material at some point, but only this one is out on tape.

KING OF NEW YORK [4]

CHRISTOPHER WALKEN, LARRY FISHBURNE, WESLEY SNIPES, STEVE BUSCEMI, DAVID CARUSO

ABEL FERRARA

ITALY/USA (AMERICAN INDEPENDENCE) 1990

100m (18)

The sinister, distracted Walken is super-cool in Ferrara's story of a drug lord, who is released from jail and plans to re-establish his supremacy in the narcotics trade in order to finance a hospital for the poor. Improbable, but amid the sex and violence Ferrara is asking the question: 'How do you decide who is good and who is evil?' At least, I think that's what it's about. Uncut. Not in widescreen format at present, but deserves to be as the present print is cropped on all four sides of the image.

THE KRAYS [3]

GARY KEMP, MARTIN KEMP, BILLIE WHITELAW, STEVEN BERKOFF

PETER MEDAK

UK (POLYGRAM) 1989

115m (18)

The makers of this biopic on the notorious rulers of 60s London gangland claim they went out of their way not to glamorise the twins – but getting twin pop stars (ex-members of Spandau Ballet) to play the gangsters hardly supports the notion, especially as the pair are far more handsome than the thugs they're portraying. Nasty and violent, but saved somewhat by Jimmy Jewel as the pair's grandpa and Steven Berkoff as victim George Cornell. Billie Whitelaw pouts a lot as the matriarch of the clan, but one suspects that the real Violet Kray was a much nicer and far more interesting lady than she's portrayed as here. The film was mooted for some time before it was actually filmed, and the same seems to be happening with a proposed sequel. Available by itself or on a two-for-one tape with *McVicar* (see page 174).

LA TAKEDOWN [3]

SCOTT PLANK, ALEX McARTHUR, ELY POUGET

MICHAEL MANN

USA (MIA) 1989

95m (15)

Interesting to see this early version of the film Mann later re-made as a big picture with De Niro and Pacino under the title *Heat* (see page 170), but the actors here are just too young for the parts. When one actor threatens 'I'll blow you outta your socks!' he is so wimpy in his delivery that it sounds like he's suggesting nothing more violent than handbags at ten paces. This is basically a sketch for *Heat*, of interest to scholars of Mann's filmic techniques but not a patch on the later film.

LAST MAN STANDING 🎬4

★ BRUCE WILLIS, BRUCE DERN, CHRISTOPHER WALKEN, ALEXANDRA POWERS

🎬 WALTER HILL

USA (ENTERTAINMENT) 1996

⏱ 101m (18)

Latest version of a movie that has been a samurai pic (*Yojimbo*), then a Western (*A Fistful Of Dollars*, see page 334) – and now a gangster film, but the story is basically the same: a stranger arrives in a town ruled by two gangs, and proceeds to sell his gun to both sides. Clint Eastwood's 'Man with No Name' is now the equally anonymous 'John Smith' (Willis), but he's still after a fistful of cash. Christopher Walken is creepy as an evil killer. Even if you've seen the other versions, this is first rate fun. Widescreen available.

LE SAMOURAI 🎬4

★ ALAIN DELON, NATHALIE DELON, FRANCOIS PERIER, CATHY ROSIER

🎬 JEAN-PIERRE MELVILLE

FRANCE (ARTIFICIAL EYE) 1967

⏱ 95m (PG)

A classic, stripped-to-essentials story of a hitman by the great Melville, with icy Alain Delon living in a bare apartment with only a caged bird for company. Caught between pursuing *flics* and treacherous hoods with only his girl on his side, Delon is impassive and menacing. In the correct ratio and subtitled.

LEPKE 🎬3

★ TONY CURTIS, ANJANETTE COMER, MICHAEL CALLAN, MILTON BERLE

🎬 MENAHEM GOLAN

USA (WARNER) 1974

⏱ 105m (18)

Cheap pic about the man who started Murder Incorporated. Curtis tries hard but he is simply too old for the scenes where Lepke is shown as a promising young thug. Directed by Golan, who later became one of the men behind Cannon Films, purveyors of much cinematic drivel.

LITTLE CAESAR 🎬4

★ EDWARD G ROBINSON, DOUGLAS FAIRBANKS Jnr, SIDNEY BLACKMER, GLENDA FARRELL

🎬 MERVYN LE ROY

USA (WARNER) 1930 B&W

⏱ 76m (PG)

Stonking tale, loosely based on the rise and fall of Al Capone. Only the names have been changed to protect the guilty. An absolute stone classic, though it may look rather theatrical and dated to today's younger viewers.

LOCK, STOCK AND TWO SMOKING BARRELS 🎬 4

⭐ VINNIE JONES, JASON FLEMYNG, JASON STATHAM, STING, STEVEN MACKINTOSH, NICK MORAN

🎬 GUY RITCHIE

UK (POLYGRAM) 1998

⏱ 107m (18)

Hit British gangster flick concerning the complex, tragicomic rivalry between various criminal outfits over money, drugs and highly prized antique shotguns. The story is occasionally hard to follow, but the London wide-boy backchat is entertaining and the violence never crosses the line into gratuitous brutality. Might be criticised for making thuggish characters into heroes, but bullet-headed footballer Vinnie Jones would hardly have done as well in a soppy love story, would he? Widescreen available.

McVICAR 🎬 3

⭐ ROGER DALTREY, ADAM FAITH, GEORGINA HALE, STEVEN BERKOFF

🎬 TOM CLEGG

UK (POLYGRAM) 1980

⏱ 107m (18)

Biog of McVicar, a hardened British criminal who studied in prison and is now a respected journalist. Gimmicky, with Who vocalist Daltrey's sloppy music heavily featured. And if you doubt my charge of frivolity, I can tell you that the original preview for journos had bread and water instead of the usual refreshments! With another ex-singer, Adam Faith, featured, it's perhaps suitable that this is on a two-for-one tape with *The Krays* (see page 172). No glamorising of crime of course, oh no indeed! Also available by itself on 4-Front.

MEAN STREETS 🎬 4

⭐ HARVEY KEITEL, ROBERT DE NIRO, DAVID PROVAL, AMY ROBINSON

🎬 MARTIN SCORSESE

USA (ELECTRIC) 1973

⏱ 108m (18)

Early hit from Scorsese, with Keitel as a young 'connected' chap torn between loyalty to his Mafia family, love for his girl and the need to help his feckless, troublesome pal Johnny Boy (De Niro). His indecision finally results in tragedy. All the Scorsese stylistic trademarks are here, set to the usual nostalgic pop beat. Invigorating.

GANGSTERS

MEN OF RESPECT

ROB STEIGER, JOHN TURTURRO, PETER BOYLE, DENNIS FARINA, STANLEY TUCCI

WILLIAM REILLY

USA (CINEMA CLUB V) 1990

109m (18)

In essence, this is *Macbeth* updated to modern Mafia environment. Doesn't quite come off in spite of a respectable cast, including the excellent Tucci, so memorable as the sybaritic tycoon in TV's *Murder One*.

MILLER'S CROSSING

GABRIEL BYRNE, JOHN TURTURRO, ALBERT FINNEY, FRANCES McDORMAND

JOEL COEN

USA (FOX) 1990

110m (18)

Classy gangsterism with Gabriel Byrne oozing charisma, but it's not in the same league as Coen's later thriller *Fargo* (see page 113). Shot by Barry Sonnenfeld, who went on to direct *Get Shorty* (see page 168).

MIAMI BLUES

FRED WARD, ALEC BALDWIN, JENNIFER JASON LEIGH, CHARLES NAPIER

GEORGE ARMITAGE

USA (VISION) 1989

92m (18)

Bizarre crime thriller based on one of the late Charles Willeford's novels about sleazy cop Hoke Mosely. Ward makes a great Mosely, out to catch a just-freed psycho who has stolen his false teeth and badge. Shame it wasn't a hit, as it would be nice to see Ward reprise the role.

MOBSTERS

CHRISTIAN SLATER, PATRICK DEMPSEY, F MURRAY ABRAHAM, MICHAEL GAMBON, ANTHONY QUINN

MICHAEL KARBELNIKOFF

USA (CIC) 1991

116m (18)

A Brat Pack-type gangster film. Just as the 'Young Guns' movies portrayed cowpoke-era baddies as fresh-faced kids, this tries to do the same for Lucky Luciano and cronies in 20s New York. It doesn't always work but hardly deserves the slagging it got on first release. The violent story is attention-holding, and Quinn and Gambon excel as old hoods reluctant to give up their empires.

NEW JACK CITY 🎬3

WESLEY SNIPES, ICE-T, MARIO VAN PEEBLES, JUDD NELSON

MARIO VAN PEEBLES

USA (WARNER) 1991

96m (18)

Black hoods take over the city's drugs trade in this amoral, violent thriller. Enjoyable, but the sort of movie that community leaders are always complaining about for giving negative images of black kids. The trouble is, it was made by black film-makers.

ONCE UPON A TIME IN AMERICA 🎬4

ROBERT DE NIRO, JAMES WOODS, ELIZABETH McGOVERN, BURT YOUNG

SERGIO LEONE

USA (WARNER) 1984

228m (18)

The third Leone film with *Once Upon A Time ...* in the title, and his final picture. It's a complex, multi-flashback/forward structured epic about a bunch of gangsters and their lives together. Great score by Ennio Morricone. Cut to 144m in the USA and re-edited into a dull, linear form, but public demand led to this long version being issued. Apparently there is a 250m European print but it is not available on tape. A moving piece of cinema from a film-making genius.

ORIGINAL GANGSTAS 🎬3

FRED WILLIAMSON, JIM BROWN, PAM GRIER, RON O'NEAL, RICHARD ROUNDTREE

LARRY COHEN

USA (FIRST INDEPENDENT) 1996

99m (18)

Cult director Cohen brings together the stars of the 'blaxploitation' movies of the 70s for a sort of class reunion, which is apt as he made his name in the genre. A deliberate 'B' movie, with the old-timers fighting the new breed of Uzi-toting twerps. Wild fun.

POINT BREAK 🎬3

KEANU REEVES, PATRICK SWAYZE, LORI PETTY, GARY BUSEY

KATHRYN BIGELOW

USA (FOX) 1991

117m (18)

Improbable tale about a young FBI man set the task of infiltrating a hedonistic gang of surfers and skydivers who finance their lifestyle by bank robberies. Bigelow overcomes the silliness by virtue of exhilaratingly-lensed action sequences, though the idea that the cop would let his prey go off and attempt suicide-by-surfboard after all the abuse he'd suffered from the man pushes disbelief-suspension a notch too far.

GANGSTERS

THE PUBLIC ENEMY [4]

JAMES CAGNEY, JEAN HARLOW, JOAN BLONDELL, MAE CLARKE

WILLIAM WELLMAN

USA (WARNER) 1931 B&W

80m (PG)

Though cut down from 96m, this is still a powerhouse story of two gangsters, and it made Cagney a star. Connoisseurs of classic scenes will recall the moment when a grumpy Cagney shoves half a grapefruit into Mae Clarke's face over breakfast.

PULP FICTION [5]

JOHN TRAVOLTA, SAMUEL L JACKSON, BRUCE WILLIS, UMA THURMAN, HARVEY KEITEL, TIM ROTH, CHRISTOPHER WALKEN

QUENTIN TARANTINO

USA (TOUCHSTONE) 1994

148m (18)

Wunderkind Tarantino's follow-up to *Reservoir Dogs* (see page 178) is a multi-layered story involving several interconnected plot threads too unremittingly bizarre to explain in the space available. The film revitalised Travolta's career and is full of actors pulling together rather than competing. This is the latest version to be made available, a widescreen print with a bonus of two cut scenes revealed for the first time with an intro by Tarantino. The censor has optically enlarged scenes of heroin injection so that the point of the needle can't be seen penetrating the skin – apparently he thinks no one will know how to take drugs if they don't see the skin being broken! Weird. Oscar: best screenplay. (Note: the brand of heroin Travolta buys in the film is called 'Bava', after one of Tarantino's heroes, late Italian director Mario Bava, who made a multi-story film called *Black Sabbath*.)

RESERVOIR DOGS 5

HARVEY KEITEL, TIM ROTH, MICHAEL MADSEN, STEVE BUSCEMI, CHRIS PENN, LAWRENCE TIERNEY, QUENTIN TARANTINO

QUENTIN TARANTINO

USA (POLYGRAM) 1992

99m (18)

The film that catapulted Tarantino from the guy who used to rent videos in a local Californian store to one of the world's top directors – I guess it really *can* happen to anybody. It's the story of a heist gone wrong and its aftermath, with undercover cop Roth bleeding to death and a patrolman having his ear severed by sadist Madsen. Hilarious dialogue and tense ensemble acting and action make this a sledgehammer debut. The title appears to be meaningless. Widescreen available. Also in pan-scan on a two-for-one tape with the excellent *Killing Zoe*.

SCARFACE 4

PAUL MUNI, GEORGE RAFT, BORIS KARLOFF, ANN DVORAK

HOWARD HAWKS

USA (CIC) 1932 B&W

86m (15)

This Hawks classic has Muni as a fictional version of Capone, manically discovering the joys of the machine-gun and wasting all in his path. Cut from 99m. A piece of cinema history that still thrills.

SCARFACE 5

AL PACINO, STEVEN BAUER, MARY ELIZABETH MASTRANTONIO, MICHELLE PFEIFFER

BRIAN DE PALMA

USA (CIC) 1983

162m (18)

Less a remake of the Hawks film than an update of its themes. Instead of an Italian exploiting the prohibition of booze in the 20s, we have a Cuban in 70s Miami tearing up the cocaine business. Ultra-violent with absurd amounts of coke being snorted, the film explores the greed of the 'Me, me me' 70s and one man's downfall. Magnificent stuff, scripted by Oliver Stone. This new widescreen print has restored a 25-second cut to the scene of a man being tortured with a chainsaw which was made to the original movie release. I guess the censor feels we have stronger stomachs these days!

SHAFT 3

RICHARD ROUNDTREE, MOSES GUNN, CHARLES CIOFFI

GORDON PARKS

USA (WARNER) 1971

100m (15)

With its hip Isaac Hayes score and the taut direction, this classic blaxploiter takes all the usual private-dick clichés and sets them in a black context. Shaft is the cool dude in search of a crime boss's missing kid. Spawned sequels, but none as hot as this. Now in widescreen.

SHARKY'S MACHINE

BURT REYNOLDS, RACHEL WARD, BRIAN KEITH, VITTORIO GASSMAN

BURT REYNOLDS

USA (WARNER) 1981

118m (18)

One of Burt's last major hits before his career began to nosedive, this is about a tough cop who sets out to protect the discarded moll of a Mob boss. Predictably, soppy romance gets in the way of the action, but not for too long. Spectacular stunts and gunplay.

STATE OF GRACE

SEAN PENN, ED HARRIS, GARY OLDMAN, BURGESS MEREDITH

PHIL JOANOU

USA (VISION) 1990

109m (18)

Uncompromising epic of Irish gangs in New York. Extremely nasty in places – many people have their civil rights most egregiously violated, I can assure you. A sadly underrated film that deserves your attention far more than most of the rubbish that fills our multiplexes week after week. Some stylish acting on display, notably from Penn and Oldman.

TRUE ROMANCE

CHRISTIAN SLATER, PATRICIA ARQUETTE, DENNIS HOPPER, CHRISTOPHER WALKEN, VAL KILMER, GARY OLDMAN, BRAD PITT

TONY SCOTT

USA (WARNER) 1993

121m (18)

Tarantino-scripted thriller about a comic-store assistant who falls in love with a hooker, kills her pimp and steals a suitcase full of cocaine before they high-tail it to California with the Mob on their trail. Cameos include a great two-hander from Hopper and Walken. Beware: this so-called uncut version is an already-censored American print that was submitted to the BBFC. The full version, out on USA laserdisc, is considerably more violent. The cuts don't detract from the picture too much, however. Widescreen available in a special box.

THE UNTOUCHABLES ★3

⭐ KEVIN COSTNER, ROBERT DE NIRO, SEAN CONNERY, ANDY GARCIA

🎬 BRIAN DE PALMA

USA (CIC) 1987

⏱ 115m (15)

Glossy, entertaining, but over-praised story of Eliot Ness and his battle against Al Capone. In spite of a pounding score by Ennio Morricone and some fine set pieces (such as a finale that replays the classic *Battleship Potemkin* scene of a pram bouncing down steps amid violence) this doesn't quite work. Costner and pals are too nicey-nice and the story is wildly inaccurate, with such non-historical scenes as Ness hurling Capone henchman Frank Nitti off a roof while making quips worthy of Schwarzenegger at his worst. Connery is the exception, and deservedly won an Oscar for his role as an Irish cop with an inexplicable Scots accent. Widescreen available.

VILLAIN ★3

⭐ RICHARD BURTON, IAN McSHANE, NIGEL DAVENPORT, FIONA LEWIS

🎬 MICHAEL TUCHNER

UK (WARNER) 1971

⏱ 93m (18)

Burton is a nasty piece of work as a brutish homosexual crime boss in London's underworld. A neglected bit of cinematic grime 'n' crime that shows what Burton could do when he was firing on all cylinders and committed to a role.

YEAR OF THE DRAGON ★4

⭐ MICKEY ROURKE, JOHN LONE, ARIANE, LEONARD TERMO

🎬 MICHAEL CIMINO

USA (4-FRONT) 1985

⏱ 129m (18)

Hurrah! A Michael Cimino film that isn't boring! Over-the-top violence in New York's Chinatown as a cop fights his own drug war. Rourke seems to have faded from view of late, but he is blistering here. Written by Oliver Stone. Maybe that's why it's worth watching!

Hong Kong

Although the 1970s fad for martial arts movies died down after the tragic death of kung fu superstar Bruce Lee, a vogue for all manner of commercial Hong Kong cinema has grown by leaps and bounds in recent years. Take a look in any major video store and you'll see a large section devoted to these movies, stacked with tapes from specialist labels such as Missing In Action's Hong Kong Classics subsidiary and Eastern Heroes. The reason for fan enthusiasm isn't hard to fathom: Hong Kong film folk seem to be completely free of the genre restraints of their western counterparts – they'll remix plot elements with abandon and incorporate ideas that USA directors would reject as smashing the bounds of credibility. A film about a true-life serial killer will have scenes of incongruous slapstick comedy, flying ghosts indulge in sexy pursuits, there are hopping vampires and sobbing hitmen …

Some of the former colony's top stars, such as comic martial arts stunt genius Jackie Chan and gunplay-actioner director John Woo, have already made inroads into the American industry. And Sammo Hung is a TV star in the UK with his USA show *Martial Law*. With Hong Kong now handed back to China, the fate of those back home remains to be seen, but in the meantime here is a small sampling of some of the better videos currently on offer.

ANGEL ENFORCERS [3]

SHARON YOUNG, RON VAN LEE, DAISY MAN

GODFREY HO

HONG KONG (HONG KONG CLASSICS/MIA) 1991

87m (18)

Flashy girly/gunfire hokum, a weird oriental version of TV's *Charlie's Angels*. Too much chat, but there are some stunning stunts mixed with nudity, gay rape and all the cheerfully offensive muddle one expects from Hong Kong cinema. Widescreen.

ANGELS [2]

MOON LEE, HIDEKO SAIJO, ALEX FU

TERESA WOO

HONG KONG (HONG KONG CLASSICS/MIA) 1988

88m (18)

More girls with guns! This time battling the dastardly Madam Sue and her fiendish torture-chamber, our heroines never take a hit or so much as smudge their mascara. Amiably mindless widescreen fun, badly dubbed.

A BETTER TOMORROW [5]

CHOW YUN FAT, LESLIE CHEUNG, LEE CHE HUNG

JOHN WOO

HONG KONG (HONG KONG CLASSICS/MIA) 1986

92m (18)

This was the movie which began Woo's rise as the master of the 'heroic bloodshed' genre, where black-suited cops and hitmen indulge in excessive shoot-outs and smouldering glances. A big influence on Quentin Tarantino, and highly charged entertainment in its own right. Subtitled and widescreen. Boxed set available too.

A BETTER TOMORROW 2 [4]

CHOW YUN FAT, LESLIE CHEUNG, TONY LEUNG

JOHN WOO

HONG KONG (MADE IN HONG KONG) 1987

100m (18)

Serviceable follow-up to Woo's earlier shoot-'em-up. Star Chow Yun Fat is reduced to playing his own identical twin (!) as his character was snuffed in the previous outing – see what I mean about Hong Kong's disregard for plot conventions? Starts slowly but soon erupts in balletic bullet mayhem. Many prefer this to the first film. Subtitled and widescreen. A third segment was helmed by producer Tsui Hark in the director's chair.

BULLET IN THE HEAD

JACKY CHEUNG, TONY LEUNG, WAISE LEE, SIMON YAM

JOHN WOO

HONG KONG (MADE IN HONG KONG) 1990

125m (18)

One of the best of Woo's films, this tells of pals who run away from their troubles in the Hong Kong of 1967 to smuggle goodies to Vietnam. But they only get into further scrapes, and are taken prisoner by the Vietcong. Probably influenced by *The Deer Hunter* (see page 320), but actually far superior and less pretentious: this is a harrowing yet enthralling movie.

EASTERN CONDORS

SAMMO HUNG, YUEN BAIO, JOYCE GODENZI

SAMMO HUNG

HONG KONG (MADE IN HONG KONG) 1986

93m (18)

Director/star Sammo Hung is one of the leading lights of the Hong Kong action scene, and this is something of a legendary film. It's rather like *The Dirty Dozen* (see page 321) in conception, with a motley band being sent to capture an enemy base (in Vietnam this time). Huge, explosive nonsense. Subtitled and widescreen. Cut by the BBFC.

ENCOUNTERS OF THE SPOOKY KIND

SAMMO HUNG, CHUNG FAT, CHAN LUNG

SAMMO HUNG

HONG KONG (MADE IN HONG KONG) 1981

98m (18)

Cuckolded hubby invokes demons to revenge himself on cheating wife. Typically mad HK movie from the prolific Hung. Silly, with wacky special effects to goggle over. Subtitled and widescreen.

ENTER THE DRAGON

BRUCE LEE, JOHN SAXON, JIM KELLY

ROBERT CLOUSE

USA/HONG KONG (WARNER) 1973

93m (18)

The charismatic Lee died just as this breakthrough kung fu epic was being released. It's a sort of James Bond effort, with Lee enlisted by secret agents to attend a martial arts tournament held by a shady businessman on his private isle – though he has personal reasons for accepting. Not much of a story but the battles are top-notch. Though this is a remastered widescreen edition, there are problems: on the copy I saw, the upper matte-line crashed down for several seconds during a fight scene, ruining the picture. And the fight with a rice-flail removed by the censor back in 1973 remains cut. Still a must-see! A version with extra scenes is out on import DVD.

FISTS OF FURY

BRUCE LEE, JAMES TIEN, MARIA YI

LO WEI

HONG KONG (POLYGRAM) 1971

99m (18)

Bruce Lee is the only good thing about his early films, frankly. Bad dubbing, shoddy sets, poor direction: and yet they cannot detract from the man's electric screen presence and dynamic skills. Not a great movie, but certainly a great star.

HAND OF DEATH

JACKIE CHAN, SAMMO HUNG, JOHN WOO

JOHN WOO

HONG KONG (HONG KONG CLASSICS/MIA) 1976

92m (18)

Very early work from Chan, Hung and Woo, made before any of the three had developed a distinctive style. Really just a messily dubbed and rather average kung fu pic, but interesting to see these artists in their formative days.

FIVE VENOMS

CHIANG SHENG, LU FENG, WEI PAI

CHANG CHEH

HONG KONG (MADE IN HONG KONG) 1978

98m (18)

Classic 70s kung fu epic from the legendary Shaw Studios, with typical plotline about a dying master who wants his star pupil to check that other students are not betraying the rules they were taught. Dubbed, but the superb stunt work is shown to advantage in this widescreen presentation.

HEROES SHED NO TEARS

EDDY KO, LAM CHING YING, LAU CHAU SANG

JOHN WOO

HONG KONG (HONG KONG CLASSICS/MIA) 1986

81m (18)

Extremely violent John Woo flick. Like Sammo Hung's *Eastern Condors* (see page 183) it's a variant on *The Dirty Dozen* (see page 321), but with an odd atmosphere all its own and some brutal scenes of impalement and dismemberment. Lacks the style of Woo's later pix, but worth seeing anyway.

HONG KONG

THE HOT, THE COOL AND THE VICIOUS 🎬 3

⭐ WONG TAO, TOMMY LEE, GEORGE WANG

🎬 LEE TSO NAM

HONG KONG (HONG KONG CLASSICS/MIA) 1979

⏱ 89m (18)

Impressively subtitled and widescreen martial arts film of the old school, with a clever plot and dazzlingly staged action scenes.

ISLAND ON FIRE 🎬 2

⭐ JACKIE CHAN, SAMMO HUNG, JIMMY WANG YU, TONY LEUNG, ANDY LAU

🎬 CHU YEN PING

HONG KONG (HONG KONG CLASSICS/MIA) 1991

⏱ 92m (18)

A veritable roll-call of HK stars should guarantee solid fun, but apparently many of the actors were filmed separately and the footage flung together later on. As you'd expect, it isn't really a coherent package, though this revenge saga does have its moments.

THE KILLER 🎬 5

⭐ CHOW YUN FAT, SALLY YEH, DANNY LEE

🎬 JOHN WOO

HONG KONG (MADE IN HONG KONG) 1989

⏱ 106m (18)

Considered by many to be Woo's best film, *The Killer*, a dizzying blend of romance, sentiment and gunplay, was first showcased at London's Institute of Contemporary Arts. The story concerns a gunman who accidentally blinds a cabaret singer and takes on a final hit to raise money for an operation on her eyes – but meanwhile the law is on his trail. Beautiful visuals and staggering shoot-outs, far beyond anything Hollywood could dream of, made this a *cause célèbre* among action fans. I believe the longest version ran 135m. Widescreen.

NAKED KILLER 🎬3

⭐ CHINGAMY YAU, SIMON YAM, CARRIE NG

🎬 CLARENCE FORD

HONG KONG (HONG KONG CLASSICS/MIA) 1992

⏱ 96m (18)

*C*razy dyke hitwoman is pursued by a cop who thinks he knows her from another life. Described by some as a HK blend of *Vertigo* (see page 304), *Basic Instinct* (see page 281) and *Nikita* (see page 355), this is a stylishly lensed erotic thriller. Avoid the dubbed/pan-scan version and go for the subtitled/widescreen print. Boxed set also available. Sequel: *Naked Killer 2*.

ONE-ARMED BOXER 🎬3

⭐ WANG YU, MA CHI, LUNG FEI

🎬 WANG YU

HONG KONG (HONG KONG CLASSICS/MIA) 1972

⏱ 88m (18)

*C*heesy-but-cheerful early kung fu classic, with the star/director battling an Indian yogi and magic monks on behalf of his martial arts school. Cheaply done but never less than breathtaking in enthusiasm and audacity.

PROJECT A 🎬4

⭐ JACKIE CHAN, SAMMO HUNG, YUEN BAIO

🎬 JACKIE CHAN

HONG KONG (IMPERIAL) 1985

⏱ 100m (PG)

*O*ne of Chan's best, with early 1900s marines sent to fight pirates on the high seas. Spectacular and such a hit that it spawned a sequel. Highly recommended as a starter if you have yet to have the Chan experience.

SATAN'S RETURN 🎬3

⭐ CHINGAMY YAU, DONNIE YEN, YUEN KING DAN

🎬 AH LUN

HONG KONG (HONG KONG CLASSICS/MIA) 1996

⏱ 95m (18)

*S*upernatural cop thriller which has been compared to *Se7en* (see page 132). Ends with gunfire, crucifixion and chainsaw violence, with humour and a convoluted plot bunged in – just the type of excess which HK cinema excels at producing. Subtitled and widescreen.

THE SEVENTH CURSE 🎬 4

⭐ CHOW YUN FAT, MAGGIE CHEUNG, ELVIS TSUI, DICK WEI

🎬 LAN WEI TSANG

HONG KONG (HONG KONG CLASSICS) 1998

⏱ 80m (18)

Deranged fare involving blood curses, baby ghosts, worm-loving tribesmen, gore and outrageous action sequences, this is the sort of anything-goes movie that Hong Kong does so well. As *The Dark Side* magazine noted, it has elements of *Alien* (see page 259) and *Raiders Of The Lost Ark* (see page 36), but looks as if the reels are in the wrong order! In widescreen, although the source print is a little rough. Slightly cut by BBFC.

SEX AND ZEN II 🎬 3

⭐ SHU QI, XU JIN JIANG, LORETTA LEE

🎬 CHIN MAN KEI

HONG KONG (HONG KONG CLASSICS) 1996

⏱ 93m (18)

Sequel to the 1993 erotic hit. A man wants to bonk more babes than anyone in history, but keeps a tight rein on his daughter, disguising her as a guy and fitting her with a chastity-preserver. Featuring a mirage lady with sexually vampiric tendencies and a man with a mechanical penis, this is a visual treat and is better than the first film. Widescreen. There is another film in the series, though it bears no relation to the earlier movies.

SNAKE IN THE EAGLE'S SHADOW 🎬 3

⭐ JACKIE CHAN, YUEN SIU TIEN, HWANG JANG LEE

🎬 YUEN SIU TIEN

HONG KONG (MADE IN HONG KONG) 1978

⏱ 97m (18)

Early Chan flick in which he plays a bullied youngster fed up with being a dogsbody at his kung fu school – so he takes instruction from the old master of the 'Snake Fist' style of the art, combines it with his own 'Cat Claw' style and manages to defeat the 'Eagle Claw' master who threatens the school (don't worry, you'll pick it up as you go along). Naff dubbing, but great in widescreen.

THE TIGERS 🎬 3

⭐ ANDY LAU, TONY LEUNG, MIU KI WAI

🎬 ERIC TSANG

HONG KONG (EASTERN HEROES) 1992

⏱ 110m (18)

Relatively serious actioner about current Hong Kong, strongly directed and with a powerful cast. If you find much of the HK stuff too frivolous, this may just be up your street. Subtitled and widescreen.

HORROR

The horror genre is a problematic one in the UK. Whatever your views on moral panics and censorship – and I'm agin 'em – the BBFC bans and demands cuts in many films, large numbers of which are horror movies freely available in Europe and the USA. Video firms are not bothered by this as they're not legally obliged to inform potential buyers that the product has been butchered – but they have been forced by the advent of specialist labels like Redemption and Pagan to rethink unadventurous releasing policies. For horror fans things can only improve! *'The Exorcist* can't stay banned forever. Can it?' I asked last time – and it's out now (see page 198).

THE ADDICTION

CHRISTOPHER WALKEN, ANNABELLA SCIORRA, LILI TAYLOR

ABEL FERRARA

USA (POLYGRAM) 1995 B&W

79m (18)

Grainy, gritty vampire story from cult director Ferrara, about a newly infected lady bloodsucker who is rampaging all over the city until a wise elder vamp (the fabulously ethereal Walken) tries to counsel her. The drug-problem parallels are obvious from the title. Quite shocking in places – as Hitchcock found in *Psycho*, blood can look even more upsetting in monochrome.

AN AMERICAN WEREWOLF IN LONDON

DAVID NAUGHTON, GRIFFIN DUNNE, JENNY AGUTTER

JOHN LANDIS

USA (ENTERTAINMENT) 1981

97m (18)

Comedy and horror are notoriously difficult to mix, but Landis hits just the right note from the opening scenes where two Yank backpackers stray into a pub full of nattering, threatening rural types and occult symbols. One boy is slaughtered by a werewolf, only to return from the dead (in increasingly decayed form) to urge his injured buddy to top himself before he too becomes a lycanthrope. So far, so funny – but the ensuing transformations (by Rick Baker) are grisly and convincing in equal measure, as are the monsters in a shock dream sequence. Scary and irreverent – do see it. Naff sequel: *An American Werewolf in Paris*.

HORROR

ANGEL HEART 🎬 3

ROBERT DE NIRO, MICKEY ROURKE, LISA BONET, CHARLOTTE RAMPLING

ALAN PARKER

USA (POLYGRAM) 1987

109m (18)

Rourke is great as a private detective stumbling into an occult conspiracy in Brit Parker's film of William Hjortsberg's novel *Falling Angel*, but as in the book the devilish clues are blindingly obvious to anyone with even a passing interest in black magic: for instance, De Niro's character is named Louis Ciphre – Lucifer, geddit? The print is slightly cut as there was a lot of huffing at the time of release over the sex scene between Bonet and Rourke.

ARACHNAPHOBIA 🎬 4

JEFF DANIELS, JULIAN SANDS, JOHN GOODMAN, HARLEY JANE KOZAK

FRANK MARSHALL

USA (TOUCHSTONE) 1990

105m (PG)

Playing on the widespread primal fear of spiders, this family-oriented scare ride features a virulent, hairy monster that comes to America from the tropics in the body of its victim, only to mate with the domestic article in the barn of arachnaphobe Daniels. Plenty of shrieks, and laughs are provided by bug-killer Goodman. Decent SFX.

THE AWFUL DOCTOR ORLOF 🎬 4

HOWARD VERNON, PERLA CRISTAL, CONRADO SAN MARTIN

JESS FRANCO

SPAIN (REDEMPTION) 1962 B&W

88m (15)

In the manner of Franju's *Les Yeux Sans Visage* (see *Eyes Without A Face*, page 199), Franco's sex 'n' surgery opus deals with a nutty doc intent on grafting stolen faces in place of that of his badly disfigured daughter. Orlof(f) became a pivotal figure in Franco's career as a director, and his *Faceless* and *Jack The Ripper* are virtual remakes (the latter nearly shot-for-shot) of this movie. Franco has undergone a critical re-evaluation of late; formerly seen as a hack with a zoom-lens fetish, he's now accepted as the master of Spanish weirdness and perversity, a man with a mania for film-making regardless of budgetary constraints. This is well made 'grue', boasting luminous black and white photography – it can hardly be chance that the great Orson Welles thought Franco good enough to shoot the acclaimed battle footage for his *Chimes At Midnight* and to take charge of the second unit on that picture. This is Jess at his best. Presented in the correct aspect ratio. Slightly cut.

BLOOD FOR DRACULA

UDO KIER, JOE DALLESANDRO, ROMAN POLANSKI

PAUL MORRISSEY

ITALY (FIRST INDEPENDENT) 1974

99m (18)

Mad, gory, sexy flick about Drac (Kier) leaving home in search of 'wirgins' to exsanguinate, but finding only whores (a houseful) whose blood makes him 'womit', he finally succumbs to the axe of priapic, commie, anti-aristo handyman Dallesandro in a climax which the censor has thankfully left intact. There has been much debate over who directed this and its companion piece *Flesh For Frankenstein* (they were made back-to-back), Morrissey or the man credited for tax reasons on Italian prints, Antonio Margheriti. The truth appears to be that the Italian (a fine horror/action director) helped with both films, less so on this one. This is hilarious and over-the-top, often billed as an Andy Warhol film – but in reality he did nothing. Morrissey made other Warhol movies, like *Heat* and *Trash*. (*Flesh For Frankenstein* is available, but in a cut version.)

BRAM STOKER'S COUNT DRACULA

CHRISTOPHER LEE, HERBERT LOM, KLAUS KINSKI, SOLEDAD MIRANDA

JESS FRANCO

SPAIN/ITALY/WEST GERMANY (4-FRONT) 1970

96m (12)

Not to be confused with Lee's Hammer classics (though a still from one appears on the cover) or Coppola's film with (almost) the same title. Cheaply shot but with a good showing by Lee as Dracula (growing gradually younger as in the novel), ably supported by a fine cast and some dodgy plastic bats. Cult director Franco could undoubtedly do better given a decent budget, but this rarely-seen version of the vampire tale is deserving of a look, especially on this budget-priced tape.

HORROR

BRAM STOKER'S DRACULA ★4

GARY OLDMAN, RICHARD E GRANT, WINONA RYDER, ANTHONY HOPKINS, KEANU REEVES, SADIE FROST

FRANCIS FORD COPPOLA

USA (COLUMBIA TRISTAR) 1992

130m (18)

Hailed as a big-budget version of the classic vampire tale, this was actually shot for a relatively modest amount compared to most Hollywood films, with director Coppola eschewing computer FX and returning to some of the oldest and simplest cinematic tricks in the book: for example, an entire battle is suggested using nothing more than red lights and a few shadows. In trying to recapture the sense of wonder engendered by such early versions as the silent German *Nosferatu*, Coppola drew giggles from some critics, who paradoxically found the camerawork so tricksy that they dubbed it a horror film for MTV pop video fans, but even if only partially successful it's a brave attempt. Gary Oldman makes a spooky Dracula in the early scenes, but as he grows younger as he feeds on blood he starts to look like Screaming Lord Sutch! The author's proprietorial credit in the title is supposed to imply that we are seeing the first movie completely faithful to the book – we're not, though it's a claim many makers of Drac flicks have made. Anyway: beautiful to look at, especially in the widescreen version.

THE BROOD ★4

SAMANTHA EGGAR, OLIVER REED, ART HINDLE

DAVID CRONENBERG

CANADA (ARROW) 1979

91m (18)

More thought-provoking sick images from Cronenberg: oddball doctor Reed treats Eggar with his therapy, urging her to give shape to her inner rage. Soon she's developing womb-like sacs outside her body – her husband isn't amused, but we are. Wonder what's in there? Yuk. Fab. Not for pregnant female viewers.

CEMETERY MAN 4

RUPERT EVERETT, ANNA FALCHI, FRANCOIS HADJI-LAZARO

MICHELE SOAVI

ITALY (ENTERTAINMENT) 1993

99m (18)

Lambasted and lauded in equal measure, Soavi's adaptation of the novel *Dellamorte Dellamore* (the film's Italian title) and the comic it inspired, *Dylan Dog*, is about a reclusive graveyard keeper troubled by lively corpses, a slobby assistant who keeps the talking severed head of his lady love in his room, and the problem that every girl he fancies looks the same. The story veers from macabre to madcap and back rather alarmingly, the rug being constantly yanked from under our feet as we're bombarded by some of the densest, most lovely imagery ever seen in a horror movie. Admired and loathed by opposing fan bases, it ends with a Wellesian flourish. A remarkable piece of cinema. Note: Everett got the title part because the face of the comic character is based on his own. (And Martin Scorsese apparently hailed it as the best film of 1993!) Sadly, Soavi has said he is quitting film to care for his sick child – a sad loss to cinema.

THE CHURCH 5

HUGH QUARSHIE, TOMAS ARANA, BARBARA CUPISTI, ASIA ARGENTO

MICHELE SOAVI

ITALY (FIRST INDEPENDENT/ REFLECTIVE) 1989

98m (18)

Soavi's second film after the slasher *Stagefright* is a visually overloaded gothic jaunt about evil from the past taking over in a sealed cathedral, and is full of historical allusions to the likes of the Knights Templar and Fulcanelli. Allegedly planned as just another in the *Demons* series – which also involve monsters in locked buildings – but Soavi expands the idea from a tired sequel to an epic that should satisfy those who look for mystery and intelligence in horror as well as gorehounds after more visceral thrills. Despite packaging which suggests producer Dario Argento is the director, Soavi stands on his own as a unique talent for those who thought Italian horror was kaput. Slightly letterboxed, though this is not noted on the box.

CRONOS [4]

FEDERICO LUPPI, CLAUDIO BROOK, RON PERLMAN

GUILLERMO DEL TORO

MEXICO (TARTAN) 1992

91m (18)

Nifty debut from the Mexican director, about an old antique dealer who finds an odd occult device which grants eternal youth – at a price. While coming to terms with the fact that he's a vampire (the scene of him lapping the residue of someone's nosebleed off the floor in a men's room is not for the squeamish) he has also to contend with the brutal son of a fading millionaire who is desperate to get his hands on the clockwork nasty. The eagle-eyed cineastes among you may detect references to other classic horror films, but that doesn't detract from the pleasure to be had from being in the hands of a genuine talent. He's now made a big American film, *Mimic* (see page 269).

THE CROW [3]

BRANDON LEE, ERNIE HUDSON, ANGEL DAVID, DAVID PATRICK KELLY

ALEX PROYAS

USA (EIV) 1994

113m (18)

Zombie rocker comes back from the grave a year after his Hallowe'en demise to tackle those who did the deed and raped and murdered his girl. Dark and weird, with cult status boosted by the eerily tragic death during filming of starring actor Lee in a gun accident on set. He was the son of the late Bruce Lee, who also died young and who believed his whole family was doomed to be stalked by a demonic entity.

CURSE OF THE DEMON [5]

DANA ANDREWS, PEGGY CUMMINS, NIALL MacGINNIS, ATHENE SEYLER

JACQUES TOURNEUR

UK (ENCORE) 1957 B&W

91m (12)

It's a mystery why the ghost stories of MR James have not been used in more movies – perhaps they're just too subtle to translate into a hit. Which brings us to critical debate over this film, based on MRJ's *Casting The Runes*, about an Aleister Crowley-type, black-tinged cult leader who disposes of his enemies by passing them, by trickery, runic curses which summon a denizen of hell to rend them in pieces. Since the film version centres on a sceptic (Andrews) gradually being convinced that he truly is in supernatural danger, many feel that it was a mistake to let us actually see the demon. I don't agree; however, the monster's inclusion in the first death scene *was* a mistake. If it had been cut, we would, like Andrews, be close to the finale before we were sure of what was going on. The cast is superb, notably MacGinnis as the evil magus, Julian Karswell, and Athene Seyler as his doting mother. This print bears the title of the shortened USA release (the longest version was issued in Britain as *Night Of The Demon*) but it has been taken from a complete master tape of the full-length version.

DAUGHTERS OF DARKNESS [4]

DELPHINE SEYRIG, JOHN KARLEN, DANIELE OUIMET

HARRY KUMEL

BELGIUM (TARTAN) 1971

97m (18)

Disturbing and sensuous arthouse horror from cult hero Kumel. In an off-season seaside hotel, two slinky lesbian babes (supposedly the undead Countess Bathory, historical blood-drinker who has inspired several movies, and her amour) seduce a young couple into kinky games – much talk of red-hot pokers and so forth. You just know it'll all end in tears, don't you? Seyrig is icily sexy, while the young hubby (Karlen) is the actor who went on to become Harvey the husband in TV's girlcop show *Cagney and Lacey*. If you're hung up on chainsaws and such, this may be a bit slow for you, but the vivid colours of the interiors contrast startlingly with the muted outdoor sequences to make cinema that glows like an accursed jewel.

HORROR

DEMENTIA 13

WILLIAM CAMPBELL, LUANA ANDERS, PATRICK MAGEE, BART PATTON

FRANCIS FORD COPPOLA

USA (SCREEN MULTIMEDIA) 1963 B&W

75m (15)

This is the full version of future *Godfather* helmsman Coppola's atmospheric cheapie, shot for producer Roger Corman (who has helped many get a foot in the door, including Martin Scorsese and Jack Nicholson) on the trip to Europe that spawned Corman's *The Young Racers*. Axe-pocalypse naff? No, just lots of hatchet killings, family secrets and spooky locations. It's the sort of thing they don't do these days, the sort that was very popular in the wake of Hitchcock's *Psycho*. With the great Magee in ham mode, Coppola makes the most of the tiny budget – check out the startling shot of a radio burbling to the bottom of a corpse-filled lake. The only thing missing here is the short intro by psychiatrist Dr William J Bryan Jnr (shot by Monte Hellman) which was shown on some American prints. Released to UK cinemas in heavily cut form as *The Haunted And The Hunted*.

DEMONS

NATASHA HOVEY, FIORE ARGENTO, URBANO BARBERINI

LAMBERTO BAVA

ITALY (SPEARHEAD) 1985

93m (18)

Directed by the son of the late, great Mario Bava (who has not inherited his pop's genius) and produced by Dario Argento, this concerns a bunch of nerds locked in a cinema while watching a movie on prophet-of-doom Nostradamus. Suddenly, audience members turn into nasties of the title and decimate the rest. Illogical, gory and quite scary. Sequel: *Demons 2*. (See review of *The Church*, page 192.)

THE DEVIL RIDES OUT

CHRISTOPHER LEE, PATRICK MOWER, CHARLES GRAY, NIKE ARRIGHI, LEON GREENE, SARAH LAWSON, PAUL EDDINGTON, GWEN FFRANGCON-DAVIES

TERENCE FISHER

UK (WARNER) 1967

95m (15)

Highly regarded cult (in all senses) movie about Satanists, scripted by Richard Matheson from Dennis Wheatley's novel. Boasts tension, a palpable sense of evil and a cast that never send the material up. One of Terence Fisher's best for Hammer, let down only by some poor FX work at the end. Greene's voice was dubbed by Patrick Allen.

DON'T LOOK NOW 🎬 4

⭐ JULIE CHRISTIE, DONALD SUTHERLAND, HILARY MASON, CELIA MATANIA

🎬 NICOLAS ROEG

UK (WARNER) 1973

⏱ 105m (18)

Short story by Daphne du Maurier inspires this creepy film about an architect who thinks he sees visions of his dead child while on a trip to Venice, with horrific results. One of Roeg's better efforts, made before his weird and dislocated style got too garbled for its own good. Contains a controversial sex scene, in which Christie and Sutherland were rumoured to be having intercourse for real.

DRACULA 🎬 5

⭐ CHRISTOPHER LEE, PETER CUSHING, MELISSA STRIBLING, MICHAEL GOUGH

🎬 TERENCE FISHER

UK (WARNER/TERRORVISION) 1958

⏱ 78m (15)

This is the first time Hammer's classic version of the famed vampire story has been available on tape in Britain. Lee makes a dashing, romantic Dracula, seducing his female victims through the sheer physicality of his presence, with Cushing as his implacably decent adversary Van Helsing. This, the first colour version, draws parallels between vampirism and drug addiction in the same way that more recent vampire films – such as Abel Ferrara's *The Addiction* (see page 188) – have done. A landmark in the horror genre. Note: this is actually the USA print (on-screen title *Horror Of Dracula*) and – in spite of the reduced running time due to the faster PAL projection speed – is longer by a few fleeting seconds of gore cut by the BBFC back in 1958. It does not, however, have the uncut version of Lee's final disintegration, which is extant only in some obscure foreign-language prints. Oscar nomination for Jack Asher's colour photography.

DRACULA 🎬 3

⭐ BELA LUGOSI, HELEN CHANDLER, EDWARD VAN SLOAN, DWIGHT FRYE, DAVID MANNERS

🎬 TOD BROWNING

USA (CIC) 1931 B&W

⏱ 75m (PG)

This first sound version of the vampire story is dated and theatrical, though Lugosi's performance and a certain weird atmosphere carry it off. This remastered version restores some censored sound effects and presents the full image, which was slightly cropped years ago when the sound (originally on discs) was added to prints which had to have the track printed on to the film stock. It's a pity that the far superior Spanish-language version, shot on the same sets at night with a different cast and crew and recently restored in the USA, is still not available here.

HORROR

DRACULA – PRINCE OF DARKNESS [4]

CHRISTOPHER LEE, BARBARA SHELLEY, ANDREW KEIR, FRANCIS MATTHEWS

TERENCE FISHER

UK (LUMIERE) 1965

87m (15)

For me, Chris Lee is the best screen Count ever, though his Hammer outings in the role diminished in quality (through no fault of his own) as they went along. Once again directed by the elegant yet robust Terence Fisher, the film-maker with the most coherent career in the genre, it has a simple yet effective plot about some silly-ass English tourists who ignore warnings and become fang-fodder for the Count's resurrection. Lee is mute, as though his bloody rejuvenation has left him in spectral form, but Barbara Shelley is outstanding as a stuffy matron transformed by Drac's bite into a bisexual babe. Sadly, this is a cut print. Original trailer included. Widescreen and pan-scan versions.

THE DRILLER KILLER [3]

JIMMY LAINE, CAROLYN MARZ, HARRY SCHULTZ

ABEL FERRARA

USA (VISUAL) 1979

75m (18)

Director Ferrara stars under the Laine pseudonym in this previously banned debut flick. It would seem that he added the gore context in an attempt to sell the thing – actually, it's an interesting little low-budget movie about an artist driven mad by failure, his girl leaving him and a rock band's rehearsals keeping him awake. That he chooses a power-drill as his method of protest seems almost incidental. Slightly cut by BBFC.

THE EVIL DEAD

BRUCE CAMPBELL, ELLEN SANDWEISS, BETSY BAKER

SAM RAIMI

USA (4-FRONT) 1982

86m (18)

Acclaimed but controversial gorefest which got caught up in the moral panic which led to the Video Recordings Act – the result was that the version available had to have numerous small cuts made in order that the BBFC could legally pass it. It's a mix of gore and frantic excess that has more in common with Raimi's beloved *Three Stooges* than with most horror pix – crazy kids in a cabin accidentally evoke demons and – whooooaaarggh! – that's it. Many directors launch a career on the back of a cheap horror film, but Raimi's only subsequent hits have been the other two 'Evil Dead' films – and the first of those wasn't even a sequel, just a bigger budget revision! Most mainstream critics didn't even notice. See the book *Seduction of the Gullible* by John Martin (Procrustes Press) for the VRA story. Raimi now produces the tackily fun *Xena* and *Hercules* TV shows. *The Evil Dead* is available in a boxed set with its two sequels which are also sold separately on the 4-Front label. The third film *(Army Of Darkness – The Medieval Dead)* is presented with two different endings.

THE EXORCIST

MAX VON SYDOW, LINDA BLAIR, ELLEN BURSTYN, LEE J COBB, JASON MILLER, JACK MacGOWRAN

WILLIAM FRIEDKIN

USA (WARNER) 1973

117m (18)

The departure of the dictatorial James Ferman has at last allowed the BBFC to pass some films against which he seemed to have a personal bias, *The Exorcist* being the first beneficiary. In truth, this tale of the demonic possession of a young girl is neither as scary nor as great a film as the video ban has made it out to be, though the myth has led numerous Brits to check it out on frequent big-screen showings or to pick up tape copies when on holiday in Euroland. William Peter Blatty's story (very loosely based on real events) is handled in a rather pedestrian manner by the director, but though the head-swivelling and pea-soup spewing FX have been superseded by today's computer morphing, the movie still has a harrowing, in-yer-face power that can't be denied. Huge (and hugely expensive) 25th anniversary box available, with extra material and a widescreen transfer.

HORROR

EYES WITHOUT A FACE

PIERRE BRASSEUR, ALIDA VALLI, EDITH SCOB

GEORGES FRANJU

FRANCE (CONNOISSEUR) 1959 B&W

87m (18)

Arthouse maverick Franju provoked outrage with this tale of a mad surgeon abducting girls in order to graft their skin on to his daughter's face, disfigured in a car crash caused by him. Like Michael Powell's career-derailing *Peeping Tom* (see page 211) and Terence Fisher's *The Curse Of Frankenstein*, the film outlived and outlasted its critics and retains its power and poetry. Stunningly lensed by Eugen Shuftan, the movie influenced a whole surgical-horror genre including films like *Corruption* and Jess Franco's *Faceless* and *The Awful Dr Orlof* (see page 189). French title: *Les Yeux Sans Visage*. This is the first time the full version has been available in the UK. Subtitled and correct aspect ratio.

THE FEARLESS VAMPIRE KILLERS

SHARON TATE, ROMAN POLANSKI, FERDY MAYNE, JACK MacGOWRAN

ROMAN POLANSKI

UK (WARNER/TERRORVISION) 1967

107m (18)

Polanski's wry tribute to Hammer is here presented in the long version and in widescreen. It has a genuine beauty amid the slapstick and gags about gay vampires, only slightly diminished on the TV screen. Original title: *Dance Of The Vampires*. Fantastic score by Krzysztof Komeda. A recent copy I ran, labelled 'remastered', was appallingly dark in places.

FEMALE VAMPIRE [4]

LINA ROMAY, ALICE ARNO, JACK TAYLOR

JESS FRANCO

FRANCE (REDEMPTION) 1973

94m (18)

With a director like Franco, who recycles footage and issues his films with titles and versions which vary from territory to territory to take account of censorship problems and ethnic preferences, it's hard to speak of a definitive print. This picture has been seen as *Erotikill, The Bare Breasted Countess, La Comtesse Noire*, etc., etc., some versions accenting horror while others insert hard-core sex shots. This seems to be the longest cut, though unsurprisingly it has been shorn of some six minutes of sex and sado-masochism by the BBFC. Franco's partner and muse Romay (who named herself after the singer of the same name from way back) appears as a nude vampire who sucks her lovers to death. And you can read that any way you wish. Falling in love with one victim, she elects to drown in a bath of blood. Much hypnotic wandering and soft-core fondling in this lovely widescreen print. I like it, but then I'm a weirdo.

THE FOG [3]

ADRIENNE BARBEAU, HAL HOLBROOK, JANET LEIGH, JAMIE LEE CURTIS

JOHN CARPENTER

USA (4-FRONT) 1979

86m (15)

One of Carpenter's lesser scare-jobs, but offers some ghostly shivers for all that. Spectres of old seadogs take revenge on a town where the people lured their ship to a rocky doom a century before. Much more whimsical and less shocking than the same director's classic *Halloween* (see page 203).

HORROR

FRANKENSTEIN 5

BORIS KARLOFF, COLIN CLIVE, MAE CLARKE, EDWARD VAN SLOAN, DWIGHT FRYE

JAMES WHALE

USA (CIC) 1931 B&W

71m (PG)

The classic first sound version of Mary Shelley's novel of a man who makes a monster from graveyard detritus and electricity has never been surpassed, and is at last available on video once more – this time in a digitally remastered print with a restoration of most of the censored snippets, most importantly the usually truncated scene where the creature (Karloff) kills a child by drowning her, albeit through ignorance rather than malice. Karloff's mute performance is deeply moving as well as scary, but the shock power of the film is obviously diminished in the light of the gorier efforts of today. Although made in the USA, the director and stars are (almost) all British.

FRANKENSTEIN MUST BE DESTROYED 5

PETER CUSHING, VERONICA CARLSON, SIMON WARD, FREDDIE JONES

TERENCE FISHER

UK (WARNER/TERRORVISION) 1969

97m (18)

As with Dracula, I've chosen not to fill these pages with numerous films based on Frankenstein; I must, however, include some from Terence Fisher's wonderful series for Hammer. And why not? Peter Cushing was a better Baron than Colin Clive, and the chosen film illustrates the way the character deepened as the series went on (a characteristic that is maintained even in a film not helmed by Fisher, Freddie Francis's *Evil Of Frankenstein*). *Frankenstein Must Be Destroyed* has a tragic tone, with Freddie Jones excellent as a man who finds his brain in a body his wife fails to see as 'him'. Ignoring Jimmy Sangster's ribald remake of *The Curse of Frankenstein* (the first in the series, which he wrote and which is also out on video at long last as *Horror Of Frankenstein*), Fisher brought the epic to a dark close in 1973's *Frankenstein And The Monster From Hell*, his last, underrated film.

FREAKS 🎬4

⭐ HARRY EARLES, OLGA BACLANOVA, WALLACE FORD

🎬 TOD BROWNING

USA (VISIONARY) 1932 B&W

⏱ 64m   (15)

This pic outraged MGM when they saw it – they disowned it and director Browning was toppled from the big time, the film being cut, retitled and sold cheap to sideshow exploitation operators. Unseen for years, it is now perhaps a tad overrated. Still, Browning knew the carnie world, and the compassionate yet unsentimental use of real freaks in a tale where they take horrible revenge on a woman who marries one of them for his money is a brave move that results in an honest film.

FROM DUSK TILL DAWN 🎬3

⭐ GEORGE CLOONEY, QUENTIN TARANTINO, HARVEY KEITEL, JULIETTE LEWIS

🎬 ROBERT RODRIGUEZ

USA (BUENA VISTA) 1996

⏱ 104m

Hotshot Tarantino dusts off one of his early efforts at scriptwriting to star with heart-throb George (*ER*) Clooney in this madcap story, which is like two different films cobbled together. First half is a heist tale, as two robber brothers kidnap a widowed preacher and his kids and force them to drive to Mexico. Once there we veer into horror as the group are trapped by vampires in a sleazy bar. Good SFX. Available in widescreen. A documentary, *Full Tilt Boogie*, has been made about the film's production. There's also a low-budget sequel.

THE FURY 🎬4

⭐ KIRK DOUGLAS, AMY IRVING, FIONA LEWIS, JOHN CASSAVETES, CARRIE SNODGRESS, DARYL HANNAH

🎬 BRIAN DE PALMA

USA (FOX) 1978

⏱ 113m   (18)

Semi-forgotten De Palma classic about a secret agent (Douglas) who has to call upon all his skills when his son, who has telekinetic powers, is kidnapped for shady experiments. Wildly gory for the time, especially a great 'exploding head' sequence which drew gasps from the audience when I was fortunate enough to attend a preview introduced by De Palma at the time of its first release. Best on a big screen, but survives on video rather well. Script by John Farris from his novel.

GOTHIC

GABRIEL BYRNE, JULIAN SANDS, NATASHA RICHARDSON, TIMOTHY SPALL

KEN RUSSELL

UK (VISION) 1986

83m (18)

Typically frantic and gleefully excessive visual feast from Ken Russell about the night in nineteenth-century Switzerland when debauched, druggy Byron, his doctor/opium supplier and Mr and Ms Shelley had a spook-story session which inspired Dr Polidori's tale *The Vampyre* and started Mary Shelley off on *Frankenstein*. Narrative flow is sacrificed to imagery which, to be fair, is often rooted in fact: for example, anti-Russellites may go spare at the sight of a woman with eyes in her nipples, but this is based on a hallucination which Shelley experienced and thoughtfully described for posterity. The four stars have gone on to bigger things. Oddly enough, two other versions of the same story were made almost simultaneously: *Haunted Summer* and *Rowing Against The Wind*.

HALLOWEEN

JAMIE LEE CURTIS, DONALD PLEASENCE, PJ SOLES

JOHN CARPENTER

USA (MIA) 1978

91m (18)

So much better than the slasher flix it inspired – and we can at last see why, as *Halloween* is made available in this full widescreen print. Carpenter is a master of the Panavision frame, painting with light and inky darkness to make the viewer jump out of his/her skin. The story is nothing: a young child commits bloody murder, grows more evil in captivity, then flees the asylum to menace babysitter Curtis. Pleasence is the shrink in hot pursuit. Works best on a big screen, but this print is the next best option. There are sequels, the best being the latest, *Halloween: H2O* (see below).

HALLOWEEN H2O

JAMIE LEE CURTIS, ADAM ARKIN, MICHELLE WILLIAMS, JANET LEIGH

STEVE MINER

USA (HOLLYWOOD) 1998

83m (18)

With the return of original star Curtis, one would expect this entry in the series to be at least slightly better than the previous string of sequels, and it is. Slightly. It's still just another slice 'n' dicer, however. Set 20 years after the first pic, it reveals that Laurie (Curtis) is actually the sister of her nemesis, and there's a guest role for her mom, Janet Leigh, replete with crass allusions to her own slasher classic *Psycho* (see page 212).

THE HAUNTING 5

	JULIE HARRIS, CLAIRE BLOOM, RICHARD JOHNSON, RUSS TAMBLYN
	ROBERT WISE
	UK (WARNER/TERRORVISION) 1963 B&W
	112m (12)

Parapsychologists check out a haunted house in Wise's adaptation of a literary ghost story by Shirley Jackson, though the film seems less concerned with revenants than the kinks of the living members of the company. As at least one critic has noted, the flick seems to suggest that Bloom's lesbianism is as monstrous as any ghost – still, the actors are fine and it's a fabulous late-night, lights-out chiller. Widescreen print. Remade in 1999 with Catherine Zeta-Jones.

HELLRAISER 3

	ANDREW ROBINSON, CLAIRE HIGGINS, ASHLEY LAURENCE
	CLIVE BARKER
	UK (CINEMA CLUB) 1987
	93m (18)

Writer/director Barker spins a neat yarn about a man who solves an occult version of Rubik's Cube, unleashing S&M-obsessed demons who torture him down to his bare bones. To revive he needs blood – and who better to get it for him than the sister-in-law he was having an affair with before things went pear-shaped. At one time Barker was thought to be the future of both horror fiction and films, but now he pens fat fantasy epics, has adopted a mid-Atlantic accent and spends his time developing movie projects that are supposed to be 'the next big thing' but which invariably flop (though the recent *Gods And Monsters*, on which he was one of the executive producers, won an Oscar). This one still packs a punch, but the body-piercing imagery has become rather *passé* over the last decade and has lost the ability to shock. Avoid the sequels: the first changes the location of the house in the story from the UK to the USA with no explanation at all. The critics didn't notice, or care.

THE HITCHER 4

	RUTGER HAUER, JENNIFER JASON LEIGH, C THOMAS HOWELL, BILL GREEN BUSH
	ROBERT HARMON
	USA (WARNER/TERRORVISION) 1986
	97m (18)

Cat-and-mouse game between a murderous drifter of seemingly supernatural abilities and the hapless boy who gives him a ride only to be blamed for his crimes. Requires massive suspension of disbelief, but it's an extremely scary and competently made horror romp with a better-than-average cast. Available in widescreen.

HORROR

THE HOWLING 🎬4

DEE WALLACE, PATRICK MacNEE, ELISABETH BROOKS, JOHN CARRADINE

JOE DANTE

USA (ENTERTAINMENT) 1980

90m (18)

If *An American Werewolf in London* (see page 188) wasn't enough, here's an equally wild comedy lycanthrope film for you. Scripted by arthouse man John Sayles, it mixed outstanding effects by Rob Bottin with a plot about a therapy retreat where our furry friends are rehabilitated for return to society. Characters are named after famous horror directors. Dante is a Roger Corman-protégé who went on to greater things, but this remains one of his best efforts. Avoid the sequels like the plague.

THE HUNGER 🎬3

SUSAN SARANDON, CATHERINE DENEUVE, DAVID BOWIE, CLIFF DE YOUNG

TONY SCOTT

USA (WARNER) 1983

92m (18)

Female vampire takes mates for centuries at a time – but the gift of extended youth she brings is not quite eternal, so she has to keep previous crumbling lovers suffering in coffins in the attic! Gory horror from the brother of director Ridley Scott, based on Whitley Streiber's novel. Available in widescreen.

INFERNO 🎬4

LEIGH McCLOSKEY, DARIA NICOLODI, ALIDA VALLI

DARIO ARGENTO

ITALY (FOX/WORLD) 1980

107m (18)

In spite of serious critical acclaim, Argento's films are still mainly available here in cut, censored, cropped, dubbed forms – and that's if they're released at all. *Inferno* follows *Suspiria* (see page 215) as the second part of the not-yet-complete 'Three Mothers' trilogy, and though slightly less amazing than its predecessor, it still weaves a distinctly strange vision of occultism and violence in Manhattan. This print does not appear to be in full widescreen, and the BBFC have been at work with the scissors again.

INTERVIEW WITH THE VAMPIRE

TOM CRUISE, BRAD PITT, CHRISTIAN SLATER, ANTONIO BANDERAS

NEIL JORDAN

USA (WARNER) 1994

117m (18)

Though the hugely popular sequels stink, Anne Rice's original source novel of a sad vampire telling all is the best bloodsucker yarn since *Dracula* – and she was wary of Tom Cruise playing her evil, manipulative anti-hero Lestat when a film version finally got the green light. She changed her mind after seeing the movie, and though this is a rather cold, empty spectacular, it is a cut above most of the other un-scary big studio horrors, and fairly faithful to the book.

THE ISLAND OF DR MOREAU

MARLON BRANDO, VAL KILMER, DAVID THEWLIS, FAIRUZA BALK

JOHN FRANKENHEIMER

USA (ENTERTAINMENT) 1996

91m (12)

This troubled version of the HG Wells tale of human/beast vivisection (director Richard Stanley was fired, but sneaked back on set as an extra!) was panned on film release, but it's a guilty pleasure to behold. Thewlis is washed-up on the mad doc's isle, where he meets Brando (sporting false gnashers that make him look like John Betjeman) and chum Kilmer. Rubbish – but absurdly fine, mad rubbish. Available in widescreen. (See also *Island Of Lost Souls*, below).

ISLAND OF LOST SOULS

CHARLES LAUGHTON, RICHARD ARLEN, BELA LUGOSI, KATHLEEN BURKE

ERLE C KENTON

USA (VISIONARY) 1932 B&W

72m (12)

Forget the more recent two versions of HG Wells' *Island Of Dr Moreau*, for in spite of the great man's dislike this is the definitive movie interpretation of the tale of the mad scientist who grafts human and animal flesh in his 'House of Pain'. Despite a great performance from Brit Laughton in the main role of the nut who wants to mate Arlen with panther woman Burke, the pic was banned in UK until 1958. Apart from the 1977 and 1997 versions, the Aurum Film Encyclopedia states that the story also inspired films in 1913 and 1959. (See how daft censorship is – banned for 26 years, yet this film is now considered okay for 12-year-olds!)

LA VAMPIRE NUE 🎬5

⭐ OLIVER MARTIN, MAURICE LEMAITRE, CAROLINE CARTIER

🎬 JEAN ROLLIN

FRANCE (REDEMPTION) 1969

⏱ 82m (18)

For years we could only read about Rollin's surreal vampire films – now, thanks to the efforts of Redemption (and writers Cathal Tohill and Pete Tombs, who ran a season at the NFT), we can see them. This is just one of several titles issued lately, a bizarre, fetishistic effort in the manner of a comic or an old serial. And yet it's very French, which makes it sad that his homeland – which has done so much for neglected filmmakers – still refuses to salute Rollin's genius.

THE LOST BOYS 🎬3

⭐ KIEFER SUTHERLAND, JASON PATRIC, DIANNE WIEST, COREY HAIM

🎬 JOEL SCHUMACHER

USA (WARNER/TERRORVISION) 1987

⏱ 97m (15)

This rather lame attempt at a modern rock 'n' roll/comic vampire fantasy for teens has inexplicably become something of a cult film. A woman and her kids move to a small Californian town only to find it infested by bloodsucking yobs battling it out with local lads who are in-the-know because they've perused the horror section in the comix store they run. Sporadic bursts of fun. Available in a widescreen special edition.

MANIAC COP 🎬3

⭐ TOM ATKINS, BRUCE CAMPBELL, SHEREE NORTH, RICHARD ROUNDTREE

🎬 WILLIAM LUSTIG

USA (POLYGRAM) 1988

⏱ 81m (18)

Jokey slash-'em-up about a monstrous vigilante policeman is quite a neat little effort from cult horror director Lustig, and inspired a series of sequels which don't match up to the original. Also available, at least for a time, on a two-for-one tape with *Maniac Cop 2*.

MARY SHELLEY'S FRANKENSTEIN

ROBERT DE NIRO, KENNETH BRANAGH, TOM HULCE, HELENA BONHAM CARTER, IAN HOLM, JOHN CLEESE, AIDAN QUINN

KENNETH BRANAGH

USA/UK (COLUMBIA TRISTAR) 1994

123m   (15)

The author's name in the title marks this as an attempt to replicate the success of the studio's *Bram Stoker's Dracula* (see page 191), but this is a less successful enterprise altogether. Critics ignorant of the genre praised the scenes set in icy wastes as being both innovative and uniquely true to the book – but this aspect, and the 'birthing' of the monster, cannot be said to be any different (or indeed any better) than amazingly similar material in a TV version of the story starring Randy Quaid which was made shortly before Branagh's film. Horror (even with a literary pedigree) is meant to be nasty, upsetting and transgressive, and big studios trying to make 'respectable' horrors will inevitably fail, because the one thing horror should never be is respectable. De Niro is awful as the creature, and the make-up isn't a patch on the old classic look Jack Pierce did on Boris Karloff. Any of Karloff's performances as the Frankenstein monster beat this hands down, so simply forget about horror and enjoy the picturesque bits! Widescreen available.

MASK OF SATAN

BARBARA STEELE, JOHN RICHARDSON, IVO GARRANI, ANDREA CECCHI

MARIO BAVA

ITALY (REDEMPTION) 1960 B&W

84m   (15)

Issued under many names, this Bava masterpiece (better known as *Black Sunday*) was banned in the UK for some years for being too horrific – but it's actually an atmospheric, ghostly story that started the career of Steele as a horror icon and is rightly regarded as a classic today. It's a tale of an evil witch who comes back from the dead after she and her man have had spiked masks hammered on to their faces – wow! This print is in the correct ratio and has the original music plus the few moments of graphic gore which were removed for US audiences.

HORROR

MR SARDONICUS 🎬4

⭐ OSCAR HOMOLKA, RONALD LEWIS, AUDREY DALTON, GUY ROLFE

🎬 WILLIAM CASTLE

USA (ENCORE) 1961 B&W

⏱ 87m (12)

Gimmick-master Castle is in his element with this version of Ray Russell's story about a surgeon summoned to a scary castle by his ex-girlfriend, now married to a cruel noble who threatens dire vengeance on both if the doc can't cure his frozen grimace caused by – well, see it for yourselves! This print happily retains the cinematic pause where the audience is asked to vote on a happy or sad ending for the beastly Baron – but don't fret, there only ever was the one climax and the baddy gets his come-uppance. Great fun.

MYSTERY OF THE WAX MUSEUM 🎬4

⭐ LIONEL ATWILL, FAY WRAY, GLENDA FARRELL

🎬 MICHAEL CURTIZ

USA (VISIONARY) 1933

⏱ 78m (PG)

Early, lovingly restored, two-strip Technicolor horror from the team that made *Doctor X* in the same process. Atwill is great and the colour is eerily rich given its technical limitations. Only the typical period humour jars. Remade as *House Of Wax* in 1953.

NEAR DARK 🎬4

⭐ ADRIAN PASDAR, JENNY WRIGHT, LANCE HENRIKSEN, BILL PAXTON

🎬 KATHRYN BIGELOW

USA (ENTERTAINMENT) 1987

⏱ 94m (18)

New slant on the vampire myth sees them as a sort of addict-breed, roving the land rather like an unwashed sub-species of the Manson Family. A lad is bitten by the befanged gal he lusts after, and the film gets to explore the moral dilemma of a new vampire reluctant to kill but having to in order to survive – nearly a decade before *Interview With The Vampire* (see page 206), too. No Tom Cruise in this one, okay? Worth seeing. Cut by the BBFC.

NIGHT OF THE LIVING DEAD

DUANE JONES, JUDITH O'DEA, KARL HARDMAN

GEORGE A ROMERO

USA (TARTAN) 1968 B&W

96m (18)

Radical reworking of zombie lore as the dead suddenly come to life for no known reason and attack the living, and we follow a group of survivors holed up in a house under siege. This unbelievably nihilistic pic shocks right up to the final moment, and was the first breakthrough 'indie' horror. It inspired other young directors to take a chance on low-budget shockers. Romero made two interesting sequels, *Dawn Of The Dead* and *Day Of The Dead*, which may be more gory and fun but will never be as historically important. There have been offshoots, like the *Return Of The Living Dead* films, and clever Italian rip-offs, while the original has been colourised and even re-made. But after years of fuzzy prints we now have a video release from the new materials used for the recent pristine USA laserdisc release. Enjoy. If that's the right word.

NOSFERATU THE VAMPYRE

KLAUS KINSKI, BRUNO GANZ, ISABELLE ADJANI, ROLAND TOPOR

WERNER HERZOG

WEST GERMANY (FOX) 1979

107m (15)

Arty genius Herzog's remake of Murnau's silent classic was shot in English and German versions. The Anglo print was deemed too naff to release to cinemas – so why is that the only version on tape? Hypnotic moments, but the subtitled print is much superior.

HORROR

PEEPING TOM 🎬5

⭐ CARL BOEHM, ANNA MASSEY, MOIRA SHEARER, SHIRLEY ANNE FIELD

🎬 MICHAEL POWELL

UK (WARNER/TERRORVISION) 1960

⏱ 97m (18)

The film that virtually destroyed the revered Powell's career. A horror pic from the company that released stuff like *Horrors Of The Black Museum* and *Circus Of Horrors* in tatty, lurid colour was not what the critics wanted from the director of *The Red Shoes*. Thanks to the efforts of Martin Scorsese and others, this is now seen as a brilliant work by a master craftsman. The story of a young focus-puller who, frightened and then filmed by his mad doctor dad, goes on to impale women on a sharpened tripod as he lenses their agony. Scoptophilia (the morbid desire to watch) didn't make for big box office in 1960 – Powell was snubbed and Boehm (aka Karl Bohm) wasn't seen again much until Fassbinder cast him years later in *Fox*. Wrongly stated in film references to be 109m, this is (allowing for the faster PAL speed) the full version. Atone for our fathers' sins and see it.

POLTERGEIST 🎬3

⭐ JO BETH WILLIAMS, CRAIG T NELSON, ZELDA RUBINSTEIN

🎬 TOBE HOOPER

USA (WARNER) 1982

⏱ 114m (15)

Producer Spielberg (that's Steve to you) is given (by some) as much credit for this gory, ghostly story of spooks and a missing child as nominal director Hooper, one critic condemning it as a 'Walt Disney horror movie'. Well, you will not be able to compare it with ol' Tobe's best work – because that's *The Texas Chainsaw Massacre* and we in the UK are not considered mature enough to see that by the powers-that-BBFC. It's certainly better than most of either man's recent stuff. Forget the sequels, though.

PSYCHO [5]

ANTHONY PERKINS, JANET LEIGH, VERA MILES, MARTIN BALSAM

ALFRED HITCHCOCK

USA (CIC) 1960 B&W

109m (15)

Shot low-budget with the crew of his TV show, Hitch's film of Robert Bloch's novel had a unique twist – you follow this gal who has nicked some money, she's played by a big star. Then, suddenly, the carpet is whisked away and the tale takes a left turn! It hadn't been done before and it still works a treat if you don't know the film. Sick, black comedy and genius film-making. Bloch's novel was inspired by the real-life killer, Ed Gein, who was also the basis for films like *The Texas Chainsaw Massacre* and *Deranged*. A restored, widescreen edition of *Psycho* (with extras including the shower scene *sans* Bernard Herrmann's great music) has been released on DVD. Remake by Gus Van Sant (see below).

PSYCHO [3]

VINCE VAUGHN, ANNE HECHE, JULIANNE MOORE, VIGGO MORTENSEN

GUS VAN SANT

USA (UNIVERSAL) 1998

99m (15)

This is almost a shot-for-shot remake of the classic Hitchcock thriller, but it's still a slick presentation and worth a look – whether you want to compare it with the original or just enjoy being scared.

RABID [4]

MARILYN CHAMBERS, FRANK MOORE, JOE SILVER, SUSAN ROMAN

DAVID CRONENBERG

CANADA (ARROW) 1976

90m (18)

Porn star Chambers takes the lead in this typical Cronenberg body horror epic about a girl who develops a vampiric, penis-like underarm appendage after being treated in a clinic for injuries from a road crash. Soon all in her path are foaming at the mouth. Lovely jubbly.

RASPUTIN THE MAD MONK [4]

CHRISTOPHER LEE, BARBARA SHELLEY, RICHARD PASCO, FRANCIS MATTHEWS

DON SHARP

UK (LUMIERE) 1965

92m (15)

Shot back-to-back with *Dracula – Prince of Darkness* (see page 197), and for legal reasons only loosely based on the real death of Rasputin (the murderer of the Russian mystic was alive at the time and had sued MGM years before). Quite why the law should protect a self-confessed murderer is beyond me, but there it is. A great, thoroughly trashy piece of nonsense, with Lee in fine form. Sadly, as is so often the case, not in widescreen ratio unless you plump for the US laserdisc and even that is cropped for technical reasons.

HORROR

ROSEMARY'S BABY

MIA FARROW, JOHN CASSAVETES, RUTH GORDON, SIDNEY BLACKMER, MAURICE EVANS

ROMAN POLANSKI

USA (CIC) 1968

137m (18)

Prestige production by shlockmeister William Castle, with Polanski helming a chilling version of Ira Levin's novel about an actor who signs on with some satanic cultists to have his wife give birth to the son of the horned one himself. Filmed in the apartment building where John Lennon was later murdered, it has an eerie, disturbing, claustrophobic feel and the coven are disturbingly mundane and believable. There's a nice joke where actress Angela Dorian (as a previous candidate for devilbirthing) agrees that she resembles 'Victoria Vetri' – this was a name she appeared under in other movies! A great book of photographs shot during production has just come out.

THE SECT

HERBERT LOM, KELLY LEIGH CURTIS, TOMAS ARANA

MICHELE SOAVI

ITALY (MARQUEE) 1991

115m (18)

A Manson-style murder in the desert. Gore in the subway. Global cults. Soavi mixes a compellingly mysterious brew that, like most of his work, will delight some and bore others. Lustrously lensed and let down only by a silly ending.

SCREAM

DAVID ARQUETTE, NEVE CAMPBELL, DREW BARRYMORE, COURTENEY COX

WES CRAVEN

USA (BUENA VISTA) 1996

107m (18)

An attempt to vary the standard slasher movie by having the cast say droll, knowing things to let the audience understand that they dig just what a silly film they're in. For some reason this has been hailed as a major breakthrough and the pic has been a runaway hit. I'm not convinced, but you might enjoy it. Sequel: *Scream 2* (see page 214).

SCREAM 2

DAVID ARQUETTE, NEVE CAMPBELL, COURTENEY COX, SARAH MICHELLE GELLAR, JADA PINKETT

WES CRAVEN

USA (BUENA VISTA) 1998

115m (18)

Having recovered from their horrific experiences, which they have tried to put behind them, the group are now struggling against a copycat killer. Slick, quick and funny, despite being violent and very scary!

THE SHINING

JACK NICHOLSON, SHELLEY DUVALL, DANNY LLOYD, SCATMAN CROTHERS

STANLEY KUBRICK

UK (WARNER) 1980

119m (18)

Overrated but still interesting epic version of Stephen King's novel about a half-crazed writer and family snowed in for the winter in a haunted hotel. Kubrick, as with his *2001* (see page 257), cut nearly 30 minutes after the American opening and only the short print is on tape. A longer cut has been seen on UK TV. (Full version runs 146m approx.) Recent TV remake.

SPIRITS OF THE DEAD

JANE FONDA, PETER FONDA, ALAIN DELON, BRIGITTE BARDOT, TERENCE STAMP

ROGER VADIM, LOUIS MALLE, FEDERICO FELLINI

FRANCE/ITALY (ARROW) 1967

121m (18)

Three Poe tales adapted by arthouse directors: Vadim's *Metzengerstein* uses the pervy idea of casting brother/sister Fondas as lovers; Malle's *William Wilson* has Alain Delon and his nemesis mixing it up with Bardot; and Fellini has Stamp being pursued by the Devil (in the form of a little girl, an idea nicked from Mario Bava): *Toby Dammit* is the title of his segment. Elegant and worthy of critical reappraisal.

HORROR

THE STRANGLERS OF BOMBAY [5]

ALLAN CUTHBERTSON, ANDREW CRUICKSHANK, GEORGE PASTELL, MARIE DEVEREUX, GUY ROLFE

TERENCE FISHER

UK (ENCORE) 1959 B&W

80m (15)

Controversial and Sadian Hammer horror about murders in the Raj period by the Thugees of India – cultists who worship Kali, a goddess who wears a necklace of skulls. She is incarnated in the flesh by the busty Devereux, a devotee who salivates as various gougings, tongue-pullings and other tortures are inflicted on hapless victims. Curiously for such a supposedly vile movie, I recall that it only rated the old 'A' certificate, which admitted youngsters when with an adult. Not in widescreen, unfortunately.

SUSPIRIA [4]

JESSICA HARPER, UDO KIER, ALIDA VALLI, JOAN BENNETT

DARIO ARGENTO

ITALY (NOUVEAUX) 1976

95m (18)

Argento's supernatural classic, for years only available here in a censored print, has at last been passed in this uncut widescreen version by the BBFC. It's a psychedelically coloured tale of a ballet school mixed up in witchy doings, with Harper making a good showing as the menaced student up to her ears in gore and mystery. The first part of Argento's unfinished 'Three Mothers' trilogy. *Inferno* (see page 205) forms the second episode.

TALOS THE MUMMY [3]

JASON SCOTT LEE, SEAN PERTWEE, CHRISTOPHER LEE, SHELLEY DUVALL

RUSSELL MULCAHY

USA/LUXEMBOURG (ENTERTAINMENT) 1997

115m (18)

This long-delayed release gets dusted off and unwrapped (ahem) in the current fashion for all things mummified in the cinema and on video. As you might expect, it's in the style of Chris Lee's Hammer flicks (one character is named Cushing in honour of his late actor pal, Peter), with foolish Victorian Brits messing with ancient Egyptian curses. A bit too flashy, but steadily helmed by Mulcahy.

THE TERROR OF DR HICHCOCK

BARBARA STEELE, ROBERT FLEMYNG, HARRIET WHITE

RICCARDO FREDA

ITALY (MOVIELAND) 1962

88m (18)

Seminal necrophiliac sleaze from one of the masters of the golden age of Italian horror. Steele looks haunting, glowering in morbid colour through the glass lid of her coffin. Not widescreen, but still a must. Box incorrectly spells the Doc's name as 'Hitchcock', like the great Alfred.

THEATRE OF BLOOD

VINCENT PRICE, DIANA RIGG, CORAL BROWNE, JACK HAWKINS

DOUGLAS HICKOX

UK (MGM/UA-WARNER) 1973

104m (18)

Stuffed with famous Brit thespians, this is a must-see for any actor who has wanted to waste his critics. An old Shakespearean barnstormer named Lionheart (cast in the Donald Wolfit, 'Sir', mode) takes to snuffing out hacks who did him down – each murder being based on a scene by the Bard. Price is wonderful, as are the supporting cast. Funny. Bloody.

THE THING

KURT RUSSELL, WILFORD BRIMLEY, RICHARD DYSART, T.K .CARTER

JOHN CARPENTER

USA (CIC) 1982

109m (18)

Spirited remake of the Hawks/Nyby classic about a monster thawed from an ice-bound flying saucer. Modern SFX enable Carpenter to go back to the source story's premise about a creature that can shapeshift to mimic any living ... er ... thing. Bleak ending. Wonderful film. Underrated when released, ripe for re-evaluation. Widescreen only on import DVD package, though a letterboxed tape was planned in 1998 but cancelled at the last minute.

TOMBS OF THE BLIND DEAD

CESAR BURNER, MARIA SILVA, JUAN CORTES

AMANDO DE OSSORIO

SPAIN/PORTUGAL (REDEMPTION) 1971

93m (18)

First of a series about nasty corpses of Templars coming back to life to abuse the populace. Overrated through non-availability. Letterboxed. Cut.

HORROR

URBAN LEGEND 🎬[3]

ALICIA WITT, JARED LETO

JAMIE BLANKS

USA (COLUMBIA TRISTAR) 1999

96m (18)

When someone begins to kill off students following the pattern of some well-known and supposedly true scare stories (known as urban legends), the horror of the stories starts to become a reality. Shocks, tension and some laughs make a good combination. Also on DVD.

THE VAMPIRE BAT 🎬[3]

LIONELL ATWILL, FAY WRAY, MELVYN DOUGLAS, DWIGHT FRYE

FRANK STRAYER

USA (REDEMPTION) 1993 B&W

67m (PG)

Mad-scientist stuff, with Atwill escaping suspicion for a time as the crimes of his creation are blamed on vampires by superstitious locals. Neat early indie horror.

VAMPIRE CIRCUS 🎬[5]

ADRIENNE CORRI, LAURENCE PAYNE, THORLEY WALTERS, LYNNE FREDERICK

ROBERT YOUNG

UK (CINEMA CLUB) 1971

87m (18)

Circus relatives of slaughtered vampire take revenge on the village that done the dirty deed. A genuine late-Hammer gem with a large cast in the manner of the old gothic novels so beloved of critic of the genre Montague Summers. The seductive-yet-menacing air that carnivals and circuses seem to exude is here in spades.

VIDEODROME 🎬[5]

JAMES WOODS, DEBBIE HARRY, LYNNE GORMAN

DAVID CRONENBERG

CANADA (CIC) 1982

89m (18)

Surreal trip in typical Cronenberg body-loathing style, about cancers inflicted by watching oddball S&M 'snuff' videos. Marvellous but confusing – it comes as no surprise to learn it was begun without a finished script. Cut for tape during the moral panic of the early 80s, but the full theatrical print is now on video. A slightly longer director's cut is on laserdisc. There is also a USA TV print which replaces violence and/or sex with dialogue out-takes.

TOP 1000 VIDEOS

WHITE ZOMBIE 🎬4

BELA LUGOSI, MADGE BELLAMY, ROBERT FRAZER

VICTOR HALPERIN

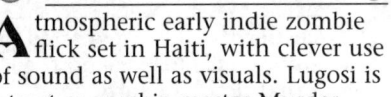

USA (ReVISION) 1932

73m (PG)

Atmospheric early indie zombie flick set in Haiti, with clever use of sound as well as visuals. Lugosi is a treat as zombie-master Murder Legendre. Also available on Redemption.

THE WICKER MAN 🎬5

EDWARD WOODWARD, CHRISTOPHER LEE, BRITT EKLAND, DIANE CILENTO, INGRID PITT

ROBIN HARDY

UK (WARNER/TERRORVISION) 1973

102/87m (18)

Heavily cut and stuck on a double bill under *Don't Look Now* (see page 196), this creepy story of pagan worship and human sacrifice on a Scottish island gained a cult rep over the years: *Cinefantastique* dubbed it 'the Citizen Kane of horror films', and it was partly restored by the BBC. Recently, in spite of all the odds, a print of the full, supposedly lost, version turned up – so why have Warners, even on a specialist label, put out the old cut-to-shreds copy once again? It's tapes like this that have led some to dub the new label, perhaps unfairly, 'TerribleVision'. Try and get hold of a copy of the uncut USA tape – it really makes all the difference. But this little classic, with Edward Woodward as the unwitting copper who thinks he's a hunter when he's really the prey, is a must-see in any version. Note: Star Lee says even the longest version is not the full film he made. Times stated are for longest and shortest extant versions.

WITCHFINDER GENERAL 🎬5

VINCENT PRICE, IAN OGILVY, HILARY DWYER, RUPERT DAVIES, PATRICK WYMARK

MICHAEL REEVES

UK (REDEMPTION) 1968

84m (18)

It was a loss to cinema when Reeves died while still in his twenties, but now we have this, his best work, in its full version at last. Loosely based on a real-life character, it concerns Price's sanctimonious and hypocritical witchfinder and his assistant in the time of Cromwell, and the way in which corrupted revenge can become as bad as the wrongs it seeks to stop. Redemption have restored violence previously cut by the BBFC, as well as nudity previously only seen in European prints. Print is rather scratchy. Box says the print is letterboxed at 1.66, but on my copy this is virtually unnoticeable.

WOLF 🎬2

⭐ JACK NICHOLSON, MICHELLE PFEIFFER, CHRISTOPHER PLUMMER, JAMES SPADER

🎬 MIKE NICHOLS

USA (COLUMBIA TRISTAR) 1994

⏱ 125m (15)

Slow horror-comedy about a businessman revitalised but troubled after being infected by lycanthropy. This old tale has been done better in *An American Werewolf In London* (see page 188).

WOLFEN 🎬4

⭐ ALBERT FINNEY, GREGORY HINES, DIANE VENORA, EDWARD JAMES OLMOS

🎬 MICHAEL WADLEIGH

USA (WARNER/TERRORVISION) 1981

⏱ 115m (18)

Ecological fable from *Woodstock* director Wadleigh, about a pack of wolves living in cities and preying on vagrants. Plenty of psychedelic animal-point-of-view shots. Letterboxed.

THE WOLF MAN 🎬4

⭐ LON CHANEY Jnr, CLAUDE RAINS, EVELYN ANKERS, BELA LUGOSI, MARIA OUSPENSKAYA

🎬 GEORGE WAGGNER

USA (CIC) 1941 B&W

⏱ 70m (PG)

Reluctant son of silent giant Chaney didn't want to be a horror star, but Junior gets one of his best roles here (in fab make-up by Jack Pierce) as the poor fellow searching for a cure after being infected by the bite of lycanthrope Lugosi. A beauty. With a real beast. Bags of foggy atmosphere.

ZOMBIE FLESH EATERS

RICHARD JOHNSON, TISA FARROW, IAN McCULLOCH, AL CLIVER

LUCIO FULCI

ITALY (VIPCO) 1979

91m (18)

The recently-deceased Fulci directed this pseudo-sequel to Romero's *Dawn Of The Dead* (an alternative, Dario Argento-edit of that film was issued in Italy as *Zombi*, so this film was known as *Zombi 2* over there) and it was passed by the BBFC for UK cinemas with cuts. Then came the moral scare of the 80s which led to the VRA, and video copies of this film – exactly the same as in the cinema version – were seized! Laughably, after all that carry-on, that same version is now out on video with a BBFC cert! So what was all the fuss about? You tell me. Vipco are one of the few firms to indicate on their boxes that films have been cut – it may not help sales but you have to admire them. They issue an uncut version of this movie in Holland. This UK version is available letterboxed. Note: Vipco seem to have stopped trading in Britain but copies of their tapes are still found in many stores. The uncut and letterboxed print of this film is also an import disc, on DVD, under the name *Zombie* and on laser as *Woodoo*.

MUSICALS

To most people, movie musicals mean only one thing: big-budget, colour extravaganzas from the heyday of the MGM studios. But the films of rock stars like the Beatles, Prince and Elvis Presley are musicals too, as are dramas such as *A Star Is Born* and *Absolute Beginners*. Whether your taste runs to golden oldies like *High Society* and *Showboat* or something a little more up-to-date such as *The Commitments*, there is a rich vein here for the viewer to mine. Best of all, somehow the addition of a few classic songs and dazzling dance routines makes even the most slender plot worth viewing over and over again, so the titles in this section are well worth adding to your permanent video collection.

ABSOLUTE BEGINNERS

EDDIE O'CONNELL, PATSY KENSIT, JAMES FOX, DAVID BOWIE, RAY DAVIES

JULIEN TEMPLE

USK (VISION) 1986

107m (15)

Ambitious musical adaptation of Colin McInnes' 1959 novel set amidst Notting Hill's racial mix. A major flop and often abused by critics, yet hardly as bad as is suggested. Though the two juvenile leads, Kensit and O'Connell, are weak (director Temple described Kensit as having 'ankles like milk bottles') there are some grand set-pieces, particularly those featuring Bowie and Kinks' singer Davies.

ALL THAT JAZZ

ROY SCHEIDER, JESSICA LANGE, JOHN LITHGOW, CLIFF GORMAN

BOB FOSSE

USA (FOX) 1979

118m (15)

Autobiographical fantasy by Fosse about a choreographer who relives his life of sex and excess as he lies ill in hospital and indulges fantasies of his wildest dance concepts. Not a big hit, but won several Oscars including one for best score. Inspired a porn version, *All That Jizz* (!).

TOP 1000 VIDEOS

AN AMERICAN IN PARIS [4]

GENE KELLY, LESLIE CARON, NINA FOCH, OSCAR LEVANT

VINCENTE MINELLI

USA (MGM/UA) 1951

108m (U)

American soldier lingers in Paris after World War Two and finds himself in love with two girls. No big surprises but a classic of sorts and satisfying entertainment. Six Oscars including best picture, score and cinematography. Highly recommended. Available on a two-for-one tape with *Gigi* (see page 227).

BLUE HAWAII [2]

ELVIS PRESLEY, ANGELA LANSBURY, JOAN BLACKMAN, NANCY WALTERS

NORMAN TAUROG

USA (4-FRONT) 1961

101m (PG)

Neither the nadir nor the zenith of Presley's numerous pix. Despite the non-existent plot, it's saved (just) by the lush locations and some reasonable tunes.

THE BOYFRIEND [4]

TWIGGY, CHRISTOPHER GABLE, MAX ADRIAN, TOMMY TUNE

KEN RUSSELL

UK (MGM/UA) 1971

125m (U)

This film, inspired by Sandy Wilson's musical show, was a radical departure for the controversial Russell, with its air of naive flapperism and choreography in the manner of Busby Berkeley. Twiggy is okay, but is outshone by Gable and the fancy footwork of young American Tune. Running time quoted is for the full version, but the current print may be cut.

BREAKING GLASS [3]

HAZEL O'CONNOR, PHIL DANIELS, JON FINCH, JONATHAN PRYCE

BRIAN GIBSON

UK (ENTERTAINMENT) 1980

104m (15)

Seedy drama of the neuroses of punky girl singer on her way to the top – and back down again. Overrated. Fictional rock stories, in my experience, rarely match up to the crazed outrageousness of the real thing. O'Connor was widely promoted but did not become a major actress (or singer, for that matter). Daniels is always worth a look, though.

BRIGADOON

GENE KELLY, CYD CHARISSE, VAN JOHNSON, ELAINE STEWART

VINCENTE MINELLI

USA (MGM/UA) 1954

103m (U)

Film version of the Lerner/Loewe musical about Yanks who stumble upon a ghostly Scottish hamlet that only comes to life once in an age. Top-notch dancing and songs make it a treat for addicts of this classic Hollywood genre.

THE BUDDY HOLLY STORY

GARY BUSEY, DON STROUD, CHARLES MARTIN SMITH, MARIA RICHWINE

STEVE RASH

USA (GUILD) 1978

110m (PG)

Inspired biopic of the short-lived 50s singer/songwriter. Oddly enough, I first saw this pic about a man who dies at the climax in a plane crash during a transatlantic flight! Busey really lived the part, and after the movie he embarked on gigs with his own band. When I worked for the original publisher of Holly's music (before the songs were sold to fan Paul McCartney) I met Holly's widow – it was odd to see this middle-aged lady living in the shadow of a man who would be a teenager for evermore. Wonderful songs, played 'live' by Busey and pals. Note: the name of Will Jordan appears twice in the credits – there are two actors with the same name!

CABARET

LIZA MINNELLI, JOEL GREY, MICHAEL YORK, HELMUT GRIEM, MARISA BERENSON

BOB FOSSE

USA (CINEMA CLUB V) 1972

123m (15)

Christopher Isherwood's tales of decadent American Sally Bowles in Berlin during the rise of Nazism, transformed into a stunning musical piece set in the sleazy cabaret of the title. All the actors perform with brio, especially Minnelli and nimble Grey as the MC. They both won Oscars, as did the score and the director. Not to be missed on any account – even if you hate musicals! Music by Ebb and Kander.

CALAMITY JANE

DORIS DAY, HOWARD KEEL, ALLYN ANN McLERIE, PHILIP CAREY

DAVID BUTLER

USA (WARNER) 1953

97m (U)

Doris Day was once considered the epitome of homely womanhood, but in recent years she has been hailed as a pre-feminist icon – and it's not too hard to see why from viewing her in this tale (highly fictionalised, of course) of the rootin', tootin', buckskin-clad Wild West gal. Great fun, and the memorable song 'Secret Love' won an Oscar.

CAMELOT 🎬 4

RICHARD HARRIS, VANESSA REDGRAVE, DAVID HEMMINGS, FRANCO NERO

JOSHUA LOGAN

USA (WARNER) 1967

175m (U)

Adaptation of the Lerner/Loewe stage musical based on the myths about the *ménage-à-trois* of King Arthur, Guinevere and Sir Lancelot. Spectacular and with a fine score, though musical form is perhaps not best served by being stretched to epic length and the actors don't entirely convince. Impressive for all that. Oscars for score, costumes and art direction.

CAN-CAN 🎬 3

FRANK SINATRA, SHIRLEY MacLAINE, MAURICE CHEVALIER, JULIET PROWSE

WALTER LANG

USA (FOX) 1960

131m (U)

Set in 90s Paris (1890s, that is) the story concerns a nightspot hassled by the police over its supposedly risqué dance routine of the title. In real life when the girls threw up their skirts their bottoms were bare, but you mustn't hope for such thrills hereabouts, I'm afraid! Saved by a good cast, especially Sinatra and MacLaine.

THE COMMITMENTS 🎬 4

ANGELINE BALL, BRONAGH GALLAGHER, ROBERT ARKINS, MICHAEL AHERNE

ALAN PARKER

USA/EIRE (FOX) 1991

113m (15)

Roddy Doyle's novel is the basis for this funny, moving and hugely appealing little pic about the adventures of a nascent soul band in Dublin. The only sad thing is that the talented cast of new faces have either returned to obscurity or have so far been given no more than cameo stints in subsequent movies, which seems a waste. A box set with documentary was available but appears to have been deleted.

CRY-BABY 🎬 3

JOHNNY DEPP, AMY LOCAINE, IGGY POP, RICKI LAKE, TRACI LORDS

JOHN WATERS

USA (CIC) 1990

81m (15)

Waters has moved increasingly away from wildly inspired filth like *Pink Flamingos* into commercially safer kitsch teen parodies of 50s trash, such as *Hairspray* and this effort. Lovingly crafted tat, with an interesting cast: Depp is now a major star, Lords is an ex-hard-porno player and Pop is the former leader of the Stooges, a genius rock and roll group with self-destruct tendencies. Lake dieted and is now a chat-show star.

MUSICALS

DADDY LONG LEGS [3]

FRED ASTAIRE, LESLIE CARON, FRED CLARK, THELMA RITTER

JEAN NEGULESCO

USA (FOX) 1955

126m (U)

'Something's Gotta Give' indeed, when Astaire fancies Caron in yet another of the many Paris-set musicals on offer. Debonair hoofing, and songs by the great Johnny Mercer. Not a great movie, but Astaire is on form.

DOCTOR DOLITTLE [3]

REX HARRISON, SAMANTHA EGGAR, RICHARD ATTENBOROUGH, ANTHONY NEWLEY

RICHARD FLEISCHER

USA (FOX) 1967

138m (U)

Colour abounds in this misguided attempt to make a musical version of Hugh Lofting's stories about a zany doc who studies animal languages. It may even soon lose novelty value as I saw a woman on TV the other day who claims to speak fluent 'cat'! And *The Horse Whisperer* (see page 118) is said to be based on truth, too! Oscars: SFX and best song for Bricusse's 'Talk to the Animals'. Now a London stage hit. 1998 non-musical remake with Eddie Murphy (see page 78).

EXPRESSO BONGO [4]

LAURENCE HARVEY, SYLVIA SYMS, CLIFF RICHARD, YOLANDE DONLAN

VAL GUEST

UK (VISION) 1959 B&W

101m (PG)

Impressive monochrome version of a Wolf Mankowitz play about Soho and its denizens. The young, not yet 'Sir', Cliff Richard is pretty insipid as are the songs, but Harvey is able as a hustling wide-boy. A cult movie nowadays, yet it gets by on more than mere camp appeal.

FAME

IRENE CARA, LEE CURRERI, GENE ANTHONY RAY, DEBBIE ALLEN

ALAN PARKER

USA (MGM/UA) 1980

128m (15)

Brit Parker's second musical foray (the first was the kiddy gangster pic *Bugsy Malone*) is the now somewhat dated, yet still exuberant, story of youngsters desperate to 'make it' (in both senses of the phrase) as they attend New York's real-life performing arts high school and cope with personal traumas. The dancing is still explosive, though the songs feel stuck in the disco era. Inspired a TV series also called *Fame*, so the film is sometimes billed as *Fame – The Movie* to differentiate. Ironic note: when the film first came out I went along to a preview with a bunch of hopeful youngsters of the type the movie was both about and aimed at, only to hear an old dear in a fur coat whisper to her pal: 'I've never seen so many dead-beats at a premiere, dear!' Some folks never get the message.

FIDDLER ON THE ROOF

TOPOL, NORMA CRANE, MOLLY PICON, PAUL MICHAEL GLASER

NORMAN JEWISON

USA (MGM/UA) 1971

172m (U)

Over-long but well-crafted film of the Broadway show about life for poor rural Jews in pre-Communist Russia. Serious themes but memorable tunes like 'If I Were a Rich Man' helped make Topol an international star. Oscars for best score, cinematography and sound. Available in widescreen.

FLASHDANCE

JENNIFER BEALS, MICHAEL NOURI, LILIA SKALA, BELINDA BAUER

ADRIAN LYNE

USA (CIC) 1983

91m (15)

Inspirational tale of female welder (!) who wants to be a dancer. Beals is great but I understand some of the dancing was doubled by a male hoofer – don't ask me how they managed it! Oscar: best song ('What a Feeling'). Not available in widescreen. Not bad, but I got tired just watching the dance sequences.

MUSICALS

FUNNY GIRL 🎬3

BARBRA STREISAND, OMAR SHARIF, ANNE FRANCIS, WALTER PIDGEON

WILLIAM WYLER

USA (CINEMA CLUB V) 1968

141m (U)

Streisand before her ego went crazy is brimming with star quality in this biopic of stage legend Fanny Brice. She won an Oscar for her performance, though she had to share the award with Katharine Hepburn in *The Lion In Winter*. This would seem to be a cut print as the original was listed on release as some ten minutes longer.

GIGI 🎬5

LESLIE CARON, MAURICE CHEVALIER, LOUIS JOURDAN, HERMIONE GINGOLD

VINCENTE MINNELLI

USA (MGM/UA) 1958

111m (PG)

Colourful Parisian (again!) froth about a boyish cutie who grows up to be a courtesan but opts for romance in this adaptation of the Colette story. I personally find the crooning of Chevalier ('Thank Heaven for Little Girls', 'I Remember It Well') sickly sweet, though Caron is perfect as the ingénue. A weighty nine Oscars (best picture, director, cinematography, editing, sets, script, costumes, score and song – 'Gigi' – plus a special award for Chevalier). Available on a two-for-one tape with *An American In Paris* (see page 222).

GREASE 🎬3

JOHN TRAVOLTA, OLIVIA NEWTON-JOHN, SID CAESAR, STOCKARD CHANNING

RANDAL KLEISER

USA (CIC) 1978

105m (PG)

Film version of ersatz rock 'n' roll teen romance musical. Cloying songs, wimpy 'Ms Neutron-Bomb' and over-the-top hip-thrusting from Travolta, yet it does have the undeniable drive and catchy songs to account for its hit status. Atrocious sequel, *Grease 2*, has nothing to commend it at all. Available in widescreen.

THE GREAT ROCK 'N' ROLL SWINDLE

THE SEX PISTOLS, MALCOLM McLAREN, RONNIE BIGGS, IRENE HANDL, LIZ FRASER

JULIEN TEMPLE

UK (POLYGRAM) 1979

100m (18)

It's hard to believe over 20 years have passed since the manufactured punk outrage of The Sex Pistols caused so much fuss in the UK press – spawning a movement that was the most exciting youth cult since the hippy daze of 1967. Svengali manager Malcolm McLaren originally planned a Pistols flick – *Who Killed Bambi?* – to be helmed by soft-core sex maestro Russ Meyer, but it fell through and this project was cobbled together in the aftermath. It has, in addition to the group, a bizarre cast of everyone from train-robber Ronnie Biggs to tragic sex star Mary Millington, plus underage nudes, dwarfs and obscene cartoon footage in a wry comment on the way the hype was created and sold. For a darker view of the band, take a look at Alex Cox's *Sid And Nancy* (see page 134).

GYPSY

ROSALIND RUSSELL, NATALIE WOOD, KARL MALDEN, PAUL WALLACE

MERVYN LEROY

USA (ENTERTAINMENT) 1962

149m (PG)

Sondheim/Styne stage musical adapted for the screen, telling the story of stripper Gypsy Rose Lee. A fizzing cast give it all they've got, but as *Radio Times* critic Derek Winnert has noted, one of the film's best tunes, 'Together Wherever We Go', has been cut out so poorly that the music trails over into the next scene. Still worth catching.

MUSICALS

HAIR

JOHN SAVAGE, TREAT WILLIAMS, BEVERLY D'ANGELO, ANNIE GOLDEN, ELLEN FOLEY

MILOS FORMAN

USA (MGM/UA) 1979

121m (15)

Forman is a Euro director who has made a career out of films giving his outsider's view of the USA. The problem with hit hippy show *Hair* was that it was neither filmed soon enough to be contemporary or late enough to have nostalgia value, but lensed in the wake of the punk era when the anti-war, flower-power ethos that fills the score was firmly out of favour. It's hard to trash work that involves people you know, but I have to say that two girl singers I became friends with in my rock-hack days, Annie Golden and Ellen Foley, have no chance to shine here: Golden has the bigger part, but her considerable vocal prowess isn't really used – she went on to good non-singing roles in TV's *Miami Vice* and the sci-fi film *12 Monkeys* (see page 257). Foley has only one song 'n' dance, but had a better acting part in *Fatal Attraction* (see page 114). As for *Hair*, watch our for the Twyla Tharp choreography, and enjoy the good songs, even if they are poorly sung.

A HARD DAY'S NIGHT

THE BEATLES, WILFRID BRAMBELL, NORMAN ROSSINGTON

RICHARD LESTER

UK (VIDEO COLLECTION) 1964 B&W

83m (U)

A veritable time-capsule of the initial excitement of the early 60s fan mania surrounding the emergence of the Beatles. Grainy, documentary feel, merged with Lester's choreographing of silent-movie-styled antics to the group's hits which set the style for pop-promo video for many years to come. Inevitably a bit dated and occasionally embarrassing, it is nevertheless filled with its share of fresh and amusing moments. For instance, Brambell was gay in real life and George Harrison at one point comments slyly on the fact that he's pictured reading a copy of *Queen* magazine! This is the best of the Fab Four's films.

229

HELLO, DOLLY! 🎬3

BARBRA STREISAND, WALTER MATTHAU, MICHAEL CRAWFORD, LOUIS ARMSTRONG

GENE KELLY

USA (FOX) 1969

146m (U)

Lengthy film of stage show based on Thornton Wilder's play *The Matchmaker*, pulled off via Streisand's remarkable vocals and stack of memorable songs. Oscars for best score, sets and sound. Available at the time of writing in a widescreen transfer video.

HELP! 🎬3

THE BEATLES, LEO McKERN, ELEANOR BRON

RICHARD LESTER

UK (VIDEO COLLECTION) 1965

92m (U)

The second Beatles movie isn't a patch on *A Hard Day's Night* (see page 229), despite the addition of colour and exotic locations. The basic concert-based plot of the first pic has been replaced by absurdist hi-jinks about a mysterious jewel, but the songs carry the day due to the compositional genius of Lennon and McCartney at their creative peak. A 60s antique.

HIGH SOCIETY 🎬4

FRANK SINATRA, BING CROSBY, GRACE KELLY, CELESTE HOLM

CHARLES WALTERS

USA (MGM/UA) 1956

103m (U)

Musical reworking of earlier play and film *The Philadelphia Story* is a light and sophisticated confection about romantic entanglements among the socialite set. This was Grace Kelly's final film before she became Princess Grace of Monaco. Great fun.

KING CREOLE 🎬4

ELVIS PRESLEY, CAROLYN JONES, DEAN JAGGER, WALTER MATTHAU, VIC MORROW

MICHAEL CURTIZ

USA (4-FRONT) 1958 B&W

116m (PG)

Presley's best film. He turns in a fair acting stint as a rebellious young would-be singer mixed up with New Orleans hoodlum Matthau, and both plot and tunes are way above average – not to mention a support cast of superb quality. Based on Harold Robbins's trashy novel *A Stone for Danny Fisher*.

MUSICALS

NEW YORK, NEW YORK [4]

ROBERT DE NIRO, LIZA MINNELLI, LIONEL STANDER, DICK MILLER

MARTIN SCORSESE

USA (WARNER) 1977

164m (PG)

Scorsese's loving tribute to the kind of glitzy musical turned out in the heyday of the form by star Minnelli's dad Vincente was savaged by critics until it was reissued in this uncut version. A simple story of the on/off love of two musical stars, but the sheer scale and style will blow you away.

OLIVER! [5]

RON MOODY, OLIVER REED, SHANI WALLIS, MARK LESTER, JACK WILD

CAROL REED

UK (COLUMBIA TRISTAR) 1968

146m (U)

Lionel Bart's evergreen fave based on *Oliver Twist* by Charles Dickens is seen here in its incarnation as the greatest Brit movie musical of all time. A raft of classic songs ('Food Glorious Food', 'Who Will Buy?', 'As Long as He Needs Me', etc.) and a perfect Fagin in Moody combine in a sumptuous treat for eye and ear. Sullen Ollie Reed, nephew of director Carol, proves that it wasn't mere nepotism that got him the part of evil Bill Sikes. Oscars: best picture, director, score, sets and more. Available in widescreen.

PAINT YOUR WAGON [2]

CLINT EASTWOOD, LEE MARVIN, JEAN SEBERG, HARVE PRESNELL

JOSHUA LOGAN

USA (CIC) 1969

167m (PG)

S-l-o-w film version of Lerner/Loewe stage success about two Californian goldrush pards who share a wife bought in an auction. Only proves the obvious: that neither Clint ('I Talk to the Trees') or Marvin ('Wandrin' Star') can sing worth a damn. However, the latter's gruff talk-a-long proved a surprise hit single. Available in widescreen.

PAL JOEY [4]

FRANK SINATRA, RITA HAYWORTH, KIM NOVAK, BOBBY SHERWOOD

GEORGE SIDNEY

USA (COLUMBIA TRISTAR) 1957 B&W

105m (PG)

A crooner in San Francisco finds himself torn between two women in this musical by Rodgers and Hart based on material by John O'Hara. Includes the legendary songs 'My Funny Valentine' and 'The Lady Is A Tramp'. Sinatra at his peak.

PINK FLOYD – THE WALL 🎬2

BOB GELDOF, JAMES LAURENSON, CHRISTINE HARGREAVES, BOB HOSKINS

ALAN PARKER

UK (POLYGRAM0 1982

92m (15)

Ever since the early departure of founder Syd Barrett, rock experimenters Pink Floyd have become more and more obsessed with overblown, crowd-pleasing bombast, and this movie is no exception: live performance, cartoons by Gerald Scarfe and pretentious thesping derail this whiny tale of the sufferings of a poor rocker, based on the smash hit album of the same name. Pink Floyd fans should enjoy it, though.

PURPLE RAIN 🎬2

PRINCE, APPOLLONIA KOTERO, MORRIS DAY, OLGA KARLATOS

ALBERT MAGNOLI

USA (WARNER) 1984

107m (15)

Prince – or whatever name he is now going by – was once an innovative artist, blending soul with guitar antics and sex-driven rock, but success has led him to change his name to a symbol and to indulge in ever-madder schemes. This was his debut flick, made when the foolishness was still amusing and the man was obsessed with the colour of the title – the story of a pop muso's efforts to make it isn't much, but the songs are ace. Oscar: best score. Also available on a two-for-one tape with Prince's subsequent, but less satisfying, *Graffiti Bridge*.

QUADROPHENIA 🎬3

PHIL DANIELS, MARK WINGETT, LESLIE ASH, STING

FRANC RODDAM

UK (FEATURE FILM CO) 1979

120m (15)

I remember this one – not because I liked it, but because the scene where a scooter breaks down was filmed opposite my flat one night in 1979 and required endless takes which kept me awake. It's a decent enough little story, based on the concept album by The Who, about the lives of mod Jimmy (Daniels) and his pals led by Ace Face (Sting). Tries for poignancy but doesn't always manage it. Daniels remains a seriously undervalued talent, but many of the cast members are now quite well known, including Mark Wingett, a staple on TV's *The Bill*. Newly reissued.

MUSICALS

THE ROCKY HORROR PICTURE SHOW [4]

TIM CURRY, SUSAN SARANDON, BARRY BOSTWICK, RICHARD O'BRIEN, CHARLES GRAY

JIM SHARMAN

UK (FOX) 1975

99m (15)

Cult film of the long-running stage show which is a daft homage to trashy rock 'n' roll and tacky 50s science-fiction flicks. A young couple stranded in the mansion of randy transvestite Curry are molested by all manner of singin', dancin' weirdos. Sick, hilarious romp, now such a cult item that some people watch it once a week and go along dressed as their favourite characters in order to shout out the dialogue along with the actors. Composer O'Brien has tried to duplicate the show's success several times but has yet to succeed.

SATURDAY NIGHT FEVER [3]

JOHN TRAVOLTA, KAREN LYNN GORNEY, BARRY MILLER

JOHN BADHAM

USA (CIC) 1978

114m (18)

The film that made Travolta a star. Based on a story about suburban disco denizens by Nik Cohn and featuring JT dancing to the music of the Bee Gees in their emasculated-shriek period, it was so popular with kids that a PG version was issued at one time (cut by 10 minutes). Dated, but a classic of sorts. Sequel: *Staying Alive*.

SEVEN BRIDES FOR SEVEN BROTHERS [5]

HOWARD KEEL, JANE POWELL, RUSS TAMBLYN, JULIE NEWMEYER

STANLEY DONEN

USA (MGM/UA) 1954

104m (U)

Classic tale of a clan of gauche hillbillies who kidnap and seek to charm into marriage a girl for each of them. Superb score, choreography and Keel in fine voice make this one of the all-time greats. Newmeyer later changed her name to Julie Newmar and found fame as Catwoman in the 60s TV series *Batman*. Available in a widescreen transfer.

SILK STOCKINGS [3]

FRED ASTAIRE, CYD CHARISSE, PETER LORRE, JANIS PAIGE

ROUBEN MAMOULIAN

USA (MGM/UA) 1957

114m (U)

Hollywood innovator Mamoulian's musical remake of *Ninotchka*, about a Russki politico babe in Paris, with a fine Cole Porter soundtrack. Based on the hit stage musical version, it goes on a bit too long, though Astaire and leggy Charisse are hot.

TOP 1000 VIDEOS

SINGIN' IN THE RAIN [5]

GENE KELLY, DONALD O'CONNOR, CYD CHARISSE, RITA MORENO, DEBBIE REYNOLDS

GENE KELLY, STANLEY DONEN

USA (MGM/UA) 1952

98m (U)

Set in Hollywood during the advent of sound film, this is a deservedly legendary picture containing one of the most famous scenes in all of motion pictures, when Kelly splashes his way through a street set in a rainstorm while performing the title song. Magical, memorable, sheer bliss. They don't make musicals like this any more.

THE SOUND OF MUSIC [3]

JULIE ANDREWS, CHRISTOPHER PLUMMER, ELEANOR PARKER, ANNA LEE

ROBERT WISE

USA (FOX) 1965

165m (U)

Twee tale of real-life family of kid singers and their flight from the Nazis. Andrews is the ersatz mom, Plummer the grumpy patriarch, and you know all the songs already! Those who love it will not listen to any criticism, and actually it works a lot better than you might expect. Widescreen. Oscars include best picture, score and director. Nun but the brave!

A STAR IS BORN [5]

JUDY GARLAND, JAMES MASON, CHARLES BICKFORD, JACK CARSON

GEORGE CUKOR

USA (WARNER) 1954

181m (U)

Cukor's film, which functions as a drama as well as a musical, is the best of several versions of the story of a drunken star who sacrifices himself to save the career of his talented wife. Heavily cut after initial release, it was restored in 1983 to something close to original length – though in some cases only the soundtrack could be found and this had to be played back with stills replacing the missing footage on screen. It is a testament to the power of Cukor's direction, the Arlen/Ira Gershwin songs and the performances of Garland and Mason that audiences were willing to accept this. Running time given is for the original but the restoration runs to 176m. For the full story of the film's loss and rebirth, read Ronald Haver's book *A Star Is Born*. Astonishingly, this 'scope classic is not out on a widescreen tape.

MUSICALS

SWEET CHARITY 🎬4

SHIRLEY MacLAINE, RICARDO MONTALBAN, CHITA RIVERA, JOHN McMARTIN

BOB FOSSE

USA (CIC/4-FRONT) 1969

142m (PG)

Fosse's first pic is a version of the Broadway hit about a bar-room tart in search of true love. Lots of pizzazz. Neil Simon's story is based on Fellini's 1957 flick *Nights of Cabiria*. No widescreen available.

THAT'LL BE THE DAY 🎬3

DAVID ESSEX, RINGO STARR, KEITH MOON, BILLY FURY

CLAUDE WHATHAM

UK (WARNER/LUMIERE) 1973

87m (15)

Real-life rock stars in this story of a singer's crawl up the greasy pole of pop success. Nice work from Essex and some okay tunes. The story was continued in the follow up, *Stardust*, and the films are available on a two-for-one tape.

THAT'S ENTERTAINMENT 🎬4

FRED ASTAIRE, GENE KELLY, FRANK SINATRA, DEBBIE REYNOLDS, MICKEY ROONEY

JACK HALEY Jnr

USA (MGM/UA) 1974

122m (U)

Compilation of classic moments from hit musicals of yore. A good idea that proved a hit with a nostalgic public. Original running time was allegedly 137m, so this appears to be a cut version. Followed by Parts 2 and 3, though by the third effort there were definite signs of barrel-scraping.

TOMMY 🎬2

OLIVER REED, ROGER DALTREY, ANN-MARGRET, JACK NICHOLSON, TINA TURNER

KEN RUSSELL

UK (POLYGRAM) 1975

111m (18)

Russell's bloated and vulgar adaptation of rock band The Who's pop opera about a psychosomatically sense-impaired boy who triumphs over his abused childhood to become a messiah. Stupid and garish and the songs were performed to better effect on the group's original album version. Still, if you need to see busty Ann-Margret lolling in a sea of baked beans, this is your chance! Good turn by the late Oliver Reed.

WEST SIDE STORY

NALALIE WOOD, RUSS TAMBLYN, GEORGE CHAKIRIS, RITA MORENO, RICHARD BEYMER

ROBERT WISE, JEROME ROBBINS

USA (MGM/UA) 1961

155m (PG)

Classy musical version of the plot of Shakespeare's *Romeo and Juliet* transposed to the tough, gang-ridden streets of New York. Great Leonard Bernstein music, Sondheim lyrics and Robbins choreography make it work. Oscars include: best picture, direction, cinematography, supporting actor (Chakiris) and supporting actress (Moreno). Available in widescreen. A classic.

THE WIZARD OF OZ

JUDY GARLAND, BERT LAHR, RAY BOLGER, JACK HALEY, MARGARET HAMILTON

VICTOR FLEMING

USA (WARNER) 1939 COL/B&W

102m (U)

The 'Oz' tales of L Frank Baum have been the subject of several films: silent, cartoon, Disney ... even a Michael Jackson vehicle. This, however, remains the classic interpretation: the glowing colour is nicely contrasted with the monochrome of 'real life' in Kansas before the young Garland is transported to the land of the Tin Man, Cowardly Lion, Wicked Witch *et al*. Enjoyable tunes and an indefinable magical quality make it a must-see for all ages. Oscars: best song ('Over The Rainbow') and score.

YANKEE DOODLE DANDY

JAMES CAGNEY, JOAN LESLIE, WALTER HUSTON, EDDIE FOY Jnr

MICHAEL CURTIZ

USA (MGM/UA) 1942 B&W

126m (U)

Biopic of songwriter/performer George M Cohan, with Cagney showing his prowess as a hoofer. Those who have only ever seen him in gangster parts will be pleasantly surprised. Oscars: best actor (Cagney), best score and sound, all well deserved. Some say this patriotic pic as made only to squash stories that Cagney was a 'lefty'. Who cares?!

ROMANCE

A romantic video can provide the perfect finishing touch for your cosy evening in *à deux* – and there seems to have been an upsurge of romantic movies of late, from the 'odd couple' of *The Piano* to street-smart stories like *Sleepless in Seattle*. But we mustn't forget that romance has always been part of film-making: the numerous versions of classics such as *Romeo and Juliet* and *Wuthering Heights* are testament to that.

ABOUT LAST NIGHT

ROB LOWE, DEMI MOORE, JAMES BELUSHI, ELIZABETH PERKINS

EDWARD ZWICK

USA (CINEMA CLUB V) 1986

102m (18)

Hip romantic comedy, based on David Mamet's play *Sexual Perversity in Chicago*, and emblematic of the modern genre. Debut for Perkins, with nice work from Lowe and Moore. Original running time listed at 113m in some sources.

THE ACCIDENTAL TOURIST

WILLIAM HURT, KATHLEEN TURNER, GEENA DAVIS, BILL PULLMAN

LAWRENCE KASDAN

USA (WARNER) 1988

116m (PG)

Travel writer rebuilds his life via an affair after his child dies in an accident – but then his estranged wife returns. What to do? Based on a novel by Anne Tyler, this romantic comedy hit won an Oscar for Geena Davis.

THE AGE OF INNOCENCE [3]

DANIEL DAY-LEWIS, MICHELLE PFEIFFER, WINONA RYDER

MARTIN SCORSESE

USA (COLUMBIA TRISTAR) 1993

138m (U)

Lives and loves of posh folk in New York of the 1870s. Not Scorsese's usual turf, but a sumptuously shot (if ennui-inducing) version of Edith Wharton's Pulitzer Prize-winning novel. Previously filmed in 1934. Widescreen available.

THE AMERICAN PRESIDENT [3]

MICHAEL DOUGLAS, ANNETTE BENING, MARTIN SHEEN, MICHAEL J FOX

ROB REINER

USA (CIC) 1995

109m (15)

Topical tale of love in the White House. Slender stuff, but with a good cast of attractive professionals and craftsman-like direction from the ever-reliable Rob Reiner it makes for an amusing evening's entertainment.

ANNE OF THE THOUSAND DAYS [3]

RICHARD BURTON, GENEVIÈVE BUJOLD, ANTHONY QUAYLE, IRENE PAPAS

CHARLES JARROTT

USA (CIC) 1969

140m (PG)

Maxwell Anderson's stage play provides the basis for this gloomy tale of one of Henry VIII's doomed wives, Anne Boleyn. Solid fare for those who dote on these historical romances. Oscar for costumes; nine nominations in all.

ROMANCE

AS GOOD AS IT GETS 🎬4

JACK NICHOLSON,
HELEN HUNT

JAMES L. BROOKS

USA (COLUMBIA TRISTAR) 1996

133m (15)

Compulsive-obsessive Nicholson is an eccentric author who takes pride in his ability to be rude and offensive. His façade cracks when he offers to pay for the medical treatment for the son of the single-mum waitress at the café where he dines every day. His unorthodox attempts to start a relationship are by turns amusing and infuriating. Meanwhile, he is forced to confront his hatred for his gay neighbour when the man is brutally attacked and comes to live with Nicholson while he recovers, and a grudging respect develops into friendship. Slightly slow to start but quality entertainment with a brilliant performance by Nicholson who has the detail to perfection. Three Golden Globes and seven Oscar nominations.

BLOOD AND SAND 🎬4

TYRONE POWER, LINDA DARNELL,
RITA HAYWORTH, LAIRD CREGAR

ROUBEN MAMOULIAN

USA (FOX) 1941

120m (PG)

Richly coloured remake of the classic Valentino silent. As handsome Tyrone Power fights his way to the top of the bullfighting world, he is pursued by women and praised by camp critic Cregar. Made once more in 1989, with Sharon Stone the only notable name in the cast.

THE BLUE LAGOON 🎬2

BROOKE SHIELDS, CHRISTOPHER
ATKINS, LEO McKERN

RANDAL KLEISER

USA (MIA) 1980

104m (15)

Sexier re-make of 1949 Brit flick about two stranded kids growing to randy maturity on a tropical isle. I met Ms Shields around the time this was made, and her mom (with commendable honesty) told me that all her daughter's pix were dire. Judge for yourself whether this is true. (See page 248, *Pretty Baby*.)

THE BODYGUARD

KEVIN COSTNER, WHITNEY HOUSTON, GARY KEMP

MICK JACKSON

USA (WARNER) 1993

130m (15)

Over-long tale of ex-secret service bodyguard who falls for his pop singer charge while protecting her from a killer. Not a favourite of mine, although it proved very popular. An inexplicable hit. Widescreen available.

BREATHLESS

RICHARD GERE, VALERIE KAPRISKY, ART METRANO

JIM McBRIDE

USA (4-FRONT) 1983

96m (18)

Cult director McBride's remake of Godard's 1959 *A Bout De Souffle*, with Gere on top form as the young crook on the run with the gorgeous Kaprisky, living for the amoral moment with no care for future consequences. Much praised by Quentin Tarantino. The censor cut a few seconds that showed how to break into a car.

THE BRIDGES OF MADISON COUNTY

CLINT EASTWOOD, MERYL STREEP

CLINT EASTWOOD

USA (WARNER) 1995

129m (12)

Brief romance between photographer Eastwood and Ms Streep ensues after they meet when he asks directions to the famous wooden bridges of Madison County while on a photographic shoot. Not for those who like action in their movies, but others might find themselves reaching for the Kleenex as Streep chooses between passion and loyalty.

CASTAWAY

OLIVER REED, AMANDA DONOHOE, GEORGINA HALE, FRANCES BARBER

NICOLAS ROEG

UK (WARNER) 1986

112m (15)

True story of a young girl who signed up for a stay on a deserted island with an older man, with Donohoe stripping off a lot and inflaming Ollie Reed's lust before it all comes to an acrimonious end. (In real life the old gent is still taking women for island jaunts, it seems.) It's amazing to see Donohoe's confident showing (!) here. A rather straightforward story for the usually convoluted-minded Nic Roeg to have handled.

ROMANCE

CHILDREN OF A LESSER GOD [3]

WILLIAM HURT, MARLEE MATLIN, PIPER LAURIE, PHILIP BOSCO

RANDA HAINES

USA (4-FRONT) 1986

118m (15)

Mark Medoff's hit play about a deaf girl's romance with her teacher provided the vehicle for real-life deaf actress Matlin to score a richly deserved Oscar. There are some awkward moments but the film never descends to maudlin sentiment, which would have been the easy option.

CITY OF ANGELS [1]

NICOLAS CAGE, MEG RYAN

BRAD SIBERLING

USA (WARNER) 1998

109m (12)

An angel's job is to roam around the Earth and offer comfort to those in difficulties – they are not meant to 'get involved'. Needless to say, that's where Nicolas Cage fails, as he would give up all his angelic qualities to be mortal and spend his time on Earth with Ryan. Lightweight romance but watchable for all that.

COMING HOME [4]

JON VOIGHT, JANE FONDA, BRUCE DERN, ROBERT CARRADINE

HAL ASHBY

USA (WARNER) 1978

122m (18)

Love-triangle in the time of the Vietnam War, with Fonda as the wife who falls for paralysed veteran while hubby is overseas doing his bit. Based on the book by Nancy Dowd, who helped pen the Oscar-winning script. Oscars too for Voight and Fonda.

FALLING IN LOVE [3]

ROBERT DE NIRO, MERYL STREEP, HARVEY KEITEL, DIANNE WIEST

ULU GROSSBARD

USA (CIC) 1984

102m (PG)

A pair of upmarket New York commuters fall madly in love in spite of the fact that they're both married. Glitzy and tiresome, but undeniably well acted by the principals.

FAR AND AWAY 🎬2

TOM CRUISE, NICOLE KIDMAN, ROBERT PROSKY, THOMAS GIBSON

RON HOWARD

USA (CIC) 1992

140m (12)

Bloated epic romance typical of the American love affair with their (imagined) roots in nineteenth-century Ireland. Cruise and Kidman play a lout and a lady who flee trouble and emigrate to the USA, scrapping and spitting all the while, but finally going gooey-eyed at the end. Nice to look at, but this is really for fans of the two leads only.

FOR THE BOYS 🎬3

BETTE MIDLER, JAMES CAAN, GEORGE SEGAL, PATRICK O'NEAL

MARK RYDELL

USA (FOX) 1991

139m (15)

Romance following Midler as she struts her stuff to entertain American 'boys' in the forces through the country's varied wars: World War Two, Korea, Vietnam. Starts off okay, but overstays its welcome somewhat. Midler fans shouldn't be bored, though.

FOREVER YOUNG 🎬3

MEL GIBSON, JAMIE LEE CURTIS, ELIJAH WOOD

STEVE MINER

USA (WARNER) 1992

102m (PG)

Gibson is a test-pilot in 1939. Believing his girlfriend is dying, he agrees to an experiment where he'll be frozen in suspended animation – but he is forgotten and left in a warehouse until being accidentally awakened in 1992. Finding his lover is still alive and now an old woman, the rapidly ageing Mel gets assistance from Curtis and her son to track her down before it's too late. Silly, but improbably moving if you're prepared to go along for the ride.

ROMANCE

FORREST GUMP 🎬 4

TOM HANKS, ROBIN WRIGHT, GARY SINISE, SALLY FIELD

ROBERT ZEMECKIS

USA (CIC) 1994

137m (12)

'Life is like a box of chocolates. You never know what you're gonna get.' Hmmm … Oscar-laden film about a man too stupid to read the menu on a choc box might not seem romantic, but America is ever-ready to take the dumb and disabled to its heart (on film, at least) and *Gump* was a smash. Simple Forrest overcomes childhood disability with the aid of his can-do mom (Field), becomes a war-hero, a business success and a national icon. Love, however eludes him as his hippy girlfriend (Wright) wants to live life to the full. She makes mistakes (shame on her) while Forrest can do no wrong – even when his mind snaps and he runs the highways of the USA sporting an ever-larger beard. Despite the dubious 'stupid-is-good' message, Oscar-winning Hanks is truly mesmerising and the ending will bring a lump to the unjaundiced throat. Widescreen.

FOUR WEDDINGS AND A FUNERAL 🎬 3

HUGH GRANT, ANDIE MacDOWELL, SIMON CALLOW, KRISTIN SCOTT THOMAS

MIKE NEWELL

UK (POLYGRAM) 1994

117m (15)

Brit romantic comedy which was staggeringly financially successful especially in the USA where the folks are always keen to revel in the eccentricities of us madcap limeys. For me it's overrated, with Hugh Grant perfecting his gauche, twitching twit routine and Andie McDowell, lovely though she is, having little of substance to do. Try it and see what you think. Attempt to repeat the formula: *Notting Hill* (1999).

THE FRENCH LIEUTENANT'S WOMAN 🎬 3

JEREMY IRONS, MERYL STREEP, DAVID WARNER, LEO McKERN

KAREL REISZ

UK (WARNER) 1981

119m (15)

Based on a John Fowles novel via a script by Harold Pinter about a doomed Victorian love affair mirrored by that of the couple playing the protagonists in a modern movie. Arty and wet but proved a box-office hit with those up for a weepy. Streep is eminently watchable, as ever.

TOP 1000 VIDEOS

GHOST

DEMI MOORE, PATRICK SWAYZE, WHOOPI GOLDBERG

JERRY ZUCKER

USA (CIC) 1990

121m (15)

Romantic fantasy about the spook of a murder victim who tries to protect his girl through a medium. Much parodied and spoofed, and has inspired the filming of other ghostly love tales. Oscars for screenplay and for supporting actress Goldberg as the dodgy spiritualist.

THE GREAT GATSBY

ROBERT REDFORD, MIA FARROW, BRUCE DERN, SAM WATERSTON, SCOTT WILSON

JACK CLAYTON

USA (CIC) 1974

135m (PG)

Second movie attempt at F Scott Fitzgerald's story of mysterious 1920s Gatsby and his tragic love. Redford is perfect as the glowingly handsome tycoon, and Waterston is wonderful as the young observer. All the cast are on form with the unfortunate exception of the insipid Farrow – in these pre-Woody Allen days one simply can't imagine a guy of Jay Gatsby's clout getting his Y-fronts in a twist over her. Patsy Kensit makes an early screen appearance as a kiddy. Oscars for score and costumes. Script by Francis Ford Coppola.

THE HUNCHBACK OF NOTRE DAME

CHARLES LAUGHTON, MAUREEN O'HARA, CEDRIC HARDWICKE, EDMOND O'BRIEN, THOMAS MITCHELL, GEORGE ZUCCO

WILLIAM DIETERLE

USA (4-FRONT) 1939 B&W

112m (PG)

Laughton stars as Quasimodo, the deformed cathedral bell-ringer, in the best-ever version of Victor Hugo's tale. His unrequited love for the gypsy girl, Esmeralda, spurs him to protect her from the lust of his master, who has commanded him to kidnap her. Criticised for sentimental style, but the compassion for the title character never bogs down the story or action. Dizzying camera-work and fantastic sets, but the crux of the film is love: those who love Esmeralda and those she loves.

ROMANCE

INDECENT PROPOSAL [4]

ROBERT REDFORD, DEMI MOORE, WOODY HARRELSON

ADRIAN LYNE

USA (CIC) 1993

119m (15)

A young couple fail to gamble themselves out of a hole in Las Vegas until rich smoothy Redford takes a shine to the wife and offers a million dollars for a night of sex. Acceptance should bring relief, but the trouble is only beginning – hubby can't handle it and the rich man starts using all his wiles to obtain second helpings. An intriguing premise, let down a little by an unrealistic ending.

LIVING OUT LOUD [3]

DANNY DeVITO, HOLLY HUNTER, QUEEN LATIFAH

RICHARD LaGRAVENESSE

USA (ENTERTAINMENT) 1998

96m (15)

Abandoned for a younger woman by her wealthy New York doctor husband, Judith Nelson begins to live a mixture of fantasy and reality. Scenes are often played out twice to contrast how she would like things to happen – and how they actually turn out. A chance meeting with an elevator operator, who is also recovering from a traumatic personal life, turns out to be a turning point and a relationship builds between the unlikely pair. Heard it before? Perhaps, but good performances and a strong script give it more appeal than your average recovering-from-trauma weepie.

LOVE FIELD [3]

MICHELLE PFEIFFER, DENNIS HAYSBERT, BRIAN KERWIN

JONATHAN KAPLAN

USA (CINEMA CLUB V) 1992

104m (15)

Dallas wife takes off for the funeral of JFK despite husband's objections. En route she meets a black man and his kid, inadvertently causing them a heap of trouble. A rather flimsy piece, but touching in places.

LOVE IS A MANY-SPLENDORED THING [2]

WILLIAM HOLDEN, JENNIFER JONES, TORIN THATCHER

HENRY KING

USA (FOX) 1955

120m (U)

Based on Han Suyin's novel *A Many Splendoured Thing*, this tells of a mixed-race female doc's affair with an American correspondent during the Korean War. Oscars for title-tune, score and costumes, but it's a so-so movie with the usual tearjerker ending one would expect.

A MATTER OF LIFE AND DEATH [5]

DAVID NIVEN, KIM HUNTER, ROGER LIVESY, MARIUS GORING

MICHAEL POWELL, EMERIC PRESSBURGER

UK (RANK) 1941 COL/B&W

104m (U)

Mooted as a World War Two propaganda piece calling for USA/UK co-operation, but in the hands of Powell and Pressburger became a classic of screen imagination. Niven is a pilot who escapes certain death only because the angel (Goring) assigned to conduct him to heaven misses him in the fog. Having fallen in love in the meantime, he's allowed to argue his case for extra life before an angry Yank prosecutor from the American War of Independence while his body undergoes a kill-or-cure op down on earth. Heaven is depicted as silvery monochrome: 'One is starved for Technicolor up there!' sighs the angel. A truly magical picture in all departments: acting, ideas, effects, design. See it again and again. American title: *Stairway To Heaven*.

ROMANCE

MOONSTRUCK 🎬 3

CHER, NICOLAS CAGE, VINCENT GARDENIA, OLYMPIA DUKAKIS

NORMAN JEWISON

USA (MGM/UA) 1987

98m (PG)

Brooklyn babe Cher gets the naughty hot-to-trots for the brother of her intended. Amusing piece of froth with some good dialogue and an ace supporting cast. Cher and Dukakis both won Oscars, as did writer John Patrick Shanly. Perennially popular with romance buffs, though I personally feel it's somewhat overrated. Worth renting.

AN OFFICER AND A GENTLEMAN 🎬 4

RICHARD GERE, DEBRA WINGER, DAVID KEITH, LOUIS GOSSETT Jnr

TAYLOR HACKFORD

USA (CIC) 1981

119m (15)

Wide-boy Gere joins US Navy to train as an officer and has the naughtiness knocked out of him by instructor Gossett Jnr (in an Oscar-winning performance). Romance and tragedy intrude when the lad and his pal take up with two slutty gals, but our hero makes good in the end. Theme tune ('Up Where We Belong') also snared an Oscar and – like the movie – was a massive hit.

OUT OF AFRICA 🎬 3

MERYL STREEP, ROBERT REDFORD, KLAUS MARIA BRANDAUER, MICHAEL KITCHEN

SYDNEY POLLACK

UK/USA (CIC) 1985

115m (PG)

Inspired by the life in Africa of Danish lady Karen Blixen (who wrote books as Isak Dinesen) and her romance with a white hunter, this smash hit picture is ace to look at but slow as treacle. Streep passes the accent test, but Redford is miscast as a stiff upper Brit. Seven Oscars: best picture/director/cinematography/script/art direction/sound/score.

PEYTON PLACE 🎬 2

LANA TURNER, HOPE LANGE, ARTHUR KENNEDY, RUSS TAMBLYN

MARK ROBSON

USA (FOX) 1957

152m (15)

The Grace Metalious potboiler inspired both this movie and a TV series. Soap opera tale about the steamy goings-on beneath the prim facade of a small New England town. David Lynch ought to do a remake – after all, what was *Blue Velvet* (see page 282) but a wilder *Peyton Place* for the 80s?

THE PIANO [3]

HARVEY KEITEL, HOLLY HUNTER, SAM NEILL, ANNA PAQUIN

JANE CAMPION

NEW ZEALAND (ENTERTAINMENT) 1983

121m (15)

Tale of a woman and child landed with an arranged marriage. When hubby leaves her precious piano on the beach she makes a deal with the estate manager to give him piano lessons in exchange for saving it. Soon the lessons are in love, rather than music. Critics have noted flaws – Keitel (as the manager) is illiterate, yet he reads a message at one point! Affecting, nevertheless. Widescreen. Highly acclaimed both at Cannes and the Academy Awards.

PRETTY BABY [4]

BROOKE SHIELDS, KEITH CARRADINE, SUSAN SARANDON, BARBARA STEELE

LOUIS MALLE

USA (CIC) 1978

106m (15)

Photographer is obsessed with 12-year-old hooker in a New Orleans brothel. Controversial films usually lose their edge with time, but, in the current climate of hysteria about child abuse, this movie (though relatively innocuous) would probably never get a studio green light were it to be proposed today. Shields is amazing: though she cannot act for toffee (see *The Blue Lagoon*, page 239), she has the body of a child and the face of a *Vogue* model, making her perfect for the part.

PRETTY IN PINK [3]

MOLLY RINGWALD, HARRY DEAN STANTON, ANDREW McCARTHY

HOWARD DEUTCH

USA (CIC) 1986

93m (15)

Rich boy and poor girl fall for each other, with all the problems one might expect from such a relationship. Plenty of teenage angst and Ringwald displays real talent as the sweet young thing.

ROMANCE

PRETTY WOMAN [4]

RICHARD GERE, JULIA ROBERTS, RALPH BELLAMY, ALEX HYDE-WHITE

GARRY MARSHALL

USA (TOUCHSTONE) 1990

115m (15)

Prostitute is hired by a rich businessman to escort him round town, but in the process of making her socially acceptable (à la *My Fair Lady*) he falls in love with her. Much-lambasted by feminists for making prostitution appear glam and a viable career opportunity – after all, most runaway girls who become hookers end up on drugs and/or in thrall to a pimp, not as the babe of a millionaire! A fun film, all the same.

ROMAN HOLIDAY [4]

GREGORY PECK, AUDREY HEPBURN, EDDIE ALBERT

WILLIAM WYLER

USA (CIC) 1953 B&W

113m (U)

Svelte Hepburn won an Oscar as the princess who tires of official duties while in Rome and falls for reporter Peck. Light comedy/romance which also garnered Oscars for story and Edith Head's costumes. Remade for TV in 1987 to no great purpose.

THE ROMANTIC ENGLISHWOMAN [3]

GLENDA JACKSON, MICHAEL CAINE, HELMUT BERGER, KATE NELLIGAN

JOSEPH LOSEY

FRANCE/UK (ODYSSEY) 1975

112m (15)

Though I've grown to see his merits, Joseph Losey made so many downbeat movies that my teenage pals and I used to call him 'Joseph Lousy' in honour of the boredom he inflicted on us. In truth, this is one of his lesser works – but with Glenda Jackson (in pre-MP days) as the spouse of a writer who gets the gibbering hots for Helmut Berger (we called him 'German Helmet') the story is an entertaining *ménage-à-trois* piece. Penned by Tom Stoppard (now Sir Tom) and Thomas Wiseman, from the latter's novel.

ROMEO AND JULIET [3]

LEONARD WHITING, OLIVIA HUSSEY, MILO O'SHEA, ROBERT STEPHENS

FRANCO ZEFFIRELLI

ITALY/UK (CIC) 1968

133m (PG)

This star-studded version of Shakespeare's play has the virtue of players who are closer to the correct ages for the parts of the young lovers than most who have undertaken the roles – Whiting was 17 and Hussey 15 when the film was made. Captures the essence of the play. Oscars for cinematography and costumes. Some sources list an original running time of 152 m. There are numerous other versions, of course, including a hard-porn one and trash expert Troma's *Tromeo and Juliet*!

SHAKESPEARE IN LOVE [4]

GWYNETH PALTROW, JOSEPH FIENNES, GEOFFREY RUSH, COLIN FIRTH, BEN AFFLECK, JUDI DENCH

JOHN MADDEN

UK (CIC) 1998

119m (15)

Oscar-winning role for Judi Dench as Queen Elizabeth I in this hugely entertaining story of love and thespians, set in the backstage milieu of Shakespeare's bustling theatrical world. Plenty of laughs and romance, with a super cast at the top of their game. The Yanks went ga-ga for it, of course, but don't let that put you off. (Note: seeing this pic inspired Prince Edward to adopt upon marriage the title Earl of Wessex used herein. You couldn't make it up.)

SCENT OF A WOMAN [3]

AL PACINO, GABRIELLE ANWAR, CHRIS O'DONNELL, RICHARD BRADFORD

MARTIN BREST

USA (CIC) 1992

151m (15)

Alcoholic ex-army man blinded when horsing about with grenades decides to get his young minder to take him out for one last wild binge before killing himself – but things don't go as planned. A feel-good picture which, though it may not be Pacino's best, won the star an Oscar which was long overdue.

SLEEPLESS IN SEATTLE [5]

TOM HANKS, MEG RYAN, BILL PULLMAN, ROSIE O'DONNELL

NORA EPHRON

USA (COLUMBIA TRISTAR) 1993

105m (PG)

Classic 'girly' movie about a man left with a child after his wife dies, the girl who's unsure about her impending marriage, and how fate brings them together via a radio show shrink. Charming, endearing, feel-good movie magic that has become something of a legend. Romance fans will not have to fake any orgasms over this one.

ROMANCE

SLIDING DOORS [3]

GWYNETH PALTROW, JOHN HANNAH, JEANNE TRIPPLEHORN, JOCK LYNCH

PETER HOWITT

USA/UK (CIC) 1997

95m (15)

Former star of TV's *Bread* directs this what-if piece of whimsy and romance. As in: what if you did/didn't make it through those closing tube doors? The effect on a couple's love life is shown with the two possible versions of events. Well acted and will no doubt trigger many viewers into reminiscing about their own missed romantic opportunities.

SOMEWHERE IN TIME [4]

CHRISTOPHER REEVE, JANE SEYMOUR, CHRISTOPHER PLUMMER, TERESA WRIGHT

JEANNOT SZWARC

USA (CIC) 1980

98m (PG)

Based on Richard Matheson's novel *Bid Time Return*, this is a romantic fantasy about a man who becomes so enraptured by the picture of an actress in an old locket that he wills himself back to 1912 to meet with her. It's never quite explained just how he manages this, but in truth you'll hardly care. Time-travel tales are always fascinating – who would not love to be free of the here-and-now? – and this is no exception. Great.

SOMMERSBY [3]

RICHARD GERE, JODIE FOSTER, BILL PULLMAN, JAMES EARL JONES

JON AMIEL

USA (WARNER) 1993

114m (15)

A man comes back from the American Civil War – but instead of the ogre who went off to fight he's now a caring chappie. His wife is well pleased, but soon begins to doubt if this is really her husband at all. Implausible (who wouldn't know their own husband, even after six years?) but engrossing reworking of the French movie *The Return Of Martin Guerre* (see page 355).

STANLEY AND IRIS [3]

ROBERT DE NIRO, JANE FONDA, SWOOSIE KURTZ

MARTIN RITT

USA (WARNER) 1989

100m (15)

Widow teaches an illiterate male workmate to read, but finds that they are growing attracted to each other. Simple tale, warmly told and considerably elevated by the power of the two leads. Based on the book *Union Street* by Pat Barker.

SUMMER OF '42 [4]

JENNIFER O'NEILL, GARY GRIMES, LOU FRIZELL, JERRY HOUSER

ROBERT MULLIGAN

USA (WARNER) 1971

98m (15)

Herman Raucher's World War Two novel is the basis for this lovely looking movie. A young woman (played by the beautiful former model O'Neill) gets news that her husband has been killed and takes a teenage boy who has been mooning after her to bed in an act of mutual consolation. There's not much more to it than that – it's an atmosphere piece all the way. Michel Legrand's music won an Oscar.

TENDER MERCIES [3]

ROBERT DUVALL, TESS HARPER, ELLEN BARKIN, WILFORD BRIMLEY

BRUCE BERESFORD

USA (WARNER) 1982

88m (PG)

Country singer is helped to reconstruct his life by a lonely widow and her boy. Unremarkable, but Duvall's Oscar-winning performance carries the film. Oscar for original screenplay, too.

TERMS OF ENDEARMENT [3]

SHIRLEY MacLAINE, DEBRA WINGER, JACK NICHOLSON, DANNY DeVITO

JAMES L BROOKS

USA (CIC) 1983

126m (15)

Sentimental film about a feuding mother and daughter, their romance, and how they finally come together when the girl contracts cancer. Oscars for pic, director, actress (MacLaine), supporting actor (Nicholson), script. Based on the Larry McMurtry novel. A sequel of sorts was attempted recently, but it sank without trace.

TESS [3]

NASTASSJA KINSKI, LEIGH LAWSON, PETER FIRTH

ROMAN POLANSKI

FRANCE/UK (GUILD) 1979

180m (PG)

To complete his epic version of Hardy's tale of a distressed cutie abused by her rich relative, Polanski had to build a replica of Stonehenge (where the climax occurs) in France – he was in danger of being extradited to the USA if he entered Britain, as he was wanted over there for allegedly abusing a distressed cutie of his own! Still, it's a fairly accurate rendering of the tragic romance, lush to look at and with a surprisingly fetching central performance from Polanski's then-paramour Kinski. Now out in widescreen.

VALENTINO

RUDOLPH NUREYEV, LESLIE CARON, MICHELLE PHILLIPS, ANTON DIFFRING

KEN RUSSELL

USA (WARNER) 1977

123m (18)

Competently-told story of the great silent star's loves, with the imaginative stroke of casting sex-god dancer Nureyev in the lead. Not our Ken's greatest moment, but there are enough visual fireworks and lusty episodes to satisfy.

THE WEDDING SINGER

ADAM SANDLER, DREW BARRYMORE, CHRISTINE TAYLOR

FRANK CORACI

USA (ENTERTAINMENT) 1998

96m (12)

Sandler is the MC who makes other folks happy on their wedding days, making the entertainment flow as smoothly as the champagne, but when his own love life fizzles out he lets his career go to hell in a handbasket – until sympathetic waitress Drew takes him in hand. Barrymore has gone from kiddie-star to wild-child to credible actress, and she and Sandler make this a reliable little romantic comedy that did well with critics and punters alike. Sandler may not mean much in the UK, but he is allegedly getting the highest single fee ever paid to an actor for the sequel to this pic, a staggering 17 million quid. And he's talking about retiring already, before most of us here have even heard of him!

WHAT DREAMS MAY COME 🎬3

ROBIN WILLIAMS, ANNABELLA SCIORRA, MAX VON SYDOW, CUBA GOODING Jnr

VINCENT WARD

USA (UNIVERSAL) 1999

109m (15)

Robin Williams finds that, for him, the afterlife is a scene in one of his partner's beautiful paintings, where anything is possible. But while he cannot bear to die without her, she cannot bear to live without him and commits suicide to try to join him. The problem is that 'suicides go to hell' and they are destined never to be together again. Undaunted, he enlists the help of The Tracker and embarks on a journey through heaven and hell to free her. Amazing and visually dazzling effects are lost a bit on the small screen but still worth a look.

WHEN HARRY MET SALLY 🎬4

BILLY CRYSTAL, MEG RYAN, CARRIE FISHER, LISA JANE PERSKY

ROB REINER

USA (ENTERTAINMENT) 1989

91m (15)

Smash hit scripted by Nora Ephron, the creator of *Sleepless In Seattle* (see page 250) with nice performances by Crystal and Ryan as two antagonistic old pals who gradually fall in love. Orgasm-faking gals of the world will love this one for its honesty and sensitivity about human relationships. Salty, smart dialogue.

WHITE PALACE 🎬3

SUSAN SARANDON, JAMES SPADER, KATHY BATES, EILEEN BRENNAN

LOUIS MANDOKI

USA (CIC) 1990

99m (18)

Glenn Savan's novel is the basis for this love story of a shy guy who falls for an older woman from a working-class background, only to realise that love doesn't automatically conquer all. Subtle characterisation makes it come alive.

WILD AT HEART 🎬4

NICOLAS CAGE, LAURA DERN, WILLEM DAFOE, DIANE LADD

DAVID LYNCH

USA (ELECTRIC) 1990

119m (18)

Lynch's typically crazed adaptation of Barry Gifford's book. Just out of jail for murder, Cage takes to the road with sexy Dern only to have her demented mama (played by Ladd, her real-life mom) send a thug on their trail. Flawed portrait of American misfits in love, and very violent. Widescreen.

ROMANCE

WOMEN IN LOVE [4]

ALAN BATES, GLENDA JACKSON, OLIVER REED, JENNIE LINDEN

KEN RUSSELL

UK (WARNER) 1970

125m (18)

Russell's flamboyant version of the DH Lawrence novel, famous for its groundbreaking male nude wrestling scene. Jackson scored the best acress Oscar for her work here. One of Ken Russell's best movies.

WUTHERING HEIGHTS [5]

LAURENCE OLIVIER, MERLE OBERON, DAVID NIVEN, FLORA ROBSON, DONALD CRISP

WILLIAM WYLER

USA (CINEMA CLUB V) 1939 B&W

104m (U)

Still the best of several film versions of the Emily Brontë story of brooding love between a high-spirited girl and the orphan boy her father adopted. Olivier and Oberon run away with the picture, and Gregg Toland's photography deservedly bagged an Oscar. Stands repeated viewings. Classic? Undoubtedly. Romantic? Definitively.

YOU'VE GOT MAIL [3]

TOM HANKS, MEG RYAN

NORA EPHRON

USA (WARNER) 1999

114m (PG)

Two business rivals – both with less-than-perfect live-in partners – are unaware that they are already involved in an on-line romance. Lightweight comedy romance with predictable performances from the two stars.

255

Science Fiction

Science Fiction has been an important facet of cinema from its earliest days; audiences over 60 years ago were as delighted by the unsophisticated silent capers of Méliès and the American Edison company's *A Trip To Mars* as we are by the hi-tech mega-bucks-budget films of today.

But in the 1990s, with special effects stretching both our imaginations and the studios' budgets almost beyond belief, it is the plots and underlying messages that are looking worryingly trite, if not downright suspect. I've no complaints about the films such as the 'Star Wars' or 'Star Trek' series: these offer pure fantasy in the best style of Flash Gordon and still manage to show that ray-guns and serious ideas need not be mutually exclusive. But when the multi-million-dollar budget of a film like *Independence Day* produces nothing more than a piece of jingoistic 'Planet USA' guff, that does make me somewhat uneasy.

Mind-boggling SFX do, without doubt, play a great part in good sci-fi films but the best should also have a few thought-provoking ideas. I am happy to say that there is enough of both in my selection in this chapter for me to have some optimism for the future of the genre. *Mars Attacks!* may be full of self-indulgent star cameos, but for me it is still great to see the best of hi-tech used to make SFX in the style of a set of bubble-gum cards I remember collecting in the 1960s. If your preference is for entertainment with a more philosophical bent, try *Blade Runner* or *12 Monkeys*. Whatever your taste, there are plenty of worthwhile titles out there for the discerning video-viewer.

SCIENCE FICTION

12 MONKEYS

BRUCE WILLIS, MADELEINE STOWE, BRAD PITT, FRANK GORSHIN, ANNIE GOLDEN

TERRY GILLIAM

USA (POLYGRAM) 1995

128m (15)

Inspired by Chris Marker's experimental short *La Jetée* (made in 1962), this complex film involves a man being sent back in time to avert the events that led to global disaster. Sent to the wrong point in the past, he's judged to be mad – and that's only the start of his troubles. To explain the whole plot of this marvellous movie would take too long and would only spoil the fun for you. Suffice to say it deals with the possibility of time travel and the problems of same in a sophisticated, moving way. Willis is on top form. Gilliam's best movie since the dark *Brazil* (see page 262). Widescreen and special boxed edition available.

2001 – A SPACE ODYSSEY

KEIR DULLEA, GARY LOCKWOOD, DOUGLAS RAIN, LEONARD ROSSITER

STANLEY KUBRICK

UK (MGM/UA-WARNER) 1968

141m (U)

Kubrick's controversial epic (based on a story by Arthur C Clarke) was nevertheless praised for its stunning visuals of ships spinning and planets rising via Oscar-winning SFX handmade in those far-off pre-digital days, all accompanied by the grand strains of classical music. The story starts with a monolithic slab which mesmerises a group of apemen; a similar object is found on the moon by mankind in 2001; it emits a signal that points us to Jupiter's moons, and a ship is sent to investigate – but the ship's talking computer (HAL, voiced by Douglas Rain, one of the movie's best features) has other ideas ... It was the one surviving astronaut's psychedelic 'stargate' trip and the ending that confused the critics – it's certainly open to many interpretations about birth, death and eternity. Does not appear to be available in widescreen, which is crazy. I saw it on one of the original Cinerama playdates and it was awesome. Cut by the director by some 20m to 141m after those dates, and now seen in 70mm or 35mm cinema prints (widescreen), it is inevitably a somewhat diminished experience. If we have to see it on TV, at least we should have it in the right ratio! The classical score was used because some of the director's co-workers, who heard the music being used temporarily during editing, said they preferred it to Alex North's original score – which is available for the curious on CD. There is a sequel to *2001*, titled *2010 – The Year We Make Contact* (see opposite).

2010 – THE YEAR WE MAKE CONTACT 🎬4

ROY SCHEIDER, HELEN MIRREN, KEIR DULLEA, BOB BALABAN, JOHN LITHGOW

PETER HYAMS

USA (MGM/UA-WARNER) 1984

116m (PG)

Any sequel to Kubrick's *2001* was going to be on a hiding to nothing from day one, and any solution to the questions posed by the original were certain to annoy those who delighted in the enigmatic qualities of the first film. It's hardy surprising then that *2010* is not highly regarded, and it has to be admitted that the functional Hyams is no Kubrick, but the pic has a lot going for it: a fine cast (including Dullea, reprising his role from *2001*); the use of Arthur C Clarke's own sequel novel as basis for the script; and meticulous recreation of sets and costumes seen in the first film – even HAL comes back-on-line, voiced once more by Douglas Rain. If you can put your preconceptions away, this much-maligned piece may entertain you, even if there are no ultimate answers or surprises. Like *2001*, the film got several Oscar nominations. It won none, while *2001* won only one, for effects.

THE ABYSS 🎬4

ED HARRIS, MARY ELIZABETH MASTRANTONIO, MICHAEL BIEHN

JAMES CAMERON

USA (FOX) 1989

140/171m (15)

This underwater epic seemed overlong when I first saw it in 1989. After being trapped while trying to locate a missing sub, our heroes suddenly discover that the aliens causing all the trouble never meant any harm in the first place! It felt like a rushed and most unsatisfying close to a claustrophobic two hours plus. The director later admitted that the film was hindered by time constraints, and he assented to a special version on laserdisc and video. Made more coherent by the extra half-hour of material, the movie paradoxically feels shorter. Both versions are available in pan-scan or widescreen, and the special edition was issued in a limited-edition box with booklet and documentary footage. For me, the letterbox version is always the preferred option, but in the booklet director Cameron disagrees. He claims that because a letterbox print has half or so of the TV screen masked-off, this makes the picture lose quality. As *Video Watchdog* critic Tim Lucas has pointed out, with this film, shot full-frame and then masked to create a widescreen image, it is simply wrong to state that the letterbox copy is any less clear – the same part of what was shot is occupying the same part of your TV whichever version you pick. Of course, with a movie that was actually shot in widescreen ratio, pan-scan does bring things up close – but you lose nearly half the picture. *The Abyss* won an Oscar for sound. The censor cut a shot of a rat being submerged in a 'breathable liquid'. Cameron went on to make that other watery effort, *Titanic* (see page 135).

SCIENCE FICTION

ALIEN [3]

SIGOURNEY WEAVER, JOHN HURT, IAN HOLM, TOM SKERRITT

RIDLEY SCOTT

UK (FOX) 1979

117m (18)

As much a horror film as it is SF, this involves a dark, scruffy spaceship invaded by an organism which grows parasitically in the body of one of the crew, only to burst forth and stalk the remaining humans. Weaver's feisty female survivor and artist HR Giger's creature ensured a cult following, leading to three sequels so far and lots of merchandising opportunities. Widescreen available.

ALIENS [4]

SIGOURNEY WEAVER, MICHAEL BIEHN, LANCE HENRIKSEN, BILL PAXTON

JAMES CAMERON

USA (FOX) 1986

137m (18)

Sequel sees Weaver awakened from the suspended-animation pod she escaped in at the climax of *Alien*. Over 50 years have passed, but the creatures are still out there. She returns to do battle with a monstrous egg-laying queen in a movie that is both a gung-ho Vietnam-in-space and a reprise of the earlier film. Henriksen is superb as a tough android who fights back even when cut in two! Oscars: sound effects and visual effects. Widescreen available, and in an extended version with 17m more footage.

ALIEN³ [3]

SIGOURNEY WEAVER, CHARLES DANCE, BRIAN GLOVER

DAVID FINCHER

USA (FOX) 1992

115m (18)

Weakest of the series. Weaver has escaped again, only to land on a prison planet full of rapists and murderers where women are not welcome. The only ally she has is the resident medic (Dance), the one man who believes that she may be telling the truth about the aliens. Despite her suicide dive at the end – in order to kill the creature spawning inside her – Weaver's Ripley character is back in yet another sequel (see opposite). Widescreen available.

ALIEN RESURRECTION [3]

SIGOURNEY WEAVER, WINONA RYDER, DAN HEDAYA, RON PERLMAN

JEAN-PIERRE JEUNET

USA (FOX) 1997

104m (18)

Desperate fourth continuation of the 'Aliens' franchise: Ripley (a zonked-out Weaver) topped herself at the end of the last movie, so we have to swallow the idea that they clone her using her DNA! After that it's business as usual – all the trademark surprises have turned to cliché, so we get the 'It's inside you ... splat!' bit, the 'White blood? You're an android!' moment, the 'I'm gonna whup yer alien butt!' battle and the last-minute escape, plus the usual selection of nerds who think they can handle the monsters until it all goes pear-shaped and they end up as cinematic cannon-fodder. All quite entertaining. Director Jeunet was hired on the strength of his work on *The City Of Lost Children* (see page 351) and he gives the pic some of that film's odd visual style and dreamlike quality – I especially enjoyed the underwater sequence with aliens zipping around like sharks. Fox issued a boxed set, comprising the previous three 'Aliens' pix and a documentary tape, now superseded by a box of all four pix (letterbox or fullscreen).

ALPHAVILLE [4]

EDDIE CONSTANTINE, ANNA KARINA, AKIM TAMIROFF, HOWARD VERNON

JEAN-LUC GODARD

FRANCE/ITALY (CONNOISSEUR) 1965 B&W

98m (PG)

Delirious mix of art movie/*film noir*/SF, with Paris standing in for Saris, the computerised city of the future where a private eye tries to rescue a boffin. Call it brilliant or pretentious, it's never boring. Godard claimed it was actually about a man from the 40s in the Paris of the 60s. Was originally to be called *Tarzan Versus IBM*. (Also available on a Warner tape).

ALTERED STATES [5]

WILLIAM HURT, BLAIR BROWN, BOB BALABAN, CHARLES HAID

KEN RUSSELL

USA (WARNER) 1980

102m (18)

Troubled movie based on Paddy Chayevsky novel. Russell replaced Arthur Penn, Chayevsky retreated behind a pseudonym. The story involves a scientist combining drugs, mysticism and flotation-tank experiments to the point where his psychedelic regression to apeman days begins to take hold physically as well as mentally. Can love save him? Much panned by critics, but stunning on a big screen. No letterbox version available.

SCIENCE FICTION

ARMAGEDDON

BRUCE WILLIS, LIV TYLER, BILLY BOB THORNTON, BEN AFFLECK, STEVE BUSCEMI

MICHAEL BAY

USA (BUENA VISTA) 1998

145m (12)

Brucie-boy stars in one of those earth-in-danger-from-a-giant-meteor movies. These things tend to arrive in groups, rather like buses. I think it just about passes muster as a late-night, after-pub pic. See the similar *Deep Impact* (page 265).

BARBARELLA

JANE FONDA, DAVID HEMMINGS, ANITA PALLENBERG, MILO O'SHEA, JOHN PHILLIP LAW

ROGER VADIM

FRANCE/ITALY (CIC) 1967

97m (15)

Part of the plan by Fonda's then-spouse Vadim to make her another of his sex-symbol stars in the Bardot manner, this adaptation of an adult comic strip (with the accent on strip) about a naive-but-cute astronaut boasts lovely fetishistic art direction and some overripe acting. Scientist Duran Duran (from whom the pop group took their name) tries to kill Barbarella with his orgasm machine, but the oversexed minx blows its fuses. You get the picture. There's actually very little bare flesh on show, and the opening anti-gravity striptease was rejigged in the USA in order to obscure a glimpse of Fonda's pubic hair. Not released on tape in widescreen, though available on USA laserdisc.

BLADE RUNNER 5

HARRISON FORD, RUTGER HAUER, SEAN YOUNG, DARYL HANNAH

RIDLEY SCOTT

USA (WARNER) 1982

117m   (15)

This film of Philip K Dick's novel *Do Androids Dream Of Electric Sheep?* is now regarded as one of the most influential SF movies of all time, with its drab, realistic look and philosophical questioning about what constitutes humanity. Ford plays a detective hunting down 'replicants', androids who've escaped. He reluctantly terminates them – until he falls in love with one and we are left to consider whether he may be a replicant himself. The world-weary voice-over was hated by many fans, and a version without it was issued recently as a 'director's cut'. In Paul M Sammon's book on the film, director Scott confesses that this new version (with a few visual changes and slightly shorter than the original) is *not* a 'director's cut', as he was not given the time he wanted to complete it. There are, it appears, several versions of the film in existence, including a more violent print and a radically different work-print. Widescreen versions are available and Sammon's book is highly recommended.

BRAZIL 4

JONATHAN PRYCE, KIM GRIEST, ROBERT DE NIRO, IAN HOLM

TERRY GILLIAM

UK (WARNER) 1985

142m   (15)

Gilliam's epic of a daydreaming everyman (Pryce) trapped in a surreal, Kafka-esque bureaucracy of the future was hampered in the USA when bosses delayed release, prompting a war of words between director and studio. While the Yanks had to suffer cut prints that destroyed the meaning of the piece, we Brits got the whole thing. Pryce tries to save the girl he loves from afar as the machinery of the law (literally) accidentally names her as a terrorist. Mad sets, great performances and just when you think everything's okay, Gilliam destroys the happy ending with a stab to the heart.

SCIENCE FICTION

CLOSE ENCOUNTERS OF THE THIRD KIND

RICHARD DREYFUSS, FRANCOIS TRUFFAUT, TERI GARR, MELINDA DILLON

STEVEN SPIELBERG

USA (COLUMBIA) 1977

135m (PG)

More a film about the search for meaning in life than an effects romp, this is quintessential Spielberg. Magical intimations of alien existence are intercut with the effects these have on the lives of several people. It's a moving film, but works best the first time you see it. In 1980 the director re-edited the material and added new footage to create a 'special edition', but in this hack's opinion it did not make for a significantly better movie. The original is the one I would recommend though you may want to rent the other out of curiosity. Widescreen available. Oscars: cinematography, sound effects editing.

COCOON

DON AMECHE, HUME CRONYN, JESSICA TANDY, WILFORD BRIMLEY

RON HOWARD

USA (FOX) 1985

117m (PG)

Whimsical piece about old folk stumbling upon a rejuvenating pool created by aliens for the purpose of rescuing stranded compadres. Starts well but turns silly, remaining amusing for all that. A sequel exists: *Cocoon 2: The Return*, made in 1988. Oscars: Ameche (supporting actor), SFX.

CONTACT 🎬4

JODIE FOSTER, JAMES WOODS, MATTHEW McCONAUGHEY, JOHN HURT, TOM SKERRITT

ROBERT ZEMECKIS

USA (WARNER) 1997

143m (PG)

This moving, low-key and thoroughly believable story about the search for extraterrestrial life was a flop at the box office, probably due to the length and the lack of flashy FX, but hopefully it'll find its audience on video. Foster is a scientist who battles against all the odds to continue her project to contact other planets, pooh-poohed by sceptics and aided only by ailing mega-rich mogul John Hurt. Just when it looks like she's on the brink of success, her place on the trip of a lifetime is nabbed by the very guy who refused to credit her theories all along! But the lady ain't about to give up that easily. Some will say this is a film for airheads who need to believe in little green men, but it has a message about hanging on to your ideals and, yes, your faith. Widescreen.

CUBE 🎬3

NICOLE de BOER, NICKY GUADAGNI, DAVID HEWLETT, WAYNE ROBSON

VINCENZO NATALI

CANADA (COLUMBIA TRISTAR) 1997

90m (15)

Gimmicky but low-tech fantasy about a group of people who find themselves thrown together in a box-like prison. Shot in under a month and agreeably bereft of FX, *Cube* relies on the acting and its near-existentialist concept to keep you watching. Flawed, but we are obviously in the presence of a director with potential.

THE DAY THE EARTH STOOD STILL 🎬5

MICHAEL RENNIE, PATRICIA NEAL, SAM JAFFE

ROBERT WISE

USA (FOX) 1951 B&W

92m (U)

Landmark SF about an alien who comes to warn earth to abjure war or face heavy measures for its own good. Naturally, he is not welcomed. Fatally wounded but temporarily revived, he leaves behind his robot (Gort) and others as planetary policemen. Well directed by Jack-of-all-genres Wise, it was a major influence on *The Abyss* (see page 258) and many other SF films. The alien catch-phrase 'Klaatu Barada Nikto' has entered into pop culture to emerge in albums by Ringo Starr of the Beatles and Beatles-imitators Klaatu, and in various movies. Now available in a digitally remastered edition.

SCIENCE FICTION

DEEP IMPACT 🎬2

ROVERT DUVALL, TEA LEONI, ELIJAH WOOD, MORGAN FREEMAN, VANESSA REDGRAVE, MAXIMILIAN SCHELL

MIMI LEDER

UK (DREAMWORKS) 1998

117m (12)

Another here-comes-the-big-one epic, about earth in danger from a meteor/asteroid/what-have-you. I personally prefer *Armageddon* (see page 261), but this has the classier cast list.

DEMON SEED 🎬4

JULIE CHRISTIE, FRITZ WEAVER, GERRIT GRAHAM

DONALD CAMMELL

USA (WARNER/BEYONDVISION) 1977

95m (15)

Cammell was the son of occultist Aleister Crowley's first biographer, and appears in Kenneth Anger's Crowleyan film *Lucifer Rising*. He died recently, having made only a handful of movies, one of which was his debut directorial effort *Performance* (see page 129), on which he shared credit with the equally radical but more commercially successful Nicolas Roeg. *Demon Seed* is about a huge, house-running computer imprisoning and impregnating the wife of its creator. Only partly a success, it's still a testament to its creator's audacious style. He will be sadly missed by fans of wild cinema. Widescreen.

DUNE 🎬4

KYLE MacLACHLAN, STING, DEAN STOCKWELL, MAX VON SYDOW

DAVID LYNCH

USA (POLYGRAM) 1984

136m (15)

This is a brave attempt to get the images and plot of Frank Herbert's epic novel on film, but it tries too hard. We open with a spoken prologue to tell us what's going on, but it confuses rather than illuminates. Beautiful to look at, however. A TV version of longer duration exists, but Lynch asked for it to be credited to Alan Smithee, the standard director-pseudonym used when a film-maker is unhappy with a product. A Japanese import laserdisc set exists containing the TV version and the widescreen cinema print.

THE EMPIRE STRIKES BACK 🎬4

HARRISON FORD, MARK HAMILL, CARRIE FISHER

IRVIN KERSHNER

UK/USA (FOX) 1980

124m (U)

Second in the hugely successful *Star Wars* series with more adventures of galactic rebellion. Confusingly, the film's storylines concern events in the middle of a planned multi-movie story. Great effects but not much of a story in this one. As a prelude to a new trilogy, the first three flicks are being reissued with new SFX. Widescreen. Oscars: SFX and sound.

TOP 1000 VIDEOS

ENEMY MINE [3]

DENNIS QUAID, LOUIS GOSSETT Jnr, BRION JAMES

WOLFANG PETERSEN

USA (FOX) 1985

93m (15)

Begun by another director (Richard Loncraine) whose footage was junked, this troubled production was cut outside the USA. It is like a space version of the war film *Hell In The Pacific*, with two enemies stranded and forced to come to terms. It also bears similarities to the 60s SF classic *Robinson Crusoe On Mars*, another butchered epic. Plot twists include the fact that one protagonist is a unisexual alien lizard who is about to give birth! Interesting.

ET – THE EXTRA-TERRESTRIAL [5]

HENRY THOMAS, DEE WALLACE, DREW BARRYMORE, PETER COYOTE

STEVEN SPIELBERG

USA (CIC) 1982

115m (U)

Disneyesque fantasy about a cuddly alien stranded on earth and rescued by kids. Spielberg remembers to instil a sense of evil in the threat posed by government men who want to experiment on the creature. Weird to see sex-symbol Barrymore and *Playboy* centrefold/actress Erika Eleniak as innocent kiddies. A classic. Oscars: SFX, sound effects editing, sound and score.

FANTASTIC VOYAGE [5]

STEPHEN BOYD, RAQUEL WELCH, DONALD PLEASENCE, ARTHUR KENNEDY

RICHARD FLEISCHER

USA (FOX) 1966

100m (U)

Mad but watchable. Scientists are shrunk and injected into the bloodstream of an injured genius with the task of piloting their submarine to a blood clot and eliminating it. Pleasures include staggering (for that time) art direction depicting human insides, and Raquel Welch's bust straining at her rubber diving suit. Parodied in *Innerspace* (see page 158). Oscars: SFX, art and set direction.

THE FIFTH ELEMENT [4]

BRUCE WILLIS, IAN HOLM, GARY OLDMAN, MILLA JOVOVICH, CHRIS TUCKER

LUC BESSON

FRANCE/USA (FOX) 1997

121m (PG)

Delirious feast for the eyes in this mad SFX romp in which Willis has to rescue an alien girl who holds the secret of world salvation. If this all sounds tired and predictable, you are in for a surprise: the visuals are wildly imaginative and so are the characters – a blue-skinned, multi-tentacled diva, Oldman's drawling killer and Tucker's camp TV host to name but three. Available in widescreen and in a hideously expensive boxed set with book. Panned by critics, unfortunately.

SCIENCE FICTION

FIRST MEN IN THE MOON 🎬4

EDWARD JUDD, MARTHA HYER, LIONEL JEFFRIES

NATHAN JURAN

UK (COLUMBIA) 1964

104m (U)

Written by Nigel Kneale and based on an HG Wells novel, this has American astronauts going to the moon only to find a faded Brit flag. Turns out some mad Victorians got there first! Tape also includes *Earth Vs The Flying Saucers* (1956). Great FX by Ray Harryhausen. Would benefit from a reissue in its widescreen form.

FLASH GORDON 🎬3

SAM JONES, MELODY ANDERSON, TOPOL, ORNELLA MUTI, MAX VON SYDOW, TIMOTHY DALTON, BRIAN BLESSED, PETER WYNGARDE

MIKE HODGES

UK (POLYGRAM) 1980

115m (PG)

Revamp, *Barbarella*-style, of the old comic-based serials, with a rock score by the group Queen, uncredited script input by philosopher Colin Wilson, and cameos from everyone from Bond-actor Dalton to some guy who used to be on *Blue Peter*! Panned on release, but much fun. Available in widescreen, though if it's the same as the USA laserdisc it may be 'blown-up' within the frame.

THE FLY 🎬4

JEFF GOLDBLUM, GEENA DAVIS, JOHN GETZ, DAVID CRONENBERG

DAVID CRONENBERG

USA (FOX) 1986

92m (18)

Update of the 50s chiller about a scientist who invents a matter teleporter and tests it on himself with horrific results. In the first version he ended up with a fly's head and the insect got a tiny human head. Cronenberg adapts the story into his own *oeuvre* of genetic rebellion by having the man gradually mutate in vile ways after he and a housefly are transported together. Goldblum is his usual eccentric self and the yukky make-up FX won an Oscar. Sequel: *The Fly 2* (1989), directed by make-up man Chris Walas, was less fun.

FORBIDDEN PLANET 🎬5

WALTER PIDGEON, ANNE FRANCIS, LESLIE NIELSEN, JACK KELLY

FRED M WILCOX

USA (MGM/UA-WARNER) 1956

98m (U)

Shakespeare's *The Tempest* as SF. Earthmen visit planet inhabited only by scientist and his daughter. But something else stalks unseen ... Scenes of the invisible 'Id' monster caught in electric rays are legendary, and Robby the Robot was revived for a film called *The Invisible Boy* – but not, as some say, for the TV show *Lost in Space*, though the robot in the show is obviously inspired by Robby. Now in a special widescreen edition.

THE ILLUSTRATED MAN [2]

ROD STEIGER, CLAIRE BLOOM, ROBERT DRIVAS

JACK SMIGHT

USA (WARNER/BEYONDVISION) 1968

103m (15)

An attempt to bring to the screen Ray Bradbury's tales told by a tattoo-covered man. Steiger gives a fine performance but the film fails to hang together, due in part to the random and episodic nature of the (rather unexciting) tales included. Interesting all the same. Widescreen.

INDEPENDENCE DAY [3]

JEFF GOLDBLUM, RANDY QUAID, WILL SMITH, BILL PULLMAN

ROLAND EMMERICH

USA (FOX) 1996

139m (12)

Admittedly visually impressive, but vastly overpraised America-saves-the-world-from-bad-aliens tale. Goldblum coasts along in his bumbling-genius autopilot mode but is always watchable. A film to sell toys by – but less than a year after release I noted they were being sold off cheap in shops. Nice explosions. Widescreen available, in fancy hologram box.

INVASION OF THE BODY SNATCHERS [4]

DONALD SUTHERLAND, BROOKE ADAMS, LEONARD NIMOY, VERONICA CARTWRIGHT

PHILIP KAUFMAN

USA (WARNER) 1978

115m (15)

Second of three extant versions of this scary story about alien seed pods which duplicate humans and take over the persona of the originals. The 1956 version may well be the one to beat, but this has superior SFX and is a laudable attempt. The director and star of the original, Don Siegel and Kevin McCarthy, have cameo parts. The third version was Abel Ferrara's more recent *Body Snatchers*. Available in widescreen.

LOGAN'S RUN [3]

MICHAEL YORK, JENNY AGUTTER, PETER USTINOV

MICHAEL ANDERSON

USA (MGM/UA-WARNER) 1976

118m (PG)

The story is set in a future where people are 'snuffed' at the age of 30. York is assigned to stop escapees – but he escapes himself with his gal and finds it's all a riot after 30. So unlike the lives of our own dear selves. Spawned a TV series. Now in widescreen special edition.

SCIENCE FICTION

MARS ATTACKS! 🎬 4

JACK NICHOLSON, GLENN CLOSE, PIERCE BROSNAN, DANNY DeVITO, ANNETTE BENING

TIM BURTON

USA (WARNER) 1996

101m   (12)

Based on a gory series of bubblegum cards I recall collecting back in the 60s, this science fiction comedy employs state-of-the-art technology to replicate the cheesy SFX of cheapo classics of yore. Pop-eyed, skull-faced aliens proclaim peace and then frazzle everything in sight with happy cries of 'Ack-ack-ack-ack!' The cast appear to enjoy themselves immensely, but audiences seem not to have surrendered to the mood and the pic was not the hit expected. Should find its true home on video. Good, light-hearted entertainment! Available in widescreen.

MEN IN BLACK 🎬 4

TOMMY LEE JONES, RIP TORN, WILL SMITH, LINDA FIORENTINO

BARRY SONNENFELD

USA (COLUMBIA TRISTAR) 1997

94m   (PG)

Based on a comic-strip (themed around the rumour that mysterious dark-clad fellows are always seen in the wake of UFO activity), this hilarious SFX-fest has cop Smith being inducted into a secret agency that polices the myriad of galactic aliens apparently already living among us. They go around keeping a lid on things by blanking people's memories of bizarre encounters while tracking renegade weirdos. Humour and science fiction don't often blend well but this is an exception: the FX, acting and Danny Elfman's score are all superb. Cut by the BBFC.

MIMIC 🎬 4

MIRA SORVINO, JEREMY NORTHAM, F MURRAY ABRAHAM, JOSH BROLIN

GUILLERMO DEL TORO

USA (HOLLYWOOD) 1998

101m   (15)

Expatriate director of the Mexican horror film *Cronos* (see page 193) moves into the big time with this adaptation of a pulp tale by Donald A Wollheim. To eradicate a child-killing disease carried by cockroaches, scientists plot to slay the beasties by releasing super-roaches that are supposed to die off after completing their mission. Only they don't. Just like Topsy, they grow and grow ... It may, being an American pic, descend into a gory shoot-'em-up at the climax, but there are enough original ideas and creepy moments here to make one think that Del Toro could turn out to be a major force in genre pix.

THE OMEGA MAN 🎬4

CHARLTON HESTON, ANTHONY ZERBE, ROSALIND CASH

BORIS SAGAL

USA (WARNER/BEYONDVISION) 1971

98m (PG)

Hammer planned a version of Richard Matheson's SF vampire novel in the 1960s – the book, *I Am Legend*, was ripe for filming, but the BBFC said any movie version would be banned. Much to their annoyance, the ditched project was made as *The Last Man On Earth* by another company in Italy with Vincent Price, and passed by the censor with no trouble! This stylised 1970s version sees Heston roaming around empty shops and battling with the undead, but it softens the book's punchline. Apparently a new version is soon to be made. Widescreen tape.

OUTLAND 🎬4

SEAN CONNERY, PETER BOYLE, FRANCES STERNHAGEN

PETER HYAMS

USA (WARNER/BEYONDVISION) 1981

109m (15)

This is *High Noon* in space, with Connery as cussed lawman probing amphetamine-style psychosis and corporate drug-dealing in the environment of a mine on one of Jupiter's moons. Great stuff – sort of 'Io-silver'! Some gruesome FX, especially when a man explodes in a decompressed airlock.

π 🎬3

SEAN GULLETTE, PAMELA HART, MARK MARGOLIS, BEN SHENKMAN

DARREN ARONOFSKY

USA (FOX PATHE) 1997 B&W

80m (15)

The maths symbol that is the title of this odd movie is 'pi' (pronounced 'pie'), and the film is as individual as its name. It concerns a brilliant but alienated young man using maths to predict patterns in the stock market. After some success he finds he is sought by a big Wall Street firm and a messianic cult, while at the same time his numerical codes threaten his sanity. Indescribably nutty, it has a wild electronic score. Boxed set available with soundtrack CD.

SCIENCE FICTION

PLAN 9 FROM OUTER SPACE 🎬 3

BELA LUGOSI, VAMPIRA, GREGORY WALCOTT, TOR JOHNSON

EDWARD D WOOD

USA (CARLTON) 1956 B&W

79m (PG)

Ed Wood has become a cult figure as (allegedly) the worst film-maker ever, due to the recent biographical volume (Rudolph Grey's *Visions Of Ecstasy*, published by Faber) and Tim Burton's movie based on it (see page 111). Actually, Wood was like many people who want to be creative – except that in his case the *outré* ideas were matched by a fierce dedication which led to him managing to get books published and movies made, however trying his personal circumstances. If you want to see how an alcoholic, transvestite *auteur* forged a film around a couple of minutes of footage of Bela Lugosi, look no further. Cheap and amateurish it may be, but *Plan 9* is enjoyable for all that.

PLANET OF THE APES 🎬 5

CHARLTON HESTON, RODDY McDOWALL, KIM HUNTER

FRANKLIN J SCHAFFNER

USA (FOX) 1968

102m (PG)

Based on a book by the man who wrote *The Bridge On The River Kwai* (see page 319), scripted by Michael Wilson (uncredited co-writer of *Lawrence Of Arabia*, page 148) and TV series *Twilight Zone*'s creator Rod Serling, this is an intelligent effort about astronauts who find themselves on a planet where apes rule and men are subservient. Makes a salient point about animal rights and racism, and the wonderful make-up (which got a special Oscar) still looks good today. Sequels followed, but couldn't match the shock ending of this film. A remake is mooted. Widescreen plus set of all the films.

QUATERMASS AND THE PIT

ANDREW KEIR, BARBARA SHELLEY, JAMES DONALD, JULIAN GLOVER

ROY WARD BAKER

UK (WARNER) 1967

97m (15)

Hammer made a cottage industry of translating Nigel Kneale's TV serials about an irascible rocket scientist to the big screen. This was their last try, and the only one in colour – a creepy science fiction gothic that posits a disturbing origin for mankind and its evil side. Even better, if you can find it, is the BBC video of the original monochrome TV serial.

RETURN OF THE JEDI

HARRISON FORD, MARK HAMILL, CARRIE FISHER

RICHARD MARQUAND

UK/USA (FOX) 1983

132m (U)

Third of the *Star Wars* films. The Ewoks are a bit too cuddly, but there is some nice creature make-up and the pace never slackens. The Ewoks, as befits cute little teddybears, appeared in spin-off TV fare. Special Oscar for FX. Widescreen. Reissued with the first two instalments in 1997, with new SFX, as an appetiser for the next trilogy. *Episode 1 The Phantom Menace* is in cinemas now.

ROBOCOP

PETER WELLER, NANCY ALLEN, DAN O'HERLIHY

PAUL VERHOEVEN

USA (ENTERTAINMENT) 1987

102m (18)

Dutch director Verhoeven uses this story of a blown-apart policeman (mutilated by gunfire in a shocking sequence) who is rebuilt as the title character to make acid comment on the state of the USA. Spoof commercials abound, and the RoboCop's have-a-nice-day demeanour as he blows away baddies is hilarious. Spawned sequels and a TV series. This first movie can be found on a tape from budget label 4-Front as well, coupled with the film *RoboCop 2*. The dark side of TV's *Six Million Dollar Man*.

SCIENCE FICTION

ROLLERBALL 🎬3

JAMES CAAN, JOHN HOUSEMAN, MAUD ADAMS, RALPH RICHARDSON

NORMAN JEWISON

USA (WARNER/BEYONDVISION) 1975

125m (15)

Prophetic and much-copied film about future sport becoming more violent and gladiatorial. The trouble is, while it sets out to condemn the sport and those who watch it, we are at the same time being given our own thrills by watching the on-screen brutality – a common contradiction in films seeking to critique spectacle. A dull tale, saved by the excellent rollerball sequences. Widescreen special edition is now available.

SOLARIS 🎬4

NATALYA BONDARCHUK, DONATAS BANIONIS, YURI JARVET

ANDREI TARKOVSKY

USSR (CONNOISSEUR) 1971

167m (PG)

Story of a planet that has the power to affect the minds of those in an orbiting space laboratory, to bad ends. Splendid visuals in the Kubrick manner, but preferred by arthouse fans as it's by a Russian. Widescreen.

SOYLENT GREEN 🎬5

CHARLTON HESTON, LEIGH TAYLOR-YOUNG, EDWARD G ROBINSON

RICHARD FLEISCHER

USA (WARNER/BEYONDVISION) 1973

97m (15)

Set in a future where the rich live in fortresses and the poor starve, this dark film has Heston as a cop who finds out just what's in the popular new nutritious stuff being offered – and not liking it. Based on the novel *Make Room, Make Room* by Harry Harrison, it offers Robinson's final, moving performance. Widescreen.

SPHERE 🎬3

DUSTIN HOFFMAN, SHARON STONE, SAMUEL L JACKSON

BARRY LEVINSON

USA (WARNER) 1998

120m (12)

Scientists investigating a spacecraft at the bottom of the ocean find it's from future America. It also contains a mysterious globe that affects each of them differently. Based on a book by Michael *Jurassic Park* Crichton, this is a fairly engrossing bit of nonsense. The cast – especially Hoffman – do their best, but the film was plagued with production problems and a new ending was lensed at huge cost after previews got the thumbs-down from audiences.

STALKER [3]

ALEKSANDR KAIDANOVSKY, NIKOLAI GRINKO, ANATOLY SOLONITSYN

ANDREI TARKOVSKY

USSR (CONNOISSEUR) 1979 COL/B/W

161m (PG)

A guide takes the curious to a forbidden zone in an industrial wasteland, searching for a room that makes dreams come true. Pessimistic arthouse stuff from Tarkovsky, one of Russia's greatest exponents of serious SF.

STAR TREK – THE MOTION PICTURE [3]

WILLIAM SHATNER, LEONARD NIMOY, JAMES DOOHAN

ROBERT WISE

USA (CIC) 1979

132m (U)

Film based on the short-lived TV series that became a cult via re-runs (see pages 314–5). Made long after the series had ended, this nevertheless spawned better sequels on film and TV. Widescreen.

STAR TREK II – THE WRATH OF KHAN [4]

WILLIAM SHATNER, LEONARD NIMOY, RICARDO MONTALBAN

NICHOLAS MEYER

USA (CIC) 1982

113m (15)

This, the second film for the Trekkies, sees Montalban reprise his role of Shatner's enemy from an episode of the TV show, spitting quotes from *Moby Dick* and torturing good guys by inserting centipedes in earholes. Nice. Widescreen.

STAR TREK III – THE SEARCH FOR SPOCK [4]

WILLIAM SHATNER, LEONARD NIMOY, JAMES DOOHAN

LEONARD NIMOY

USA (CIC) 1984

105m (PG)

Nimoy directs himself as Spock in this far-fetched tale about the reincarnation (or whatever) of the pointy-eared hero who gave his life heroically at the climax of the previous flick. Widescreen.

SCIENCE FICTION

STAR TREK IV – THE VOYAGE HOME

WILLIAM SHATNER, LEONARD NIMOY, JAMES DOOHAN, CATHERINE HICKS

LEONARD NIMOY

USA (CIC) 1986

119m (PG)

Ecological, supposed comedy-romp, where the space heroes spend too much time on the earth of the past in search of whales. Rather slow-moving and mainly for Trekkies. Widescreen.

STAR TREK V – THE FINAL FRONTIER

WILLIAM SHATNER, LEONARD NIMOY, DAVID WARNER

WILLIAM SHATNER

USA (CIC) 1989

106m (PG)

The boys meet God – honest. Absurd, but fun, like it should be. Also available is *Star Trek – The Undiscovered Country*. This was followed by *Star Trek – Generations*, in which the old-timers hand over the reins of the filmic 'Trek' to the stars of the superior TV offshoot, *The Next Generation* (see pages 314–15). The cast of the latter, which blends serious philosophical questions with hokum far better than the originals ever did, have since appeared in the first of their own movies (see below). Widescreen.

STAR TREK – FIRST CONTACT

PATRICK STEWART, ALICE KRIGE, BRENT SPINER, LEVAR BURTON

JONATHAN FRAKES

USA (CIC) 1996

106m (12)

Superb big-screen outing for the *Next Generation* team, with Captain Picard (Stewart) matching wits with a slinky Krige as the nasty alien queen. Few TV shows transfer well to the cinema as punters are often unwilling to shell out for characters they're used to seeing free, but the Trekkers are the exception. As befits a movie, the FX are bigger/better, but they work just as well on video. Widescreen. Sequel: *Star Trek – Insurrection (see below)*.

STAR TREK – INSURRECTION

PATRICK STEWART, JONATHAN FRAKES, BRENT SPINER

JONATHAN FRAKES

USA (CIC) 1999

99m (PG)

A community are being forcibly removed from their home by those who want to exploit the secret of their eternal youth. Jean-Luc and his crew follow the dictates of their consciences rather than their orders to come to their aid. The usual high quality we've come to expect of the *Next Generation* team, a well-crafted and entertaining movie with first-rate SFX.

STAR WARS [5]

MARK HAMILL, HARRISON FORD, CARRIE FISHER, PETER CUSHING, ALEC GUINNESS

GEORGE LUCAS

UK/USA (FOX) 1977

121m (U)

First and best of Lucas's *Flash Gordon*-inspired ray-gun romps. Currently on show in revamped form to herald a new series of 'prequels'. Oscars: sets, editing, effects, costumes, sound, score and sound effects. Later prints are subtitled as *Episode IV: A New Hope*.

STARMAN [3]

JEFF BRIDGES, KAREN ALLEN, CHARLES MARTIN SMITH, RICHARD JAECKEL

JOHN CARPENTER

USA (VIDEO COLLECTION) 1984

110m (PG)

Delightful, if slender, tale of an alien who assumes the form of a dead man and cajoles his wife into helping him escape nasty secret-agent types. Oddly touching, with a fine performance from Bridges. Inspired a flop TV series.

STARSHIP TROOPERS [4]

CASPER VAN DIEN, MICHAEL IRONSIDE, JAKE BUSEY, NEIL PATRICK HARRIS, DENISE RICHARDS

PAUL VERHOEVEN

USA (BUENA VISTA) 1997

124m (15)

Space-opera based on (allegedly fascist) Robert Heinlein novel about gung-ho astronautical grunts battling giant alien insects is turned into a blend of *Aliens* (see page 259) and *Beverley Hills 90210* as director Verhoeven attempts, with limited success, to repeat the outsider critique of America of his original *RoboCop* (see page 272). Super digital SFX, though the actors are bronzed ciphers – but maybe that's the whole idea. A Chinese takeaway accompaniment supreme!

THX 1138 [3]

ROBERT DUVALL, DONALD PLEASENCE

GEORGE LUCAS

USA (WARNER/BEYONDVISION) 1970

95m (15)

Nice widescreen tape of Lucas's debut, based on a film he made as a student. A *1984*-derived story about a man determined to escape from a restrictive underground society of the future where men have numbers instead of names. Allegedly, the title number was the registration of the director's first car – it appears in most of his films and THX is also the name of his sound-system for cinemas, laserdiscs, etc.

SCIENCE FICTION

THE TIME MACHINE 🎬5

⭐ ROD TAYLOR, ALAN YOUNG, YVIETTE MIMIEUX, WHIT BISSELL

🎬 GEORGE PAL

USA (WARNER/BEYONDVISION) 1960

⏱ 103m (PG)

My favourite SF film, from the marvellous score to the robust playing of Taylor. A fine version of HG Wells' story of a man who invents a device for time travel, only to find a future where lotus-eating wimps are preyed on by cannibals. Inevitably simplified – when our hero helps the good guys (Eloi) destroy a few cannibal (Morlock) tunnels, we're expected to accept that the war is over. Yet surely the whole world is supposed to be full of the devils? The SFX were Oscar-winners and are excellent, apart from an atomic war sequence which seems to be made from custard and Dinky toys. A hugely enjoyable film and stunning to look at.

TOTAL RECALL 🎬4

⭐ ARNOLD SCHWARZENEGGER, RACHEL TICOTIN, SHARON STONE

🎬 PAUL VERHOEVEN

USA (GUILD) 1990

⏱ 113m (18)

Complex spectacular with Oscar-winning effects about a man who has been having dreams of Mars. He can't afford a holiday, so 'buys' someone else's memories. This brings on the realisation that he's an agent who has been submerged into a boring everyday life ... The sequence where he is told to kill himself in order to prove that he is only dreaming is particularly unnerving. Well, would *you* do it? The only flaw is that it's hard to accept Arnie as an ordinary guy in the first place. Based on a crazed PK Dick tale.

WAR OF THE WORLDS 🎬4

⭐ GENE BARRY, ANN ROBINSON, ROBERT CORNTHWAITE

🎬 BYRON HASKIN

USA (CIC) 1953

⏱ 85m (PG)

SFX Oscar-winner which updates HG Wells' story of Martian invaders to modern times. The Martians are bizarre in the extreme, and the film had an 'X' certificate on first UK release. Let down somewhat by actors, but great anyway. Narration by Sir Cedric Hardwicke.

WESTWORLD 🎬 3

⭐ YUL BRYNNER, RICHARD BENJAMIN, JAMES BROLIN

🎬 MICHAEL CRICHTON

USA (WARNER/BEYONDVISION) 1973

⏱ 89m (15)

Now a hit novelist and film-maker, Crichton made his directorial debut with this story of a futuristic Disneyland where several eras are recreated and guests can kill and have sex with realistic robots. It all goes wrong and the robot underclass fights back; Brynner in particular as a killer gunslinger just will not lie down. A duff sequel entitled *Futureworld* was made in 1976.

THE X-FILES MOVIE 🎬 3

⭐ GILLIAN ANDERSON, DAVID DUCHOVNY, BLYTHE DANNER, TERRY O'QUINN, MARTIN LANDAU

🎬 ROB BOWMAN

USA (FOX) 1998

⏱ 122m (15)

Dependable big-screen outing for TV's Mulder and Scully, combining a new adventure with attempts to tie up loose ends from the series. We find aliens from the Texas of 35 million years BC still causing repercussions in present-day Dallas, as well as low-flying super-bees and low-flying helicopters: you really do get the lot here, including Mark Snow's amazing soundtrack music. Available in widescreen. Certain *X-Files* TV episodes are also available on tape (see page 314).

YOU ONLY LIVE TWICE 🎬 4

⭐ SEAN CONNERY, DONALD PLEASENCE, AKIKO WAKABAYASHI

🎬 LEWIS GILBERT

USA (MGM/UA-WARNER) 1967

⏱ 116m (PG)

Many James Bond films qualify as science fiction and none more so than this, with mini-copters and stolen spaceships, the SPECTRE (ha) of World War Three and a mechanical volcano. Connery is still the best Bond ever in my book. Script by Roald Dahl.

ZARDOZ 🎬 4

⭐ SEAN CONNERY, CHARLOTTE RAMPLING, JOHN ALDERTON

🎬 JOHN BOORMAN

UK (FOX) 1974

⏱ 105m (15)

Stunning visuals in Boorman's idea of a future world rather like that of *The Time Machine* (see page 277), with wimpy lotus-eaters in protected zones being attacked by thuggish killers on the prowl. Things get interesting when Connery and Rampling, members of opposing factions, get involved and attempt to solve the mystery at the heart of their society and (ultimately) their god. Boorman's script doesn't really gel, but it's a dazzling curio and a real cult gem.

THRILLERS

Video fans in search of a true 'thrill' might profitably investigate several other sections of this book – Gangsters (see pages 163–80) and Horror (see pages 188–220) should prove especially fruitful. For many, the pinnacle of the genre is the work of Alfred Hitchcock, movies which prove that art and entertainment need not be mutually exclusive cinematic notions; but in recent years the thriller has come to be defined by the sleazy psychosexual whodunnit as purveyed by writer Joe Eszterhas in pix such as *Jagged Edge* (see page 292) and *Basic Instinct* (see page 281) – films which provide a momentary frisson but offer little depth. A friend of mine dubs them 'hamburger movies': enjoyable products, but instantly forgotten the moment you step out into the real world. Pay your money and take your choice ...

8mm

NICOLAS CAGE, JOAQUIN PHOENIX, PETER STORMARE

JOEL SCHUMACHER

USA (COLUMBIA TRISTAR) 1999

118m (15)

An elderly widow finds some old footage among her late husband's possessions which seems to show the murder of a young girl. She hires private 'tec Cage to find out the truth, which leads him to LA's seedy underground sex industry. Dark and sometimes disturbing thriller.

10 RILLINGTON PLACE

RICHARD ATTENBOROUGH, JUDY GEESON, JOHN HURT, ISOBEL BLACK

RICHARD FLEISCHER

UK (CINEMA CLUB V) 1970

110m (15)

Ludovic Kennedy's book on the Christie case provides the groundwork for USA director Fleischer's surprisingly able grasp of post-war London *mis-en-scène*. Christie (Attenborough) was a serial killer who eluded capture for years, even giving evidence against simpleton Tim Evans (Hurt) in order to see him hanged (for allegedly murdering his wife and baby) before the truth about his own guilt came to light too late. There is still much debate about what Evans did or didn't do, but there's no doubt that he should never have hanged. Attenborough gives a creepy portrayal of a seedy, weedy monster.

ANGEL OF VENGEANCE

ZOE TAMERLIS, STEVE SINGER, JACK THIBEAU, PETER YELLEN

ABEL FERRARA

USA (WARNER) 1980

78m (18)

Long-banned female revenge flick from cult director Ferrara, also known by the title *Ms 45*. It's about a mute seamstress who goes over the edge after being raped twice in one day. She kills the second assailant, chops his body into bits, then proceeds to use his gun to blow away every leering male she encounters. Teenage Tamerlis, who went on to script later films for the director under the name Zoe Lund, gives a powerful performance, all the more remarkable given her age (16) and the fact that she has no dialogue. This is a pristine print, though cut by the BBFC. Note: the tape was issued then withdrawn for remastering, due to what a Warner's source (who refused to give his name) calls 'technical problems' – in fact, the first copies shipped in early September 1997 were accidentally issued *sans* cuts! If your copy has the number 082897 on the side of the tape, it is uncut. Even in censored form, though, this is a gripping picture.

THRILLERS

BASIC INSTINCT 3

⭐ MICHAEL DOUGLAS, SHARON STONE, JEANNE TRIPPLEHORN, GEORGE DZUNDZA

🎬 PAUL VERHOEVEN

USA (GUILD) 1992

⏱ 128m   (18)

Improbable tale about a bisexual thrill-killing babe who enjoys writing novels which tease the cops by mirroring her real-life crimes. There's lots of sex and slashing, with Douglas plodding along as the infatuated policeman and Stone uncrossing her legs in the no-panties scene which made her a star (she later claimed she didn't realise it was being shot). Picketed by gays in the USA for suggesting that lesbianism and murder go hand-in-hand. Widescreen available.

THE BIG SLEEP 5

⭐ HUMPHREY BOGART, LAUREN BACALL, JOHN RIDGELY, ELISHA COOK Jnr

🎬 HOWARD HAWKS

USA (WARNER) 1944 B&W

⏱ 110m   (PG)

Raymond Chandler's first hard-boiled novel makes a compelling *noir* with gumshoe Marlowe up to his eyes in complex intrigues. It is pretty much accepted – even by those who made it – that the film makes little sense, but it's still a wonderfully atmospheric classic. The pic wasn't issued to the public until 1946, but a simpler version was shown to USA troops abroad in 1944.

THE BIRDS 4

⭐ ROD TAYLOR, TIPPI HEDREN, SUZANNE PLESHETTE, JESSICA TANDY

🎬 ALFRED HITCHCOCK

USA (CIC) 1963

⏱ 113m   (15)

Based on the Daphne du Maurier tale of the same name, this Hitchcock oddity has the amorous desires of a spoiled rich girl (Hedren) and a smart lawyer (Taylor) upset by the intrusion of the irrational forces of nature, incarnated here by the sudden revolt of all avian life against humankind. The aura of dislocation is aided by a weird soundtrack created by Bernard Herrmann and a strange musical invention developed by Oskar Skala.

BLOOD SIMPLE 4

⭐ FRANCES McDORMAND, JOHN GETZ, DAN HEDAYA, M EMMET WALSH

🎬 JOEL COEN

USA (POLYGRAM) 1983

⏱ 95m   (18)

Breakthrough pulp fiction from the brothers Coen. Sleazy bar boss hires a detective to murder his cheating wife and her lover, but with everyone concerned either misunderstanding or double-crossing at every twist it turns into a sick, funny rollercoaster of trashy Texas malice in blunderland. Walsh is marvellous as the bent detective. Also sold in a boxed set with Coen's *Fargo* (see page 113).

BLOW OUT 🎬 4

JOHN TRAVOLTA, NANCY ALLEN, JOHN LITHGOW, DENNIS FRANZ

BRIAN DE PALMA

USA (FOX) 1981

108m (18)

Clever variation of the theme of *Blow Up* – instead of spotting a murder in a snap, however, Travolta is a sound engineer who accidentally records the gunshot that causes a car to smash, plunging him into a maelstrom involving a hooker, a politician and a psycho hitman. One of De Palma's best, working on many levels and constantly undermining audience perceptions as to what is really happening.

BLUE STEEL 🎬 4

JAMIE LEE CURTIS, RON SILVER, CLANCY BROWN, LOUISE FLETCHER

KATHRYN BIGELOW

USA (FIRST INDEPENDENT) 1989

97m (18)

Unlikely story of a rookie policewoman involved in a relationship with a seemingly respectable chap who goes off the rails when he stumbles upon a robbery and picks up a gun dropped at the scene. Starts off well, but gradually becomes more and more unbelievable as it rolls along, though Ron Silver as the killer compels attention right to the very end.

BLUE VELVET 🎬 5

KYLE MacLACHLAN, LAURA DERN, DENNIS HOPPER, ISABELLA ROSSELLINI, DEAN STOCKWELL

DAVID LYNCH

USA (ELECTRIC) 1986

115m (18)

Weirdo Lynch's masterful exploration of the corruption behind the white-picket-fence image of small-town America, with MacLachlan and Dern as the two kids who come up against a bunch of ambisexual, druggy, violent pervos in the oddest rite-of-passage ever lensed. One of those films which scholars love to discuss in terms of symbolism and metaphor, but don't let that put you off. Seriously strange. Widescreen available.

BODY DOUBLE 🎬5

CRAIG WASSON, DEBORAH SHELTON, MELANIE GRIFFITH, DENNIS FRANZ

BRIAN DE PALMA

USA (CINEMA CLUB V) 1984

109m (18)

One of De Palma's numerous reworkings of Hitchcockian themes – this time both *Rear Window* and *Vertigo* are thrown into the mix, with Wasson as a jobbing actor afflicted by claustrophobia who witnesses sexy goings-on from the vantage point of a pal's apartment. (The film also uses themes alleged to be based on Hitch's own life, since biographers have stated that Grace Kelly once agreed to strip naked while he spied on her from his house by telescope.) Often dismissed by critics, this is one of De Palma's best. Slightly cut by the BBFC for gore content, which is actually minimal.

THE BODY SNATCHER 🎬5

BORIS KARLOFF, BELA LUGOSI, HENRY DANIELL, RUSSELL WADE

ROBERT WISE

USA (4-FRONT) 1945 B&W

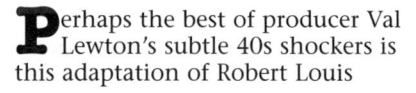

79m (PG)

Perhaps the best of producer Val Lewton's subtle 40s shockers is this adaptation of Robert Louis Stevenson's grave-robbing tale inspired by Burke and Hare, the Edinburgh duo who supplemented their supply of bodies for medical schools by murder. Karloff is great as Gray, the strangely sympathetic 'graveyard rat' and killer who blackmails his cold medical adversary (the enigmatic Daniell) into operating to help a paralysed child. This is the first time the complete film has been seen here, as the old UK print often shown on TV was cut by the BBFC to remove all mentions of Burke and Hare. (My thanks to Brad Stevens for this information.)

THE BOYS FROM BRAZIL 🎬3

GREGORY PECK, LAURENCE OLIVIER, JAMES MASON, LILLI PALMER

FRANKLIN J SCHAFFNER

USA (4-FRONT) 1979

120m (18)

Absurd version of an Ira Levin novel, with caricatures of Nazi scientist Josef Mengele (Peck) and nemesis Simon Wiesenthal (Olivier) battling over a plot to create a race of Hitler clones. It remains bizarre fun, but one can't avoid the niggling feeling that men who were involved in such terrible and serious recent historical events in the holocaust ought not to be seen as comic-strip characters, lest today's kids fail to realise that Hitler's ideas of racial purity were not only dangerous but deadly serious.

BRUBAKER

ROBERT REDFORD, YAPHET KOTTO, JANE ALEXANDER, M EMMET WALSH
STUART ROSENBERG
USA (FOX) 1980
130m (15)

Oscar-nominated script about a young prison governor who sets out to reform the rural penitentiary he's appointed to run, by pretending to be an inmate in order to unearth murder and corruption in the system. The kind of over-worthy pic Hollywood likes to applaud itself for undertaking, but well-honed and featuring a decent, understated star turn from Redford as the tow-headed zealot. Similar setting to the same director's *Cool Hand Luke* (see page 105).

BULLITT

STEVE McQUEEN, ROBERT VAUGHN, JACQUELINE BISSET, ROBERT DUVALL
PETER YATES
USA (WARNER) 1969
109m (15)

Classic San Francisco car-chase flick features McQueen as a wooden-faced cop battling intrigue and gunshots in the hands of former 'Man from UNCLE' Vaughn. Undemanding, fast and just a bit too good to be a mere hamburger movie. Based on the hard-boiled novel *Mute Witness* by Robert L Pike. Oscar for best editing. Widescreen now available.

CAPE FEAR

ROBERT MITCHUM, GREGORY PECK, MARTIN BALSAM
J LEE THOMPSON
USA (CIC) 1961 B&W
106m (15)

Evil ex-convict stalks the family of the lawyer who put him in jail in this taut, grim adaptation of a novel *(The Executioner)* by John D MacDonald. Mitchum is downright scary as the sadistic, misogynistic criminal and Peck his usual upright self in an unusual thriller dealing with the (now topical) theme of the cops being powerless to stop stalkers. The original cinema release back in 1961 was cut by the BBFC as the violence was extreme for the time, but this appears to be the full print.

THRILLERS

CAPE FEAR 🎬 4

ROBERT DE NIRO, NICK NOLTE, JESSICA LANGE, JULIETTE LEWIS

MARTIN SCORSESE

USA (CIC) 1991

122m (18)

Interesting reworking of the 1961 thriller. Scorsese makes the film morally ambiguous – this time the lawyer who sent the crook to jail was not the prosecutor but his own defence attorney, who thought he was 'doing the right thing' in betraying his evil client. Stalked by the baddy (an impressively mad De Niro) the lawyer adopts equally unlawful methods to see him off. Not quite in the same class as the original, but still powerful stuff. Features cameo appearances by Mitchum, Peck and Balsam in parts different from the ones they played in the first version.

COMA 🎬 3

MICHAEL DOUGLAS, GENEVIÈVE BUJOLD, RICHARD WIDMARK, ED HARRIS, TOM SELLECK

MICHAEL CRICHTON

USA (WARNER) 1978

113m (15)

Written and directed by the author of *Jurassic Park* (see page 29) this is another of Crichton's effective technology-runs-rampant fancies, set in a hospital where a young doctor (Bujold) has difficulty convincing her associates she's not mad when she starts insisting that the bosses are killing healthy patients to run a lucrative spare-parts racket in organ transplants. Based on Robin Cook's novel, it manages to keep your attention, and has the bonus of sounding just plausible enough to be true.

COPLAND 🎬 3

ROBERT DE NIRO, HARVEY KEITEL, SYLVESTER STALLONE, RAY LIOTTA

JAMES MANGOLD

USA (BUENA VISTA) 1997

101m (18)

Highly praised cop story about a small town ruled by corrupt police, but I have to say I was slightly underwhelmed by the film, which feels much longer than it actually is. Always a bad sign. Amid a raft of highly regarded thesps, most praise has surprisingly gone to Sylvester Stallone: in his first serious role for years he gained weight to play the local cop who finally rebels against his dodgy bosses. Worth a look for this aspect alone.

COPYCAT

- SIGOURNEY WEAVER, HARRY CONNICK Jnr
- JON AMIEL
- USA (WARNER) 1995
- 118m (18)

Weaver battles a nutter, played by crooner Connick Jnr, who is copying the styles of famous serial killers of the past in this rather far-fetched but tense thriller. Note: in real-life the nemesis of anti-capital punishment campaigner Sister Helen Prejean (see *Dead Man Walking* on page 107) is Harry Connick Snr, who is a pro-death penalty prosecutor!

CRIMSON TIDE

- GENE HACKMAN, DENZEL WASHINGTON, VIGGO MORTENSEN, GEORGE DZUNDZA
- TONY SCOTT
- USA (HOLLYWOOD) 1995
- 112m (15)

A do-it-by-the-book submarine commander clashes with his new subordinate over whether they should launch nuclear weapons in this nail-biting cold war thriller. Hackman is on top form as the martinet – 'We're here to defend democracy, not to practise it' – up against the mutinous refusenik Washington. An uncredited Quentin Tarantino adds some comic relief dialogue here and there. Tony Scott, brother of Ridley, keeps the tension screwed down tight right until the end. A corker.

CRUISING

- AL PACINO, PAUL SORVINO, KAREN ALLEN, JOE SPINELL
- WILLIAM FRIEDKIN
- USA (WARNER) 1980
- 102m (18)

Sleazoid epic about a cop who goes undercover to probe killings among New York's gay sadomasochist community, only to end up being corrupted by the fascinating, leather-clad milieu he is forced to inhabit. Controversial and sordid, but well made and featuring a compelling and powerful central performance by star Pacino. Cruising for a bruising! Cut on original release and again on tape.

CUJO

- DEE WALLACE, CHRISTOPHER STONE, DANNY PINTAURO
- LEWIS TEAGUE
- USA (MIA) 1983
- 87m (18)

Average adaptation of Stephen King novel about people trapped in a car by a rabid St Bernard. Not as silly as it sounds, but director Teague doesn't make as much of it as Hitchcock or De Palma would.

THRILLERS

THE DAY OF THE JACKAL [4]

EDWARD FOX, ALAN BADEL, ERIC PORTER, DONALD SINDEN

FRED ZINNEMANN

FRANCE/UK (CIC/4-FRONT) 1973

136m (15)

Methodical recounting of a lone assassin's preparations for the shooting of President de Gaulle, with Fox smooth and cold as a snake as the hitman of the title. Based on a smash novel of the same name by Frederick Forsyth. Loose update, *The Jackal*, released in 1998 (see page 27).

THE DEAD ZONE [4]

CHRISTOPHER WALKEN, MARTIN SHEEN, HERBERT LOM, BROOKE ADAMS

DAVID CRONENBERG

USA (ENTERTAINMENT) 1983

99m (18)

A Stephen King story of a man who comes out of a coma to find he can tell the future, but also finds himself confronted by that age-old problem: if you knew there was a future Hitler standing in front of you, but couldn't prove it, would you kill him? Director Cronenberg directs with his usual flair for plots dealing with bodies and minds rebelling against themselves, aided by a haunting turn from Walken as a man isolated by his unlooked-for psychic talents.

DIAL M FOR MURDER [4]

RAY MILLAND, GRACE KELLY, ROBERT CUMMINGS, ANTHONY DAWSON

ALFRED HITCHCOCK

USA/UK (WARNER) 1954

100m (PG)

Originally shot in 3D (which accounts for the odd, intrusive close-ups of thrusting objects), this is a tight thriller about a man who plots to have his wife murdered by a down-at-heel crook. Full of ingenious, old-fashioned twists, it struggles to escape its stage-play origins – most of the action takes place in one room – though the cast give it their best shot. Remade for TV in 1981 and recent stage revival.

DOA [4]

EDMUND O'BRIEN, PAMELA BRITTON, NEVILLE BRAND

RUDOLF MATE

USA (2nd SIGHT) 1949 B&W

84m (PG)

Strange but effective tale of a man who is 'dead on arrival' – but still alive. He's been poisoned with a radioactive substance for which there's no cure, and decides to spend the last few hours of his life tracking down his killer. Remade in 1969 as *Color Me Dead* and again under the original title in 1988 (see page 288).

DOA

DENNIS QUAID, MEG RYAN, CHARLOTTE RAMPLING

ROCKY MORTON, ANNABEL JANKEL

USA (TOUCHSTONE) 1988

93m (15)

Reworking of the 1949 thriller about a man trying to catch the person who poisoned him before the drug takes effect. Motivation is reduced to the trivial, car chases and romance are added but it's all to no real gain. Kinetic and watchable, but the original remains your best bet. Cut.

ENEMY OF THE STATE

WILL SMITH, GENE HACKMAN

TONY SCOTT

USA (BUENA VISTA) 1998

127m (15)

Smith plays a lawyer who is given a video tape which ties a top national security officer into a political murder. Targeted by surveillance operatives who think he is involved, he becomes enmeshed in a conspiracy and is forced to go on the run to try to stay alive while he proves his innocence. Action-packed with a good performance by Smith and the professional presence you would expect from Hackman.

ESCAPE FROM ALCATRAZ

CLINT EASTWOOD, PATRICK McGOOHAN, ROBERTS BLOSSOM, DANNY GLOVER

DON SIEGEL

USA (CIC/4-FRONT) 1979

112m (15)

Fact-based drama from Eastwood's long-time collaborator Siegel about an escape from the former USA island prison. No one knows what happened to the escapees – they were never heard of again – but the movie drops an optimistic (if unrealistic) hint that they got away and avoided the death by drowning that was said to await all in the dangerous waters off San Francisco. Tough entertainment with a typically stoic act from the star.

FLATLINERS

KIEFER SUTHERLAND, JULIA ROBERTS, KEVIN BACON, WILLIAM BALDWIN

JOEL SCHUMACHER

USA (CINEMA CLUB V) 1990

109m (15)

Bizarre tale of overweening medical students who hijack equipment and experiment with stopping their own hearts in order to explore near-death experiences. Interestingly, the film chooses to deal with matters of memory, guilt and personal conscience rather than crazy supernatural guff. Great effects.

THRILLERS

FOREIGN CORRESPONDENT 🎬5

JOEL McCREA, LARAINE DAY,
HERBERT MARSHALL, GEORGE
SANDERS

ALFRED HITCHCOCK

USA (VIDEO SPECIALS) 1940 B&W

115m (PG)

Spy 'meller' set in pre-war Europe of the 30s with McCrea as a hack caught up in intrigue and Nazi espionage. Hurtles to a great finale. Definitely one of Hitch's best, with a surprisingly gory (for its time) shooting scene in which a man is blasted in the face by an assassin posing as a cameraman.

FRENZY 🎬4

JON FINCH, ALEC McCOWEN,
ANNA MASSEY, BARRY FOSTER

ALFRED HITCHCOCK

UK (CIC) 1972

111m (18)

Another of Hitchcock's 'wrong man' thrillers in which a bumbling innocent is wanted for crimes he didn't commit. This time it's Finch being set up by his serial-killer pal Foster to take the rap for the latter's murderous spree. As always, Hitch isn't interested in concealing whodunnit but is relentless in making us identify (at different times) with both the dupe and the killer – check out the scene where Foster is in the back of a lorry trying to wrest an incriminating ring from the stiff fingers of a victim. Like *Psycho* (see page 212), in its time, this was much lambasted on release for being tasteless and too explicit. A few seconds were cut by the censor. Fine Covent Garden location filming.

THE FUGITIVE 🎬4

HARRISON FORD, TOMMY LEE
JONES, SELA WARD, JEROEN KRABBE

ANDREW DAVIS

USA (WARNER) 1994

131m (15)

Update of the 60s television series about an escaped prisoner on the trail of the one-armed man who killed his wife and left him to be wrongly convicted of the crime. Ford adopts the hesitant, stressed style of a man on the run to perfection and Tommy Lee Jones all but steals the show as a dogged cop who cares about the law, not justice. Begins with a magical piece of effects work in the best train crash ever seen on screen and zooms off from there. A real crowd-pleaser. Sequel: *US Marshals*.

GET CARTER 4

MICHAEL CAINE, JOHN OSBORNE, IAN HENDRY, BRITT EKLAND

MIKE HODGES

UK (WARNER) 1970

112m (18)

Gutsy actioner about internecine warfare and revenge among northern England's criminal fraternity. Caine is believable as the implacable gangster, and there's a fine cameo performance from playwright Osborne as a local crime boss. Very violent and atmospheric and now something of a cult film.

THE HAND THAT ROCKS THE CRADLE 3

ANNABELLA SCIORRA, REBECCA DE MORNAY, JULIANNE MOORE, MATT McCOY

CURTIS HANSON

USA (TOUCHSTONE) 1992

106m (15)

In some ways slightly reminiscent of a Bette Davis film called *The Nanny*, this is a malevolent melodrama about a thoroughly nasty girl taken on as childminder by a young woman who is unaware of her secret agenda of revenge. Not quite as scary or jolting as the publicity suggests, but worth seeing all the same. Widescreen available.

HOMICIDE 4

JOE MANTEGNA, VING RHAMES, NATALIJA NOGULICH, WILLIAM H MACY

DAVID MAMET

USA (FIRST INDEPENDENT) 1991

97m (15)

Unusual film from writer/director Mamet, about a murder squad cop roped into a case which makes him question whether his loyalty to the law is more important than his Jewish heritage. Thought-provoking with a fine lead performance from Joe Mantegna and an odd (but plausible) plot. Mamet also wrote *The Untouchables* (see page 180).

HOUSE OF GAMES 5

JOE MANTEGNA, LINDSAY CROUSE, LILIA SKALA, STEVE GOLDSTEIN

DAVID MAMET

USA (CONNOISSEUR) 1987

98m (15)

Mamet's masterpiece, concerning a psychologist who is drawn into the world of a group of conmen only to have her illicit fascination with, and complicity in, their crimes lead to tragedy. The 'cons' are lovingly staged and played out and the actors (particularly Mantegna) first-rate. Do not miss.

THRILLERS

I KNOW WHAT YOU DID LAST SUMMER [3]

SARAH MICHELLE GELLAR, FREDDIE PRINZ Jnr, JENNIFER LOVE HEWITT

JIM GILLESPIE

USA (ENTERTAINMENT) 1997

97m (15)

Scripted by Kevin Williamson of *Scream* (see page 213) and its sequels, this is a daft little chiller about a bunch of ambitious teens who have a guilty secret that could ruin their fortunes: they ran a guy over, decided to dump the body in the sea, but found at the last minute he was still alive – so now it's murder! In the wake of a note, saying 'I know what you did last summer', comes violent retribution. Sequel: *I Still Know What You Did Last Summer*.

I WAKE UP SCREAMING [5]

BETTY GRABLE, CAROLE LANDIS, VICTOR MATURE, LAIRD CREGAR

BRUCE HUMBERSTONE

USA (FOX) 1941 B&W

79m (PG)

It was a great loss to cinema when plump, lisping, character actor Laird Cregar died after completing only a handful of films. Here he plays a slimy, nasty cop determined to frame Mature for the murder of a beautiful girl. He spits out insane dialogue while creepily toying with a miniature hangman's noose to taunt his victim. One of the best *noirs*, and an essential part of cinema's soft, white underbelly. Wild.

IN THE HEAT OF THE NIGHT [5]

SIDNEY POITIER, ROD STEIGER, WARREN OATES, SCOTT WILSON

NORMAN JEWISON

USA (WARNER) 1967

95m (15)

Landmark 1960s thriller about a black policeman wrongly arrested while waiting for a train in America's Deep South. When his identity is proven, white police chief Steiger calls him in to solve a local murder. The interplay and gradually-increasing respect between Steiger and the detective (Poitier) is well handled, and the plot is engrossing. Steiger is careful to make his character more than a comic-book racist and the southern atmosphere feels authentic. Oscars for best picture, script, actor (Steiger) and more. There was a lacklustre sequel, *They Call Me Mr Tibbs*, with Poitier investigating another case. Recent cinema restoration.

IN THE LINE OF FIRE [5]

CLINT EASTWOOD, RENE RUSSO, JOHN MALKOVICH, DYLAN McDERMOTT

WOLFGANG PETERSEN

USA (COLUMBIA TRISTAR) 1993

127m (15)

Eastwood is a secret service man haunted by guilt because he failed to stop the assassination of President Kennedy in 1963, who hopes to redeem himself when a dangerous loony challenges him to a battle of wits with the life of the current incumbent of the White House as prize. Great action sequences, including an edge-of-the-seat rooftop chase, and Eastwood (unlike many other stars) never tries to hide his age – in fact he makes it an important part of the plot. Malkovich is unsettling as the nut-case and Russo makes a good love interest – check out the scene where she and Clint have to divest themselves of all manner of hardware before they can get into a clinch. Petersen came to the attention of Hollywood with his submarine picture *The Boat* (see page 318). Widescreen available.

INTERNAL AFFAIRS [4]

RICHARD GERE, ANDY GARCIA, NANCY TRAVIS, WILLIAM BALDWIN

MIKE FIGGIS

USA (CIC/4-FRONT) 1990

110m (18)

Gere is a crooked cop under investigation by internal affairs detective Garcia, who pushes him into more and more acts of violence and corruption. Tough, rough atmosphere and heavyweight acting from the two leads make for a gruelling, uncompromising picture. This film proved that Gere could still deliver the goods when given the right material to work with.

JAGGED EDGE [4]

JEFF BRIDGES, GLENN CLOSE, PETER COYOTE, ROBERT LOGGIA

RICHARD MARQUAND

USA (VCI CINEMA CLUB) 1985

105m (18)

A good example of writer Joe Eszterhas's sleaze thriller style. Lawyer Close defends smoothie Bridges on a charge of brutally butchering his wife. She gets him off and falls for him in the process. Ah, but was he guilty after all? Jumpy, fraught 'meller', with a lovely hard-boiled performance by Robert Loggia as Close's private investigator buddy. Eszterhas's best effort.

THRILLERS

JENNIFER EIGHT

ANDY GARCIA, UMA THURMAN, LANCE HENRIKSEN, JOHN MALKOVICH

BRUCE ROBINSON

USA (CIC) 1992

124m (15)

Complicated story from *Withnail And I* (see page 94) director Robinson. Despite an all-star cast, this convoluted tale of a cocky young copper never got a cinema release in the UK due to studio intransigence – which is a great shame. It may tend to ramble towards the end but it has a great deal to commend it. Worth renting, at least.

KALIFORNIA

BRAD PITT, JULIETTE LEWIS, DAVID DUCHOVNY, MICHELLE FORBES

DOMINIC SENA

USA (COLUMBIA TRISTAR) 1993

118 (18)

The trend a while back was for fraught domestic situations: the nanny from hell (*The Hand That Rocks The Cradle*, see page 290), the tenant from hell (*Pacific Heights*, see page 128), the flatmate from hell (*Single White Female*, see page 301), the lover from hell (*Fatal Attraction*, see page 114), etc. This one might be subtitled the car-sharers from hell: disgusting slob Pitt and his trailer-trash girlfriend (Lewis). Violent but very well acted, especially by Lewis and Pitt.

KLUTE

DONALD SUTHERLAND, JANE FONDA, ROY SCHEIDER, CHARLES CIOFFI

ALAN J PAKULA

USA (WARNER) 1971

109m (18)

Oscar-winning role for Fonda as a disturbed prostitute involved with a detective on the track of a maniacal killer. Depressing and dark atmosphere, but the actors force you to keep looking.

LEON

JEAN RENO, GARY OLDMAN, NATALIE PORTMAN, DANNY AIELLO

LUC BESSON

FRANCE/USA (TOUCHSTONE) 1995

106m (18)

Wonderfully off-beat thriller about a lonely hitman (Reno), and his relationship with a neglected little girl who helps him deal with corrupt cop Oldman and shifty boss Aiello. Also in widescreen. A laserdisc director's cut extends the film with more detail on the friendship of the child and the killer. A neat film in any version.

THE LONG GOODBYE [5]

ELLIOTT GOULD, STERLING HAYDEN, NINA VAN PALLANDT, MARK RYDELL

ROBERT ALTMAN

USA (WARNER) 1973

111m (18)

Altman's best in my book is this laconic update to 70s amorality and drift of Raymond Chandler's 'tec tale. It begins with a search for the purrfect brand of cat food, ends with murder in Mexico, and along the way we meet a gallery of grotesques, including Hayden's beautiful, drunken loser and Rydell's wacky gangster. Not to be missed. Widescreen.

THE LONG GOOD FRIDAY [4]

BOB HOSKINS, HELEN MIRREN, EDDIE CONSTANTINE, DAVE KING

JOHN MacKENZIE

UK (CIC) 1980

109m (18)

Already a legendary pic, this stars Hoskins as cockney criminal Harold Shand. On the eve of a lucrative deal with the American Mafia, he finds himself under attack from unknown forces. Explosively violent, but Hoskins has a sort of crude dignity – when the Mafia are scared off by trouble, he delivers a paean to the greatness of criminal Britain that mirrors the xenophobic speeches of 'respectable' politicians defending Little England, raising cheers in London cinemas by describing the Yank boss as 'a long streak of paralysed piss'! Unlovely he may be, but you can't take your eyes off Mr Shand. Made for TV but rejected as too violent, though it has since been shown on the box.

THE MANCHURIAN CANDIDATE

LAURENCE HARVEY, FRANK SINATRA, JANET LEIGH, ANGELA LANSBURY

JOHN FRANKENHEIMER

USA (WARNER) 1962 B&W

126m (15)

Based on a novel by Richard Condon, this cold war epic, about a soldier returned to the USA by the Commies as a brainwashed assassin, was out of circulation for many years at the behest of Sinatra, who felt it paralleled too strongly the murder of his friend President Kennedy which occurred the year after it was released. The right-wing mater of the killer as portrayed by Lansbury provides a sardonic swipe at Mom and apple pie. Harvey does his best-ever work as the disturbed assassin. Sinatra made another assassination film, *Suddenly*, also rarely seen.

MANHUNTER

BRIAN COX, WILLIAM PETERSEN, KIM GREIST, TOM NOONAN, DENNIS FARINA

MICHAEL MANN

USA (BMG) 1986

115m (18)

Marvellous film based on Thomas Harris's novel *Red Dragon*. It concerns a weird FBI agent who is called out of retirement because he has the ability to track serial sex killers by identifying with their thoughts. It wasn't a hit but has attained cult status as it has an appearance by Brian Cox as imprisoned murderer Hannibal 'The Cannibal' Lecter – the character who became much talked-about when portrayed by Anthony Hopkins in the movie of the sequel novel, *The Silence Of The Lambs* (see page 301). Cox's version of the character is very different, and – in spite of Hopkins winning an Oscar – critically preferred. A beautifully shot film which will make your skin crawl. Now out in widescreen. A 124m version was prepared in 1996 by Mann, but is unavailable, though BMG are trying to get the rights. Fullscreen copy is said to be pan-scan, but actually has more image to replace black areas. See note on Super 35 on page 13.

MARATHON MAN 〖3〗

DUSTIN HOFFMAN, LAURENCE OLIVIER, ROY SCHEIDER, MARTHE KELLER

JOHN SCHLESINGER

USA (CIC/4-FRONT) 1976

119m (18)

This is the story of a young guy (Hoffman) unwittingly dragged into trouble by the death of his secret agent brother. The most talked-about scene is the one where Nazi Olivier uses crude dental skills to torture Hoffman in the hope of making him divulge important information. Over-praised by mainstream critics, in my opinion, but worth a look nevertheless.

MARNIE 〖3〗

SEAN CONNERY, TIPPI HEDREN, BRUCE DERN, DIANE BAKER

ALFRED HITCHCOCK

USA (CIC) 1964

130m (15)

Melodrama about a thieving girl and her husband (Connery), who naturally wants to find out just why she's a frigid kleptomaniac. The story may be trite, but Hitchcock films it lovingly and there's a dreamy score by his fave composer Bernard Herrmann.

MISERY 〖4〗

KATHY BATES, JAMES CAAN, FRANCES STERNHAGEN, LAUREN BACALL

ROB REINER

USA (CINEMA CLUB V) 1990

102m (18)

This version of Stephen King's novel is mainly a two-hander between Caan and Bates. He's a novelist injured in a car crash, she's the obsessive fan who finds him. She happens to be a nurse and is delighted to have him recuperate in her isolated home – but when she finds he has killed off her favourite romantic character, Misery Chastain, to write serious books, she goes off the rails in a big way. Sadistic, unnerving, and very gripping. Oscar: best actress (Bates).

MISSISSIPPI BURNING 〖3〗

GENE HACKMAN, WILLEM DAFOE, FRANCES McDORMAND, BRAD DOURIF

ALAN PARKER

USA (ENTERTAINMENT) 1988

121m (18)

Fact-based thriller about FBI investigations into the murder of civil rights workers in America's Deep South, with sterling acting all round – notably from McDormand as the wife of a guilty man. The film was criticised for concentrating on white characters as the 'saviours' of black victims, but it still works as a thriller and the cinematography rightly won an Oscar.

MONA LISA

BOB HOSKINS, CATHY TYSON, MICHAEL CAINE, ROBBIE COLTRANE, SAMMI DAVIS

NEIL JORDAN

UK (CIC) 1986

104m (18)

Hoskins impresses as an ex-con driving tart Tyson to her clients – but then he falls for her. Gritty story with an adult theme, carried by good performances from Hoskins, Tyson and the ever-reliable Caine. Widescreen available.

THE NEGOTIATOR

SAMUEL L JACKSON, KEVIN SPACEY, JOHN SPENCER, J.T. WALSH, RON RIFKIN, DAVID MORSE

GARY GRAY

USA (WARNER) 1999

134m (15)

Given short shrift (oddly) by most critics, this is a drama with a twist. A negotiator in hostage crimes, cop Jackson is framed for murder and embezzlement of his comrades' disability fund. So he seizes a bunch of people, including the man he believes set him up, in an attempt to get at the truth. Question: how can the cops 'talk down' a man who knows everything they're going to say before they say it, since he's the expert in hostage negotiations? Spiffing cast, especially Jackson and his opponent-in-negotiations, Spacey. Look out too for craggy Spencer, who you may recall from TV's *LA Law*. This one's as tight as they come, and the lengthy running time zips by.

NIGHT MOVES

GENE HACKMAN, JENNIFER WARREN, JAMES WOODS, MELANIE GRIFFITH

ARTHUR PENN

USA (WARNER) 1975

96m (18)

Dark detective thriller with characters whose lives suggest the unravelling of 70s American society. Early appearances from James Woods and Melanie Griffith, daughter of Tippi Hedren. Her part here, as a sexually precocious teenager, mirrored her real-life antics at the time. Sloppily directed by Penn, with boom mikes occasionally intruding into the top of the frame, but an effective picture for all that. Special edition available.

NIGHTWATCH 🎬 4

⭐ NIKOLAJ WALDAU, SOFIE GRAABOEL, KIM BODNIA, ULF PILGAARD

🎬 OLE BORNEDAL

DENMARK (TARTAN) 1994

⏱ 104m (18)

Acclaimed creepy thriller about evil goings-on in a mortuary. As is often the case with foreign thrillers, the director is has been wooed into making an English-language version with US and UK stars. It turned out to be inferior to the original, so if you can cope with subtitles this is for you. Issued in widescreen.

NO WAY OUT 🎬 3

⭐ KEVIN COSTNER, GENE HACKMAN, SEAN YOUNG, HOWARD DUFF

🎬 ROGER DONALDSON

USA (SPEARHEAD) 1987

⏱ 110m (15)

Loosely based on *noir The Big Clock*, this is a tricksy double-agent story with sex and violence thrown in for bad measure. Costner proves he can act as well as look handsome, and while hardly an important film it'll provide a decent night's entertainment.

NORTH BY NORTHWEST 🎬 5

⭐ CARY GRANT, EVA MARIE SAINT, JAMES MASON, LEO G CARROLL, MARTIN LANDAU

🎬 ALFRED HITCHCOCK

USA (WARNER) 1959

⏱ 131m (PG)

The pinnacle of Hitch's 'wrong man' epics, with Grant charming as the playboy fated to be drawn into a spy chase – the scene where he's pursued in a field by a crop sprayer plane is a classic, and modern audiences always howl with laughter at the final shot: after we see Grant and Eva Marie Saint embrace in a railway carriage, there's a Freudian cut to the train roaring into a tunnel! Super score by Bernard Herrmann. A classic.

PAYBACK 🎬 3

⭐ MEL GIBSON, ALEXIS LUI, JAMES COBURN, WILLIAM DEVANE, KRIS KRISTOFFERSON, GREGG HENRY

🎬 BRIAN HELGELAND

USA (WARNER) 1999

⏱ 130m (18)

For once, Gibson plays the bad guy; a violent criminal who is shot and left for dead by his sado-mascochist, double-crossing partner and his unfaithful wife after a robbery. Once he recovers, he sets about getting his cut of the money in ruthless and violent style – although he spikes the tension with some well-aimed, sharp humour. Also on DVD. Based on the same source novel as Point Blank (see page 299).

THRILLERS

PERDITA DURANGO [3]

ROSIE PEREZ, JAVIER BARDEM, AIMEE GRAHAM

ALEX DE LA IGLESIA

USA/SPAIN/MEXICO (FOX PATHE) 1997

99m (18)

Directed by cult movie-maker Iglesia *(Accion Mutante, Day Of The Beast)*, this is based on a story by Barry Gifford, who wrote the source novel for *Wild At Heart* (see page 254) – indeed, the title character of this pic featured in that film, albeit played by Isabella Rossellini. Here Perdita (Perez) and her man kidnap a couple for a black magic sacrifice and smuggle foetuses into Las Vegas! Over-the-top and perversely compelling viewing.

A PERFECT MURDER [2]

MICHAEL DOUGLAS, GWYNETH PALTROW, VIGGO MORTENSEN

ARNOLD KOPELSON

USA (WARNER) 1998

103m (15)

A wealthy businessman, his beautiful wife and her lover form the eternal triangle in this offering loosely based on Hitchcock's *Dial M For Murder* (see page 287). The husband, played by Douglas, devises what he believes is the perfect plan to murder his wife. Elegant psychological suspense thriller.

POINT BLANK [5]

LEE MARVIN, ANGIE DICKINSON, KEENAN WYNN, CARROL O'CONNOR

JOHN BOORMAN

USA (WARNER) 1967

92m (18)

Based on a character created by Richard Stark (pseudonym for Donald E Westlake), this is a merciless revenge thriller about a hood (Marvin) demanding the return of money given to the Mob by a bent accomplice, but finding modern gangland is run by men in suits with nothing but credit cards. He responds in a one-man war of attrition. Brutal and brilliantly directed by Brit Boorman. Recently revived in cinemas. Remake: *Payback* with Mel Gibson (see page 298).

PRIMAL FEAR [4]

RICHARD GERE, FRANCES McDORMAND, EDWARD NORTON, LAURA LINNEY

GREGORY HOBLIT

USA (CIC) 1996

124m (18)

Gripping story about the sleazy underbelly of the USA legal system. Gere is a flashy lawyer defending a seemingly feckless kid (the wonderful Norton) accused of murdering a top churchman. The lawyer appears to know all the tricks – but who is really manipulating whom? Underrated on cinema release, this nifty thriller ought to find its audience on video.

RAISING CAIN 🎬3

⭐ JOHN LITHGOW, LOLITA DAVIDOVICH, STEVEN BAUER, FRANCES STERNHAGEN

🎬 BRIAN DE PALMA

USA (CIC) 1992

⏱ 92m (15)

De Palma descends to self-parody with this story of a fractured persona at the mercy of his crazy child-psychologist dad. Not content with borrowing from Hitchcock, the theme of Michael Powell's *Peeping Tom* (see page 211) is added to the witch's brew. Critics chuckled at press screenings, but there's no denying the director's skill or John Lithgow's talent as an actor.

RANSOM 🎬4

⭐ MEL GIBSON, RENE RUSSO, GARY SINISE, DELROY LINDO

🎬 RON HOWARD

USA (TOUCHSTONE) 1996

⏱ 116m (18)

Fine update of the 1955 thriller. Wealthy Gibson gets fed up of being messed about when his child is kidnapped and goes on TV to announce (much to the horror of his wife) that he will not pay the ransom, but will give the cash to anyone who grasses the baddies up. Pulse-pounding stuff, with real emotion rather than big bangs.

REPULSION 🎬3

⭐ CATHERINE DENEUVE, IAN HENDRY, PATRICK WYMARK, YVONNE FURNEAUX

🎬 ROMAN POLANSKI

UK (ODYSSEY) 1965 B&W

⏱ 104m (18)

Dank story of a disturbed girl and her murderous assaults. It has too much of the 'art-film' about it to hold the viewer's attention to the end, but has its moments, notably the great surreal scene of hands coming out of walls in a corridor.

RONIN 🎬3

⭐ ROBERT DE NIRO, JEAN RENO, NATASHA McELHONE, STELLAN SKARSGARD, SEAN BEAN, JONATHAN PRYCE

🎬 JOHN FRANKENHEIMER

USA (WARNER) 1999

⏱ 117m (15)

A group of mercenaries are hired to steal a top-secret briefcase from a mysterious client in Paris, but it turns out that they are not the only ones with their eyes on the briefcase – but they have to compete with some other ruthless underground organisations. Fast, action-packed and violent with some astonishing car chases.

THRILLERS

SEA OF LOVE 🎬3

⭐ AL PACINO, ELLEN BARKIN, JOHN GOODMAN, MICHAEL ROOKER

🎬 HAROLD BECKER

USA (CIC) 1989

⏱ 108m — 18

Gripping thriller about a cop investigating a chain of murders linked to 'lonely hearts' adverts, who finds himself involved with a woman who may be the killer. Not as luridly satisfying as its rep suggests, but driven along neatly by a taut Richard Price screenplay and a good Pacino performance.

THE SILENCE OF THE LAMBS 🎬4

⭐ JODIE FOSTER, ANTHONY HOPKINS, SCOTT GLENN, TED LEVINE

🎬 JONATHAN DEMME

USA (COLUMBIA TRISTAR) 1991

⏱ 113m — 18

Gory version of Thomas Harris's novel about a caged serial killer (Hopkins) and his relationship with FBI rookie Foster as they track down another murderer. It won several Oscars, including best actor for Hopkins, but many feel his stint as Hannibal Lecter is inferior to that of Brian Cox in *Manhunter* (see page 295). There's a cameo performance from director/producer Roger Corman, who gave director Demme his start years before. The film was condemned for equating transsexuality with murder, leading Demme to make the sympathetic AIDS drama *Philadelphia* (see page 129) to silence not the lambs, but his critics. Hopkins is set to star in a film of a new Harris novel, *Hannibal*.

SINGLE WHITE FEMALE 🎬2

⭐ BRIDGET FONDA, JENNIFER JASON LEIGH, STEVEN WEBER

🎬 BARBET SCHROEDER

USA (CINEMA CLUB V) 1992

⏱ 108m — 18

Flatmate from hell movie. Revenge, rage and lunacy abound, but I find it to be the least thrilling of the '... from hell' genre which was in vogue some years ago. Though the story is a bit tired, the two leads give decent performances.

SLEEPERS ⭐⭐⭐

ROBERT DE NIRO, DUSTIN HOFFMAN, BRAD PITT, KEVIN BACON, JASON PATRIC

BARRY LEVINSON

USA (POLYGRAM) 1996

141m (18)

Controversial movie about boys abused in a kids' home who grow up and go separate ways until two of them, now gangsters, meet and kill one of their molesters. Another boy who has become a lawyer takes on the defence. It's allegedly all true, but investigating journalists could find no record of the case. And much as we all loathe child abuse, it's worrying to see a supposedly quality pic suggesting it's okay to take the law into your own hands and then lie and cheat (with the help of your priest!) in order to get away with it. It'd be all right if some doubt were voiced, but this never happens. All the more disturbing for being so well acted. Available in widescreen.

SLEUTH ⭐⭐⭐⭐

LAURENCE OLIVIER, MICHAEL CAINE

JOSEPH L MANKIEWICZ

UK/USA (MIA) 1972

132m (15)

Anthony Shaffer's play makes a fine two-handed duel for Olivier and Caine as rivals in love engaged in a class-based battle of wits and mutual humiliation. The trouble is that the central visual deception, which I can't reveal as it would spoil the plot for you, didn't fool me for a minute. On stage it would pass, but on the big screen I saw through it right off. But the actors make it worthwhile. Agreeably crisp and salty dialogue.

SNAKE EYES ⭐⭐

NICOLAS CAGE, GARY SINISE, JOHN HEARD, CARLA GUGINO

BRIAN DE PALMA

USA (TOUCHSTONE) 1999

95m (15)

Cage stars as a corrupt cop doing security at a big boxing match. When a murder takes place he takes it as a personal affront, orders the stadium sealed and spends the rest of the film trying to solve the mystery. A good idea by De Palma (trying to make a film that unfolds in one space, like his hero Hitchcock's *Rope*) fails to gel in spite of some bravura technical flourishes and an energetic stint by Cage.

TAXI DRIVER

ROBERT DE NIRO, JODIE FOSTER, HARVEY KEITEL, CYBILL SHEPHERD, PETER BOYLE, ALBERT BROOKS, JOE SPINELL, MARTIN SCORSESE

MARTIN SCORSESE

USA (COLUMBIA TRISTAR) 1976

114m (18)

Those that love it call it a work of genius, those that hate it say it's just a big-budget exploitation movie. Both statements may be true. De Niro is Travis Bickle, a Vietnam veteran who can't sleep and takes a night job as a taxi driver. Horrified by the life he sees on the street, his inability to form a relationship with the girl he worships and his failure to persuade a child prostitute to quit, he embarks on an apocalyptic explosion of violence – with surprising results. Paul Schrader's screenplay is still as relevant as ever to our mad, sad world. Fine score from Bernard Herrmann. Recently reissued in a remastered widescreen edition. Slight BBFC cut, but seen intact on TV.

THE THIRD MAN

ORSON WELLES, JOSEPH COTTEN, ALIDA VALLI, TREVOR HOWARD, BERNARD LEE

CAROL REED

UK (WARNER) 1949 B&W

105m (PG)

A masterpiece. Writer Cotten is looking for his elusive pal Harry Lime (Welles) in post-World War Two Vienna – is he dead or alive, a nice guy or a monster? This version of Graham Greene's story is full of mysterious shadows and teasing menace. Check out the zither music, Welles looming out of a doorway (surely one of the greatest entrances in cinema), his self-penned speech about morality, money, death and cuckoo clocks, the chase through the sewers ... Welles revived Lime as a not-*quite*-so-bad guy for radio, and there was a TV series with Michael Rennie in the role.

TOM CLANCY'S NETFORCE 🎬3

SCOTT BAKULA, BRIAN DENNEHY, KRIS KRISTOFFERSON, JUDGE REINHOLD

ROBERT LIEBERMAN

USA (HIGH FLIERS) 1999

154m (15)

It's the year 2005 and FBI man Bakula is on the trail of the killer of one of his Internet team, but he has to contend with mad computer boss Reinhold. Solid material and a reliable cast make this lengthy pic the sort of fun you might want to stretch over a couple of evenings. Clancy, of course, is the hit novelist behind stuff like *Patriot Games* (see page 34) and *The Hunt For Red October* (see page 26).

TWILIGHT 🎬2

PAUL NEWMAN, SUSAN SARANDON, GENE HACKMAN

ROBERT BENTON

USA (CIC) 1999

91m (15)

An ageing private detective gets involved in a murder mystery which is linked to some old, unsolved cases amid the backdrop of the sleazy side of Hollywood. Sound performances from all three stars, as you would expect with their pedigree.

VERTIGO 🎬5

JAMES STEWART, KIM NOVAK, BARBARA BEL GEDDES, TOM HELMORE

ALFRED HITCHCOCK

USA (CIC) 1958

122m (PG)

Hitch was miffed to have missed out on the rights to the novel which inspired the French thriller *Les Diaboliques*, so the authors penned a book specially for him to adapt. The result was this classic about a man who attempts to remake his new gal in the image of the lady he failed to save due to his suffering from the affliction of the title, only to discover he's been duped. Music by Hitchcock's favourite composer Herrmann is a great part of the package. The film has recently been somewhat controversially restored and reissued in 70mm, so this tape may well be superseded at a future date. Many critics say this original version is preferable. Note: As we went to press, the restored cut was issued as part of the Hitchcock centenary onslaught, though the box cover seems to play down the restoration, doubtless because of the bad press it's had.

TV & Special Interest

Video is not just about feature films – indeed, there is a whole world of tapes available that have nothing to do with cinema: sex and sex education, travel, trains, wildlife, DIY, painting, photography, gardening, the Royal Family, petcare, war, cookery, computers, cars, religion, the paranormal, sport, music, natural history, birdwatching, etc. The list of categories is virtually endless! Browse round the shelf markers in your local store or ask the staff to look up specific areas for you, as they tend to be 'special interest' rather than appealing to the wider video-buying/renting public. Some videos – such as *Edward and Sophie, The Royal Wedding* – will have a short shelf-life. If there are any areas you'd like to see covered in future editions of this guide please let us know. In the meantime, here is a selection of the most popular TV and Special Interest tapes available at present ...

COMEDY

There are loads of one-off shows by great stand-up comedians either TV-derived or based on live shows, and you should find that the best of your favourite performers are in stock or available to order. Here are just a few of the performers who offer the best video box-office.

Pure Video catalogues are a good source of what is available and they provide a list of ordering serial numbers. You can find them for sale at major HMVs or similar stores.

BILLY CONNOLLY
Loud and rude efforts from Scottish favourite Billy are available on Vision Video (mainly rated 18). They are mostly derived from live concerts. *Billy Connolly – Erect for 30 Years* and *Billy Connolly – Two Night Stand Live* are good examples.

EDDIE IZZARD
Popular alternative comedian with off-the-wall style.

OTHER COMEDY
Vision Video have released a number of comedians, including the droll **Jack Dee** and even **Jim Davidson** (certificate 18). Other favourites on video include **Roy Chubby Brown**, **Steve Coogan**, **Dave Allen** and **Lily Savage**.

FITNESS

These tapes are rated E, exempt from BBFC classification. Numerous other celebrity and fitness-regime videos are currently in print and these are among the most popular. Since their different styles will suit different people, it is best to match your needs and fitness level to what is on offer.

CHER FITNESS – A NEW ATTITUDE
(Fox)
Tips from the superstar actress/singer.

JANE FONDA – TOTAL BODY SCULPTING
(Warner)
One of several fitness vids from the seemingly ageless star.

BEVERLEY CALLARD – THE ULTIMATE RESULTS
(VCI)
Coronation Street star's workout/get-fit regime.

SOCCER

These tapes are rated E, exempt from BBFC classification. Similar volumes around for most major teams. You'll find the range is often extended pre-Christmas and for Father's Day in June.

ARSENAL 1896–96 CENTENARY
(BBC)
History of the great London team.

TV AND SPECIAL INTEREST

BRYAN ROBSON'S GREAT MOMENTS IN SOCCER
(Beckmann)

CELTIC A–Z
(John Williams)
One of several tapes on the Glasgow champs from this label.

LIVERPOOL – 300 LIVERPOOL GOALS
(Doherty)
Compilation of the scouse team's top scores.

MANCHESTER UNITED – 300 PREMIERSHIP GOALS
(Manchester Utd)
One of 50 or more tapes devoted to the nation's faves, the bulk of which appear on the team's own video label.

TV CHILDREN'S

There are oodles of children's videos available – both new offerings and old favourites – and the great thing about young children, in particular, is that they can watch the same thing over and over again without tiring of it! It's almost impossible to select 'the best' because that will be different for every child, but here are a few of the most popular favourites.

BATMAN – THE ANIMATED SERIES
(Warner)
Remaining high in the popularity stakes, this was made in bright and bouncy (Zap! Powee!) style before the dark and eerie Gotham City of the latest Batman creations.

THE COMPLETE BAGPUSS
(Polygram)
Well over 20 years old but still voted the best-loved children's TV character ever, those visiting or revisiting this classic stop-frame animation about the saggy old cloth cat and his mice friends will be captivated by its innocent charm.

HANNA BARBERA
(First Independent/Hanna Barbera)
Hanna Barbera character videos include Fred Flintstone and Yogi Bear.

THE MUPPETS
(Colombia TriStar)
The Very Best of the Muppet Show is among a range of tapes of this favourite TV series featuring songs and sketches from Kermit, Fozzie and friends.

TELETUBBIES
(BBC)
You love 'em or hate 'em but you can't ignore 'em! *Big Hug!* Is the video the under-threes will love.

WALT DISNEY
(Disney)
Pick your favourite Disney character and there'll be a selection of videos featuring everyone from the old favourites such as **Donald** and **Mickey** to newer arrivals like **Winnie the Pooh**.

WARNER BROS.
(Warner)
Warner Bros. characters include **Bugs Bunny, Daffy, Sylvester** and **Tweetie Pie**.

OTHER TV CHILDREN'S

Other popular titles include the recently released *The Clangers* (Polygram), *Sesame Street* (Columbia TriStar), the educational programme, that perennial favourite *Postman Pat* and the charming tales of *Gran*, a sort of female Heath Robinson in carpet slippers. You can also find classics like *Noddy* and *The Magic Roundabout, Top Cat* and *Rupert Bear* or new additions like Jane Hissey's *Old Bear*.

TV ANIMATION

These are adult titles – although *The Simpsons* has a broad appeal. Look under TV Children's (page 307) for other cartoon favourites.

BEAVIS AND BUTTHEAD
USA (CIC)   (PG)(12)(15)

A host of tapes, with titles like *Work Sucks*, giving an idea of the philosophical outlook of the dynamic duo. B&B has characters as crude as the animation: two retarded adolescents who sit in front of their TV and comment nastily on the awful rock videos they (and we) witness; they also wear short pants but lust after women. Weird, but very funny too.

THE SIMPSONS
USA (FOX)   (PG)

Several tapes available of the dysfunctional all-American family headed by the dumb Homer, but really ruled by young Bart 'Eat my shorts!' Simpson, including *Too Hot For TV*. You either love it or hate it.

SOUTH PARK
USA (WARNER)   (15)

Inane, deliberately badly animated fable about a sick, small town peopled by hypocritical, pompous adults and precocious little brats (one of whom gets killed every week yet is back in the next show). The humour is clever-but-filthy; I especially love the black school chef (voiced by Isaac Hayes) who urges us in song to suck on his 'chocolate salty balls'. Individual tapes and boxed sets available. 'Oh my God, they've killed Kenny!'

TV – COMEDY

ABSOLUTELY FABULOUS

⭐ DAWN FRENCH, JENNIFER SAUNDERS, JOANNA LUMLEY, JUNE WHITFIELD, JULIA SAWALHA, JANE HORROCKS

UK (BBC) (15)

Complete boxed set of the hilarious cult show about two relentlessly trendy pals in the fashion world growing old disgracefully. Also available: series 1, series 2, plus various individual tapes.

BLACKADDER

⭐ ROWAN ATKINSON, STEPHEN FRY, HUGH LAURIE, TONY ROBINSON, MIRANDA RICHARDSON

UK (BBC) (15)

Complete boxed set of all four series involving various nasty members of the Blackadder family through the ages, all played by Atkinson and all having a dogsbody named Baldrick (Robinson). Brilliant. Also: all four series available separately, as well as individual tapes.

CHEERS

⭐ TED DANSON, KELSEY GRAMMER, KIRSTIE ALLEY, WOODY HARRELSON, etc.

USA (CIC) (PG)(15)

Boxed set and six best-of tapes of this comedy set in a Boston bar named Cheers. Precursor to the hit *Frasier*.

TV AND SPECIAL INTEREST

THE FALL AND RISE OF REGINALD PERRIN

⭐ LEONARD ROSSITER

UK (SECOND SIGHT) (PG)

When last screened on TV in 1991, it attracted eight million viewers. Now this classic is available as a boxed set.

FAWLTY TOWERS

⭐ JOHN CLEESE, ANDREW SACHS, CONNIE BOOTH, PRUNELLA SCALES

UK (BBC) (PG)

Boxed set of the comedy classic about a manic hotel owner. Also single tapes. Despite its popularity only a handful of shows were ever made.

FRASIER

⭐ KELSEY GRAMMER, JANE LEEVES, DAVID HYDE-PIERCE, JOHN MAHONEY, PERI GILPIN

USA (CIC) (PG)

Six best-of volumes available of this hit follow-on from *Cheers*, about the life, loves, family and pals of a wacky radio phone-in shrink in Seattle. Very funny and sophisticated humour with a healthy dash of vulgarity. Boxed episodes also on sale.

TOP 1000 VIDEOS

FRIENDS

⭐ JENNIFER ANISTON, DAVID SCHWIMMER, COURTENEY COX, LISA KUDROW, MATT LE BLANC, MATTHEW PERRY

USA (WARNER) (PG)(12)(15)

Numerous tapes of this popular romantic comedy series about the love lives and problems of a group of young Americans. So popular that Aniston's hairstyle became a worldwide cult.

HARRY ENFIELD AND CHUMS

⭐ HARRY ENFIELD, PAUL WHITEHOUSE, KATHY BURKE

UK (BBC) (15)

Several tapes of impersonator/comic Enfield's hilarious character-based shows. Superb.

MONTY PYTHON'S FLYING CIRCUS

⭐ JOHN CLEESE, GRAHAM CHAPMAN, MICHAEL PALIN, TERRY JONES, ERIC IDLE, TERRY GILLIAM

UK (BBC) (PG)(12)(15)

Many tapes available of this madcap, surreal and innovative comedy series of yore. See also *Comedy* section for movies.

ONLY FOOLS AND HORSES

⭐ DAVID JASON, BUSTER MERRYFIELD*, NICHOLAS LYNDHURST (*Early shows have LENNARD PEARCE)

UK (BBC) (PG)

Multiple tapes of this long-running show about semi-crooked, endearingly inept entrepreneurs trying to get rich in Peckham. Wonderfully observed. A set of every show is out via Britannia, FREEPOST, Romford, Essex RM50 1JP.

OTHER TV COMEDY

There are numerous BBC shows on tape – *Bottom, Dad's Army, Last Of The Summer Wine, One Foot In The Grave, Porridge, Rab C Nesbitt, Steptoe & Son, Yes Minister* and *The Young Ones* to name but a few series, most rated PG.

TV AND SPECIAL INTEREST

TV DRAMA

THE AVENGERS

PATRICK MacNEE, HONOR BLACKMAN, DIANA RIGG, LINDA THORSON

UK (CONTENDER) (PG)

Classic 60s spy-spoof series starring urbane Macnee and a succession of glam sidekicks. Boxed set available plus individual tapes. Follow-up *The New Avengers* – with MacNee, Gareth Hunt and Joanna Lumley – also on release (tapes rated 12).

CADFAEL

DEREK JACOBI

UK (CENTRAL) (PG)(15)

New slant on sleuthing with Jacobi as an ancient monk solving crimes, rather in the style of the film *The Name of the Rose* (see page 126). Several volumes available.

CRACKER

ROBBIE COLTRANE

UK (GRANADA) (15)(18)

Many tapes of this hit series about psychological criminal profiler helping the police to catch killers while dealing with his collapsing marriage and gambling addiction. Remade in America with US actors under the name *Fitz*, but that version appears not to be on tape yet, though it has been on TV.

I CLAUDIUS

DEREK JACOBI, BRIAN BLESSED, JOHN HURT, etc.

UK (BBC) (15)

Two double-tape sets give the complete run of this superb 70s adaptation of Robert Graves's story of intrigue in ancient Rome, with marvellous acting throughout. Starts slowly but soon takes off.

INSPECTOR MORSE

JOHN THAW, KEVIN WHATELY

UK (CENTRAL) (PG)(12)(15)

Numerous volumes of this series based on Colin Dexter's stories of the Jag-driving detective and his assistant Sergeant Lewis. See *Only Fools and Horses* entry (page 310) for address of Britannia, from whom it's possible to collect the full run by mail order.

PRIDE AND PREJUDICE

COLIN FIRTH, JENNIFER EHLE, etc.

UK (BBC) (U)

Recent rightly celebrated adaptation of Jane Austen's classic romance on two-tape set.

PRIME SUSPECT

HELEN MIRREN, TOM BELL

UK (GRANADA) (15)(18)

Five stories so far starring Mirren as forceful cop Jane Tennison. Immensely popular on TV.

THE SCARLET PIMPERNEL

☆ RICHARD E. GRANT, ELIZABETH McGOVERN, MARTIN SHAW, etc.

UK (CARLTON)   (PG)(12)

Trio of tapes available separately of this latest TV version of the adventures of fop Sir Percy, who is secretly the elusive Pimpernel, hero of the aristos in the French revolution.

SHARPE

☆ SEAN BEAN

UK (CENTRAL)   (PG)(12)(15)

All the adventures of the upwardly mobile oik-to-officer hero of Wellington's army are out on tape, with Bean in the lead part. Based on Bernard Cornwell's novels.

SHERLOCK HOLMES

☆ JEREMY BRETT, EDWARD HARDWICKE, CHARLES GRAY

UK (GRANADA)   (PG)

After the initial shock at his eccentric style, fans soon took to the late Brett's incarnation of Conan Doyle's Baker Street sleuth and he is now rated alongside Rathbone and Cushing as one of the best screen Holmeses ever. All episodes available.

SMILEY'S PEOPLE

☆ ALEC GUINNESS, BERNARD HEPTON, MAUREEN LIPMAN, etc.

UK (BBC)   (15)

Follow-up to *Tinker, Tailor, Soldier, Spy*, this is another adaptation of a John Le Carré thriller, with Guinness super-cool as the dry spymaster Smiley. Directed by Simon Langton in 1982. Two-tape set.

OTHER TV DRAMA

Everything from *The Man From UNCLE* to *London's Burning* to *The Onedin Line* to *Soldier, Soldier* ... in short, a plethora of TV drama, covering 60s kitsch spy stuff to current hits to ancient BBC serials. Again, the *Pure Video* catalogue from HMV lists currently available tapes. There are also comprehensive volumes of soap series around: *Coronation Street, Brookside, Emmerdale, EastEnders*, etc. The BBC tend to issue new dramas like *Our Mutual Friend*, within weeks of the TV showing. If you can't find what you want, your store may be able to order it for you.

TV AND SPECIAL INTEREST

TV SCIENCE FICTION

BABYLON 5

This cult series about a space station where various species interact (not always amicably) has fared better on video over here than back in the USA, where it is only now being made available. Set in 2257, a decade after a space war that nearly obliterated Earth, it was dreamed up as a five-year series of 110 episodes taking place aboard a galactic UN. There are about 40 tapes out on Warner (usually PG or 12), including pilot show *The Gathering* and separate TV films *In The Beginning* and *Thirdspace*. In 1997 the pilot was recut to fit in with the storyline of the series and a new music score was added, so you may want to check which version you're buying or renting.

DR WHO

There seem to be about 50 or so BBC videos of episodes from the various incarnations of the famed Time Lord and his TARDIS machine. However, the Beeb has a notoriously slapdash attitude to archive material, often only realising the cult value of stuff after master tapes are wiped! Some material has therefore been provided by collectors or obscure foreign stations who bought material when it was new and just happened to keep a copy. I saw a new boxed set *(The Crusade And The Space Museum)* the other day, featuring the first Doc (William Hartnell), that only had parts 1 and 3 of a story, with the middle segment missing and viewers having to rely on linking commentary and a booklet to fill them in on the plot! This only seems to make the collectors even more devoted. Tapes are U or PG.

STAR TREK

Quite apart from the feature films (see pages 274–5), there are around a staggering 200 single tapes or sets currently available derived from the original series and its offshoots! When the relatively short-lived 60s show with William Shatner as Kirk and Leonard Nimoy as Spock was revived for cinema, fans were delighted. Not so when a follow-up called *The Next Generation*, with new stars like Patrick Stewart, Jonathan Frakes, Michael Dorn, LeVar Burton, Brent Spiner, Marina Sirtis, Whoopi Goldberg and others was mooted for TV. However, the protests were soon forgotten and the new show lasted a lot longer than the original, eventually transferring itself to the big screen as new strands *Deep Space Nine* and *Voyager* took over the box. Currently, just about everything seems to be available: the original series (as well as a pilot starring Jeffrey Hunter instead of Shatner); *The Next Generation*, mainly in sequential tapes with two episodes apiece, but also in sets devoted to shows featuring particular characters (like android Data) or villains (The Borg, Q, etc.); and *Deep Space Nine/Voyager*, again mainly on standard two-episode tapes. All are on CIC, and most are rated PG (with some U and an occasional 12). The series often cleverly use metaphor and analogy to deal with problems we have to face in the real world, like racism and sexism, which has sometimes caused controversy. I believe one *Next Generation* show was refused a showing by the BBC because it was deemed to suggest sympathy for the IRA, though I've been unable to determine if it is out on tape at present. The *Pure Video* catalogues regularly issued and sold in big shops like HMV are a good source of what is currently in stock or available to order.

X-FILES

Fox has released episode tapes of this popular series starring Gillian Anderson and David Duchovny as well as boxed sets of complete series, usually rated 12 or 15, although the boxed set of Series 2 is rated 18 as it includes an 18-rated tape. Fans of the series will already be familiar with the FBI duo and their dark and sometimes disturbing forays into alien sightings and conspiracy theory.

OTHER TV SCIENCE FICTION

The BBC has made available cult material like **Blake's 7** (PG), **The Hitchhiker's Guide To The Galaxy** (PG) and even the original **Quatermass & The Pit** (PG) – all over multiple tapes except the last, a three-hour compilation of the six original monochrome episodes of Nigel Kneale's (third) story of his maverick scientist creation. Warners have also released the *V* series on a brace of 15-rated tapes. Fox have issued tapes, rated 15, of the *X-Files'* creator's superb serial-killer/science fictional **Millennium**, though this second Chris Carter series has not caught the public imagination on such a big scale. Nevertheless, it's something of a cult and has inspired two non-official guidebooks. Kids' stuff like **UFO** (Polygram, U/PG), **Space 1999** (ITC, U/PG) and **Thunderbirds** (MGM/UA, U) are also available on multiple tapes.

WAR

War films can be crash, bang, smash-'em-up entertainment, patriotic propaganda, historical adventure or polemics on the futility of armed conflict and there are plenty of all kinds available on video. Strangely enough, though, in spite of the potential for both action and human interest, very few directors seem to specialise in the genre. The great maverick Sam Fuller made several low-budget classics, but the only one of his war pix I could find currently available is his mutilated masterpiece *The Big Red One*. Oliver Stone at one time looked to be making a career of modern war epics, with films such as *Born On The Fourth Of July*, *Platoon* and *Salvador*, but he's since moved on to more controversial political and social dramas. Spielberg has recently scored with *Saving Private Ryan*. It would be nice if we lived in a world where war films were invariably set in the distant past – but it looks as if mankind will go on providing movie-makers with up-to-the-minute genocidal storylines for the forseeable future. How sad.

633 SQUADRON

GEORGE CHAKIRIS, CLIFF ROBERTSON, MARIA PERSCHY

WALTER GRAUMAN

UK (WARNER) 1964

92m (PG)

Exciting World War Two story of preparation for and execution of an extremely difficult bombing raid. Thrill-a-minute and a rousing score combine with a good cast to create a picture that remains a perennial favourite. Also available on a two-for-one tape with *The Battle Of Britain* (see page 316). Note: this appears to be a cut print.

ALL QUIET ON THE WESTERN FRONT

LEW AYRES, LOUIS WOLHEIM, JOHN WRAY

LEWIS MILESTONE

USA (CIC) 1930 B&W

103m (PG)

Based on Erich Maria Remarque's anti-war novel, this is the tale of German kids who volunteer for World War One. They rapidly change from gung-ho patriots to sad and scared cynics. This is a heavily cut version. The film spawned a sequel and was remade in the 70s. Oscar: best picture.

APOCALYPSE NOW ▶5

★ MARLON BRANDO, MARTIN SHEEN, ROBERT DUVALL, FREDERIC FORREST, DENNIS HOPPER

🎬 FRANCIS FORD COPPOLA

USA (CIC) 1979

⏱ 146m (18)

Coppola's multi-million dollar epic relocates the action of Joseph Conrad's novel *Heart Of Darkness* to the Vietnam conflict, with Sheen as a soldier sent on a mission into Cambodia in order to kill Kurtz (Brando), a high-ranking officer who has gone mad and is conducting his own war with the help of native tribesmen. The boat journey upriver in the company of LSD-taking troops has been said to parallel an acid trip (indeed, the film was allegedly at one point titled *The Psychedelic Soldier*), and the acting and images often border on the surreal. Brando's dialogue was improvised and sounds it. The production took a toll on the physical, mental and financial health of several of those involved, and while some dismiss it as pretentious twaddle it remains one of the most spectacular, audacious and talked-about films of all time. There is a fine documentary on the making of the movie, *Hearts Of Darkness*. Oscars: cinematography and sound. Note: widescreen available, but the ratio is badly cropped.

THE BATTLE OF BRITAIN ▶3

★ LAURENCE OLIVIER, ROBERT SHAW, MICHAEL CAINE, SUSANNAH YORK

🎬 GUY HAMILTON

UK (WARNER) 1969

⏱ 110m (PG)

Worthy attempt to tell the story of the decisive World War Two fight between the RAF and the Luftwaffe. Great music and aerial dogfights, and loads of stars popping up for stiff-upper-lip cameos. This appears to be a cut print (down from 132m). Also available on two-for-one tape with *633 Squadron* (see page 315), another war-in-the-air showpiece.

THE BATTLE OF MIDWAY ▶3

★ CHARLTON HESTON, TOSHIRO MIFUNE, HENRY FONDA, ROBERT MITCHUM, GLENN FORD, JAMES COBURN

🎬 JACK SMIGHT

USA (CIC/4-FRONT) 1976

⏱ 126m (PG)

Account of a 1942 Pacific ocean battle between Japanese and Yanks. Suffers from similar star overload to *The Battle Of Britain* (see above), but is a tad more coherent and gripping a prospect. Most of the star performers underplay to good effect. Convincing battle scenes.

WAR

BATTLE OF THE BULGE 3

HENRY FONDA, ROBERT RYAN, ROBERT SHAW, CHARLES BRONSON

KEN ANNAKIN

USA (WARNER) 1965

132m (PG)

Yet another account of a decisive World War Two fight – this time the final German attack of 1944 in the Ardennes – finds itself smothered in heavyweight acting cameos. Saved by Fonda's measured performance. Available in widescreen, which is the only way to see it.

THE BIG RED ONE 5

LEE MARVIN, MARK HAMILL, ROBERT CARRADINE, BOBBY DI CICCO

SAM FULLER

USA (WARNER) 1980

82m (15)

Sam Fuller's autobiographical masterpiece was cut by the studio but remains a powerful story of a World War Two infantry division. The title refers to the figure '1' on the soldiers' badges, but misinterpretation of this was no doubt the reason for the (hilarious) seizure of the video in the 'nasties' debacle of the early 1980s! Police were confounded to find that they'd seized a worthy war film and not a hard-core porno flick. This is one picture that merits rediscovery and restoration to full director's cut length.

THE BLUE MAX 5

GEORGE PEPPARD, JAMES MASON, URSULA ANDRESS, JEREMY KEMP

JOHN GUILLERMIN

USA (FOX) 1966

146m (PG)

Excellently acted and visually thrilling tale of German World War One flying aces. Peppard is the working-class yob who causes offence when his aviation skills gain him entry into the aristocratic world of fighter pilots, while Kemp is his resentful comrade. By chasing after the coveted 'Blue Max' medal, seducing the wife of a senior officer and generally ignoring the rules of chivalry and gentlemanly behaviour, Peppard becomes a hero to the people and a thorn in the side of his bosses. One of the best air-war pix ever. Available in a widescreen version, but unfortunately from a cut print.

THE BOAT 🎬5

JURGEN PROCHNOW, HERBERT GRONEMEYER, KLAUS WENNEMANN

WOLFGANG PETERSEN

WEST GERMANY (COLUMBIA TRISTAR) 1981

143m (15)

This U-Boat adventure was the most expensive German film ever at the time it was made. The claustrophobic, sweaty, fear-inducing world of the cramped 'boat' is shown in a way that outdoes all the Hollywood submarine pix. The movie was shown in a dubbed 128m version outside Germany, but acclaim led to a subtitled 143m print being released as *Das Boot*, the German title. That is the print available on this widescreen tape, subtitles (ha ha) and all. An epic 300m German TV series version has been shown on BBC TV. Director Petersen and lead actor Prochnow have gone on to Hollywood success.

BORN ON THE FOURTH OF JULY 🎬4

TOM CRUISE, WILLEM DAFOE, JOHN GETZ, STEPHEN BALDWIN, TOM BERENGER

OLIVER STONE

USA (CIC) 1989

138m (18)

Perhaps the best of director Stone's series of Vietnam movies is based on the autobiography of Ron Kovic, a young man who was an enthusiastic soldier but changed his mind (as you do) after coming home crippled. The film ably moves from mindless patriotism on Kovic's part through degradation of body and spirit until his final realisation that he's been duped. Cruise's finest acting role. Oscars for direction and editing. Available in widescreen.

THE BRIDGE ON THE RIVER KWAI 🎬4

ALEC GUINNESS, WILLIAM HOLDEN, JACK HAWKINS, SESSUE HAYAKAWA

DAVID LEAN

UK (COLUMBIA TRISTAR) 1957

155m (PG)

Based on a novel by Pierre Boulle, who wrote the source story for *Planet Of The Apes*, this factually inspired story of Allied troops on the notorious Burma railway built at the behest of the Japanese in World War Two is not without problems. Essentially a character study of two stubborn men (Guinness as the Brit and Hayakawa as the Jap) with different ideas of 'honour', it actually soft-pedals the Japanese atrocities in an attempt at psychological analysis. Guinness wants to show Brit superiority, but actually ends up collaborating with the enemy. Flawed, but still won several Oscars, including best film, director, cinematography and actor (Guinness).

WAR

CASUALTIES OF WAR 🎬 4

MICHAEL J FOX, SEAN PENN, DON HARVEY, THUY THU LE

BRIAN DE PALMA

USA (CINEMA CLUB V) 1989

108m (18)

Based on a true story of a group of young American troops who kidnapped, sexually abused and shot a Vietnamese girl, and the one man who refused to be a party to the crime. Fox is believable as the lad who refuses to be pressured or threatened into burying the facts, proving that he's a capable actor when given something other than the usual comedy rubbish to work with. Often derided – maybe the Americans dislike the truth – this is one of De Palma's best and least showy pix. Quentin Tarantino rates it as a classic, if that helps. Cut from 120m.

THE COLDITZ STORY 🎬 3

JOHN MILLS, ERIC PORTMAN, BRYAN FORBES, LIONEL JEFFRIES

GUY HAMILTON

UK (WARNER) 1954 B&W

93m (U)

Classic escape story of Allied captives in World War Two, ingenious and full of famous British faces. Also available in a two-for-one tape with *Ice Cold In Alex* (see page 323), which also stars Mills. The two films complement each other nicely.

CROSS OF IRON 🎬 4

JAMES COBURN, MAXIMILIAN SCHELL, JAMES MASON, DAVID WARNER

SAM PECKINPAH

UK/WEST GERMANY (WARNER) 1977

127m (18)

Peckinpah's men-stick-together ethos transported from the West to a wild bunch of German soldiers on the Russian front in World War Two. Coburn is the cynical leader, Schell the idiot desperate for the Iron Cross medal of the title. Solidly anti-war, though Peckinpah's version was undercut by his being forced to quit shooting before he had all the material he needed. Richard Burton took the Coburn part in a sequel shot by another director. Now in widescreen.

THE CRUEL SEA 🎬 4

JACK HAWKINS, STANLEY BAKER, DENHOLM ELLIOTT, MOIRA LISTER

CHARLES FREND

UK (WARNER) 1953 B&W

121m (PG)

Nicholas Monsarrat's novel of the men aboard a Brit corvette in World War Two, with understated playing from all concerned. Sentimental in parts, but much of its time is spent in effective portrayal of life at sea.

THE DAM BUSTERS

MICHAEL REDGRAVE, RICHARD TODD, NIGEL STOCK, JOHN FRASER

MICHAEL ANDERSON

UK (WARNER) 1954 B&W

120m (U)

Story of the invention by Barnes Wallis of the bouncing bomb, and its subsequent use against German dams on the Ruhr in 1943. While it was probably a necessary act of war, it's easy in the excitement of the piece to forget that many ordinary civilians lost their lives in the process. Fine acting from Redgrave as the boffin.

THE DEER HUNTER

ROBERT DE NIRO, CHRISTOPHER WALKEN, JOHN SAVAGE, MERYL STREEP

MICHAEL CIMINO

USA (WARNER) 1978

175m (18)

Cimino is the master of the overblown, with this and *Heaven's Gate* (see page 336) the most obvious examples. This tale of friends and families torn by the Vietnam war certainly has some memorable sequences, but these are interspersed with some slower stretches. When I saw it on first release, the audience groaned and shifted in their seats throughout and at the point where the weeping family sit around the table crooning 'God Bless America' the woman seated next to me exclaimed 'Oh for God's *sake!*' and made a noisy exit. Nevertheless, it is a moving tale, and won Oscars for best film, director and supporting actor (Walken), amongst others. To my mind Cimino's best film remains his simple, effective debut, the Clint Eastwood vehicle *Thunderbolt And Lightfoot,* but he seems to prefer weighty epics.

THE DESERT FOX

JAMES MASON, CEDRIC HARDWICKE, JESSICA TANDY, RICHARD BOONE

HENRY HATHAWAY

USA (FOX) 1951 B&W

85m (PG)

Life of German World War Two Field Marshall Erwin Rommel, from his desert war with adversary Montgomery to his part in the plot to kill Hitler. Mason is on top form here. He played Rommel again two years later in *The Desert Rats,* made to cash in on the success of this film.

WAR

THE DIRTY DOZEN 5

LEE MARVIN, ROBERT RYAN, TELLY SAVALAS, DONALD SUTHERLAND, JOHN CASSAVETES, CHARLES BRONSON

ROBERT ALDRICH

USA (WARNER) 1967

146m (15)

Based on EM Nathanson's bulky novel about a group of killers and World War Two deserters given the choice of joining a suicide mission instead of jail or execution. Highly enjoyable nonsense, and for once the parade of stars are allowed to act their socks off rather than simply make cameo appearances. Inspired several duff TV sequels and not a few rip-offs. Widescreen tape is available. Aldrich has become something of a cult director in recent years, but somewhat unjustly, this is not one of his more highly regarded pictures. Cut by 24 seconds.

FULL METAL JACKET 3

MATTHEW MODINE, ADAM BALDWIN, LEE ERMEY, VINCENT D'ONOFRIO

STANLEY KUBRICK

USA/UK (WARNER) 1987

112m (18)

Late entry in the Vietnam movie stakes by the coldest of directors. Kubrick insisted on recreating Vietnam in London's docklands, with limited success. The movie follows the familiar pattern of showing a tough instructor training raw recruits, followed by a look at how the lads do in combat. The innovation here is that one bullied recruit loads his gun with real ammo (the full metal jacket of the title) and blows the bullying drill leader away! The Vietnam sequence which follows loses momentum, but perhaps that's what real war is like. The film has, in my opinion, an inflated reputation – see it and judge for yourself.

GALLIPOLI 3

MARK LEE, MEL GIBSON, BILL HUNTER, BILL KERR

PETER WEIR

AUSTRALIA (CIC) 1981

106m (PG)

Two pals tough it out in World War One Gallipoli landings. Decent acting and action. Available in widescreen. Note: one of Gibson's first big parts after the success of *Mad Max* (see page 31). He's now a major star, of course.

GLORY

MATTHEW BRODERICK, DENZEL WASHINGTON, MORGAN FREEMAN, CARY ELWES

EDWARD ZWICK

USA (COLUMBIA TRISTAR) 1989

117m (15)

Black section of the Union army in the American Civil War. Well acted and beautifully shot (actor Washington won a best support Oscar and Freddie Francis was rewarded for his cinematography) but some of the sentiments are questionable. I wonder how an actor of the calibre of Morgan Freeman could mouth dialogue about how whites had been doing all the fighting for blacks and that it was now time for them to pay back the debt – especially when we now know that the North's motives were as much economic as anything else. Some critics call *Glory* an anti-war film, but it seems (even in its title) to be gung-ho for battle. All that aside, a watchable piece. This appears to be a cut version, as sources list the original running time at 128m. Available in widescreen.

THE GREAT ESCAPE

STEVE McQUEEN, JAMES GARNER, DONALD PLEASENCE, JAMES COBURN, RICHARD ATTENBOROUGH, CHARLES BRONSON, DAVID McCALLUM

JOHN STURGES

USA (WARNER) 1963

165m (PG)

Detailed account of World War Two Allied escape from a German prison camp, the fun and games being undercut by a brutal ending. All the actors acquit themselves well. Remade for TV in 1988. A widescreen tape is now available. Note: the musical score has become as famous as the film due to the catchy theme tune.

THE GUNS OF NAVARONE

GREGORY PECK, DAVID NIVEN, STANLEY BAKER, ANTHONY QUINN

J LEE THOMPSON

UK/USA (COLUMBIA TRISTAR) 1961

157m (PG)

Based on an Alistair MacLean novel, this lengthy adventure concerns a World War Two Allied team attempting to destroy German guns on a Greek island because they threaten shipping lanes. Performance-driven with much intrigue involving treacherous behaviour, the pic nevertheless won the Oscar for SFX. A lacklustre sequel was made many years later.

HAMBURGER HILL 🎬3

⭐ ANTHONY BARRILE, MICHAEL PATRICK BOATMAN, TIM QUILL

🎬 JOHN IRVIN

USA (CINEMA CLUB V) 1987

⏱ 110m (18)

True story with cast of unknowns, set in Vietnam during bloody attempt to secure the hill of the title. Irvin is always a dependable director, and it's a pity the film is not better known.

ICE COLD IN ALEX 🎬3

⭐ JOHN MILLS, SYLVIA SIMS, ANTHONY QUAYLE, HARRY ANDREWS

🎬 J LEE THOMPSON

UK (WARNER) 1960 B&W

⏱ 125m (PG)

World War Two desert trek by a varied group in a clapped-out ambulance. A neat little picture with some fine acting on display. Also on a two-for-one tape with *The Colditz Story* (see page 319), another Mills starrer.

KELLY'S HEROES 🎬3

⭐ CLINT EASTWOOD, DONALD SUTHERLAND, CARROLL O'CONNOR

🎬 BRIAN G HUTTON

USA/YUGOSLAVIA (WARNER) 1970

⏱ 143m (PG)

Unlikely story (in *M*A*S*H* style) of slovenly, rebellious US troops in World War Two deciding to go in for private enterprise by hijacking Nazi gold from bank vaults. The film is on the long side, but is saved by Eastwood, Sutherland and O'Connor.

THE LONG AND THE SHORT AND THE TALL 🎬3

⭐ RICHARD TODD, LAURENCE HARVEY, RICHARD HARRIS, RONALD FRASER

🎬 LESLIE NORMAN

UK (WARNER/LUMIERE) 1960 B&W

⏱ 101m (PG)

World War Two conscience-drama set in Malaysia, where Brits have to decide whether to kill a captive. Based on the play by Willis Hall, directed by father of film critic Barry Norman. Good acting, especially from Ronald Fraser, who sadly passed away in 1997.

THE LONGEST DAY

JOHN WAYNE, ROD STEIGER, ROBERT RYAN, ROBERT MITCHUM, HENRY FONDA

KEN ANNAKIN, ANDREW MARTON, BERNHARD WICKI

USA (FOX) 1962 B&W

170m (PG)

Epic account of Normandy landings by the Allies in World War Two, recently shown more realistically in *Saving Private Ryan*. Someone once stated that black and white widescreen was the most redundant of filmic styles, and you can sample it for yourselves on this tape. Too many stars, too little story (or too much?), but it still won Oscars for cinematography and effects work. Colourised for TV showings in recent years.

MEMPHIS BELLE

MATTHEW MODINE, ERIC STOLTZ, BILLY ZANE, TATE DONOVAN

MICHAEL CATON-JONES

USA (WARNER) 1990

103m (PG)

True tale of World War Two B-17 bomber crew previously told in a wartime documentary. A slow build-up to the final mission lets us get to grips with the featured characters. Well crafted and definitely worth seeing.

THE NAKED AND THE DEAD

CLIFF ROBERTSON, ALDO RAY, RAYMOND MASSEY, RICHARD JAECKEL

RAOUL WALSH

USA (ODYSSEY) 1958

130m (PG)

Somewhat anodyne adaptation of Normal Mailer's novel of Americans versus Japanese in World War Two. The performers are up to scratch, but Mailer's gutsy prose doesn't get the translation it deserves. Still worth a glance, if only for Raymond Massey as a thoroughly nasty officer.

NIGHT OF THE GENERALS

OMAR SHARIF, PETER O'TOOLE, TOM COURTENAY, JOANNA PETTET

ANATOLE LITVAK

FRANCE/UK (CINEMA CLUB V) 1967

138m (15)

Underrated and unusual war movie, with O'Toole as a German general in World War Two. He's also a serial killer, and when he's about to be found out he tries to implicate his underling in order to escape justice. Based on the novel by HH Kirst. This is a cut print, unfortunately, as far as I can determine.

WAR

PATTON [5]

GEORGE C SCOTT, KARL MALDEN, STEPHEN YOUNG, MICHAEL STRONG

FRANKLIN J SCHAFFNER

USA (FOX) 1970

169m (PG)

Magnificent epic on the life of flamboyant US general Patton, with a mesmerising performance by Scott in the title role. Opens with a fantastic image of Patton addressing troops in front of a huge stars 'n' stripes and never pauses for breath. A real warts-and-all portrayal. Seven Oscars, including best picture, director, actor (Scott) and screenplay (Francis Ford Coppola and EH North). Widescreen edition available. Aka *Patton: Lust For Glory*. Scott refused his Oscar but reprised the role in a TV film on Patton's last years.

PLATOON [4]

TOM BERENGER, WILLEM DAFOE, CHARLIE SHEEN, KEVIN DILLON

OLIVER STONE

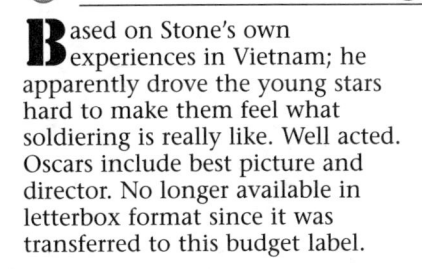

USA (CINEMA CLUB V) 1986

115m (15)

Based on Stone's own experiences in Vietnam; he apparently drove the young stars hard to make them feel what soldiering is really like. Well acted. Oscars include best picture and director. No longer available in letterbox format since it was transferred to this budget label.

RED DAWN [4]

CHARLIE SHEEN, PATRICK SWAYZE, POWERS BOOTHE, BEN JOHNSON

JOHN MILIUS

USA (WARNER) 1984

109m (15)

High-school kids look out on the playing fields and see Commie troops landing by parachute in an invasion of the USA. They take to the hills and form guerilla bands, going so far as to court-martial and execute 'traitors'. Okay, so it's militaristic, right-wing guff, but I simply can't help liking John Milius and his pix. He's the last mad individualist of his kind in Hollywood-land and we must treasure him. Fun, and the young cast do a decent job, with help from seasoned performers such as Ben Johnson.

RUN SILENT, RUN DEEP [3]

CLARK GABLE, BURT LANCASTER, JACK WARDEN, BRAD DEXTER

ROBERT WISE

USA (WARNER) 1958 B&W

89m (U)

Best of the old Hollywood submarine romps, with an all-star cast. However, I'm afraid after *The Boat* (see page 318), Germany's epic of claustrophobia and fear, films like this tend to pale into insignificance. Worth a look, though, as Wise is always a reliable purveyor of craftsman-like entertainment.

SALVADOR 🎬 4

JAMES WOODS, JAMES BELUSHI, JOHN SAVAGE, MICHAEL MURPHY

OLIVER STONE

USA (VIDEO COLLECTION) 1986

117m (18)

Sleazy photographer goes with his pal for some adventures in war-torn El Salvador, only to become involved as he sees how his own government is supplying the bad guys. Stone's picture is based on a true story. Woods is magnificent as usual, and Belushi (brother of late comic John) is watchable too. Super film, and far superior to Stone's political biopix of JFK and Nixon.

SANDS OF IWO JIMA 🎬 3

JOHN WAYNE, JOHN AGAR, FORREST TUCKER, MARTIN MILNER

ALLAN DWAN

USA (4-FRONT) 1949 B&W

108m (PG)

Tough Marines story set in World War Two, neatly directed by veteran Dwan. Lots of action and a fine showing by Wayne – his performance was nominated for an Oscar, although he did not win one until the end of his career and one of his last Westerns, *True Grit* (see page 346).

SAVING PRIVATE RYAN 🎬 4

TOM HANKS, MATT DAMON, TOM SIZEMORE, EDWARD BURNS, TED DANSON

STEVEN SPIELBERG

USA (CIC) 1998

162m (15)

Bravery, cowardice, compassion, insensitivity, murder, humour and brutality, all in an acclaimed epic about the attempt to save the sole remaining soldiering son of a family from death in World War Two. What got most attention, however, was the stunning opening sequence depicting the carnage suffered by the Americans at Omaha Beach during the Normandy landings – strange how some movies are praised for explicit gore and violence while others are condemned for the same thing. Over-hyped, perhaps, but honest about how men act in war, and boasting another fine performance by Hanks. Five Oscars, including best director. Lovely quality tape transfer, pin-sharp and almost TV broadcast definition.

WAR

SERGEANT YORK

GARY COOPER, WALTER BRENNAN, JOAN LESLIE, NOAH BEERY Jnr

HOWARD HAWKS

USA (WARNER) 1941 B&W

129m (U)

Classic World War One tale: true (if glamorised) story of a country hick who became an American legend. One of Hawks' best pictures. Cooper is delightful – he won an Oscar for best actor as the pacifist who captured 132 Germans all by himself.

SINK THE BISMARCK

KENNETH MORE, DANA WYNTER, CARL MOHNER, LAURENCE NAISMITH

LEWIS GILBERT

UK (FOX) 1960 B&W

97m (U)

This story of the search for the Nazi battleship is saved from being a dry and impersonal saga by the moving acting of More as the navy's desk-man – the scene where we hear him crying behind closed doors when he learns his son has been rescued from the sea is powerful indeed. A British classic of the old school. Based on CS Forester's book.

STALAG 17

WILLIAM HOLDEN, OTTO PREMINGER, PETER GRAVES, DON TAYLOR

BILLY WILDER

USA (CIC) 1953 B&W

115m (PG)

Oscar-winning acting from Holden as the wiseguy in a World War Two POW camp, suspected of treachery by his compatriots because they can't manage to escape. An odd mix of laughs and drama, based on a hit play. Not one of Billy's best, I'm afraid, but still considered an important movie in its day.

TAPS

TIM HUTTON, SEAN PENN, GEORGE C SCOTT, TOM CRUISE

HAROLD BECKER

USA (FOX) 1981

121m (PG)

Unusual story of students of a military academy who, faced with a closedown, start a small war by seizing control of the building. Veteran Scott is very nearly outshone by his youthful co-stars, especially Penn (in his screen debut) and Cruise. Do yourself a favour and get hold of a copy.

TORA! TORA! TORA! 🎬4

MARTIN BALSAM, JOSEPH COTTEN, JASON ROBARDS, TAKAHIRO TAMURA

RICHARD FLEISCHER AND OTHERS

JAPAN/USA (FOX) 1970

138m (U)

Pearl Harbor attack re-run in an epic that looks at both the Japanese and the American sides of the story. Legendary Japanese director Akira Kurosawa was contracted to do the non-American sequences, but was so unfamiliar with this sort of stuff that he failed to notice when a full-size model of a battleship was built with guns facing the wrong way round! Fleischer finally did the film with the help of three other assistant directors, the result being explosive enough to win an Oscar for effects work. Available in widescreen.

THE TRAIN 🎬4

BURT LANCASTER, JEANNE MOREAU, PAUL SCOFIELD

JOHN FRANKENHEIMER

FRANCE/ITALY (WARNER) 1964 B&W

128m (PG)

French resistance hijacks Nazi trainload of stolen art treasures. Lancaster is unmissable as the train driver and Scofield pulls considerable weight as the scheming German officer. This is a letterbox version but appears to be from a cut print. Still, it's nice to see a war movie that works because of character acting rather than lots of explosions.

VON RYAN'S EXPRESS 🎬3

FRANK SINATRA, TREVOR HOWARD, BRAD DEXTER, JOHN LEYTON

MARK ROBSON

USA (FOX) 1965

112m (PG)

Slick World War Two caper. Sinatra is the new, top-ranking Yank officer in a POW camp hitherto dominated by the Brits. He rubs them up the wrong way and is accused of collaborating with the enemy commandant, but finally gains respect when he hijacks a German military train. Plenty of action.

WHERE EAGLES DARE 🎬4

RICHARD BURTON, CLINT EASTWOOD, PATRICK WYMARK, MARY URE

BRIAN G HUTTON

USA/UK (WARNER) 1969

148m (PG)

Far superior to Hutton's *Kelly's Heroes* (see page 323), which also featured Eastwood, this *Boy's Own*-style adventure was written for the screen by Alistair MacLean and later fashioned into a novel by him. It starts off reasonably simply, as what Quentin Tarantino has called 'a guys-on-a-mission movie' – but it soon gets unbelievably complex as it is revealed that the rescue attempt on a Nazi-occupied alpine castle is only part of the plan to unearth traitors at the heart of Allied command. It really has to be seen on a huge screen to appreciate the scale, but the currently available widescreen print is pretty good.

WESTERNS

The Western genre is undoubtedly one of the best-served on video. That being said, however, there are still some gaps: while huge numbers of John Wayne 'oaters' seem to be perennially available, some crucial work by directors like Sam Peckinpah and Budd Boetticher is missing from the shelves, as are many highly-regarded 'spaghetti' Westerns from Italian film-makers. Still, I had no trouble finding enough classics to fill this section; indeed, I could have filled it twice over ... which can only be good news for video viewers!

THE ALAMO

JOHN WAYNE, RICHARD WIDMARK, LAURENCE HARVEY, RICHARD BOONE, CHILL WILLS

JOHN WAYNE

USA (WARNER) 1960

192m (PG)

Star/director Wayne's dream project about Davy Crockett and pals holding off the Mexican army at the eponymous Texas mission was long considered a bit naff – but with the recent writing of a book on the picture and the restoration of this full-length widescreen version it is now being given its due. It's a bit like a Texas version of *Zulu* (three men and a dog against a howling mob) and with uncredited help from director John Ford, it's surely worth a look. Spectacular climax.

THE BALLAD OF CABLE HOGUE

JASON ROBARDS, STELLA STEVENS, DAVID WARNER, STROTHER MARTIN

SAM PECKINPAH

USA (WARNER) 1970

121m (PG)

Tragicomic tale of a loser left to die in the desert who finds water 'where it wasn't' – and with it love, friendship, compassion and death. Beautifully shot by Lucien Ballard and featuring some of Peckinpah's stock company of actors, it'll come as a surprise to those expecting another *The Wild Bunch* (see page 348). David Warner as a sleazy preacher is especially fine.

THE BIG COUNTRY [4]

GREGORY PECK, CHARLTON HESTON, JEAN SIMMONS, CARROLL BAKER

WILLIAM WYLER

USA (WARNER) 1958

163m (PG)

Family-feud epic, with Peck as the seaman pitched into a battle for (ironically) water-rights when he leaves the ocean to marry. He rejects the macho posturing of his new environment to the dismay of all, but comes good in the end. A major hit, it remains a classic of big-style Hollywood movie-making. Great punch-up between Heston and Peck! And that theme ...

A BULLET FOR THE GENERAL [5]

GIAN-MARIA VOLONTE, LOU CASTEL, KLAUS KINSKI, MARTINE BESWICK

DAMIANO DAMIANI

ITALY (AKTIV/4-FRONT) 1966

113m (18)

After the movies of Sergio Leone, this film is regarded as one of the best spaghettis ever. A meditation on revolution and corruption, it unfolds slowly as the bandit (Volonte, excellent as always) is tempted from the socialist path by Castel. Unfortunately this is a cut print. Nice mad-prophet antics from Kinski. Widescreen.

BUTCH CASSIDY AND THE SUNDANCE KID [3]

PAUL NEWMAN, ROBERT REDFORD, KATHERINE ROSS, STROTHER MARTIN

GEORGE ROY HILL

USA (FOX) 1969

105m (PG)

Based on the true story of two Old West gunmen who fled to South America, this was a huge hit in its day – but it has dated badly compared to other Westerns of the same era (like *The Wild Bunch*, see page 348) due to the smug humour and that sickly tune, 'Raindrops Keep Falling On My Head'. Oscars include script, music and cinematography.

CHISUM [2]

JOHN WAYNE, BEN JOHNSON, FORREST TUCKER

ANDREW V McLAGLEN

USA (WARNER) 1970

110m (PG)

Yet another version of the Billy the Kid legend (and his involvement in the Lincoln County Wars) this suffers from making the peripheral figure of Chisum (Wayne) the hero, and from sidelining the Kid (ineffectually played as a pretty boy by Geoffrey Deuel). Wayne is entertaining as usual, but the same story has been done better in films such as *Young Guns* (see page 349). Widescreen available.

COMPAÑEROS

FRANCO NERO, TOMAS MILIAN, JACK PALANCE, FERNANDO REY

SERGIO CORBUCCI

ITALY/SPAIN/WEST GERMANY (AKTIV) 1970

110m (18)

Deliriously over-the-top political spaghetti Western by the other Sergio – Corbucci, creator of the notorious *Django* (see page 332). Mercenary Nero and revolutionary Milian unite to rescue the pacifist Rey. They are pursued by Palance, a dope-smoking nutter who has a wooden hand, gained when Nero left him crucified to a tree and his faithful pet hawk freed him by eating his hand off! Crazy and utterly marvellous – the only negative is that this is a faded, cut and crudely pan-scanned print.

DANCES WITH WOLVES

KEVIN COSTNER, MARY McDONNELL, GRAHAM GREENE

KEVIN COSTNER

USA (GUILD) 1990

173/225m (15)

Oscar-winning story of a cavalryman who is tired of war and gets himself posted to the limits of the frontier. There he makes a pet of a wolf and is initiated into Sioux tribal ways. Wonderful cinematography by Dean Semler, and Costner's confident acting and directing make this a magical film – though some have said it goes too far in its idealised portrait of the Native American. The movie was such a smash that a special version was issued with an extra 50 minutes or so of footage. Both versions are available on video. Widescreen.

DEAD MAN

JOHNNY DEPP, GABRIEL BYRNE, ROBERT MITCHUM, GARY FARMER

JIM JARMUSCH

USA (POLYGRAM) 1996 B&W

115m (18)

When Depp survives a bullet in this old West story, the fact that he's named William Blake leads injun Farmer to believe he's the immortal incarnation of the legendary visionary and poet of the same name. Strange stuff, shot in luminous monochrome, with a super cameo by Mitchum.

DEATH RIDES A HORSE [4]

⭐ LEE VAN CLEEF, JOHN PHILLIP LAW, ANTHONY DAWSON, LUIGI PISTILLI, MARIO BREGA

🎬 GIULIO PETRONI

ITALY (MGM/UA) 1967

⏱ 110m   (12)

After his success in the Sergio Leone/Clint Eastwood films, American character actor Van Cleef became a star in his own right in several more spaghetti Westerns. This one, at long last available on video, reguarly features in critics' Top 20 lists for the genre: old gunhand Van Cleef teaches a young man how to shoot so he can revenge himself on those who slaughtered his folks – but what'll happen when he finds out his mentor was present at the massacre? Great stuff! Budget-price tape.

DJANGO [5]

⭐ FRANCO NERO, EDUARDO FAJARDO, JOSE BODALO

🎬 SERGIO CORBUCCI

ITALY/SPAIN (ART HOUSE/4-FRONT) 1966

⏱ 95m   (18)

Controversial spaghetti (banned in the UK for ages) by Corbucci, which spawned a legion of dodgy sequels – often producers dubbing an Italian Western into English simply changed the title character's name to Django. Oddly enough, some of these *faux*-Djangos are better than the one official sequel (again with Nero), the 1980s sleazefest *Django Strikes Again* (see opposite). This first Django film begins with Nero dragging his gatling-gun (in a coffin) through the muddy streets of a hellish town, and doesn't let up until the final frames of cruelty and mutilation.

DJANGO THE BASTARD [4]

⭐ ANTHONY STEFFEN, PAOLO GOZLINO, LU KANANTE

🎬 SERGIO GARRONE

ITALY (AKTIV) 1969

⏱ 95m   (15)

Nice widescreen transfer of one of the 30 or so unofficial 'Django' films. This one has a somewhat mysterious revenge theme that has led some critics to speculate that it inspired the US Clint Eastwood hit *High Plains Drifter* (see page 336). Often appears on critical lists of the Top 20 spaghettis – and rightly so!

WESTERNS

DJANGO STRIKES AGAIN

FRANCO NERO, DONALD PLEASENCE, CHRISTOPHER CONNOLLY

TED ARCHER (NELLO ROSSATI)

ITALY (AKTIV/4-FRONT) 1987

88m (18)

Twenty years on and our gunfighter has become a monk – but he's lured out of retirement to rescue a daughter in some vile Amazonian jungle, where she's being held by a sadistic gunboat diplomatist with a passion for rare butterflies! Only Italians can make Westerns this insane. Pleasence plays a Scots entomologist (!) as he did in Dario Argento's horror flick *Phenomena* (aka *Creepers*).

FACE TO FACE

GIAN-MARIA VOLONTE, TOMAS MILIAN, WILLIAM BERGER

SERGIO SOLLIMA

ITALY/SPAIN (AKTIV) 1967

102m (15)

Unusual Euro-Western which sees ailing prof Volonte, in the west for his health, captured by bandit Milian only to use his brains to take over gradually as gang leader. Finally, it is the supposed bad guy who has to subdue the increasingly nasty professor. Entertainment with an anti-fascist message. This is a shortened print, but it is in widescreen.

EL DORADO

JOHN WAYNE, ROBERT MITCHUM, JAMES CAAN

HOWARD HAWKS

USA (CIC/4-FRONT) 1967

127m (PG)

Rather a bleak re-run of his earlier *Rio Bravo* (see page 343), this is still Hawks at his very best. Wayne, Caan and boozy Mitchum fight for right against cattle king Ed Asner (TV's Lou Grant), and only the most mean-spirited churl will fail to enjoy being along for the ride. Admired as bravura movie-making by everyone from your grandad to Quentin Tarantino – and I should jolly well think so too!

A FISTFUL OF DOLLARS 🎬 4

CLINT EASTWOOD, GIAN-MARIA VOLONTE, MARIANNE KOCH

SERGIO LEONE

ITALY/WEST GERMANY/SPAIN (MGM/UA) 1964

94m (15)

The first in the 'Man With No Name' trilogy directed by Leone, which made Eastwood a star and caused spaghetti Westerns to be taken seriously when it was finally issued in English-speaking countries in 1967. It's a remake of Akira Kurosawa's samurai flick *Yojimbo* (which was itself said to be based on Budd Boetticher's oater *Buchanan Rides Alone*), with the same plot: a stranger rides into a corrupt town and sells his services to both sides in a gang feud. The laconic, poncho-clad Clint, Leone's delirious direction and Ennio Morricone's music make this an essential part of any Western fan's education. The film has recently been remade yet again, this time by Walter Hill, as the Bruce Willis gangster thriller *Last Man Standing* (see page 173). Restored letterbox copy now out.

FOR A FEW DOLLARS MORE 🎬 5

CLINT EASTWOOD, LEE VAN CLEEF, GIAN-MARIA VOLONTE

SERGIO LEONE

ITALY/WEST GERMANY/SPAIN (MGM/UA) 1965

128m (15)

The second 'Man With No Name' film (though he actually has a different name in each) boasts a much bigger budget and a rather more complex plot. Clint and rival Van Cleef cut up rough with each other and form an uneasy truce to snare the sadistic bandit Volonte. At last out in a widescreen, restored version.

FORT APACHE 🎬 4

JOHN WAYNE, HENRY FONDA, WARD BOND

JOHN FORD

USA (4-FRONT) 1948 B&W

127m (U)

Ford is the acknowledged master of the classic Western form, and this is one of his best. New commander Fonda blunders but Wayne covers up in the interests of the cavalry. A masterful film. Note: also available as a bargain two-in-one tape on the same label, coupled with Ford's *Stagecoach* (see page 346).

WESTERNS

GERONIMO [5]

GENE HACKMAN, ROBERT DUVALL, WES STUDI, JASON PATRIC

WALTER HILL

USA (COLUMBIA) 1994

111m (12)

With Peckinpah gone, Hill is the one man left making serious Westerns. This is an accurate version by John Milius of the tale of this famous Apache, but it lost out at the box office in the US when a simultaneous competing version was shown on TV. Then, in the UK, BBC TV critic Barry Norman wrongly told viewers Hill's movie was just a cut-down theatrical release of that TV film! Despite great reviews and a prestige London run it sank – don't miss it now. Wes Studi, villain of *The Last Of The Mohicans* (see page 148), is Geronimo.

THE GOOD, THE BAD AND THE UGLY [5]

CLINT EASTWOOD, LEE VAN CLEEF, ELI WALLACH

SERGIO LEONE

ITALY (MGM/UA) 1966

161m (18)

The final part of Leone's Eastwood trilogy sees the three protagonists (and antagonists) of the title dodging through civil war lines in search of a coffin full of cash. Restored version on import DVD includes outtakes. Widescreen tape now available here.

THE GUNFIGHTER [3]

GREGORY PECK, MILLARD MITCHELL, KARL MALDEN

HENRY KING

USA (FOX) 1950 B&W

84m (U)

Peck excels as the old gunfighter trying to settle down with the girl he loves but being forced into a final shoot-out by a glory-seeking punk. This may seem old hat now, but at the time the dark tone was something new. Nice performance from Karl Malden as the hero-worshipping bartender, and Peck is marvellously understated.

HANG 'EM HIGH [3]

CLINT EASTWOOD, INGER STEVENS, ED BEGLEY, BEN JOHNSON

TED POST

USA (WARNER) 1967

114m (18)

Clint's first US Western recalls the brutal realism of his Leone trilogy. In fact Leone was offered this film and refused. Although it is credited to Ted Post, a pal from his TV days, Eastwood directed much of the picture. The opening scenes are shocking, as the ex-lawman turned cattle-rancher is hanged and left for dead by a posse of vigilantes who wrongly suspect him of rustling and murder. Saved by Ben Johnson, he takes up the badge again to hunt down his enemies with unflinching violence, while forming an odd relationship with a woman searching for those who killed her husband.

HEAVEN'S GATE 🎬 4

KRIS KRISTOFFERSON, CHRISTOPHER WALKEN, JOHN HURT, ISABELLE HUPPERT

🎬 MICHAEL CIMINO

USA (WARNER) 1980

⏱ 205m (18)

Based on the Johnson County Wars, this is the film that infamously brought down a studio with its squandering of a reported $50 million budget. A flop with punters and critics on first release and then cut by over an hour, the full-length version has since come to be regarded as something of a masterwork of big-scale cinema. This is supposed to be the uncut print, but it emerged in 1997 that the initial release was actually longer still at 220m and a print was shown at the National Film Theatre. Rather slow, but very beautiful. For the full tale read the book *Final Cut*, and think of what you could have done with the money!

HIGH NOON 🎬 5

GARY COOPER, GRACE KELLY, KATY JURADO, LEE VAN CLEEF, LON CHANEY Jnr, LLOYD BRIDGES, THOMAS MITCHELL

🎬 FRED ZINNEMANN

USA (4-FRONT) 1952 B&W

⏱ 85m (U)

New edition of the classic Western about a town lawman who learns that his wedding day is about to be interrupted by the return of the baddie he jailed. We follow his progress – or lack of it – as the townspeople who had once lauded him now refuse to help him fight the outlaws, and even his intended urges him to run. A host of rich cameos, but Cooper stands out as the hero. Bonus trailer and documentary on this tape. Oscars include best actor for Cooper and one for that famed 'Do Not Forsake Me ...' song heard throughout. Allegedly Howard Hawks so loathed the film that he made *Rio Bravo* (see page 343) as a kind of riposte to the idea of lawmen needing help.

HIGH PLAINS DRIFTER 🎬 3

CLINT EASTWOOD, VERNA BLOOM, JACK GING, MITCHELL RYAN

🎬 CLINT EASTWOOD

USA (CIC) 1973

⏱ 100m (18)

Eerie, strange Western about a gunman hired by a town to keep the baddies off – but his methods prove harsh and nearly as bad as the problem he's there to solve. Slowly we begin to wonder if he is not the ghost of a sheriff the town failed to help many years before. It doesn't entirely work but it has its moments. Some critics allege it was inspired by the Italian Western *Django The Bastard* (see page 332).

WESTERNS

THE HORSE SOLDIERS [3]

JOHN WAYNE, WILLIAM HOLDEN, CONSTANCE TOWERS, HOOT GIBSON

JOHN FORD

USA (WARNER) 1959

119m (PG)

Perhaps this is one of Ford's lesser cavalry romps (I recall being bored by it as a child), but the friction between Wayne's soldier and Holden's medic is well handled and the film has a glorious look. Ripe for re-evaluation, methinks?

HOW THE WEST WAS WON [4]

SPENCER TRACY (narrator), HENRY FONDA, JAMES STEWART, JOHN WAYNE

HENRY HATHAWAY, JOHN FORD, GEORGE MARSHALL

USA (MGM/UA-WARNER) 1962

165m (PG)

An epic dealing with different parts of Western history (the rivers, the railroad, the plains, the outlaws, the Civil War) through one family's story. The first feature in the giant-screen Cinerama process, this patchy film has some spectacular scenes that are reduced in power on the small screen. Ford's Civil War bit works best, but the movie has always posed a problem on video as Cinerama involved three projectors side-by-side – leaving a pair of rather noticeable lines down the screen that are even more intrusive on video. Enjoyable all the same, and part of cinema history. Also available in a special edition.

JEREMIAH JOHNSON [4]

ROBERT REDFORD, WILL GEER, STEPHAN GIERASCH, ALLYN ANN McLERIE

SIDNEY POLLACK

USA (WARNER) 1972

108m (PG)

This would have been a very different movie had it been made by the original choice for director, Sam Peckinpah – but it's still a wonderful picture about a man who rejects civilisation to become a mountain trapper, schooled in the ways of the wild by grizzled Will Geer. Written by the eccentric John Milius, last of the rugged individualists, it's a hauntingly shot tale of one man's battles with himself, the Crow tribe and nature itself. Worth several return visits.

JESSE JAMES [2]

TYRONE POWER, HENRY FONDA, RANDOLPH SCOTT, HENRY HULL

HENRY KING

USA (FOX) 1939

105m (U)

Idealised Hollywood biopic of the legendary outlaw and folk-hero. James is portrayed as a hero fighting injustice, emphasised by the casting of Power and Fonda – well loved stars – in the main outlaw parts. A smash hit, it spawned a sequel, *The Return Of Frank James* with Fonda returning in the title role. The James story has been more honestly told in other movies, notably Walter Hill's fabulous *The Long Riders* (see page 339).

KEOMA ... THE VIOLENT BREED
[4]

⭐ FRANCO NERO, WOODY STRODE, WILLIAM BERGER, DONALD O'BRIEN

🎬 ENZO G CASTELLARI

ITALY (AKTIV/4-FRONT) 1975

⏱ 96m (15)

Released in some countries as yet another phoney 'Django' film (probably due to Nero's presence, he being the original), this powerful story with its nagging music certainly makes an impact. Nero is an alienated half-breed returning to clean up his racist home town. This is taken from a nicely restored and cleaned widescreen print. A sterling effort – if only all video firms would take such trouble over relatively minor releases like this.

THE LEFT-HANDED GUN
[4]

⭐ PAUL NEWMAN, HURD HATFIELD, JOHN DEHNER

🎬 ARTHUR PENN

USA (WARNER) 1958 B&W

⏱ 102m (PG)

Penn, who went on to make *Little Big Man* (see below) and *Bonnie and Clyde* (see page 165), got his movie break by directing this version of a Gore Vidal script he'd already made for TV – a gritty look at the Billy the Kid legend. Though Paul Newman is first-rate as the Kid, his movie-star handsomeness tends to undercut the realism the piece aims for. Still, this remains one of the best versions of the tale.

THE LIFE AND TIMES OF JUDGE ROY BEAN
[3]

⭐ PAUL NEWMAN, STACY KEACH, AVA GARDNER, ANTHONY PERKINS

🎬 JOHN HUSTON

USA (WARNER) 1972

⏱ 124m (15)

Derided upon first release, this has now been judged to be one of Huston's classics. Not by me, though! While the John Milius script is neat, the story of the half-mad Bean's obsession with law and order and Lillie Langtry (not necessarily in that order) is rather fragmented. A curiosity.

LITTLE BIG MAN
[3]

⭐ DUSTIN HOFFMAN, FAYE DUNAWAY, MARTIN BALSAM, CHIEF DAN GEORGE

🎬 ARTHUR PENN

USA (FOX) 1970

⏱ 147m (15)

Penn seems to have fallen from favour – and this film shows why. Its jokey, debunking tone seems dated (like that of *Butch Cassidy And The Sundance Kid,* see page 330). It tells the reminiscences of a 121-year-old man who claims to be the one white survivor of Custer's Last Stand – great material, as the source novel proves to anyone who's read it – but what seemed gut-achingly wry in 1970 is a little embarrassing today. You may well disagree – rent it and decide!

WESTERNS

THE LONG RIDERS

DAVID CARRADINE, KEITH CARRADINE, ROBERT CARRADINE, JAMES KEACH, STACY KEACH, DENNIS QUAID, RANDY QUAID, CHRISTOPHER GUEST, NICHOLAS GUEST

WALTER HILL

USA (WARNER) 1980

99m (18)

The Jesse James story has inspired great movies from directors such as Sam Fuller, Nicholas Ray and Philip Kaufman, but Walter Hill's piece takes some beating. It has an authentic, inbred, rural feel, helped by the inspired casting of several sets of real-life brothers as the siblings in the story, and we see how the James gang gets a somewhat undeserved Robin Hood image due to the old North/South hatreds and the accidental killing of an innocent boy by Pinkerton agents. Don't miss it, if only for the wonderfully staged bank robbery sequence.

THE MAGNIFICENT SEVEN

YUL BRYNNER, ELI WALLACH, STEVE McQUEEN, JAMES COBURN, HORST BUCHOLZ, CHARLES BRONSON, ROBERT VAUGHN

JOHN STURGES

USA (MGM/UA-WARNER) 1960

138m (PG)

Like *A Fistful Of Dollars* (see page 334), this is based on a Kurosawa samurai film. It replicates the plot of *Seven Samurai* precisely, with Brynner gathering together his group of violent men and convincing them uncharacteristically to 'do the right thing' and help run bandits out of a village for meagre pay. Spawned sequels, but none of them came close to the original. Great score.

THE MAN WHO SHOT LIBERTY VALANCE

JOHN WAYNE, JAMES STEWART, LEE MARVIN, WOODY STRODE

JOHN FORD

USA (CIC) 1962 B&W

122m (U)

Pivotal Ford, undercutting the mythical West many of his earlier movies celebrated. Peaceable Stewart gets famous for shooting Valance (Marvin as a sleazy outlaw), only to find that things are not quite as they seem. But Stewart gets the girl (Vera Miles) and becomes a senator, while his pal Wayne fades into the dark, just as he did on the night of the shooting. A dark and bittersweet film about the conflict between truth and legend.

THE MISSOURI BREAKS 🎬 4

MARLON BRANDO, JACK NICHOLSON, KATHLEEN LLOYD, RANDY QUAID

ARTHUR PENN

USA (WARNER) 1976

126m (15)

One of Penn's better works, and unlike *Little Big Man* (see page 338), the oddball tone hasn't dated. Rustler Nicholson plays cat and mouse with weird hired killer Brando, who adopts strange accents and outfits (including a dress) to stalk his victims. At the same time, Nicholson romances the daughter of the man who is paying Brando to see him off. As bizarre as any spaghetti opus.

MY DARLING CLEMENTINE 🎬 4

HENRY FONDA, VICTOR MATURE, WALTER BRENNAN

JOHN FORD

USA (FOX) 1946 B&W

96m (U)

Ford actually knew Wyatt Earp (he lived until 1929) and so, while this may seem a mythologised version of his story, there are claims for the accuracy of the final shoot-out at the OK Corral. But it's the overall feel of the movie, filled with rich characters, that makes it work. It takes nothing away from *Clementine* if I say that other films about the lawman, like *Tombstone* (see page 346) and *Wyatt Earp* (see page 348) may well be more accurate. Whatever that means.

ONCE UPON A TIME IN THE WEST 🎬 5

CHARLES BRONSON, HENRY FONDA, JASON ROBARDS, CLAUDIA CARDINALE

SERGIO LEONE

ITALY (CIC) 1968

168m (15)

From the incredible credits sequence, where Bronson eliminates three killers at a train station, this is an unquestionable masterpiece from Leone. Casting the upright Fonda as a villain in the pay of the railroad trying to steal Cardinale's land was a clever bit of business, and the whole picture has an epic feel while never losing sight of the characters and their motives. This is the full-length print (though an even longer one is rumoured to exist) and is available in widescreen, which is the only way to see it. After the 'Man With No Name' films, this forms another trilogy of sorts with *Once Upon A Time ... The Revolution* (released here as *A Fistful Of Dynamite*, see page 144) and *Once Upon A Time In America*, see page 176.

ONE-EYED JACKS 🎬 4

⭐ MARLON BRANDO, KARL MALDEN, BEN JOHNSON, KATY JURADO

🎬 MARLON BRANDO

USA (CIC) 1961

⏱ 141m (PG)

This was Brando's baby from the start, based on a novel (*The Authentic Death Of Hendry Jones* by C Neider), loosely inspired by Billy the Kid, and he soon got rid of proposed directors Sam Peckinpah and Stanley Kubrick – which certainly calls for some big ego! When it got out that the footage was cut down from a five-hour version critics expected the worst, but this is actually a pretty fine film. Brando tracks down his old outlaw buddy, who left him to be captured but is now a respected figure with a family, and it is only a matter of time before scores must be settled. A flawed but brilliant piece.

THE OUTLAW JOSEY WALES 🎬 4

⭐ CLINT EASTWOOD, CHIEF DAN GEORGE, SONDRA LOCKE, JOHN VERNON

🎬 CLINT EASTWOOD

USA (WARNER) 1976

⏱ 134m (18)

When the Western was thought to be all but a dead form in the USA, along came Eastwood to give new life (once again) to the genre with this great picture. A farmer who becomes a killer after his family are slain in war, he gradually assembles a bunch of misfits around him and tries to make a new life for himself. Around this simple premise Eastwood weaves a film that is thoughtful, humorous and explosively violent.

PALE RIDER 🎬 3

⭐ CLINT EASTWOOD, MICHAEL MORIARTY, CARRIE SNODGRESS, CHRIS PENN

🎬 CLINT EASTWOOD

USA (WARNER) 1985

⏱ 115m (15)

Pale all right in my opinion – a pale imitation of the George Stevens 1953 Western classic *Shane* (see page 344), even down to certain shots and sequences: in *Shane*, a mystery man helps a young couple and their boy to fight nasty landowners who want to drive homesteaders out. He shows his strength by helping dig out a tree stump. In the end he leaves as he knows the wife fancies him and the kid likes him better than dad, and he doesn't want to cause trouble. In *Pale Rider*, a mystery man helps a couple and daughter fight mine owners, shows strength by smashing a huge rock, and he leaves because the woman and her daughter fancy him. (I haven't read AD Foster's source novel, so I can't say if it, too, rips off Jack Schaefer's novel *Shane*). All this apart, it's a well acted, entertaining Western and is now reissued in a widescreen version. Glowingly lensed by Bruce Surtees.

PAT GARRETT AND BILLY THE KID

JAMES COBURN, KRIS KRISTOFFERSON, BOB DYLAN, SLIM PICKENS

SAM PECKINPAH

USA (MGM/UA) 1973

122m (18)

Like much of his work, Peckinpah's version of the Billy the Kid story was mutilated by the studio that made it – but it remains an essential film. This version, though longer than the studio cut, is not perfect: touted as 'the director's cut', it is actually a work print, with one essential scene missing and many others lacking the fine-tuning present in the cut print's scenes. A proper restoration, presented in widescreen, would be most welcome, as this is one of Peckinpah's finest films. Coburn is magnificent as the regretful Garrett, doomed to kill his old pal just to keep his head above water. A stunning movie, both in its glowing look and in its performances.

PURGATORY

SAM SHEPARD, ERIC ROBERTS, RANDY QUAID

ULI EDEL

USA (WARNER) 1998

91m (PG)

Weird Western about a bunch of baddies who wind up in a town full of undead gunmen condemned to wander the Earth for ever. Daft, but the cast of respected actors almost get you to believe in the premise. Late-night lunacy.

RED RIVER

JOHN WAYNE, MONTGOMERY CLIFT, JOANNE DRU, WALTER BRENNAN

HOWARD HAWKS

USA (MGM/UA) 1948 B&W

125m (U)

Wayne is a ruthless rancher (we see him kill when his right simply to steal some land is challenged at the start of the film) who adopts Clift and begins a cattle dynasty. They fall out on a cattle-drive, and only Clift's gal (Dru) stops them killing each other at the climax. This ending has been rightly criticised as a cop-out, as it conflicts with all we've learned about Wayne's character up to that point. Nevertheless, this is one of Hawks's greats. Now available in a 'director's cut' version.

WESTERNS

RIDE THE HIGH COUNTRY 🎬5

⭐ RANDOLPH SCOTT, JOEL McCREA, MARIETTE HARTLEY, JAMES DRURY

🎬 SAM PECKINPAH

🎞 USA (MGM/UA) 1962

⏱ 94m — (15)

An object lesson in how to make the most of a simple story. Two old 'pards' take work carrying gold from a mining camp – but, saddled with a misguided young girl in search of love, and a feisty young sidekick, they end up (not without conflict between themselves and with outsiders) having to decide whether cash or honour matters most. Treated as just one more oater by the studio and sold abroad as *Guns In The Afternoon*, it still managed acclaim and is now considered a masterpiece. See it.

RIO BRAVO 🎬5

⭐ JOHN WAYNE, DEAN MARTIN, RICKY NELSON, WALTER BRENNAN

🎬 HOWARD HAWKS

🎞 USA (WARNER) 1959

⏱ 141m — (PG)

First-rate Hawks film. Wayne and assorted chums form a family to fight the encroaching baddies – a theme returned to in his *El Dorado* (see page 333) and *Rio Lobo* (see facing), and perhaps inspiring Eastwood's *The Outlaw Josey Wales* (see page 341)? If you need any more nudging, it's one of Quentin Tarantino's fave flicks, okay? John Carpenter reworked it as *Assault On Precinct 13*.

RIO GRANDE 🎬2

⭐ JOHN WAYNE, MAUREEN O'HARA, BEN JOHNSON, VICTOR McLAGLEN

🎬 JOHN FORD

🎞 USA (4-FRONT) 1950 B&W

⏱ 105m — (U)

Part of Ford's '7th Cavalry' trio, with *Fort Apache* (see page 334) and *She Wore A Yellow Ribbon*. Not his best – the hokey songs are off-putting – but even Ford at half-cock is not to be sniffed at.

RIO LOBO 🎬3

⭐ JOHN WAYNE, JACK ELAM, JENNIFER O'NEILL

🎬 HOWARD HAWKS

🎞 USA (FOX) 1970

⏱ 114m — (PG)

Hawks' last film. Not in the league of *Rio Bravo* (see above) and *El Dorado* (see page 333), it's still an enjoyable romp with Wayne as an ex-army officer on the trail of traitors who sold him out in the Civil War – rather implausibly helped out by the southerners who dealt with the traitors during the conflict! Jennifer O'Neill is competent and beautiful, while Jack Elam is always good value.

THE SEARCHERS

JOHN WAYNE, JEFFREY HUNTER, VERA MILES, WARD BOND, NATALIE WOOD

JOHN FORD

USA (WARNER) 1956

119m (U)

A pristine widescreen print of Ford's epic about the quest for a girl kidnapped by Comanches. Wayne is like you've never seen him – a rootless man who, it's hinted, may be an outlaw, he embarks on a crazy search for the missing child. He's full of hate and anger throughout the picture, and we – along with Hunter at his side every step of the way – feel that he might as soon kill the girl as rescue her when he finds her, for the 'crime' of being defiled by the 'red men'. When he finally returns home he has completed his task, but the final image of a door closing while he remains outside shows that he is forever excluded from the inner circle. Much beloved of Martin Scorsese, and very influential: the NFT ran a season of films possibly inspired by *The Searchers*.

SHANE

ALAN LADD, VAN HEFLIN, JEAN ARTHUR, JACK PALANCE

GEORGE STEVENS

USA (CIC) 1953

118m (PG)

Loner Ladd (possibly a reformed bad man?) puts up his guns and helps a family of homesteaders – but when the local range king hires nasty Palance to slaughter the 'sodbusters' he's forced to pick up them shootin' irons again. Despite the admiration of the whole family, he has to ride off into the sunset – the implication being that, a) he may be dying of a bullet wound and doesn't want the boy who idolises him to see the end, and b) he likes the family too much to let the unspoken attraction betwen him and the woman of the house come to any kind of fruition. Clint Eastwood made a not entirely satisfactory unofficial remake: *Pale Rider* (see page 341).

WESTERNS

THE SHOOTING

JACK NICHOLSON, WARREN OATES, WILL HUTCHINS, MILLIE PERKINS

MONTE HELLMAN

USA (LABYRINTH MEDIA) 1966

81m (PG)

Existential piece made by Hellman and Nicholson back-to-back with the equally bizarre *Ride In The Whirlwind* (82m), which is also on this budget tape, marketed as 'The Jack Nicholson Westerns'. *Whirlwind* sees Nicholson and Cameron Mitchell accidentally being mistaken for outlaws to whom they've innocently given hospitality and chased endlessly through grim landscapes. *The Shooting* has a döppelganger theme, with a vengeful woman leading Oates to his twin brother in the final denouement. These two films show what can be done on a minuscule budget. Sadly, the prints used have seen better days.

THE SHOOTIST

JOHN WAYNE, LAUREN BACALL, RON HOWARD, JAMES STEWART, HUGH O'BRIAN, RICHARD BOONE

DON SIEGEL

USA (CIC/4-FRONT) 1976

100m (PG)

Bleak but satisfactory story of a gunman dying of cancer (as Wayne was when he made this, his last film) who chooses to go out in a blaze of glory rather than waste away. Wayne underplays beautifully, whether duelling verbally with landlady Bacall or educating her wild kid Howard in the ways of the world. Siegel chooses to have the boy reject violence at the end by throwing away the old man's gun, whereas in the source novel he struts off to become just another gunslinger (we are led to assume). Howard gave up acting and is now a top director – he recently made the Mel Gibson vehicle *Ransom* (see page 300). Apparently serial killer Ian Brady's favourite film.

SOLDIER BLUE

CANDICE BERGEN, PETER STRAUSS, DONALD PLEASENCE

RALPH NELSON

USA (ENTERTAINMENT/4-FRONT) 1970

114m (18)

Jobbing director Nelson attained a short-lived notoriety with this love story twixt feisty bitch and innocent cavalryman set amidst much gushing gore and severed limbs as soldiers massacre native Americans. See once for curiosity value – but the climax was heavily cut in Britain by the BBFC on initial release and probably remains so.

STAGECOACH

JOHN WAYNE, CLAIRE TREVOR, THOMAS MITCHELL, JOHN CARRADINE

JOHN FORD

USA (ENTERTAINMENT) 1939 B&W

96m (U)

Also available on a two-film tape with Ford's *Fort Apache* (see page 334), this is the movie that made Wayne a star. Who today would risk appearing as 'The Ringo Kid' – those were the days. Savour them.

TOMBSTONE

KURT RUSSELL, VAL KILMER, BILL PAXTON, CHARLTON HESTON

GEORGE P COSMATOS

USA (ENTERTAINMENT) 1993

135m (15)

Made at the same time as the Kevin Costner epic *Wyatt Earp* (see page 348), which deals with Earp's whole life, this smaller reworking of the OK Corral tale was expected to be a box office joke ... but the laughs were on the big boys as Russell's superior, gutsy portrayal and Kilmer's dandified Doc proved to be a surprise hit. Works fine on tape too – but make sure you get the widescreen copy.

TRUE GRIT

JOHN WAYNE, KIM DARBY, GLEN CAMPBELL, ROBERT DUVALL, DENNIS HOPPER

HENRY HATHAWAY

USA (CIC) 1969

128m (PG)

Surprise Oscar-bestowing smash hit for Wayne as a gruff ruffian turned marshal, hired by a young girl to get the killer of her father and forced to take both her and a Texas ranger along for the trip. The script and the photography of Lucien Ballard help make it a delight for eyes and ears. Do yourself a favour one wet afternoon and rent or buy this tape.

WESTERNS

UNFORGIVEN

CLINT EASTWOOD, MORGAN FREEMAN, GENE HACKMAN, RICHARD HARRIS

CLINT EASTWOOD

USA (WARNER) 1992

131m (15)

Made from a script Eastwood had been saving until he felt he'd reached the right age for the part, this is a film about a reformed murderer and gunman living on a crappy farm with his kids. The wife who reformed him is gone, and he is tempted by the offer of money made by some whores to revenge one of their number who was slashed by a cowboy. It's a very dark movie, with no real good guys and no truly bad ones either. Gene Hackman's lawman tries to keep the peace, but is a cruel bully at heart. Richard Harris poses as a posh type, but turns out to be a cowardly cockney. And Eastwood is colder than we've ever seen him. 'For Sergio and Don' reads the dedication, for Clint's mentors Leone and Siegel. He learned from masters, and it shows. A cruel classic.

WILD BILL

JEFF BRIDGES, ELLEN BARKIN, BRUCE DERN, KEITH CARRADINE, DAVID ARQUETTE, DIANE LANE, JOHN HURT

WALTER HILL

USA (MGM/UA) 1995

94m (15)

Incredibly, Walter Hill's wonderful film about legendary gunfighter Wild Bill Hickok did not get a UK cinema release (apart from a short run at London's National Film Theatre) – outrageous, when you consider some of the drivel that fills our screens week after week. Depicting a series of episodes from Hickok's life, culminating in his death at the hands of a disturbed boy, it's perhaps the first Western since Peckinpah's *The Wild Bunch* (see page 348) to show the true horror and brutal unpredictability of gunfighting. Bridges makes a wild and woolly anti-hero, and the other actors are a match for him: Barkin as Calamity Jane (raunchier than Doris Day, that's for sure), Hurt as the archetypal Anglo-buddy, and Dern as a madman who challenges Hickok to a sit-down shoot-out after their earlier fight has confined him to a wheelchair! A masterful combination of sepia realism and elegaic myth, and a must-see for fans of Hill's earlier *Geronimo* (see page 335).

347

THE WILD BUNCH

WILLIAM HOLDEN, ROBERT RYAN, WARREN OATES, BEN JOHNSON, EDMOND O'BRIEN, ERNEST BORGNINE

SAM PECKINPAH

USA (WARNER) 1969

145m (18)

Sam Peckinpah's revisionist Western follows a gang of outlaws from when they're ambushed in a small town until they decide to go out in a final blast, fighting against impossible odds in support of one of their own, because they know that in 1912 men of their kind have outlived their usefulness. Both Holden as the boss outlaw and Ryan as the man he left to die (now his nemesis, not through choice but because it's the only way out of jail) are magnificent, as indeed are all the players. Derided for showing the effects of bullets on flesh at the time of release, it is now accepted as a classic. The recent restoration is problematic – it is relevant solely to the USA as that is the only place where the restored parts were cut! This means, sadly, that since the restored print is now used worldwide, the existing European print, which was always full-length and contained slight differences, is unlikely to be seen outside film archives. Peckinpah scholar Paul Seydor thinks that people like myself who mention this are nitpickers (see exchange of letters in *Sight and Sound* in late 1996) but many people agree with me. One good thing – at least the restoration means a widescreen print is now out on video. Masterful camera work yet again from Lucien Ballard. If you only see one Western, see this one.

WYATT EARP

KEVIN COSTNER, DENNIS QUAID, GENE HACKMAN, JEFF FAHEY

LAWRENCE KASDAN

USA (WARNER) 1994

183m (12)

This epic about frontier lawman Earp was overshadowed at the box-office by *Tombstone* (see page 346), which only deals with one part of the man's life and is all the better for it. Neither film managed to deflate the Earp myth, however, as the rather dubious character still retains his basically heroic image. Ambitious, but flawed, with Costner too lightweight for the role. Fine support cast, though.

WESTERNS

YOUNG GUNS 4

EMILIO ESTEVEZ, KIEFER
SUTHERLAND, CHARLIE SHEEN,
TERENCE STAMP, LOU DIAMOND
PHILLIPS, JACK PALANCE

CHRISTOPHER CAIN

USA (CINEMA CLUB) 1988

107m (18)

Denounced as an 'MTV-Western' on release, this is actually one of the better versions of the early part of Billy the Kid's career in the Lincoln County Wars – accurately told, with Stamp as his mentor Tunstall, taking a (gay?) interest in his young trail bums, and Palance as Murphy, the schemer who orders the man's death and provokes an explosion of revenge. The young cast are excellent to a man, or boy.

YOUNG GUNS II 3

WILLIAM PETERSEN, EMILIO
ESTEVEZ, KIEFER SUTHERLAND,
CHRISTIAN SLATER, LOU DIAMOND
PHILLIPS

GEOFF MURPHY

USA (FOX) 1990

104m (15)

Useful follow-up flick which completes the Billy the Kid story, with his supposed murder by Pat Garrett. Cleverly told in flashback by utilising the true tale of a man who, circa 1950, claimed to be the real Kid grown old. In real life the man's story was disbelieved, but for the purpose of this film ... well, it's intriguing, ain't it? It's not *The Left-Handed Gun* (see page 338) or *Pat Garrett And Billy The Kid* (see page 342), but it'll do.

WORLD GREATS

In recent years, ordinary film fans have been tempted in ever greater numbers to brace themselves and brave the world of dubbed or subtitled 'arthouse' films; they have not been disappointed. Popular hits, like the lavish Provence soap opera pairing of *Jean De Florette* and *Manon Des Sources* and the action-packed films of director Luc Besson, as well as the tendency of the USA studios to remake many French successes, have shown that international cinema is not all doom and gloom. What follows is a (very) short selection of world cinema films available on videotape. It's not possible to include swathes of Bergman and Kurosawa reviews, but if these examples tempt you then those classics are out there for rental or purchase.

AGUIRRE, THE WRATH OF GOD

KLAUS KINSKI, HELENA ROJO, CECILIA RIVERA, RUY GUERRA

WERNER HERZOG

WEST GERMANY (TARTAN) 1972

94m (15)

The late Kinski (dad of pouting Nastassja) had a great face and used it to perfection in countless spaghetti Westerns, horror pix and thrillers, but his best work came from his love-hate relationship with half-mad director Herzog. This tale of a maniacal conquistador's doomed trip along the Amazon has some stunning scenes: an exploding cannon pitching over a cliff, Kinski adrift amidst a horde of chattering monkeys ... all backed by the hypnotic music of Popol Vuh, Herzog's perennial soundtrack collaborators. Imaginative epic entertainment.

THE AMERICAN FRIEND

DENNIS HOPPER, BRUNO GANZ, NICHOLAS RAY, SAM FULLER

WIM WENDERS

WEST GERMANY (CONNOISSEUR) 1977

127m (PG)

Based on Patricia Highsmith's novel *Ripley's Game*. Ganz is a hapless artisan, willing to be hired for murder by Hopper because he believes he's dying and wants to have cash to leave to his family. Oddly distant yet compelling, with cameos from expatriate USA directors Ray and Fuller. Very much a cult picture these days and I personally find it a better bet than many of Wenders' more acclaimed ramblings. Hopper is wonderful as ever, of course.

WORLD GREATS

AND GOD CREATED WOMAN

BRIGITTE BARDOT, CURT JURGENS, JEAN LOUIS TRINTIGNANT

ROGER VADIM

FRANCE (ARROW) 1956

90m (18)

BB' gets her kit off for the delectation of several dirty old men. The film 'made' Bardot as well as St Tropez. Vadim, who used the same title for another story in 1987, was very adept at turning his paramours into sex symbols (see *Barbarella* on page 261). Widescreen.

BELLE DE JOUR

CATHERINE DENEUVE, MICHEL PICCOLI, JEAN SOREL, GENEVIEVE PAGE

LOUIS BUNUEL

FRANCE/ITALY (ELECTRIC) 1967

100m (18)

A massive hit when revived in the early 90s, this seductive story of an upper-class wife who has a secret life as a hooker retains its power 30 years after it was made. Buñuel chips away, as always, at the complacent veneer of polite society.

CINEMA PARADISO

PHILIPPE NOIRET, SALVATORE CASCIO, ANDREA MORRICONE

GIUSEPPE TORNATORE

ITALY/FRANCE (TARTAN) 1989

122m (PG)

A delightful film about the power of cinema to transform lives. A small boy forms a friendship with a grumpy old projectionist who runs the local film shows in their village. There's a great scene where all the clips cut by the censorious local priest are shown in tandem, to the delight of the now grown-up boy. Won an Oscar for best foreign film. Widescreen. Available in several different sets including one boxed with the script and one in an extended 155m version. Whichever you choose you'll be smiling at the end!

THE CITY OF LOST CHILDREN

RON PERLMAN, JEAN-CLAUDE DREYFUS, GENEVIEVE BRUNET

JEAN-PIERRE JEUNET, MARC CARO

FRANCE (ENTERTAINMENT) 1995

108m (15)

From the makers of cult arthouse film *Delicatessen*, this is a bizarre adult fairy tale: in a dark, decaying seaside dive, a circus strongman helps an orphan regain a pal from the clutches of a mad scientist who steals people's dreams. The baddy hangs out on a rotting oil rig surrounded by freaks and eye-dazzling retro machinery. Daft, but it's a treat for the senses. With killer fleas and a brain floating in an aquarium, the pic led to Jeunet directing the latest 'Aliens' episode, *Alien Resurrection* (see page 260).

CYRANO DE BERGERAC ▸ 4

- GERARD DEPARDIEU, ANNE BROCHET, VINCENT PEREZ
- JEAN-PAUL RAPPENEAU
- FRANCE (ARTIFICIAL EYE) 1990
- 138m (U)

Depardieu excels in this colour-packed version of Edmond Rostand's play about the long-nosed romancer, and rightly won the best actor award at Cannes. Nimble subtitling by Anthony Burgess makes this the most authentic of all the versions of this classic story to be lensed. Widescreen and boxed set available.

THE DIARY OF A CHAMBERMAID ▸ 3

- JEANNE MOREAU, MICHEL PICCOLI, FRANCOISE LUGAGNE
- LUIS BUNUEL
- FRANCE/ITALY (ELECTRIC) 1964
- 79m (15)

Buñuel's typically subversive version of Octave Mirbeau's story, updated to the 30s and taking a stab at right wing/bourgeois mores. Previously filmed in the USA by Jean Renoir in 1946. Widescreen.

ELVIRA MADIGAN ▸ 3

- PIA DEGERMARK, THOMMY BERGGREN, LENNART MALMER
- BO WIDERBERG
- SWEDEN (TARTAN) 1967
- 95m (PG)

Lush slow-motion romance which was a big hit worldwide and bagged Degermark the actress of the year award at Cannes. Widescreen.

FUNNY GAMES ▸ 3

- SUSANNE LOTHAR, ULRICH MUHE, FRANK GIERING, ARNO FRISCH
- MICHAEL HANEKE
- AUSTRIA (TARTAN) 1997
- 106m (18)

Challenging and harrowing account of two young men who visit a family on holiday, progressing from insolence to sickening violence against their hosts. In the tradition of *Man Bites Dog* (see page 354), it draws the audience in and questions their morality in agreeing to watch. Uncut and unflinching. Widescreen.

WORLD GREATS

JEAN DE FLORETTE [5]

GERARD DEPARDIEU, YVES MONTAND, DANIEL AUTEUIL, ELISABETH DEPARDIEU

CLAUDE BERRI

FRANCE (ELECTRIC) 1986

121m (PG)

Shot back-to-back with *Manon Des Sources* (see page 354), this tells author Marcel Pagnol's epic tale of love and greed in his beloved Provence. Depardieu is a city fellow thwarted by wily countrymen led by scheming patriarch Montand. Deservedly a smash. The first subtitled movie I ever managed to get my mother to sit through until the end and, like audiences the world over, she loved it. You will too! Widescreen.

LA DOLCE VITA [3]

MARCELLO MASTROIANNI, ANITA EKBERG, ANOUK AIMEE, NICO

FREDERICO FELLINI

ITALY (ELECTRIC) 1960 B&W

173m (15)

Fellini's view of the depraved, sleazy underbelly of 60s café society, seen via the lives of journalists, strippers and starlets who come (!) together in a final licentious orgy. Best film winner at Cannes. Widescreen available.

LES DIABOLIQUES [4]

SIMONE SIGNORET, VERA CLOUZOT, PAUL MEURISSE, CHARLES VANEL

HENRI GEORGES CLOUZOT

FRANCE (ARROW) 1954 B&W

114m (18)

This classy thriller comes from the Boileau/Narcejac team which later wrote *Vertigo* for Hitchcock (see page 304). A dingy school is the setting for a plot by two women to murder the man in their lives; but is he really dead? Grisly stuff, remade twice to no great purpose. This remains the top version.

M [5]

PETER LORRE, OTTO WERNICKE, GUSTAV GRUNDGENS

FRITZ LANG

GERMANY (REDEMPTION) 1931 B&W

118m (PG)

Lorre's debut, in which he stars as a childkiller pursued through pre-war Germany by a temporary alliance of cops and crooks. Lang and Lorre manage the unlikely feat of making a serial murderer a sympathetic character, even as he admits his guilt. Also released in a newly restored version, available from the BFI. 1951 remake by Joseph Losey.

MAN BITES DOG

BENOIT POELVOORDE, NELLY PAPPAERT, MALOU MADOU

REMY BELVAUX, ANDRE BONZEL, BENOIT POELVOORDE

BELGIUM (TARTAN) 1992 B&W

96m (18)

Outrageous fake documentary in which a film crew follow a serial killer around as he talks them through his acts of rape and butchery, gradually seducing them with his charmingly savage persona. Made by triumvirate of film students, it won three prizes at Cannes. Widescreen and boxed set available.

MANON DES SOURCES

YVES MONTAND, DANIEL AUTEUIL, EMMANUELLE BEART, ELISABETH DEPARDIEU

CLAUDE BERRI

FRANCE (ELECTRIC) 1986

114m (PG)

Sequel to *Jean De Florette* (see page 353) in which the daughter of crafty Yves Montand's victim grows up to take her revenge on the village for causing her dad's death. Wonderful entertainment, shot in beautiful golden colours. Widescreen. (Both films are based on *L'Eau Des Collines* by Marcel Pagnol).

MEPHISTO

KLAUS MARIA BRANDAUER, ILDIKO BANSAGI, KRYSTYNA JANDA

ISTVAN SZABO

HUNGARY (ARTHOUSE) 1981

144m (15)

The film that shot Brandauer to stardom. Based on a novel by Klaus Mann about his real-life actor uncle Gustav Grundgens (who appears in *M*, see page 353). The film sees him find acclaim from the Nazis for his stage portrayal of the Devil, as he sells his soul for fame and rejects his black girlfriend at the behest of the fascists. Brandauer is magnetic in the starring role. Oscar for best foreign film.

MISHIMA:
A LIFE IN FOUR CHAPTERS

KEN OGATA, KANJI SAWADA, YASOSUKE BANDO

PAUL SCHRADER

JAPAN/USA (WARNER) 1985 COL/B&W

120m (15)

Schrader (who wrote such hits as *Taxi Driver*, see page 303) intersperses the life of gay Japanese writer Mishima with excerpts from his work. Oddly, he wanted a return to strict militarism after World War Two and tried to stage a coup. When it failed he committed hara-kiri. Great score by Philip Glass. For those who snipe at the commercial *oeuvres* of Francis Ford Coppola and George Lucas, note that they both helped finance this wondrous (but uncommercial) movie.

NIKITA 🎬 4

⭐ ANNE PARILLAUD, JEAN RENO, JEANNE MOREAU

🎬 LUC BESSON

FRANCE/ITALY (ARTIFICIAL EYE) 1990

⏱ 117m   (18)

Improbably wild but entertaining story of a junkie girl reprieved from a death sentence (after a shoot-out at a chemist's shop) and subsequently groomed as a hit woman for the state. Remade in the USA in 1993 as *Point Of No Return* aka *The Assassin* with Bridget Fonda in the lead. Besson has become a major director with films like *Leon* (see page 293) and *The Fifth Element* (see page 266). Widescreen. (Inspired Hong Kong *Black Cat* series of pix.)

ONIBABA 🎬 4

⭐ NOBUKO OTOWA, YITSUKO YOSHIMURA, KEI SATO

🎬 KANETO SHINDO

JAPAN (TARTAN) 1964 B&W

⏱ 104m   (15)

Scary Japanese horror about two women who ambush stray samurai – but lust intervenes. Atmospheric and very disturbing film that makes the most of the small cast and smaller budget. Highly recommended for fans of the bizarre. Widescreen.

THE RETURN OF MARTIN GUERRE 🎬 3

⭐ GERARD DEPARDIEU, NATHALIE BAYE, MAURICE BARRIER

🎬 DANIEL VIGNE

FRANCE (ARROW) 1982

⏱ 123m   (15)

Medieval story of a man who returns to his wife and home a changed fellow: but is it really him? Intriguing fable, later remade in the USA as *Sommersby* (see page 251).

A SHORT FILM ABOUT KILLING 🎬 4

⭐ MIROSLAW BAKA, KRZYSZTOF GLOVISZ, JAN TESARZ

🎬 KRZYSZTOF KIESLOWSKI

POLAND (TARTAN) 1988

⏱ 84m   (18)

The fifth of the director's 'Ten Commandments' series is a sad little story about a youth who murders a taxi driver for no apparent reason, only to suffer the death penalty. Shows how sordid both the crime and the punishment inevitably are. A Cannes winner which is credited with causing a temporary hold on capital punishment in Poland. Widescreen.

FURTHER READING

Magazines

There are numerous video consumer titles in newsagents such as *Video World*, and fans of populist cinema might try *Empire* or *Total Film*. For serious film fans, there is the BFI magazine *Sight and Sound*, or US imports *Film Comment* and *American Cinematographer*. Also from the USA is the more sociopolitically minded *Cineaste*.

Horror fans should enjoy *The Dark Side*; or the mind-boggling, book-length *Flesh & Blood* (sex/horror/exploitation), and from the same stable, *Eyeball*. Write for information on those last two titles to PO BOX 178, Guildford, Surrey, GU3 2YU.

If you're keen on knowing about cuts/variant versions, the best mag is *Video Watchdog*, PO BOX 5283, Cincinnati, OH 45205-0283, USA. Or *Uncut?*, Midnight Media, The Barn, Upton Lodge, Hamerton Road, Upton, Cambs PE17 5YA is useful.

Serious special effects fans must buy *Cinefex*, a US import.

Books

The Aurum Film Encyclopedia is now in four separate volumes, *The Western, Horror, Science Fiction* and *Gangsters*, all indispensable. A fifth, *Noir,* is eagerly awaited. Edited by Phil Hardy (Aurum Press).

Epic Films by Gary A Smith (McFarland).

Immoral Tales (Sex and Horror Cinema in Europe 1956–84) by Cathal Tohill and Pete Tombs (Titan) and *Mondo Macabro* by Pete Tombs (Titan), a guide to horror film around the globe in countries like Brazil and India.

Radio Times Film & Video Guide by Derek Winnert (Hodder & Stoughton).

Red Hot and Blue: A Smithsonian Salute to the American Musical by Amy Henderson and Dwight Blocker Bowers (Smithsonian).

Sergio Leone by Oreste de Fornari (Gremese).

Sex and Zen and a Bullet in the Head: the Essential Guide to Hong Kong's Mind-bending Films by Stefan Hammond and Mike Wilkins (Titan).

Spaghetti Westerns by Thomas Weisser (McFarland).

The X Factory by Anthony Petkovich (Critical Vision) is one of several background guides to the US sex film industry. Also *Babylon Blue* by David Flint (Creation).

This is just a selection of the numerous books/magazines available on all genres. If you can't find what you need locally, write, call or visit the following:

Zwemmers, 80 Charing Cross Road, London, WC2H 0BB (0171 240 4157). Film books/mags from Europe and USA.

Cinema Bookshop, 14 Great Russell Street, London, WC1B 3NH (0171 637 0206). New and out-of-print books, stills, etc.

Cinema Store, 4b/c Orion House, Upper St Martin's Lane, London, WC2H 9EJ (0171 379 7838). Everything film-related.

Forbidden Planet, 71 New Oxford Street, London, WC1A 1DG (0171 836 4179). Branches in larger cities. A comic/science fiction shop with lots of film and TV stuff.

Psychotronic Video, Unit 30C, 1st Floor, Camden Lock Buildings, Chalk Farm Road, Camden Town, London, NW1 8AF (0181 699 5375). Collectors' store.

Cinema Store, Forbidden Planet and Psychotronic also sell videos; Cinema Store specialises in DVD laserdisc/imports and Psychotronic in rare material, such as deleted box-sets, movie props, toys and ephemera. Tell 'em I sent you!

INDEX

TOP 1000 VIDEOS – INDEX. Notes: Entries in **bold** are film titles. Chinese, Japanese and Vietnamese personal names are not generally inverted (eg Chow Yun Fat is indexed under C). However, when the names are westernized they are inverted (eg Bruce Lee is indexed under L).

7th Voyage Of Sinbad, The 56
8mm 280
9½ Weeks 43
10 66
10 Commandments, The 139
10 Rillington Place 280
12 Monkeys 257
13 Ghosts 153
48 Hours 13
55 Days At Peking 139
101 Dalmations 56
633 Squadron 315
1941 66
2001 – A Space Odyssey 257
2010 – The Year We Make Contact 258
About Last Night 237
Abraham, F Murray 126, 175, 269
Abrahams, Jim 67, 82
Absence Of Malice 95
Absolute Beginners 221
Absolutely Fabulous 309
Abyss, The 258
Accidental Tourist, The 237
Accused, The 95
Ace Ventura: Pet Detective 66
Acid House, The 66
Ackland, Joss 72
Adams, Brooke 268, 287
Adams, Maud 273
Addams Family, The 67
Addams Family Values 67
Addiction, The 188
Addy, Mark 80
Adjani, Isabelle 210
Adrian, Max 108, 222
Adventures Of Pinocchio, The 153
Adventures Of Robin Hood, The 13
Affleck, Ben 116, 250, 261
African Queen, The 14
Agar, John 326
Age of Innocence, The 238
Aguirre, The Wrath Of God 349
Agutter, Jenny 160, 188, 268
Ah Lun 186
Aherne, Michael 224
Ai No Borei 43
Aiello, Danny 109, 293
Aimee, Anouk 352
Air Force One 14
Airplane 67
Akiko Wakabayashi 278
Akira Kurosawa 151
Al Capone 164
Aladdin 57
Alamo, The 328
Albert, Eddie 249
Alda, Alan 76
Alderton, John 278
Aldrich, Robert 23, 321
Alexander, Jane 284
Alien 259
Aliens 259
Alien3 259

Alien Resurrection 260
All Quiet On The Western Front 315
All That Jazz 221
All The President's Men 96
Allen, Debbie 226
Allen, Irwin 136
Allen, Joan 24
Allen, Karen 36, 276, 286
Allen, Nancy 66, 272, 282
Allen, Tim 64
Allen, Todd 97
Allen, Woody 58, 69, 76, 81, 93
Allers, Roger 61
Alley, Kirstie 309
Almodovar, Pedro 46
Alonso, Maria Conchita 37, 167
Alphaville 260
Altered States 260
Altman, Robert 294
Ameche, Don 92, 263
American Buffalo 96
American Friend, The 350
American Gigolo 96
American Graffiti 67
American In Paris, An 222
American President, The 238
American Tail, An 57
American Werewolf In London, An 188
Amiel, Jon 251, 286
Amistad 96
Anaconda 14
Anastasia 57
And God Created Woman 351
And Now For Something Completely Different 68
Anders, Luana 195
Anderson, Gillian 278
Anderson, Lindsay 74
Anderson, Melody 267
Anderson, Michael 268, 320
Anderson, Paul Thomas 44
Andress, Ursula 22, 93, 317
Andrews, Dana 194
Andrews, Harry 79, 142, 323
Andrews, Julie 66, 159, 234
Angel Enforcers 182
Angel Heart 189
Angel Of Vengeance 280
Angels 182
Animal Crackers 68
Animal House 68
Aniston, Jennifer 310
Ankers, Evelyn 219
Ann-Margret 104, 235
Annakin, Ken 161, 162, 317, 324
Annaud, Jean-Jacques 126, 133
Anne Of The Thousand Days 238
Annie Hall 69
Annis, Francesca 149
Antz 58
Anwar, Gabrielle 250
Apocalypse Now 316
Apollo 13 97
Apostle, The 97
Apostoloff, Stephen C 50
Apted, Michael 116
Arachnaphobia 189
Arana, Tomas 192, 213
Archer, Anne 18, 34, 114
Archer, Ted 334
Argento, Asia 192

INDEX

Argento, Dario 205, 215
Argento, Fiore 195
Ariane 180
Arkin, Adam 203
Arkin, Alan 89
Arkins, Robert 224
Arlen, Richard 206
Armageddon 261
Armitage, George 175
Armstrong, Louis 230
Armstrong, Robert 60
Armstrong, Todd 60
Arno, Alice 200
Arnold, Tracy 117
Aronofsky, Darren 270
Arquette, David 213, 214, 347
Arquette, Patricia 179
Arquette, Rosanna 45, 99
Arrighi, Nike 195
Arsenal 1896-96 Centenary 306
Arsenic And Old Lace 69
Art Of Love, The 43
Arthur 69
Arthur, Jean 344
As Good As It Gets 239
Ash, Leslie 232
Ashby, Hal 241
Ashcroft, Peggy 128
Ashton, Joseph 155
Asphalt Jungle, The 164
Asquith, Anthony 83
Assante, Armand 88, 170
Astaire, Fred 225, 233, 235
Astin, Sean 92
Atherton, William 21
Atkins, Christopher 239
Atkins, Tom 30, 207
Atkinson, Jayne 156
Atkinson, Rowan 309
Attenborough, Richard 29, 31, 106, 112, 145, 225, 280, 322
Atwill, Lionel 18, 209, 217
Aubrey, Juliet 90
Auger, Claudine 40
Austin Powers – International Man Of Mystery 70
Austin, Sean 156
Auteuil, Daniel 353, 354
Avengers, The 311
Avildsen, John G 132, 159
Awakenings 97
Awful Doctor Orlof, The 189
Axton, Hoyt 81
Aykroyd, Dan 66, 73, 78, 80, 92
Ayres, Lew 315

Babe 154
Babenco, Hector 120
Babylon 5 313
Bacall, Lauren 171, 281, 296, 345
Back To The Future 15
Back To The Future Part 2 15
Back To The Future Part 3 15
Backdraft 97
Baclanova, Olga 202
Bacon, Kevin 97, 288, 302
Bad And The Beautiful, The 98
Bad Day At Black Rock 98
Bad Lieutenant 164
Bad Taste 70
Badel, Alan 287
Badham, John 17, 22, 233
Baka, Miroslaw 355
Baker, Betsy 198
Baker, Carroll 330

Baker, Diane 28, 296
Baker, Joe Don 25, 40
Baker, Roy Ward 272
Baker, Stanley 152, 167, 319, 322
Bakula, Scott 304
Balaban, Bob 95, 258, 260
Baldwin, Adam 321
Baldwin, Alec 23, 26, 33, 71, 94, 121, 175
Baldwin, Stephen 120, 137, 318
Baldwin, William 97, 288, 292
Bale, Christian 112
Balk, Fairuza 206
Balkan, Florinda 144
Ball, Angeline 168, 224
Ballard, Carroll 156
Ballard Of Cable Hogue, The 329
Balsam, Martin 96, 99, 164, 212, 284, 328, 338
Bancroft, Anne 81, 111, 115
Banderas, Antonio 33, 129, 206
Banerjee, Victor 128
Banionis, Donatas 273
Bansagi, Ildiko 354
Barabbas 140
Barbarella 261
Barbeau, Adrienne 200
Barber, Frances 240
Barber, Paul 80
Barberini, Urbano 195
Bardem, Javier 299
Bardot, Babette 45, 50
Bardot, Brigitte 214, 351
Barker, Clive 204
Barkin, Ellen 252, 301, 347
Barr, Jean-Marc 99, 101
Barrier, Maurice 355
Barrile, Anthony 323
Barringer, Pat 50
Barron, Steve 153, 161
Barry, Gene 277
Barrymore, Drew 213, 253, 266
Barrymore, Lionel 171
Barton Fink 98
Basic Instinct 281
Basil, The Great Mouse Detective 58
Basinger, Kim 16, 43, 120
Basquiat 98
Bass, Alfie 84
Bassett, Angela 52, 101
Bates, Alan 146, 255
Bates, Kathy 88, 115, 135, 254, 296
Batman 16
Batman – The Animated Series 307
Batman And Robin 16
Batman Forever 16
Batman Returns 16
Battle Of Britain, The 316
Battle Of Midway, The 316
Battle Of The Bulge 317
Bauer, Belinda 226
Bauer, Steven 178, 300
Bava, Lamberto 195
Bava, Mario 208
Baxter, Anne 139
Bay, Michael 37, 261
Baye, Nathalie 355
Beaches 99
Beals, Jennifer 226
Bean, Sean 25, 34, 114, 301, 312
Beart, Emanuelle 33, 354
Beatles, The 229, 230
Beatty, Ned 20, 82
Beatty, Warren 20, 165, 166
Beauty And The Beast 58
Beavis And Butthead 308

TOP 1000 VIDEOS

Becker, Harold 33, 301, 327
Becket 140
Bedazzled 70
Bedelia, Bonnie 21
Bedford Incident, The 99
Beery, Noah, Jnr 327
Beethoven 71
Beetlejuice 71
Begley, Ed 335
Bel Geddes, Barbara 304
Bell, Tom 311
Bellamy, Madge 218
Bellamy, Ralph 92, 249
Belle De Jour 351
Belushi, James 237, 326
Belushi, John 66, 68, 73
Belvaux, Remy 354
Ben-Hur 140
Bening, Annette 38, 166, 170, 238, 269
Benjamin, Richard 85, 278
Bennent, David 29
Bennett, Jill 74
Bennett, Joan 215
Benny, Jack 83
Benson, Jodi 61
Benson, Robby 58
Benton, Robert 165, 304
Benveniste, Michael 49
Berenger, Tom 22, 114, 318, 325
Berenson, Marisa 223
Beresford, Bruce 78, 252
Bergen, Candice 145, 346
Berger, Helmut 249
Berger, Ludwig 161
Berger, William 333, 338
Berggren, Thommy 352
Bergin, Patrick 34
Bergman, Ingrid 102
Bergman, Sandahl 19
Berkely, Elizabeth 51
Berkoff, Steven 36, 71, 172, 174
Berle, Milton 173
Bernard, Susan 49
Bernhard, Sandra 84
Berri, Claude 353, 354
Bertolucci, Bernardo 147
Besson, Luc 99, 266, 293, 355
Beswick, Martine 62, 330
Better Tomorrow, A 182
Better Tomorrow 2, A 182
Beverley Callard – The Ultimate Results 306
Beverly Hills Cop 71
Beymer, Richard 236
Beyond The Valley Of The Dolls 44
BFG, The 58
Bickford, Charles 234
Biehn, Michael 37, 39, 258, 259
Big 154
Big Blue, The 99
Big Country, The 330
Big Red One, The 317
Big Sleep, The 281
Big Wednesday 99
Bigelow, Kathryn 52, 176, 209, 282
Biggins, Christopher 48
Biggs, Ronnie 228
Bikel, Theodore 107
Bill And Ted's Bogus Adventure 72
Bill And Ted's Excellent Adventure 72
Billionaire Boys Club 100
Billy Bathgate 165
Billy Liar 72
Binoche, Juliette 112
Birdman Of Alcatraz, The 100

Birds, The 281
Birkin, Jane 47
Birman, Serafima 147
Bisley, Steve 31
Bissell, Whit 277
Bissett, Jacqueline 284
Black, Isobel 280
Black Rain 165
Blackadder 309
Blackboard Jungle, The 100
Blackman, Honor 26, 60, 311
Blackman, Joan 222
Blackmer, Sidney 173, 213
Blade 17
Blade Runner 262
Blair, Linda 198
Blakely, Colin 22
Blanche 44
Blanchett, Cate 112
Blanks, Jamie 217
Blazing Saddles 73
Blessed, Brian 267, 311
Blethyn, Brenda 84
Blondell, Joan 177
Blood And Sand 239
Blood for Dracula 190
Blood Simple 281
Bloom, Claire 19, 76, 204, 268
Bloom, Verna 336
Blossom, Roberts 288
Blow Out 282
Blue Hawaii 222
Blue Lagoon, The 239
Blue Max, The 317
Blue Steel 282
Blue Thunder 17
Blue Velvet 282
Blues Brothers, The 73
Blum, Mark 76
Bluth, Don 57
Boat, The 318
Boatman, Michael Patrick 323
Bob Roberts 73
Bodalo, Jose 332
Bodnia, Kim 298
Body Double 283
Body Heat 100
Body Snatcher, The 283
Bodyguard, The 240
Boehm, Carl 211
Bogart, Humphrey 14, 102, 171, 281
Boiling Point 17
Bolger, Ray 236
Bond, Ward 335, 344
Bondarchuk, Natalya 273
Bondarchuk, Sergei 152
Bonet, Lisa 189
Bonham Carter, Helena 208
Bonnie And Clyde 165
Bonzel, Andre 354
Boogie Nights 44
Boone, Pat 28
Boone, Richard 320, 329, 345
Boorman, John 20, 143, 168, 278, 299
Booth, Connie 309
Boothe, Powers 325
Borgnine, Ernest 23, 24, 35, 151, 348
Born Free 101
Born On The Fourth Of July 318
Bornedal, Ole 298
Borowczyk, Walerian 43, 44, 49
Bosco, Philip 241
Bostwick, Barry 233
Bounty, The 101

360

INDEX

Bowie, David 98, 148, 205, 221
Bowman, Rob 278
Boyd, Stephen 140, 144, 145, 266
Boyfriend, The 222
Boyle, Danny 136
Boyle, Peter 94, 175, 270, 303
Boys From Brazil, The 283
Boyz 'n' The Hood 101
Bracco, Lorraine 170
Bradford, Richard 250
Braga, Sonia 120
Bram Stoker's Count Dracula 190
Bram Stoker's Dracula 191
Brambell, Wilfrid 229
Brambilla, Marco 20
Branagh, Kenneth 146, 208
Brand, Neville 100, 287
Brandauer, Klaus Maria 34, 247, 354
Brando, Marlon 39, 127, 149, 169, 206, 316, 340, 341
Branice, Ligia 44
Brass, Tinto 49, 141
Brasseur, Pierre 199
Braveheart 141
Brazil 262
Breakfast Club, The 74
Breaking Glass 222
Breaking The Waves 101
Breast Men 101
Breathless 240
Brega, Mario 332
Bremner, Ewen 66, 136
Brennan, Eileen 88, 254
Brennan, Walter 327, 340, 342, 343
Brest, Martin 71, 123, 250
Breton, Michele 129
Brett, Jeremy 312
Bridge On The River Kwai, The 318
Bridges, Jeff 276, 292, 347
Bridges, Lloyd 67, 82, 157, 336
Bridges Of Madison County, The 240
Brigadoon 223
Brimley, Wilford 95, 216, 252, 263
Bring Me The Head Of Alfredo Garcia 165
Britannia Hospital 74
Britton, Pamela 287
Broadbent, Jim 84
Broadcast News 74
Brochet, Anne 352
Broderick, Matthew 61, 75, 322
Brodie, Don 62
Broken Arrow 17
Brolin, James 278
Brolin, Josh 156, 269
Bron, Eleanor 70, 230
Bronson, Charles 317, 321, 322, 339, 340
Bronx Warriors 166
Brood, The 191
Brook, Claudio 193
Brooks, Albert 74, 85, 303
Brooks, Elisabeth 205
Brooks, James L 74, 239, 252
Brooks, Mel 73, 89, 94
Brooks, Randy 167
Brooks, Ray 155
Brooks, Richard 100, 103, 112, 149
Brosnan, Pierce 19, 25, 40, 269
Brown, Blair 260
Brown, Bryan 116
Brown, Clancy 26, 282
Brown, Jim 37, 176
Browne, Coral 216
Browning, Tod 196, 202
Brubaker 284
Brunet, Genevieve 351

Bryan Robson's Great Moments In Soccer 307
Brynner, Yul 139, 151, 278, 339
Bucholz, Horst 339
Bucquoy, Jean 51
Buddy Holly Story, The 223
Bug's Life, A 59
Bugsy 166
Bujold, Geneviève 153, 238, 285
Bull, Peter 14
Bullet For The General, A 330
Bullet In The Head 183
Bullitt 284
Bullock, Sandra 20, 38, 39, 118, 135
Buñuel, Luis 351, 352
Burbs, The 74
Burke, Kathleen 206
Burke, Kathy 91, 112, 126, 310
Burner, Cesar 216
Burns, Edward 326
Burns, Tim 31
Burroughs, William S 110
Burstyn, Ellen 198
Burton, Levar 275
Burton, Richard 137, 140, 142, 150, 180, 238, 328
Burton, Tim 16, 71, 111, 156, 269
Buscemi, Steve 18, 24, 98, 113, 136, 172, 178, 261
Busey, Gary 22, 30, 99, 176, 223
Busey, Jake 276
Bush, Bill Green 204
Butch Cassidy And The Sundance Kid 330
Butler, David 223
Butler, Yancy 22
Byrne, Gabriel 137, 175, 203, 331

Caan, James 29, 169, 242, 273, 296, 333
Cabaret 223
Cable Guy, The 75
Cabot, Bruce 60
Cadfael 311
Caesar, Sid 227
Caffrey, David 77
Cage, Nicolas 18, 24, 37, 241, 247, 254, 280, 302
Cagney, James 177, 236
Cain, Christopher 349
Caine, Michael 27, 77, 79, 81, 84, 152, 249, 290, 297, 302, 316
Caine Mutiny, The 102
Calamity Jane 223
Caligula 141
Callan, Michael 173
Callard, Beverley 306
Callow, Simon 59, 243
Calloway, Cab 73
Camelot 224
Cameron, James 39, 40, 41, 135, 258, 259
Cammell, Donald 129, 265
Campbell, Bruce 198, 207
Campbell, Glen 346
Campbell, Martin 25, 33, 48
Campbell, Neve 213, 214
Campbell, William 195
Campion, Jane 248
Can-Can 224
Canada, Ron 121
Candy, John 87, 92, 119, 157
Cantona, Eric 112
Capaldi, Peter 106
Cape Fear (1961) 284
Cape Fear (1991) 285
Capone 166
Capra, Frank 69
Capri, Alaina 45
Capshaw, Kate 27, 165
Captain Blood 18

TOP 1000 VIDEOS

Cara, Irene 226
Cardinale, Claudia 340
Carey, Philip 223
Carey, Tim 171
Carlin, George 72
Carlito's Way 166
Carlson, Veronica 201
Carlyle, Robert 80, 136
Caro, Marc 351
Caron, Leslie 222, 225, 227, 253
Carpenter, John 24, 200, 203, 216, 276
Carradine, David 339
Carradine, John 116, 205, 346
Carradine, Keith 23, 248, 339, 347
Carradine, Robert 241, 317, 339
Carrere, Tia 41, 93
Carrey, Jim 16, 66, 75, 78, 136
Carriere, Mathieu 47
Carroll, Leo G 298
Carry On ... 75
Carson, Jack 103, 234
Carter, T.K. 216
Cartier, Caroline 207
Cartwright, Veronica 268
Caruso, David 25, 172
Carver, Steve 166
Carvey, Dana 93
Casablanca 102
Casanova's Big Night 75
Casares, Maria 144
Cascio, Salvatore 351
Casey, Bernie 72
Cash, Rosalind 270
Casino 167
Cassavetes, John 166, 171, 202, 213, 321
Cassel, Seymour 171
Cassidy, Jack 23
Cassidy, Joanna 64
Cassinelli, Claudio 144
Castaway 240
Castel, Lou 330
Castellari, Enzo G 166, 338
Castle, William 153, 209
Casualties Of War 319
Cat On A Hot Tin Roof 103
Cates, Phoebe 81
Caton-Jones, Michael 27, 36, 324
Cattaneo, Peter 80
Cazale, John 109
Cecchi, Andrea 208
Cei, Pina 50
Celi, Adolfo 40
Celtic A-Z 307
Cemetery Man 192
Cepeda, Laura 46
Chaffey, Don 60, 62
Chakiris, George 236, 315
Chamber, The 103
Chamberlain, Wilt 19
Chambers, Marilyn 212
Chan, Jackie 37, 184, 185, 186, 187
Chan Lung 183
Chan-a-Hung, Meredith 54
Chandler, Helen 196
Chaney, Lon, Jnr 107, 219, 336
Chang Cheh 184
Channing, Stockard 134, 227
Chapman, Graham 68, 85, 86, 310
Charge Of The Light Brigade, The 142
Chariots Of Fire 103
Charisse, Cyd 223, 233, 234
Charles, Josh 207
Charleson, Ian 103
Chase, Chevy 87

Cheers 309
Chelsom, Peter 82
Chen, Joan 147
Chen, Pauline 48
Cher 93, 247, 306
Cher Fitness – A New Attitude 306
Cherkassov, Nikolai 147
Cheung, Jacky 183
Cheung, Leslie 182
Cheung, Maggie 187
Chevalier, Maurice 158, 224, 227
Chiang Sheng 184
Children Of A Lesser God 241
Children's TV, other 308
Chin Man Kei 187
Chinatown 103
Chingamy Yau 186
Chisum 330
Chitty Chitty Bang Bang 154
Chomsky, Marvin J 100
Chong, Rae Dawn 105
Chow Yun Fat 182, 185, 187
Christie, Julie 72, 143, 196, 265
Chu Yen Ping 185
Chung Fat 183
Church, The 192
Cilento, Diane 218
Cimino, Michael 180, 320, 336
Cincinnati Kid, The 104
Cinema Paradiso 351
Cioffi, Charles 178, 293
Citizen Cane 104
City Of Angels 241
City Of Lost Children, The 351
City Slickers 76
Clark, Candy 17
Clark, Fred 225
Clarke, Mae 177, 201
Clarke, Warren 24
Clayton, Jack 244
Clear And Present Danger 18
Cleese, John 68, 80, 85, 86, 162, 208, 309, 310
Clegg, Tom 174
Clemente, Ron 57, 58, 61
Cleopatra 142
Cliffhanger 18
Clift, Montgomery 115, 147, 342
Clive, Colin 201
Cliver, Al 220
Clooney, George 16, 35, 202
Close Encounters Of The Third Kind 263
Close, Glenn 106, 114, 131, 146, 269, 292
Clouse, Robert 183
Clouzot, Henri Georges 353
Clouzot, Vera 353
Clunes, Martin 66
Cobb, Lee J 127, 198
Coburn, James 87, 144, 298, 316, 319, 322, 339, 342
Cocoon 263
Coen, Joel 83, 98, 113, 175, 281
Cohen, Larry 176
Cohen, Rob 19, 155
Colditz Story, The 319
Cole, George 142
Coleman, Dabney 127
Collinson, Peter 27
Color Of Money, The 104
Color Purple, The 105
Colors 167
Colouris, George 34, 104
Coltrane, Robbie 155, 297
Columbus, Chris 134, 157
Coma 285
Comer, Anjanette 173

INDEX

Coming Home 241
Comingore, Dorothy 104
Commitments, The 224
Common-Law Cabin 45
Compañeros 331
Compere, Jean-Henri 51
Complete Bagpuss, The 307
Con Air 18
Conan The Barbarian 19
Conan The Destroyer 19
Connery, Sean 22, 26, 27, 34, 37, 40, 126, 155, 180, 270, 278, 296
Connick, Harry, Jnr 118, 286
Connolly, Billy 62, 90, 125, 306
Connolly, Christopher 166, 333
Constantine, Eddie 260, 294
Contact 264
Coogan, Steve 162
Cook, Elisha, Jnr 23, 281
Cook, Peter 70
Cool Hand Luke 105
Cooper, Chris 101
Cooper, Gary 327, 336
Cooper, Merian C 60
Coote, Robert 35
Copland 285
Coppola, Andrea 47
Coppola, Francis Ford 169, 191, 195, 316
Coppola, Sofia 169
Copycat 286
Coraci, Frank 253
Corbucci, Sergio 331, 332
Cornthwaite, Robert 277
Corrente, Michael 96
Corri, Adrienne 217
Cortes, Juan 216
Cosgrove, Brian 58
Cosmatos, George P 36, 346
Costa, Mary 63
Costner, Kevin 91, 115, 119, 180, 240, 298, 331, 348
Cottafavi, Vittorio 146
Cotten, Joseph 104, 303, 328
Couffer, Jack 161
Coulson, Bernie 95
Courage Under Fire 105
Courtenay, Tom 72, 324
Coward, Noel 27
Cox, Alex 134
Cox, Brian 36, 295
Cox, Courteney 66, 213, 214, 310
Cox, Ronny 20, 71
Coyote, Peter 266, 292
Craig, Daniel 122
Craig, Michael 62
Crane, Norma 226
Crash 45
Craven, Wes 213, 214
Crawford, Michael 230
Creed-Miles, Charles 126
Cregar, Laird 239, 291
Crenna, Richard 25, 36, 100
Crichton, Charles 80, 84
Crichton, Michael 278, 285
Crimes And Misdemeanors 76
Crimes Of Passion 45
Criminal, The 167
Crimson Tide 286
Crisp, Donald 38, 118, 255
Cristal, Perla 189
Criswell 50
Crocodile Dundee 76
Cromwell 142
Cromwell, James 154, 155
Cronenberg, David 45, 91, 126, 191, 212, 217, 267, 287

Cronos 193
Cronyn, Hume 263
Crosby, Bing 230
Cross, Ben 103
Cross Of Iron 319
Crothers, Scatman 214
Crouse, Lindsay 290
Crow, The 193
Crowden, Graham 74
Crowe, Cameron 83
Crowe, Russell 120
Cruel Sea, The 319
Cruickshank, Andrew 215
Cruise, Tom 29, 33, 41, 83, 104, 114, 131, 206, 242, 318, 327
Cruising 286
Cry Freedom 106
Cry In The Dark, A 105
Cry-Baby 224
Crying Game, The 106
Crystal, Billy 76, 160, 254
Cube 264
Cujo 286
Cukor, George 234
Culkin, Macaulay 92, 157
Cummings, Robert 287
Cummins, Peggy 194
Cupisti, Barbara 192
Curreri, Lee 226
Curry, Tim 26, 29, 233
Curse Of The Demon 194
Curtis, Jackie 54
Curtis, Jamie Lee 41, 80, 92, 200, 203, 242, 282
Curtis, Kelly Leigh 213
Curtis, Tony 107, 134, 151, 173
Curtis-Hall, Vondie 116
Curtiz, Michael 13, 18, 38, 102, 209, 230, 236
Curzon, Jill 155
Cusack, Cyril 155
Cusack, Joan 67
Cusack, John 18, 57, 124, 170
Cushing, Peter 155, 196, 201, 276
Cuthbertson, Allan 215
Cuthbertson, Iain 116, 160
Cyrano De Bergerac 352
Czerny, Henry 33

Daddy Long Legs 225
Dafoe, Willem 18, 39, 112, 148, 254, 296, 318, 325
Dahl, Arlene 28
Daleks – Invasion Earth 2150 AD 155
Dallesandro, Joe 190
Dalton, Audrey 29
Dalton, Timothy 267
Daltrey, Roger 174, 235
Dam Busters, The 320
Damiani, Damiano 330
Damon, Matt 116, 326
Dance, Charles 117, 259
Dances With Wolves 331
D'Angelo, Beverly 87, 229
Dangerous Game 106
Dangerous Liaisons 106
Daniell, Henry 283
Daniels, Jeff 78, 156, 189
Daniels, Phil 222, 232
Danner, Blythe 278
Danny Champion Of The World 155
Danson, Ted 100, 309, 326
Dante, Joe 63, 74, 81, 158, 205
Dante's Peak 19
Danvers, Lise 49
Darabont, Frank 133
Darby, Kim 346

363

TOP 1000 VIDEOS

Dark Habits 46
Dark Side Of Love, The 46
Darnell, Eric 58
Darnell, Linda 32, 239
Darwell, Jane 116
Daughters Of Darkness 194
Davenport, Nigel 180
Daves, Delmer 143
Davi, Robert 51, 156
David, Angel 193
Davidovich, Lolita 17, 300
Davidson, Bruce 45
Davidson, Jaye 106
Davies, Jeremy 51
Davies, Ray 221
Davies, Rupert 218
Davis, Andrew 289
Davis, Brad 124
Davis, Geena 31, 71, 91, 237, 267
Davis, Judy 98, 126, 128
Davis, Ossie 109
Davis, Sammi 297
Dawson, Anthony 287, 332
Day At The Races, A 76
Day, Doris 223
Day, Laraine 289
Day, Morris 232
Day Of The Jackal, The 287
Day The Earth Stood Still, The 264
Day-Lewis, Daniel 101, 118, 125, 148, 238
Daylight 19
de Boer, Nicole 264
De Bont, Jan 38, 39, 41
De Havilland, Olivia 13, 18, 145
De Jonge, Marc 36
De La Croix, Raven 53
De La Iglesia, Alex 299
De Luise, Dom 57, 73
De Mornay, Rebecca 290
De Niro, Robert 84, 97, 130, 167, 169, 170, 171, 174, 176, 180, 189, 208, 231, 241, 251, 262, 285, 301, 302, 303, 320
De Ossorio, Amando 216
De Palma, Brian 33, 166, 178, 180, 202, 282, 283, 300, 302, 319
De Vito, Danny 16, 28, 37, 92, 120, 128, 159, 168, 245, 252, 269
De Young, Cliff 205
Dead Man 331
Dead Man Walking 107
Dead Men Don't Wear Plaid 77
Dead Poets Society 107
Dead Zone, The 287
Dean, James 110
Dean, Loren 165
Dearden, Basil 147
Death Becomes Her 77
Death Rides A Horse 332
Deep Impact 265
Deer Hunter, The 320
Defiant Ones, The 107
Degermark, Pia 352
Dehner, John 338
Del Rey, Marina 51
Del Toro, Benicio 79
Del Toro, Guillermo 193, 269
Delaney, Dana 156
Deliverance 20
Delon, Alain 173, 214
Delon, Nathalie 173
Dementia 13 195
Demetrius And The Gladiators 143
DeMille, Cecil B 139, 150

Demme, Jonathan 129, 301
Demolition Man 20
Demon Seed 265
Demons 195
Dempsey, Patrick 175
Dench, Judi 125, 250
Deneuve, Catherine 205, 300, 351
Dennehy, Brian 25, 130, 304
Dennis, Sandy 137
Dennison, Michael 83
Depardieu, Elisabeth 353, 354
Depardieu, Gerard 352, 353, 355
Depp, Johnny 79, 111, 156, 167, 224, 331
Derek, Bo 66
Dern, Bruce 74, 173, 241, 244, 296, 347
Dern, Laura 29, 254, 282
Desert Fox, The 320
Detour 108
Deutch, Howard 248
Devane, William 298
Devereux, Marie 215
Devil Rides Out, The 195
Devil's Advocate 108
Devils, The 108
Dexter, Brad 325, 328
Di Cicco, Bobby 317
Dial M For Murder 287
Diary Of A Chambermaid, The 352
Diaz, Cameron 90
DiCaprio, Leonardo 135
Dick Tracy 20
Dickinson, Angie 299
Die Hard 21
Dieterle, William 244
Diffring, Anton 253
Digard, Uschi 52
Dillon, Kevin 109, 325
Dillon, Matt 90, 91, 110
Dillon, Melinda 263
Dirty Dozen, The 321
Dirty Harry 21
Dirty Rotten Scoundrels 77
Dirty Weekend 46
Disclosure 109
Divorcing Jack 77
Django 332
Django Strikes Again 333
Django The Bastard 332
Dmytryk, Edward 102
Do The Right Thing 109
Doa (1949) 287
Doa (1988) 288
Doctor Doolittle (1967) 225
Doctor Zhivago 143
Dog Day Afternoon 109
Dogs Of War, The 22
Doherty, Shannen 82
Donald, James 272
Donaldson, Roger 19, 101, 298
Donen, Stanley 70, 233, 234
Donlan, Yolande 225
Donner, Clive 93
Donner, Richard 30, 39, 156
Donnie Brasco 167
D'Onofrio, Vincent 321
Donohoe, Amanda 122, 240
Donovan, Martin 87
Donovan, Tate 324
Don't Look Now 196
Doohan, James 274, 275
Doors, The 109
Dorff, Stephen 17
Douglas, Kirk 98, 151, 202

INDEX

Douglas, Melvyn 217
Douglas, Michael 28, 37, 92, 109, 113, 114, 137, 165, 238, 281, 285, 299
Dourif, Brad 128, 296
Dow, Peggy 82
Dr Dolittle (1998) 78
Dr No 22
Dr Strangelove, Or How I Learned To Stop Worrying And Love The Bomb 78
Dr Who 313
Dracula (1931) 196
Dracula (1958) 196
Dracula – Prince Of Darkness 197
Dragonheart 155
Dragoti, Stan 85
Drake, Claudia 108
Dravic, Milena 54
Dreyfus, Jean-Claude 351
Dreyfuss, Richard 28, 59, 67, 129, 263
Driller Killer, The 197
Drivas, Robert 268
Driver, Minnie 116
Driving Miss Daisy 78
Drop Zone 22
Dru, Joanne 342
Drugstore Cowboy 110
Drury, James 343
Duchovny, David 278, 293
Duff, Howard 298
Dukakis, Olympia 247
Duke, Bill 35
Dullea, Keir 257, 258
Dumb And Dumber 78
Dumont, Margaret 68
Dunaway, Faye 103, 136, 165, 338
Dunbar, Adrian 82, 168
Dune 265
Dunne, Griffin 188
Dunst, Kirsten 57, 63, 90, 158
Durning, Charles 83, 91, 109
Duvall, Robert 29, 97, 113, 167, 169, 252, 265, 276, 284, 316, 335, 346
Duvall, Shelley 214, 215
Dvorak, Ann 178
Dwan, Allan 326
Dwyer, Hilary 218
Dylan, Bob 342
Dysart, Richard 216
Dzundza, George 281, 286

Earles, Harry 202
East Of Eden 110
Eastern Condors 183
Eastwood, Clint 21, 23, 24, 124, 231, 240, 288, 292, 323, 328, 335, 335, 336, 341, 347
Easy Rider 111
Eaton, Shirley 26
Eccleston, Christopher 112
Ed Wood 111
Eddington, Paul 195
Edel, Uli 120, 342
Edge, The 23
Educating Rita 79
Education Of Little Tree, The 155
Edward Scissorhands 156
Edwards, Blake 66, 89
Edwards, Cliff 62
Eggar, Samantha 191, 225
Egon Schiele Excesses 47
Ehle, Jennifer 91, 138, 311
Eiger Sanction, The 23
Eisenstein, Sergei 147
Ekberg, Anita 203
Ekland, Britt 218, 290

El Cid 143
El Dorado 333
Elam, Jack 343
Eleman, Herb 87
Elephant Man, The 111
Elfman, Danny 64
Elizabeth 112
Elizondo, Hector 96
Elliott, Chris 81
Elliott, Denholm 27, 319
Elmer Gantry 112
Elphick, Michael 94
Elvira Madigan 352
Elwes, Cary 41, 82, 160, 322
Emmerich, Roland 268
Emperor Of The North 23
Empire Of The Sun 112
Empire Strikes Back, The 265
Encounters Of The Spooky Kind 183
Endfield, Cy 62, 152
Enemy Mine 266
Enemy Of The State 288
Enfield, Harry 310
English Patient, The 112
Englund, Robert 99
Enter The Dragon 183
Entertaining Mr Sloane 79
Ephron, Nora 250, 255
Ermey, Lee 321
Erotic Dreams Of Cleopatra, The 47
Erotika 47
Escape From Alcatraz 288
Escape From Brothel 48
Escape From LA 24
Escape From New York 24
Eskimo Nell 48
Esposito, Giancarlo 73
Essex, David 235
Estevez, Emilio 74, 349
ET – The Extra-Terrestrial 266
Eubank, Shari 52
Evans, Edith 83
Evans, Maurice 213
Everett, Rupert 122, 192
Evil Dead, The 198
Evil Senses 48
Excalibur 143
Exorcist, The 198
Expresso Bongo 225
Eyer, Richard 56
Eyes Without A Face 199

Face To Face 333
Face/Off 24
Fahey, Jeff 348
Fail Safe 5
Faiman, Peter 76
Fairbanks, Douglas, Jnr 173
Faith, Adam 174
Fajardo, Eduardo 332
Falchi, Anna 192
Falk, Peter 160
Fall And Rise Of Reginald Perrin, The 309
Fall Of The Roman Empire, The 144
Falling Down 113
Falling In Love 241
Fame 226
Fantasia 59
Fantastic Voyage 266
Far And Away 242
Fargas, Antonio 54
Fargo 113
Farina, Dennis 175, 295
Farmer, Gary 331

TOP 1000 VIDEOS

Farmer, Mimsy 48
Farrell, Glenda 173, 209
Farrely, Bobby 90
Farrely, Peter 78, 90
Farrow, Mia 76, 81, 213, 244
Farrow, Tisa 220
Faster, Pussycat! Kill ... Kill 49
Fatal Attraction 114
Fauna, Flora 51
Fawcett, Farrah 97
Fawlty Towers 309
Fear And Loathing In Las Vegas 79
Fearless Vampire Killers, The 199
Feldman, Corey 74, 156
Feldman, Marty 94
Fellini, Federico 214, 353
Female Vampire 200
Fenn, Sherilyn 127
Ferrara, Abel 106, 164, 172, 188, 197, 280
Ferrer, Mel 152
Ferris, Pam 159
Few Good Men, A 114
Ffrangcon-Davies, Gwen 195
Fiddler On The Roof 226
Fiedler, Jon 87
Field of Dreams 115
Field, Sally 95, 243
Field, Shirley Anne 82, 125, 211
Field, The 114
Fields, Suzanne 49
Fiennes, Joseph 250
Fiennes, Ralph 52, 112, 130, 132
Fifth Element, The 266
Figgis, Mike 292
Finch, Jon 149, 222, 289
Fincher, David 132, 259
Finney, Albert 175, 219
Fiorentino, Linda 269
Firefox 24
First Blood 25
First Men In The Moon 267
First Wives Club 79
Firth, Colin 250, 311
Firth, Peter 252
Fish Called Wanda, A 80
Fishburne, Larry 101, 172
Fisher, Carrie 73, 74, 81, 254, 265, 272, 276
Fisher, Frances 135
Fisher, Terence 195, 196, 197, 201, 215
Fistful Of Dollars, A 335
Fistful Of Dynamite, A 144
Fists Of Fury 184
Five Venoms 184
Flash Gordon 267
Flashdance 226
Flatliners 288
Flavia The Heretic 144
Fleischer, Richard 19, 140, 151, 225, 266, 273, 280, 328
Fleming, Victor 145, 236
Flemyng, Gordon 155
Flemyng, Jason 174
Flemyng, Robert 216
Flesh And Blood 25
Flesh Gordon 49
Fletcher, Louise 101, 128, 282
Fly Away Home 156
Fly, The 267
Flynn, Errol 13, 18, 38
Focas, Spiros 28
Foch, Nina 222
Fog, The 200
Foley, Dave 59
Foley, Ellen 91, 114, 229
Foley, James 103
Fonda, Bridget 171, 301
Fonda, Henry 113, 116, 127, 152, 316, 317, 324, 335, 337, 340
Fonda, Jane 127, 214, 241, 251, 261, 293, 306
Fonda, Peter 24, 111, 214
Fong, Alen 48
Fontaine, Joan 75
For A Few Dollars More 335
For The Boys 242
Forbes, Bryan 319
Forbes, Michelle 293
Forbidden Planet 267
Force Of Evil 168
Ford, Clarence 186
Ford, Glenn 100, 316
Ford, Harrison 14, 18, 27, 34, 36, 38, 67, 94, 130, 138, 262, 265, 272, 276, 289
Ford, John 116, 118, 335, 337, 339, 340, 343, 344, 346
Ford, Wallace 202
Foreign Correspondent 289
Forever Young 242
Forlani, Clare 123
Forman, Milos 128, 129, 229
Forrest, Frederic 113, 316
Forrest Gump 243
Forster, Robert 171
Forsythe, William 170
Fort Apache 335
Fosse, Bob 121, 221, 223, 235
Foster, Barry 289
Foster, Jodie 95, 251, 264, 301, 303
Four Weddings And A Funeral 243
Fowler, Harry 89
Fox, Edward 34, 101, 287
Fox, James 129, 131, 221
Fox, Michael J 15, 238, 319
Foy, Eddie, Jnr 236
Frakes, Jonathan 275
Francis, Anne 98, 100, 227, 267
Franco, Jess 53, 189, 190, 200
Francq, Noe 51
Franju, Georges 199
Frankenheimer, John 100, 206, 295, 301, 328
Frankenstein 201
Frankenstein Must Be Destroyed 201
Franz, Dennis 96, 282, 283
Fraser, John 143, 320
Fraser, Liz 228
Fraser, Ronald 323
Frasier 309
Frazer, Robert 218
Freaks 202
Frears, Stephen 106, 125, 130, 170
Freberg, Stan 61
Freda, Riccardo 216
Frederick, Lynne 217
Free Willy 156
Freeman, Morgan 34, 78, 132, 133, 265, 322, 347
Freeman, Paul 36
French, Dawn 153, 309
French Lieutenant's Woman, The 243
Frend, Charles 319
Frenzy 289
Frewer, Matt 158
Fricker, Brenda 114, 135, 125
Fried Green Tomatoes At The Whistle Stop Cafe 115
Friedenberg, Richard 155
Friedkin, William 198, 286
Friedland, Alice 171
Friends 310
Frisch, Arno 352
Frizell, Lou 252

INDEX

Frobe, Gert 26
From Dusk Till Dawn 202
From Here To Eternity 115
Frost, Sadie 191
Fry, Stephen 138, 162, 309
Frye, Dwight 196, 201, 217
Fu, Alex 182
Fugitive, The 289
Fulci, Lucio 220
Full Metal Jacket 321
Full Monty, The 80
Fuller, Sam 317, 350
Funny Games 352
Funny Girl 227
Furlong, Edward 40
Furneaux, Yvonne 300
Fury, Billy 235
Fury, The 202

Gable, Christopher 222
Gable, Clark 145, 325
Gabriel, Mike 62
Gallagher, Bronagh 224
Galligan, Zach 81
Gallipoli 321
Gallo, Carla 51
Gambon, Michael 175
Gandhi 145
Ganolfini, James 39
Ganz, Bruno 210, 350
Garcia, Andy 165, 169, 180, 292, 293
Gardenia, Vincent 247
Gardner, Ava 139, 338
Garfield, John 168
Garland, Judy 147, 234, 236
Garner, James 322
Garr, Teri 91, 94, 263
Garrani, Ivo 208
Garrone, Sergio 332
Gassman, Vittorio 179
Gavin, Erica 54
Gazzara, Ben 166, 171
Geer, Will 337
Geeson, Judy 280
Geldof, Bob 232
Geller, Sarah Michell 214, 291
General, The 168
Genghis Khan 145
Genn, Leo 150
George, Chief Dan 338, 341
Geraghty, Marita 81
Gere, Richard 27, 240, 247, 249, 251, 292, 299
Geronimi, Clyde 56, 61, 63
Geronimo 335
Gershon, Gina 24, 51
Gerson, Betty Lou 56
Gertz, Jami 41
Get Carter 290
Get Shorty 168
Getaway, The 168
Getz, John 267, 281, 318
Ghost 244
Ghostbusters 80
GI Jane 115
Gibson, Brian 90, 222
Gibson, Hoot 337
Gibson, Mel 30, 31, 32, 62, 101, 141, 146, 242, 298, 300, 321
Gibson, Thomas 242
Gielgud, John 69, 103, 111, 133, 141, 142, 145
Gierasch, Stephan 337
Giering, Frank 352
Gigi 227
Gilbert, Brian 138

Gilbert, Lewis 79, 278, 327
Gillespie, Jim 291
Gilliam, Terry 68, 79, 85, 257, 262, 310
Gilpin, Peri 309
Ging, Jack 336
Gingold, Hermione 227
Girotti, Massimo 43
Glaser, Paul Michael 37, 226
Gleeson, Brendan 168
Glenn, Scott 26, 105, 150, 301
Glenville, Peter 140
Glory 322
Glover, Brian 259
Glover, Danny 30, 105, 138, 288
Glover, Julian 27, 272
Glovisz, Krzysztof 355
Godard, Jean-Luc 260
Godenzi, Joyce 183
Godfather, The 169
Godfather Part II, The 169
Godfather Part III, The 169
Golan, Menahem 173
Goldberg, Eric 62
Goldberg, Whoopi 105, 244
Goldblum, Jeff 29, 31, 267, 268
Golden, Annie 229, 257
Goldeneye 25
Goldfinger 26
Goldman, Gary 57
Goldstein, Steve 290
Golino, Valeria 131
Gomez, Thomas 168
Goncalves, Milton 120
Gone With The Wind 145
Good Morning, Vietnam 80
Good, The Bad And The Ugly, The 335
Good Will Hunting 116
Goodall, Caroline 132
Goodfellas 170
Gooding, Cuba, Jnr 83, 101, 254
Goodman, John 98, 189, 301
Goonies, The 156
Gordon, Don 34
Gordon, Ruth 213
Gordon, Steve 69
Gorillas In The Mist 116
Goring, Marius 246
Gorman, Cliff 221
Gorman, Lynne 217
Gorney, Karen Lynn 233
Gorshin, Frank 257
Gosnell, Raja 157
Gossett, Louis, Jnr 247, 266
Gothard, Michael 108
Gothic 203
Gotti 170
Gough, Michael 16, 196
Gould, Elliott 294
Gozlino, Paolo 332
Graaboel, Sofie 298
Grable, Betty 291
Graduate, The 81
Graham, Aimee 299
Graham, Gerrit 265
Graham, Heather 31, 44
Grahame, Gloria 98
Grammer, Kelsey 57, 309
Grandi, Serena 49
Granger, Stewart 35
Grant, Cary 69, 298
Grant, Hugh 243
Grant, Kathryn 56
Grant, Richard E 94, 191, 311
Grapes Of Wrath, The 116

367

TOP 1000 VIDEOS

Grapewin, Charley 116
Grauman, Walter 315
Graves, Peter 327
Gray, Charles 195, 233, 312
Gray, Gary 297
Gray, Spalding 99
Grease 227
Great Escape, The 322
Great Gatsby, The 244
Great Rock 'n' Roll Swindle, The 228
Green, Michael 85
Green, Nigel 60, 152
Green, Pamela 50
Greene, Ellen 119
Greene, Graham 155, 331
Greene, Leon 195
Greenstreet, Sidney 102
Greenwood, Joan 62, 83, 84
Gregory, Mark 166
Greist, Kim 262, 295
Gremlins 81
Grey, Joel 223
Greystoke 145
Gridlock'd 116
Griem, Helmut 223
Grier, Pam 171, 176
Griffith, Melanie 94, 128, 283, 297
Griffiths, Hugh 140
Griffiths, Rachel 77, 117
Griffiths, Richard 94
Grifters, The 170
Grimes, Gary 252
Grinko, Nikolai 274
Grodin, Charles 71
Gronemeyer, Herbert 318
Grossbard, Ulu 241
Groundhog Day 81
Grundgens, Gustav 353
Guadagni, Nicky 264
Guardino, Harry 21, 166
Guccione, Bob 141
Guerra, Ruy 350
Guerritore, Monica 46, 48, 50
Guest, Christopher 90, 339
Guest, Nicholas 339
Guest, Val 225
Gugino, Carla 302
Guillaume, Robert 61
Guillermin, John 136, 317
Guinness, Alec 84, 128, 142, 143, 144, 148, 276, 312, 318
Guintoli, Neil 117
Gullette, Sean 270
Gulpilil, David 76
Gunfighter, The 335
Gunn, Moses 160, 178
Guns Of Navarone, The 322
Gwynne, Fred 86
Gypsy 228

Haas, Lukas 138
Hackett, Buddy 61
Hackford, Taylor 108, 247
Hackman, Gene 35, 39, 58, 94, 103, 129, 165, 168, 286, 288, 296, 297, 298, 304, 335, 347, 348
Hadji-Lazaro, Francois 192
Hagerty, Julie 67, 85
Hagman, Larry 88, 113
Haid, Charles 260
Haim, Corey 207
Haines, Randa 241
Haing S Ngor 120
Hair 229
Haji 49, 52

Hale, Georgina 108, 174, 240
Haley, Jack 236
Haley, Jack, Jnr 235
Hallahan, Charles 19
Halloween 203
Halloween H2O 203
Halperin, Victor 218
Hamburger Hill 323
Hamer, Robert 84
Hamill, Mark 265, 272, 276, 317
Hamilton, George 85
Hamilton, Guy 26, 316, 319
Hamilton, Linda 19, 39, 40
Hamilton, Margaret 153, 236
Hamilton, Murray 28
Hamlet 146
Hand Of Death 184
Hand That Rocks The Cradle, The 290
Handl, Irene 228
Haneke, Michael 352
Hang 'Em High 335
Hanks, Tom 64, 74, 97, 129, 154, 243, 250, 255, 326
Hanna Barbera 307
Hannah And Her Sisters 81
Hannah, Daryl 137, 202, 262
Hannah, John 251
Hanson, Curtis 120, 290
Hard Day's Night, A 229
Hardman, Karl 210
Hardwicke, Cedric 244, 320
Hardwicke, Edward 312
Hardy, Robin 218
Hargreaves, Christine 232
Harlin, Renny 18, 31
Harlow, Jean 177
Harmon, Robert 170, 204
Harper, Jessica 215
Harper, Tess 252
Harrelson, Woody 93, 129, 245, 309
Harris, Barbara 77
Harris, Ed 37, 97, 134, 136, 150, 179, 258, 285
Harris, James B 17, 99
Harris, Julie 110, 116, 204
Harris, Neil Patrick 276
Harris, Richard 114, 142, 149, 224, 323, 347
Harrison, Rex 142, 225
Harrison, Susan 134
Harry, Debbie 217
Harry Enfield And Chums 310
Hart, Ian 91
Hart, Pamela 270
Hartley, Mariette 343
Harvey 82
Harvey, Don 319
Harvey, Laurence 225, 295, 323, 329
Haskin, Byron 277
Hatcher, Teri 40
Hatfield, Hurd 143, 338
Hathaway, Henry 320, 337, 346
Hathaway, Noah 160
Hauer, Rutger 25, 204, 262
Haunting, The 204
Havers, Nigel 103, 112, 128
Hawke, Ethan 107
Hawkins, Jack 140, 148, 149, 152, 216, 318, 319
Hawks, Howard 178, 281, 327, 333, 342, 343
Hawn, Goldie 77, 79, 88
Hawthorne, Nigel 20, 24, 96, 122
Hayden, Sterling 78, 164, 294
Hayes, Isaac 24
Hayes, Patricia 160
Hayman, David 134
Hays, Robert 67
Haysbert, Dennis 245

INDEX

Hayward, Susan 143
Hayworth, Rita 231, 239
Hazuki Hotaru 53
Headly, Glenne 77
Hear My Song 82
Heard, John 97, 99, 154, 157, 302
Heat 170
Heathers 82
Heaven's Gate 336
Heche, Anne 167, 300
Hedaya, Dan 19, 67, 260, 281
Hedren, Tippi 281, 296
Heerman, Victor 68
Heflin, Van 344
Helgeland, Brian 298
Hellman, Monte 345
Hello, Dolly 230
Hellraiser 204
Helmore, Tom 304
Help! 230
Hemmings, David 142, 224, 261
Hendry, Ian 290, 300
Henreid, Paul 102
Henriksen, Lance 39, 109, 209, 259, 293
Henry – Portrait Of A Serial Killer 117
Henry – Portrait Of A Serial Killer 2 117
Henry, Gregg 298
Henry V 146
Henry VIII And His Six Wives 146
Henshall, Douglas 91
Hepburn, Audrey 152, 249
Hepburn, Katharine 14, 127
Hepton, Bernard 312
Herbert, Charles 153
Heche, Anne 38
Hercules Conquers Atlantis 146
Herek, Stephen 72
Herman, Mark 84
Heroes Shed No Tears 184
Hershey, Barbara 81, 99, 113
Herzog, Werner 210, 350
Heston, Charlton 139, 140, 143, 147, 270, 271, 273, 316, 330, 346
Hewitt, Jennifer Love 291
Hewitt, Peter 72
Hewlett, David 264
Hickox, Douglas 79, 216
Hicks, Catherine 275
Hicks, Scott 133
Hideko Saijo 182
Higgins, Claire 204
High Noon 336
High Plains Drifter 336
High Society 230
Highlander 26
Hilary And Jackie 117
Hill, Benny 27, 154
Hill, Bernard 135
Hill, George Roy 330
Hill, James 154
Hill, Walter 13, 173, 335, 339, 347
Hiller, Wendy 149
Hindle, Art 191
Hines, Gregory 219
Hingle, Pat 170
Hitchcock, Alfred 212, 281, 287, 289, 296, 298, 304
Hitcher, The 204
Ho, Godfrey 182
Hoag, Judith 161
Hoblit, Gregory 299
Hodges, Mike 267, 290
Hoffman, Dustin 20, 34, 81, 91, 96, 121, 124, 131, 165, 273, 296, 302, 338
Hoffman, Gaby 90

Hogan, Paul 76
Holbrook, Hal 96, 200
Holden, William 136, 246, 318, 327, 337, 348
Holloway, Stanley 84
Holly, Lauren 78
Holm, Celeste 230
Holm, Ian 103, 122, 126, 145, 208, 259, 262, 266
Home Alone 157
Home Alone 2 157
Home Alone 3 157
Homicide 290
Homolka, Oscar 209
Honey, I Blew Up The Kid 157
Honey, I Shrunk The Kids 158
Hooper, Tobe 211
Hope, Bob 75
Hope Floats 118
Hopkins, Anthony 23, 33, 96, 101, 111, 121, 123, 131, 191, 301
Hopkins, Bo 29, 124
Hopkins, Stephen 31
Hopper, Dennis 17, 38, 98, 105, 111, 167, 179, 282, 316, 346, 350
Hordern, Michael 155
Horne, Victoria 82
Horrocks, Jane 84, 309
Horse Soldiers, The 337
Horse Whisperer, The 118
Hoskins, Bob 64, 232, 294, 297
Hot Shots 82
Hot, The Cool And The Vicious, The 185
House Of Games 290
Houseman, John 273
Houser, Jerry 252
Houston, Whitney 240
Hovey, Natasha 195
How Green Was My Valley 118
How The West Was Won 337
Howard, Arliss 31
Howard, Leslie 145
Howard, Ron 67, 97, 242, 263, 300, 345
Howard, Trevor 89, 142, 149, 303, 328
Howell, C Thomas 204
Howes, Sally Ann 154
Howitt, Peter 251
Howling, The 205
Hoyt, John 49
Hudson, Ernie 193
Hudson, Hugh 103, 145
Hudsucker Proxy, The 83
Hughes, John 74, 92
Hughes, Ken 142, 154
Hulce, Tom 68, 208
Hull, Henry 337
Hull, Josephine 82
Humberstone, Bruce 291
Hunchback Of Notre Dame, The 244
Hunger, The 205
Hunt, Bonnie 71
Hunt For Red October, The 26
Hunt, Helen 41, 239
Hunt, Linda 62
Hunt, Martita 140
Hunter, Bill 321
Hunter, Holly 45, 74, 245, 248
Hunter, Jeffrey 344
Hunter, Kim 246, 271
Huppert, Isabelle 336
Hurley, Elizabeth 70
Hurt, John 36, 111, 114, 124, 259, 264, 280, 311, 336, 347
Hurt, William 31, 74, 100, 120, 134, 237, 241, 260
Hussein, Waris 146
Hussey, Olivia 250

369

Huston, Anjelica 67, 170
Huston, John 14, 103, 164, 171, 338
Huston, Walter 236
Hutchins, Will 345
Hutton, Brian G 323, 328
Hutton, Lauren 96
Hutton, Tim 327
Hwang Jang Lee 187
Hyams, Peter 258, 270
Hyde, Jonathan 158
Hyde-Pierce, David 309
Hyde-White, Alex 249
Hyde-White, Wilfred 158
Hyer, Martha 267
Hytner, Nicholas 122

I Claudius 311
I Know What You Did Last Summer 291
I Wake Up Screaming 291
Ice Cold In Alex 323
Ice Cube 14, 101
Ice-T 176
Idle, Eric 68, 85, 162, 310
Illustrated Man, The 268
Immoral Tales 49
Importance Of Being Earnest, The 83
In Search Of The Castaways 158
In The Heat Of The Night 291
In The Line Of Fire 292
In The Name Of The Father 118
Indecent Proposal 245
Independence Day 268
Indiana Jones & The Last Crusade 27
Indiana Jones & The Temple Of Doom 27
Inferno 205
Ingham, Barrie 58
Ingram, Rex 161
Innerspace 158
Inspector Morse 311
Internal Affairs 292
Interview With The Vampire 206
Invasion Of The Bodysnatchers 268
Irons, Jeremy 61, 131, 155, 243
Irons, Samuel 155
Ironside, Michael 276
Irvin, John 22, 323
Irving, Amy 202
Isaacs, Jason 77
Ishiwara Yuri 53
Island Of Dr Moreau, The 206
Island Of Lost Souls 206
Island On Fire 185
Isuzu Yamada 151
Italian Job, The 27
It's a Mad, Mad, Mad, Mad World 83
Ivan The Terrible 147
Ives, Burl 103
Ivey, Dana 77
Ivory, James 131
Izzard, Eddie 306

Jackal, The 27
Jackie Brown 171
Jackson, Glenda 249, 255
Jackson, Mick 240
Jackson, Peter 70
Jackson, Samuel L 31, 135, 171, 177, 273, 297
Jackson, Wilfred 61
Jacobi, Derek 122, 146, 311
Jaeckel, Richard 276, 324
Jaffe, Sam 164, 264
Jaffrey, Saeed 125
Jagged Edge 292
Jagger, Dean 112, 230

Jagger, Mick 129
James And The Giant Peach 59
James, Brion 266
James, Sidney 84
Jameson, Jenna 88
Janda, Krystyna 354
Jane Fonda – Total Body Sculpting 306
Jankel, Annabel 288
Jarmusch, Jim 331
Jarrott, Charles 238
Jarvet, Yuri 273
Jason And The Argonauts 60
Jason, David 58, 310
Jaws 28
Jean De Florette 353
Jeffrey, Peter 161
Jeffries, Lionel 154, 160, 267, 319
Jenkins, Tamara 89
Jennifer Eight 293
Jeremiah Johnson 337
Jerry Maguire 83
Jesse James 337
Jeter, Michael 22
Jeunet, Jean-Pierre 260, 351
Jewel Of The Nile, The 28
Jewison, Norman 104, 226, 247, 273, 291
JFK 119
Joanou, Phil 179
Joffe, Roland 120
Johns, Glynis 159
Johnson, Ben 168, 325, 330, 335, 341, 343, 348
Johnson, Don 91
Johnson, Joe 158
Johnson, Richard 147, 204, 220
Johnson, Tim 58
Johnson, Tor 271
Johnson, Van 102, 223
Johnston, Joe 158
Jones, Angela 50
Jones, Carolyn 230
Jones, Dean 71
Jones, Dickie 62
Jones, Duane 210
Jones, Freddie 24, 111, 201
Jones, Gemma 108
Jones, Grace 19
Jones, James Earl 18, 19, 61, 115, 251
Jones, Jennifer 246
Jones, L.Q. 33
Jones, Sam 267
Jones, Shirley 112
Jones, Terry 68, 85, 86, 162, 310
Jones, Tommy Lee 16, 63, 119, 269, 289
Jones, Vinnie 174
Jordan, Neil 123, 206, 297
Jory, Victor 34
Jourdan, Louis 227
Journey To The Center Of The Earth 28
Jovovich, Milla 266
Judd, Edward 267
Judgment At Nuremberg 147
Julia, Raul 67, 120, 130
Jumanji 158
Jurado, Katy 336, 341
Juran, Nathan 56, 267
Jurassic Park 29
Jurgens, Curt 149, 351

Kahn, Madeline 73, 94
Kaidanovsky, Aleksandr 274
Kalifornia 293
Kanante, Lu 332
Kane, Carol 69
Kane, David 91

INDEX

Kaneto Shindo 355
Kanji Sawada 354
Kaplan, Jonathan 95, 245
Kaprisky, Valerie 240
Kapur, Shekhar 112
Karate Kid, The 159
Karbelnikoff, Michael 175
Karina, Anna 260
Karlatos, Olga 232
Karlen, John 194
Karloff, Boris 178, 201, 283
Kasdan, Lawrence 100, 237, 348
Katt, William 99
Kaufman, Christine 47
Kaufman, Philip 150, 268
Kaye, Stubby 64
Kazan, Elia 110, 127
Kazuko Yoshiyuki 43
Ke Huy Quan 27
Keach, James 339
Keach, Stacy 24, 338, 339
Keaton, Diane 69, 79, 169
Keaton, Michael 16, 71, 128, 171
Keel, Howard 223, 233
Keen, Geoffrey 154
Kei Sato 355
Keighley, William 13
Keir, Andrew 155, 197, 272
Keir, Udo 101
Keitel, Harvey 106, 133, 134, 148, 164, 166, 174, 177, 178, 202, 241, 248, 285, 303
Keith, Brian 179
Keith, David 247
Keller, Marthe 296
Kelly, David Patrick 193
Kelly, Gene 222, 223, 230, 234, 235
Kelly, Grace 230, 287, 336
Kelly, Jack 267
Kelly, Jim 183
Kelly's Heroes 323
Kemp, Gary 172, 240
Kemp, Jeremy 317
Kemp, Martin 172
Kennedy, Arthur 140, 148, 247, 266
Kennedy, George 23, 86, 105
Kensit, Patsy 30, 221
Kenton, Erle C 206
Keoma ... The Violent Breed 338
Kernochan, Sarah 90
Kerr, Bill 320
Kerr, Deborah 35, 115, 150
Kershner, Irvin 34, 265
Kerwin, Brian 245
Key Largo 171
Khartoum 147
Kidder, Margot 39
Kidman, Nicole 16, 35, 91, 165, 242
Kier, Udo 17, 153, 190, 215
Kieslowski, Krzysztof 355
Killer 119
Killer Elite, The 29
Killer, The 185
Killing Fields, The 120
Killing Of A Chinese Bookie, The 171
Kilmer, Val 16, 41, 109, 170, 179, 206, 346
Kind Hearts And Coronets 84
King Creole 230
King, Dave 294
King, Henry 246, 335, 337
King Kong 60
King Of Comedy 84
King Of New York 172
Kingsley, Ben 132, 145, 266
Kinnear, Roy 48

Kino Mahito 53
Kinski, Klaus 190, 210, 330, 350
Kinski, Nastassja 39, 252
Kirby, Bruno 76
Kirk, Tommy 161
Kiss Of The Spider Woman 120
Kitchen, Michael 247
Kleiser, Randal 157, 227, 239
Kline, Kevin 80, 106
Klute 293
Ko, Eddy 184
Koch, Marianne 335
Komenich, Rich 117
Kopelson, Arnold 299
Korda, Alexander 161
Korda, Zoltan 161
Koster, Henry 82, 150
Kotcheff, Ted 25
Koteas, Elias 45, 161
Kotero, Appollonia 232
Kotto, Yaphet 37, 284
Kove, Martin 159
Kozak, Harley Jane 189
Kozlowski, Linda 76
Krabbe, Jeroen 289
Kramer, Stanley 83, 107, 147
Krays, The 172
Krige, Alice 275
Kristofferson, Kris 121, 165, 298, 304, 336, 342
Kubrick, Stanley 78, 151, 214, 257, 321
Kudrow, Lisa 87, 310
Kumel, Harry 194
Kurtz, Swoosie 251

LA Confidential 120
La Dolce Vita 353
LA Takedown 172
La Vampire Nue 207
Lacey, Ronald 25
Ladd, Alan 344
Ladd, Diane 254
Lady And The Tramp 61
LaGravenesse, Richard 245
Lahr, Bert 236
Laine, Jimmy 197
Lake, Ricki 224
Lam Ching Ying 184
Lamarr, Hedy 150
Lambert, Christopher 26, 145
Lan Wei Tsang 187
Lancaster, Burt 100, 112, 115, 134, 147, 325, 328
Lancaster, Stuart 49
Landau, Martin 76, 111, 142, 153, 278, 298
Landis, Carole 291
Landis, John 68, 73, 92, 188
Lane, Diane 347
Lane, Nathan 61
Lane, Priscilla 69
Lang, Fritz 353
Lang, Stephen 120
Lang, Walter 224
Lange, Hope 247
Lange, Jessica 36, 91, 221, 285
Langella, Frank 63
Lanovoi, Vasily 152
Lansbury, Angela 57, 58, 150, 222, 295
Lapaglia, Anthony 136
Lasseter, John 59, 64
Last Emperor, The 147
Last Exit To Brooklyn 120
Last Man Standing 173
Last Of The Mohicans, The 148
Last Temptation Of Christ, The 148
Latifah, Queen 245

TOP 1000 VIDEOS

Lau, Andy 185, 187
Lau Chau Sang 184
Laughton, Charles 151, 206, 244
Laurence, Ashley 204
Laurenson, James 232
Laurie, Hugh 309
Laurie, Piper 241
Lavender Hill Mob, The 84
Lavia, Gabrielle 48, 50
Law, John Phillip 261, 332
Law, Jude 124, 138
Lawrence Of Arabia 148
Lawson, Leigh 252
Lawson, Sarah 195
Lazar, John 44
Le Blanc, Matt 31, 310
Le Gros, James 110
Le Samouraï 173
Lean, David 128, 143, 148, 318
Leder, Mimi 35, 265
Lee, Anna 118, 234
Lee, Bernard 22, 303
Lee, Brandon 193
Lee, Bruce 183, 184
Lee Che Hung 182
Lee, Christopher 66, 190, 195, 196, 197, 212, 215, 218
Lee, Danny 185
Lee, Jason Scott 215
Lee, Loretta 187
Lee, Mark 321
Lee, Peggy 61
Lee, Spike 109
Lee, Tommy 185
Lee Tso Nam 185
Leeves, Jane 59, 309
Left-Handed Gun, The 338
Legend 29
Legends Of The Fall 121
Lehmann, Michael 82
Lehne, Fredric 100
Leigh, Janet 151, 200, 203, 212, 295
Leigh, Jennifer Jason 25, 83, 120, 175, 204, 301
Leigh, Vivien 145
Lemaitre, Maurice 207
Lemmon, Jack 87, 119
Lena Lorenzo 46
Lenny 121
Leon 293
Leonard, Bridget 50
Leonard, Robert Sean 107, 119
Leone, Sergio 144, 176, 335, 335, 340
Leoni, Tea 265
Lepke 173
LeRoy, Mervyn 150, 173, 228
Les Diaboliques 353
Leslie, Joan 236, 327
Lester, Mark 231
Lester, Richard 229, 230
Lethal Weapon 30
Lethal Weapon 2 30
Lethal Weapon 3 30
Lethal Weapon 4 30
Leto, Jared 217
Letscher, Matt 33
Leung, Tony 182, 183, 185, 187
Levant, Brian 71
Levant, Oscar 222
Levin, Henry 28, 145
Levine, Ted 301
Levinson, Barry 80, 109, 131, 166, 273, 302
Lewis, Fiona 180, 202
Lewis, Jerry 83, 84
Lewis, Juliette 52, 202, 285, 293
Lewis, Ronald 209

Leyton, John 328
Li, Jet 30
Lieberman, Robert 304
Life And Times Of Judge Roy Bean, The 338
Linden, Jennie 255
Lindo, Delroy 17, 300
Lindsay, Robert 77
Linney, Laura 136, 299
Linz, Alex D 157
Lion King, The 61
Lion King II – Simba's Pride, The 61
Liotta, Ray 115, 170, 285
Lipman, Maureen 79, 312
Lister, Moira 319
Lithgow, John 18, 221, 258, 282, 300
Little Big Man 338
Little Caesar 173
Little, Cleavon 73
Little Mermaid, The 61
Little Voice 84
Litvak, Anatole 324
Liverpool – 300 Liverpool Goals 307
Livesy, Roger 246
Living Out Loud 245
Llosa, Luis 14
LLoyd, Christopher 15, 57, 64, 67, 128
LLoyd, Danny 214
LLoyd, Kathleen 340
Lo Wei 184
Loc, Tone 66
Locaine, Amy 324
Lock, Stock And Two Smoking Barrels 174
Locke, Sondra 341
Lockwood, Gary 257
Logan, Joshua 224, 231
Logan's Run 268
Loggia, Robert 154, 292
Lohan, Lindsay 160
Lollobrigida, Gina 151
Lom, Herbert 62, 89, 143, 151, 152, 190, 213, 287
Lone, John 147, 180
Lone Star 121
Long And The Short And The Tall, The 323
Long Good Friday, The 294
Long Goodbye, The 294
Long Kiss Goodnight, The 31
Long Riders, The 339
Longest Day, The 324
Longo, Malisa 49
Looking For Richard 121
Lopez, Jennifer 14
Lord Jim 149
Lords, Traci 17, 224
Loren, Sophia 143, 144
Lorre, Peter 69, 102, 233, 353
Losey, Joseph 167, 249
Lost Boys, The 207
Lost In America 85
Lost In Space 31
Lost World: Jurassic Park, The 31
Lothar, Susanne 352
Louis-Dreyfus, Julia 59
Love At First Bite 85
Love, Courtney 129
Love Field 245
Love Is a Many-Splendored Thing 246
Love Is The Devil 122
Lovett, Lyle 87
Lowe, Rob 93, 237
Lu Feng 184
Lucas, George 67, 276
Luchini, Fabrice 49
Luddy, Barbara 61, 63
Lugagne, Francoise 352

INDEX

Lugosi, Bela 196, 206, 218, 219, 271, 283
Lui, Alexis 298
Lukoye, Peter 154
Lumet, Sidney 109, 113
Lumley, Joanna 309
Lund, Zoe 164
Lung Fei 186
Lunghi, Cherie 143
Lunn, Porsche 47
Lupone, Patti 78
Luppi, Federico 193
Luske, Hamilton S 56, 61, 62
Lustig, William 207
Lynch, David 111, 254, 265, 282
Lynch, Jock 251
Lynch, Kelly 110
Lyndhurst, Nicholas 310
Lyne, Adrian 43, 114, 226, 245
Lynn, Jonathan 86
Lyonne, Natasha 89

M 353
Ma Chi 186
MacArthur, James 99, 161
Macbeth 149
Macchio, Ralph 86, 159
MacDonald, Edmund 108
MacDowell, Andie 81, 133, 145, 243
MacGinnis, Niall 60, 194
MacGowran, Jack 198, 199
MacGraw, Ali 168
Mackay, Fulton 74
MacKendrick, Alexander 134
MacKenzie, John 294
Mackintosh, Steven 174
MacLachlan, Kyle 51, 109, 265, 282
MacLaine, Shirley 129, 224, 235, 252
MacMurray, Fred 102
MacNee, Patrick 205, 311
MacPherson, Elle 23
Macy, William H 113, 290
Mad Max 31
Mad Max 2: The Road Warrior 32
Mad Max: Beyond Thunderdome 32
Madden, John 125, 250
Madigan, Amy 92, 115
Madness Of King George, The 122
Madonna 20, 106
Madou, Malou 354
Madsen, Michael 109, 156, 167, 178
Magee, Patrick 89, 167, 195
Magnificent Seven, The 339
Magnoli, Albert 232
Maguire, Tobey 79
Mahoney, John 309
Makavejev, Dusan 54
Mako 19, 128, 133
Malden, Karl 100, 104, 127, 228, 325, 335, 341
Malik, Art 41
Malkovich, John 18, 106, 112, 120, 127, 292, 293
Malle, Louis 214, 248
Malleson, Miles 84
Malmer, Lennart 352
Mamet, David 290
Mamoulian, Rouben 32, 233, 239
Man Bites Dog 354
Man, Daisy 182
Man For All Seasons, A 149
Man Who Shot Liberty Vallance, The 339
Man With The Golden Arm, The 122
Manchester, Melissa 58
Manchester United – 300 Premiership Goals 307
Manchurian Candidate, The 295
Mandoki, Louis 254

Mangano, Silvano 140
Mangold, James 285
Manhunter 295
Maniac Cop 207
Mankiewicz, Joseph L 142, 302
Mann, Anthony 143, 144
Mann, Michael 148, 170, 172, 295
Manners, David 196
Manni, Ettore 146
Manning, Katy 48
Manon Des Sources 354
Mantegna, Joe 166, 290
Marathon Man 296
Margolis, Mark 270
Margolyes, Miriam 59
Margulies, David 43
Marin, Cheech 91
Mark Of Zorro, The 32
Marks, George Harrison 50
Marnie 296
Marquand, Richard 272, 292
Mars Attacks! 269
Mars, Kenneth 61, 89
Marshall, Frank 189
Marshall, Garry 85, 99, 249
Marshall, George 337
Marshall, Herbert 289
Marshall, Penny 97, 154
Martin, Dean 343
Martin, Oliver 207
Martin, Steve 77
Martin, Strother 105, 329, 330
Marton, Andrew 324
Marvin, Lee 23, 98, 102, 231, 299, 317, 321, 339
Marx Brothers, The 68, 76
Mary Poppins 159
Mary Shelley's Frankenstein 208
Marz, Carolyn 197
Mask Of Satan 208
Mask Of Zorro, The 33
Mason, Hilary 196
Mason, James 28, 35, 144, 145, 149, 234, 283, 298, 317, 319, 320
Massey, Anna 211, 289
Massey, Raymond 69, 110, 324
Masterson, Mary Stuart 115
Mastrantonio, Mary Elizabeth 104, 178, 258
Mastroianni, Marcello 353
Matania, Celia 196
Matarazzo, Heather 90
Mate, Rudolf 287
Matheson, Tim 66, 68
Mathis, Samantha 17
Matilda 159
Matlin, Marlee 241
Matter Of Life And Death, A 246
Matthau, Walter 87, 113, 119, 230
Matthews, Francis 197, 212
Matthews, Kerwin 56
Mattison, Burny 58
Mature, Victor 143, 150, 291, 340
Maura, Carmen 46
Maybury, John 122
Mayne, Ferdy 199
McAnally, Ray 125
McArthur, Alex 172
McBride, Jim 240
McCallum, David 46, 82, 322
McCallum, Robert 47
McCarthy, Andrew 248
McCarthy, Kevin 158
McCloskey, Leigh 205
McCole, Stephen 66
McConaughey, Matthew 96, 121, 135, 264

McCormack, Catherine 91
McCormack, Mary 88
McCowen, Alec 106, 289
McCoy, Matt 290
McCrea, Joel 289, 343
McCulloch, Ian 220
McDermott, Dylan 292
McDonald, Christopher 39
McDonald, Peter 36
McDonnell, Mary 331
McDormand, Frances 113, 121, 175, 281, 296, 299
McDowall, Roddy 35, 118, 142, 271
McDowell, Malcolm 17, 141
McElhone, Natascha 136
McElhone, Natasha 301
McEnery, Peter 79
McGann, Paul 94
McGavin, Darren 122
McGee, Vonetta 23
McGillis, Kelly 41, 95, 138
McGoohan, Patrick 135, 141, 288
McGovern, Elizabeth 176, 311
McGregor, Ewan 84, 136
McGuigan, Paul 66
McGuire, Dorothy 161
McKean, Michael 90
McKenna, Virginia 154, 161
McKern, Leo 149, 230, 239, 243
McKidd, Kevin 66
McLaglen, Andrew V 330
McLaglen, Victor 343
McLaren, Malcolm 228
McLeod, Norman Z 75
McLerie, Allyn Ann 223, 337
McMamara, Brian 100
McMartin, John 235
McMillan, Roddy 161
McNaughton, Ian 68
McNaughton, John 117
McQueen, Steve 34, 104, 136, 168, 284, 322, 339
McRae, Scooter 51
McShane, Ian 180
McTiernan, John 21, 26, 35
McVicar 174
Mean Streets 174
Meaney, Colm 18
Meaning Of Life, The 85
Medak, Peter 172
Meet Joe Black 123
Melville, Jean-Pierre 173
Melvin, Murray 108
Memphis Belle 324
Men In Black 269
Men Of Respect 175
Menzies, William Cameron 161
Mephisto 354
Mercury Rising 33
Meredith, Burgess 132, 179
Merrill, Gary 62
Merryfield, Buster 310
Mervyn, William 160
Metcalf, Laurie 92
Metcalfe, Tim 119
Metrano, Art 240
Meurisse, Paul 353
Meyer, Nicholas 274
Meyer, Russ 44, 45, 49, 50, 52, 53, 54
Miami Blues 175
Michael Collins 123
Michell, Keith 146
Michener, Dave 58
Midler, Bette 79, 99, 242
Midnight Cowboy 124
Midnight Express 124

Midnight In The Garden Of Good And Evil 124
Mighty Joe Young 159
Miles, Sarah 162
Miles, Sylvia 124
Miles, Vera 212, 344
Milestone, Lewis 149, 315
Milian, Tomas 331, 333
Milius, John 19, 99, 325
Milland, Ray 287
Millar, Gavin 155
Miller, Barry 233
Miller, Dennis 109
Miller, Dick 231
Miller, George 31, 32, 93
Miller, Jason 198
Miller, Jonny Lee 136
Miller, Penelope Anne 97, 166
Miller's Crossing 175
Mills, Hayley 158
Mills, John 145, 161, 319, 323
Milner, Martin 134, 153, 326
Mimic 269
Mimieux, Yvette 277
Miner, Jan 121
Miner, Steve 203, 242
Minett, Mike 70
Minghella, Anthony 112
Mingozzi, Gianfranco 144
Minkoff, Rob 61
Minnelli, Liza 69, 223, 231
Minnelli, Vincente 98, 222, 223, 227
Minoru Chiaki 151
Minty, Emil 32
Miranda 49
Miranda, Soledad 53, 190
Mirren, Helen 122, 141, 143, 258, 294, 311
Misery 296
Mishima: A Life In Four Chapters 354
Mission Impossible 33
Mississippi Burning 296
Missouri Breaks, The 340
Mitchell, Millard 335
Mitchell, Thomas 244, 336, 346
Mitchum, Robert 284, 316, 324, 331, 333
Miu Ki Wai 187
Mobsters 175
Modine, Matthew 128, 321, 324
Mohner, Carl 327
Molina, Alfred 130
Mona Lisa 297
Mondo Topless 50
Monroe, Marilyn 164
Montalban, Ricardo 235, 274
Montand, Yves 353, 354
Monty Python And The Holy Grail 85
Monty Python's Flying Circus 310
Monty Python's Life Of Brian 86
Moody, Ron 231
Moon, Keith 235
Moon Lee 182
Moonstruck 247
Moore, Demi 109, 114, 115, 237, 244, 245
Moore, Dudley 66, 69, 70
Moore, Frank 212
Moore, Julianne 31, 44, 290, 300
Moorhead, Agnes 104
Moran, Nick 174
Moranis, Rick 80, 157, 158
More, Kenneth 327
Moreau, Jeanne 328, 352, 355
Moreno, Rita 234, 236
Morgan, Freeman 96
Moriarty, Cathy 130
Moriarty, Michael 341

INDEX

Morita, Noriyuki 'Pat' 159
Morley, Robert 14, 142, 162
Morricone, Andrea 351
Morris, Haviland 157
Morrissey, Paul 190
Morrow, Jo 153
Morrow, Vic 100, 166, 230
Morse, David 297
Mortensen, Viggo 17, 19, 115, 166, 286, 299, 300
Morton, Gary 121
Morton, Rocky 288
Mostel, Zero 89
Mower, Patrick 195
Mr Sardonicus 209
Mrs Brown 125
Mueller-Stahl, Armin 35, 133
Muhe, Ulrich 352
Mulcahy, Russell 26, 215
Mulligan, Robert 252
Muni, Paul 178
Muppets, The 307
Murakami, Rena 48
Murdock, Jack 131
Murphy, Eddie 13, 71, 78, 87, 92
Murphy, Geoff 349
Murphy, Michael 326
Murray, Bill 80, 81, 91, 111
Musker, John 57, 58, 61
Muti, Ornella 267
Mutiny On The Bounty 149
My Beautiful Laundrette 125
My Cousin Vinny 86
My Darling Clementine 340
My Left Foot 125
Myers, Cynthia 44
Myers, Mike 70, 93
Myers, Nancy 160
Myles, Bruce 105
Mysterious Island 62
Mystery Of The Wax Museum 209

Nagisa Oshima 43
Nail, Jimmy 90
Naismith, Laurence 327
Naked – As Nature Intended 50
Naked And The Dead, The 324
Naked Gun 86
Naked Killer 186
Naked Lunch 126
Name Of The Rose, The 126
Napier, Alan 63
Napier, Charles 36, 52, 175
Natali, Vincenzo 264
National Lampoon's Vacation 87
Natividad, Kitten 53
Naughton, David 188
Neal, Patricia 264
Neal, Tom 108
Neame, Ronald 35
Near Dark 209
Neeson, Liam 36, 101, 123, 132
Negotiator, The 297
Negulesco, Jean 225
Neill, Sam 29, 105, 118, 248
Neiuwenhuijs, Victor E 54
Nelligan, Kate 249
Nelson, Craig T 108, 211
Nelson, Judd 74, 100, 176
Nelson, Ralph 346
Nelson, Ricky 343
Nelson, Sean 96
Nero, Franco 224, 331, 332, 333, 338
Never Say Never Again 34
Neverending Story, The 160

New Jack City 176
New York, New York 231
Newell, Mike 167, 243
Newley, Anthony 225
Newman, Paul 83, 95, 103, 104, 105, 136, 304, 330, 338
Newmeyer, Julie 233
Newton, Thandie 116
Newton-John, Olivia 227
Ng, Carrie 186
Nichols, Mike 81, 88, 94, 129, 137, 219
Nicholson, Jack 16, 74, 93, 103, 111, 114, 128, 214, 219, 235, 239, 252, 269, 340, 345
Nico 353
Nicolodi, Daria 205
Nielsen, Leslie 86, 267
Night Moves 297
Night Of The Generals 324
Night Of The Living Dead 210
Nightwatch 298
Nighy, Bill 90
Nikita 355
Nil By Mouth 126
Nimoy, Leonard 268, 274, 275
Niven, David 139, 246, 255, 322
No Way Out 298
Nobuko Otowa 355
Nogulich, Natalija 290
Noiret, Philippe 351
Nolte, Nick 13, 285
Noonan, Chris 154
Noonan, Tom 295
Norman, Leslie 323
Norman, Zack 37
Norrington, Stephen 17
North By Northwest 298
North, Sheree 207
Northam, Jeremy 269
Norton, Edward 299
Nosferatu The Vampyre 210
Nouri, Michael 226
Novak, Gilla 46
Novak, Kim 122, 231, 304
Noyce, Philip 18, 34
Nureyev, Rudolph 253
Nutty Professor, The 87

O'Brian, Hugh 345
O'Brien, Donald 338
O'Brien, Edmond 244, 287, 348
O'Brien, Richard 233
O'Connell, Eddie 221
O'Connor, Carrol 299, 323
O'Connor, Donald 234
O'Connor, Hazel 222
O'Dea, Judith 210
O'Donnell, Chris 16, 103, 250
O'Donnell, Rosie 250
O'Hara, Catherine 157
O'Hara, Maureen 118, 244, 343
O'Hara, Paige 58
O'Herlihy, Dan 113, 272
O'Herne, Peter 70
O'Malley, J Pat 56
O'Neal, Patrick 242
O'Neal, Ron 176
O'Neill, Amy 157
O'Neil, Lawrence 101
O'Neill, Jennifer 252, 343
O'Quinn, Terry 278
O'Shea, Milo 250, 261
O'Sullivan, Maureen 76
O'Toole, Annette 13
O'Toole, Peter 93, 140, 141, 147, 148, 149, 324

TOP 1000 VIDEOS

Oates, Warren 17, 165, 291, 345, 348
Oberon, Merle 255
Occhipinti, Andrea 49
Odd Couple, The 87
Of Mice And Men 127
Officer And A Gentleman, An 247
Ogata, Ken 354
Ogilvie, George 32
Ogilvy, Ian 218
Oldman, Gary 14, 31, 119, 126, 130, 134, 179, 191, 266, 293
Oliver! 231
Oliver, Barrett 160
Olivier, Laurence 101, 147, 151, 255, 283, 296, 302, 316
Olmos, Edward James 219
Omega Man, The 270
On Golden Pond 127
On The Waterfront 127
Once Upon A Time In America 176
Once Upon A Time In The West 340
One Flew Over The Cuckoo's Nest 128
One Million Years BC 62
One-Armed Boxer 186
One-Eyed Jacks 341
Onibaba 355
Only Fools And Horses 310
Opposite Sex, The 87
Orgy Of The Dead 50
Original Gangstas 176
Ormond, Julia 121
Osborne, John 290
Ouimet, Daniele 194
Ouspenskaya, Maria 219
Out Of Africa 247
Outbreak 34
Outland 270
Outlaw Josey Wales, The 341
Oz, Frank 77

π 270
Pacific Heights 128
Pacino, Al 20, 108, 109, 121, 166, 167, 169, 170, 178, 250, 286, 301
Page, Genevieve 351
Page, Harrison 54
Paige, Janis 233
Paint Your Wagon 231
Pakula, Alan J 96, 130, 293
Pal, George 277
Pal Joey 231
Palance, Jack 16, 76, 140, 331, 344, 349
Pale Rider 341
Palin, Michael 68, 80, 85, 86, 310
Pallenberg, Anita 129, 261
Palmer, Geoffrey 125
Palmer, Lilli 283
Palminteri, Chazz 137
Paltrow, Gwyneth 132, 250, 251, 299
Paluzzi, Luciana 40
Papas, Irene 238
Papillon 34
Pappaert, Nelly 354
Paquin, Anna 156, 248
Parello, Chuck 117
Parent Trap, The 160
Parfrey, Woodrow 34
Parillaud, Anne 355
Park, Reg 146
Parker, Alan 124, 189, 224, 226, 232, 296
Parker, Eleanor 122, 234
Parker, Mary Louise 115
Parker, Sarah Jessica 111
Parks, Gordon 178

Parson, Beatrice 168
Parsons, Estelle 165
Pasco, Richard 212
Pascual, Cristina S 46
Pasdar, Adrian 209
Passage To India, A 128
Pastell, George 215
Pat Garrett And Billy The Kid 342
Patch Adams 88
Patinkin, Mandy 160
Patric, Jason 39, 207, 302, 335
Patrick, Robert 40
Patriot Games 34
Patton 325
Patton, Bart 195
Paxton, Bill 41, 97, 135, 159, 209, 259, 346
Payback 298
Payne, Laurence 217
Peacemaker, The 35
Pearce, Lennard 310
Peck, Gregory 249, 283, 284, 322, 330, 335
Peckinpah, Sam 29, 165, 168, 319, 329, 342, 343, 348
Peeping Tom 211
Penn, Arthur 165, 297, 338, 340
Penn, Chris 178, 341
Penn, Sean 107, 166, 167, 179, 319, 327
People vs Larry Flynt, The 129
Peppard, George 317
Perdita Durango 299
Perez, Rosie 93, 299
Perez, Vincent 352
Perfect Murder, A 299
Performance 129
Perier, Francois 173
Perkins, Anthony 45, 212, 338
Perkins, Elizabeth 154, 237
Perkins, Millie 345
Perlman, Rhea 159
Perlman, Ron 126, 193, 260, 351
Perrine, Valerie 121
Perry, Matthew 310
Perschy, Maria 315
Persky, Lisa Jane 254
Persoff, Nehemiah 57, 164
Pertwee, Sean 215
Pesci, Joe 30, 86, 119, 130, 157, 167, 170
Peter Sellers 89
Petersen, William 295, 349
Petersen, Wolfgang 14, 34, 160, 266, 292, 318
Petrelli, Marcella 47
Petroni, Giulio 332
Pettet, Joanna 324
Petty, Lori 156, 176
Peyton Place 247
Pfeiffer, Michelle 16, 93, 106, 178, 219, 238, 245
Philadelphia 129
Phillips, Lou Diamond 105, 349
Phillips, Michelle 253
Phoenix, Joaquin 91, 280
Piano, The 248
Picasso, Paloma 49
Piccoli, Michel 351, 352
Pickens, Slim 78, 168, 342
Pickles, Wilfred 72
Picon, Molly 226
Pidgeon, Walter 98, 118, 227, 267
π 270
Pierce, Bradley 158
Pierro, Marina 43
Pilgaard, Ulf 298
Pink Floyd – The Wall 232
Pinkett, Jada 87, 214
Pinocchio 62
Pintauro, Danny 286

INDEX

Pistilli, Luigi 332
Pitt, Brad 121, 123, 132, 133, 179, 206, 257, 293, 302
Pitt, Ingrid 218
Placido, Michelle 43
Plan 9 From Outer Space 271
Planet Of The Apes 271
Plank, Scott 172
Platoon 325
Pleasence, Donald 24, 146, 203, 266, 276, 278, 322, 333, 346
Pleshette, Suzanne 281
Plummer, Christopher 57, 144, 152, 219, 234, 251
Pocahontas 62
Poelvoorde, Benoit 354
Point Blank 299
Point Break 176
Poitier, Sidney 27, 99, 100, 107, 291
Polanski, Roman 103, 149, 190, 199, 213, 252, 300
Pollack, Sydney 91, 95, 247, 337
Pollard, Michael J 165
Polonsky, Abraham 168
Poltergeist 211
Pop, Iggy 224
Porter, Eric 287
Portman, Eric 319
Portman, Natalie 293
Poseidon Adventure, The 35
Post, Ted 335
Postcards From The Edge 129
Postlethwaite, Peter 31, 96, 118, 137
Potter, Terry 70
Potts, Annie 45
Pouget, Ely 172
Powell, Dick 98
Powell, Jane 233
Powell, Michael 161, 211, 246
Power, Tyrone 32, 239, 337
Powers, Alexandra 173
Predator 35
Preminger, Otto 122, 327
Presley, Elvis 222, 230
Presley, Priscilla 86
Presnell, Harve 113, 231
Pressburger, Emeric 246
Preston, Kelly 83, 92
Presumed Innocent 130
Pretty Baby 248
Pretty In Pink 248
Pretty Woman 249
Price, Dennis 53, 84
Price, Vincent 58, 75, 156, 216, 218
Prick Up Your Ears 130
Pride And Prejudice 311
Primal Fear 299
Primary Colors 88
Prime Suspect 311
Prince 232
Princess Bride, The 160
Prinz, Freddie, Jnr 291
Prisoner Of Zenda, The 35
Private Benjamin 88
Private Parts 88
Prochnow, Jurgen 318
Procter, Emily 101
Producers, The 89
Project A 186
Prosky, Robert 107, 242
Proval, David 174
Prowse, Juliet 224
Proyas, Alex 193
Pryce, Jonathan 40, 222, 262, 301
Psycho (1960) 212
Psycho (1998) 212
Public Enemy, The 177

Pullman, Bill 237, 250, 251, 268
Pulp Fiction 177
Purgatory 342
Purple Rain 232
Pyriev, Eric 147

Quadrophenia 232
Quaid, Dennis 129, 150, 155, 158, 160, 266, 288, 339, 348
Quaid, Randy 87, 124, 268, 339, 340, 342
Quarshie, Hugh 26, 192
Quatermass And The Pit 272
Quayle, Anna 48
Quayle, Anthony 148, 238, 323
Quill, Tim 323
Quinn, Aidan 121, 208
Quinn, Anthony 140, 148, 170, 175, 322
Quivers, Robin 88
Quiz Show 130
Quo Vadis 150

Rabid 212
Raft, George 178
Raging Bull 130
Raiders Of The Lost Ark 36
Railway Children, The 160
Raimi, Sam 198
Rain, Douglas 257
Rain Man 131
Rains, Claude 13, 38, 102, 148, 219
Raising Cain 300
Rambo: First Blood Part 2 36
Rambo 3 36
Ramis, Harold 81, 87
Rampling, Charlotte 146, 189, 278, 288
Randall, Tony 84
Ransom 300
Rappeneau, Jean-Paul 352
Rash, Steve 223
Rasputin The Mad Monk 212
Rathbone, Basil 13, 18, 32, 75
Ratner, Brett 37
Raven, Stark 51
Ray, Aldo 324
Ray, Gene Anthony 226
Ray, Nicholas 139, 350
Rea, Stephen 90, 106, 123
Read, Dolly 44
Red Dawn 325
Red River 342
Redford, Robert 96, 118, 130, 244, 245, 247, 284, 330, 337
Redgrave, Jemma 66
Redgrave, Lynn 90, 133
Redgrave, Michael 83, 320
Redgrave, Vanessa 108, 130, 138, 224, 265
Reed, Carol 231, 303
Reed, Donna 115
Reed, Oliver 108, 191, 231, 235, 240, 255
Reeve, Christopher 39, 131, 251
Reeves, Keanu 38, 72, 106, 108, 176, 191
Reeves, Michael 218
Reicher, Frank 60
Reid, Beryl 79
Reilly, William 175
Rein, Adele 45
Reiner, Carl 77
Reiner, Rob 90, 114, 160, 238, 254, 296
Reinhold, Judge 71, 81, 304
Reisz, Karel 243
Reitherman, Wolfgang 56, 63
Reitman, Ivan 38, 80, 92
Remains Of The Day 131
Remar, James 13, 110

377

Rennie, Michael 143, 150, 264
Reno, Jean 99, 293, 301, 355
Repulsion 300
Reservoir Dogs 178
Return Of Martin Guerre, The 355
Return Of The Jedi 272
Reversal Of Fortune 131
Rey, Fernando 331
Reynolds, Burt 20, 44, 179
Reynolds, Debbie 234, 235
Rhames, Ving 18, 290
Rhys-Davies, John 36
Ricci, Christina 87
Richard, Cliff 225
Richard Gere 96
Richards, Denise 276
Richardson, Ian 46
Richardson, John 62, 208
Richardson, Miranda 106, 112, 309
Richardson, Natasha 160, 203
Richardson, Ralph 145, 147, 273
Richardson, Tony 142
Richter, Jason James 156
Richwine, Maria 223
Rickman, Alan 21, 73, 123
Ride The High Country 343
Ridgely, John 281
Rifkin, Ron 297
Rigg, Diana 216, 311
Right Stuff, The 150
Ring Of Bright Water 161
Ringwald, Molly 74, 248
Rio Bravo 343
Rio Grande 343
Rio Lobo 343
Ritchie, Guy 174
Ritt, Martin 251
Ritter, Thelma 100, 225
Rivera, Cecilia 350
Rivera, Chita 235
Roach, Jay 70
Rob Roy 36
Robards, Jason 96, 129, 328, 329, 340
Robbins, Jerome 236
Robbins, Tim 73, 83, 107, 133
Robe, The 150
Roberts, Eric 342
Roberts, Julia 123, 134, 249, 288
Roberts, Steve 89
Roberts, Tony 69
Robertson, Cliff 315, 324
Robinson, Amy 174
Robinson, Andrew 204
Robinson, Andy 21
Robinson, Ann 277
Robinson, Bruce 90, 94, 293
Robinson, Edward G 104, 139, 171, 173, 273
Robinson, Philip Alden 115
Robinson, Tony 309
Robocop 272
Robson, Flora 38, 139, 255
Robson, Mark 247, 328
Robson, Wayne 264
Rock, Chris 30
Rock, The 37
Rocky 132
Rocky Horror Picture Show, The 233
Roddam, Franc 232
Roeg, Nicolas 129, 196, 240
Röeves, Maurice 148
Rogers, Mimi 31, 70, 109
Rojo, Helena 350
Roland, Gilbert 98
Rolfe, Guy 209, 215

Rollerball 273
Rollin, Jean 207
Roman Holiday 249
Roman, Susan 212
Romancing The Stone 37
Romantic Englishwoman, The 249
Romay, Lina 200
Romeo And Juliet 250
Romero, George A 210
Ronin 300
Rooker, Michael 18, 117, 119, 301
Rooney, Mickey 235
Root, Amanda 58
Rosemary's Baby 213
Rosenberg, Stuart 105, 284
Rosier, Cathy 173
Ross, Don 87
Ross, Katherine 81, 330
Ross, Ted 69
Rossati, Nello 333
Rossellini, Isabella 77, 282
Rossi, Leo 95
Rossington, Norman 229
Rossiter, Leonard 74, 257, 309
Rossitto, Angelo 32
Roth, Lillian 68
Roth, Tim 36, 116, 177, 178
Roundtree, Richard 176, 178, 207
Rourke, Mickey 43, 100, 180, 189
Rowlands, Gena 118
Rubinstein, Zelda 211
Ruggiero, Anthony 164
Run Silent, Run Deep 325
Running Man, The 37
Rush, Geoffrey 112, 133, 250
Rush Hour 37
Russell, David O 51
Russell, Ken 45, 54, 108, 203, 222, 235, 253, 255, 260
Russell, Kurt 24, 97, 216, 346
Russell, Rosalind 228
Russell, Theresa 54
Russo, James 106
Russo, Rene 30, 34, 91, 168, 292, 300
Ryan, Meg 57, 105, 109, 158, 204, 250, 254, 255, 288
Ryan, Mitchell 336
Ryan, Robert 98, 317, 321, 324, 348
Rydell, Mark 127, 242, 294
Ryder, Winona 71, 82, 121, 156, 191, 238, 260

Saad, Margit 167
Sabella, Ernie 61
Sabu 161
Sachs, Andrew 309
Sagal, Boris 270
Saint, Eva Marie 127, 298
Saito, James 161
Sakata, Harold 26
Saks, Gene 87
Saldana, Theresa 130
Salvador 326
Sammo Hung 183, 184, 185, 186
Samperi, Salvatore 46
Samples, Candy 53
Sampson, Will 128
Samson And Delilah 150
Samuel, Joanne 31
San Martin, Conrado 189
Sanders, George 89, 150, 151, 158, 289
Sandler, Adam 253
Sands, Julian 120, 126, 189, 203
Sands Of Iwo Jima 326
Sandweiss, Ellen 198
Sanjay 54
Santoni, Reni 21, 77

INDEX

Sara, Mia 29
Sarafian, Deran 39
Sarandon, Chris 64
Sarandon, Susan 59, 93, 107, 134, 205, 233, 248, 254, 304
Satana, Tura 49
Satan's Return 186
Saturday Night Fever 233
Saunders, Jennifer 309
Savage, Ann 108
Savage, John 229, 320, 326
Savalas, Telly 321
Savelyeva, Ludmila 152
Saving Private Ryan 326
Savoy, Teresa Ann 141
Sawalha, Julia 309
Saxon, John 183
Sayles, John 121
Scacchi, Greta 130
Scales, Prunella 309
Scandalous Gilda 50
Scarborough, Adrian 122
Scarface (1932) 178
Scarface (1983) 178
Scarlet Pimpernel, The 312
Scent Of A Woman 250
Schaffner, Franklin J 34, 271, 283, 325
Scheider, Roy 17, 28, 126, 221, 258, 293, 296
Schell, Maximilian 265, 319
Schepisi, Fred 105
Schindler's List 132
Schlesinger, John 72, 124, 128, 296
Schnabel, Julian 98
Schneider, Sophie 51
Schoedsack, Ernest 60
Schrader, Paul 96, 354
Schroeder, Barbet 131, 301
Schultz, Harry 197
Schumacher, Joel 16, 113, 135, 207, 280, 288
Schwarzenegger, Arnold 16, 19, 35, 37, 39, 40, 41, 92, 277
Schwimmer, David 101, 310
Sciorra, Annabella 131, 188, 254, 290
Scob, Edith 199
Scofield, Paul 130, 146, 149, 328
Scorsese, Martin 84, 104, 130, 148, 167, 170, 174, 231, 238, 285, 303
Scorupco, Isabella 25
Scott, Dougray 91
Scott, George C 78, 325, 327
Scott, Randolph 337, 343
Scott, Ridley 29, 115, 165, 259, 262
Scott, Tony 41, 179, 205, 286, 288
Scream 213
Scream 2 214
Se7en 132
Sea Hawk, The 38
Sea Of Love 301
Searchers, The 344
Seberg, Jean 231
Sect, The 213
Segal, George 137, 242
Selick, Henry 59, 64
Selleck, Tom 285
Sellers, Peter 78, 93
Sena, Dominic 293
Sergeant York 327
Sessue Hayakawa 318
Seth, Roshan 125
Se7en 132
Seven Brides For Seven Brothers 233
Seven Years In Tibet 133
Seventh Curse, The 187
Sevigny, Chloe 136

Sewell, Rufus 46
Sex And Zen II 187
Sex Pistols, The 228
Sexual Life Of The Belgians, The 51
Seyferth, Maartje 54
Seyler, Athene 194
Seymour, Jane 251
Seyrig, Delphine 194
Shadrach 133
Shadyac, Tom 66, 87, 88
Shaft 178
Shakespeare In Love 250
Shakur, Tupac 116
Shane 344
Sharif, Omar 143, 145, 148, 227, 324
Sharky's Machine 179
Sharman, Jim 233
Sharp, Don 212
Sharpe 312
Sharpsteen, Ben 59, 62
Shatner, William 274, 275
Shatter Dead 51
Shaw, Fiona 125
Shaw, Martin 149, 311
Shaw, Robert 28, 149, 316, 317
Shawn, Dick 85, 89
Shawn, Wallace 130
Shawshank Redemption 133
Shearer, Harry 90
Shearer, Moira 211
Sheedy, Ally 74
Sheen, Charlie 39, 82, 137, 325, 349
Sheen, Martin 133, 145, 238, 287, 316
Shelley, Barbara 197, 212, 272
Shelton, Deborah 283
Shelton, Ron 91, 93
Shenar, Paul 99
Shenkman, Ben 270
Shepard, Sam 150, 342
Shepherd, Cybill 303
Sher, Anthony 125
Sheridan, Dinah 160
Sheridan, Jim 114, 118, 125
Sherlock Holmes 312
Sherwood, Bobby 231
Shields, Brooke 239, 248
Shine 133
Shining, The 214
Shire, Talia 132
Shirley, Bill 63
Shooting, The 345
Shootist, The 345
Short Film About Killing, A 355
Short, Martin 158
Shot In The Dark, A 89
Showgirls 51
Shu Qi 187
Shue, Elisabeth 159
Siberling, Brad 241
Sid And Nancy 134
Sidney, George 231
Siege, The 38
Siegel, Don 21, 288, 345
Siemaszko, Casey 127
Signoret, Simone 353
Silence Of The Lambs, The 301
Silk Stockings 233
Silva, Maria 216
Silva, Rita 47
Silver, Fawn 50
Silver, Joe 212
Silver, Ron 100, 131, 282
Silvers, Phil 83
Silverstone, Alicia 16

379

Simmons, Jean 112, 150, 151, 330
Simon, Michel 44
Simon, Paul 69
Simpson, O.J. 86
Simpsons, The 308
Sims, Sylvia 323
Sinatra, Frank 115, 122, 224, 230, 231, 235, 295, 328
Sinden, Donald 287
Singer, Bryan 137
Singer, Steve 280
Singin' In The Rain 234
Single White Female 301
Singleton, John 101
Sinise, Gary 97, 127, 243, 300, 302
Sink The Bismarck 327
Sinn, Nikki 47
Sir Henry At Rawlinson End 89
Six Days, Seven Nights 38
Sizemore, Tom 326
Skala, Lilia 226, 290
Skarsgard, Stellan 301
Skerritt, Tom 41, 259, 264
Slater, Christian 17, 82, 126, 175, 179, 206, 349
Slater, Helen 76
Sleepers 302
Sleeping Beauty 63
Sleepless In Seattle 250
Sleuth 302
Sliding Doors 251
Sloane, Everett 104
Slums Of Beverly Hills 89
Small Soldiers 63
Smight, Jack 268, 316
Smiley's People 312
Smith, Charles Martin 67, 223, 276
Smith, Gregory 63
Smith, Will 268, 269, 288
Smoke 134
Snake Eyes 302
Snake In The Eagle's Shadow 187
Snipes, Wesley 17, 20, 22, 93, 172, 176
Snodgress, Carrie 202, 341
Soavi, Michele 192, 213
Solaris 273
Soldier Blue 346
Soles, PJ 203
Solima, Sergio 333
Solomon And Sheba 151
Solonitsyn, Anatoly 274
Somewhere In Time 251
Sommer, Elke 89
Sommersby 251
Sondergaard, Gale 32
Sonnenfeld, Barry 67, 168, 269
Sorel, Jean 351
Sorenson, Ricky 63
Sorvino, Mira 269
Sorvino, Paul 20, 170, 286
Sound Of Music, The 234
South Park 308
Soylent Green 273
Spacek, Sissy 119
Spacey, Kevin 59, 120, 121, 124, 132, 135, 137, 297
Spader, James 45, 219, 254
Spain, Fay 146, 164
Spall, Timothy 90, 203
Spanking The Monkey 51
Spartacus 151
Spector, Phil 111
Speed 38
Speed 2 – Cruise Control 39
Spence, Bruce 32
Spencer, John 297
Spheeris, Penelope 93

Sphere 273
Spielberg, Steven 27, 28, 29, 31, 36, 66, 96, 105, 112, 132, 263, 266, 326
Spinell, Joe 286, 303
Spiner, Brent 275
Spirits Of The Dead 214
Spottiswoode, Roger 40
St James, Susan 85
Stack, Robert 67
Stagecoach 346
Stalag 17 327
Stalker 274
Stallone, Sylvester 18, 19, 20, 25, 36, 58, 132, 166, 285
Stamp, Terence 137, 214, 349
Stander, Lionel 231
Stanley And Iris 251
Stanshall, Vivian 89
Stanton, Harry Dean 148, 248
Star Is Born, A 234
Star Trek (TV) 313–315
Star Trek – The Motion Picture 274
Star Trek II – The Wrath Of Khan 274
Star Trek III – The Search For Spock 274
Star Trek IV – The Voyage Home 275
Star Trek V – The Final Frontier 275
Star Trek – First Contact 275
Star Trek – Insurrection 275
Star Wars 276
Starman 276
Starr, Ringo 235
Starship Troopers 276
State Of Grace 179
Statham, Jason 174
Steele, Barbara 208, 216, 248
Steenburgen, Mary 15, 129
Steffen, Anthony 332
Steiger, Rod 127, 143, 144, 152, 164, 175, 268, 291, 324
Stephens, Robert 250
Stepmom 134
Stern, Daniel 157
Stern, Howard 88
Sternhagen, Frances 270, 296, 300
Stevens, George 344
Stevens, Inger 335
Stevens, Stella 329
Stevenson, Robert 158, 159
Stewart, Elaine 223
Stewart, James 82, 304, 337, 339, 345
Stewart, Patrick 275
Still Crazy 90
Stiller, Ben 75, 90
Sting 174, 232, 265
Stock, Nigel 320
Stockwell, Dean 14, 265, 282
Stokowski, Leopold 59
Stoltz, Eric 324
Stone, Christopher 286
Stone, Oliver 109, 119, 137, 318, 325, 326
Stone, Sharon 58, 167, 273, 277, 281
Stormare, Peter 113, 280
Stowe, Madeleine 148, 257
Strange Days 52
Stranglers Of Bombay, The 215
Strassman, Marcia 157, 158
Strauss, Peter 346
Strayer, Frank 217
Streep, Meryl 77, 105, 129, 240, 241, 243, 247, 320
Streisand, Barbra 227, 230
Stribling, Melissa 196
Stride, John 149
Strike! 90
Strode, Woody 338, 339

INDEX

Stroemburg, Ewa 53
Strong, Michael 325
Strong, Samantha 47
Stroud, Don 223
Stuart, Gloria 135
Studi, Wes 148, 335
Sturges, John 98, 322, 339
Styron, Susanna 133
Sullivan, Barry 98
Summer of '42 252
Superman – The Movie 39
Supervixens 52
Suspiria 215
Sutherland, Donald 34, 97, 109, 119, 135, 196, 268, 293, 321, 323
Sutherland, Kiefer 114, 135, 207, 288, 349
Sutton, Dudley 108
Swayze, Patrick 176, 244, 325
Sweet Charity 235
Sweet Smell Of Success, The 134
Swinton, Tilda 122
Swiss Family Robinson 161
Sword In The Stone, The 63
Syms, Sylvia 46, 225
Szabo, Istvan 354
Szwarc, Jeannot 251

Takahiro Tamura 43, 328
Takakura, Ken 165
Talos The Mummy 215
Tamahorn, Lee 23
Tamblyn, Russ 204, 233, 236, 247
Tamerlis, Zoe 280
Tamiroff, Akim 260
Tandem 53
Tandy, Jessica 78, 115, 263, 281, 320
Taps 327
Tarantino, Quentin 171, 177, 178, 202
Tarita 149
Tarkovsky, Andrei 273, 274
Tate, Sharon 199
Tatsuya Fuji 43
Taurog, Norman 222
Taxi Driver 303
Taylor, Christine 253
Taylor, Deems 59
Taylor, Don 327
Taylor, Elizabeth 103, 137, 142
Taylor, Ginny 63
Taylor, Jack 200
Taylor, Lili 188
Taylor, Robert 150
Taylor, Rod 56, 277, 281
Taylor-Young, Leigh 273
Teague, Lewis 28, 286
Teenage Mutant Ninja Turtles 161
Teletubbies 308
Temple, Julien 221, 228
Tender Mercies 252
Terminal Velocity 39
Terminator 2: Judgement Day 40
Terminator, The 39
Termo, Leonard 180
Terms Of Endearment 252
Terror Of Dr Hichcock, The 216
Terry, Nigel 143
Terry-Thomas 83, 162
Tesarz, Jan 355
Tess 252
Thatcher, Torin 56, 246
That'll Be The Day 235
That's Entertainment 235
Thaw, John 106, 311
Theatre of Blood 216

There's Something About Mary 90
Theron, Charlize 108, 159
Thewlis, David 59, 77, 133, 155, 206
Thibeau, Jack 280
Thief Of Bagdad 161
Thing, The 216
Third Man, The 303
Thiry, Raymond 54
This Is Spinal Tap 90
This Year's Love 91
Thomas, Betty 78, 88
Thomas, Henry 266
Thomas, Jonathan Taylor 153
Thomas, Kristin Scott 112, 118, 243
Thomas, Terry 83, 162
Thompson, Emma 88, 118, 131, 146
Thompson, J Lee 284, 322, 323
Thompson, Jack 25, 124
Thompson, Lea 15
Thorn, Frankie 164
Thorne, Angela 58
Thornton, Billy Bob 88, 261
Thorpe, Richard 35
Thorson, Linda 311
Those Magnificent Men In Their Flying Machines 162
Thring, Frank 32
Throne Of Blood 151
Thunderball 40
Thurman, Uma 16, 106, 177, 293
Thuy Thu Le 319
THX 1138 276
Ticotin, Rachel 18, 277
Tien, James 184
Tierney, Lawrence 178
Tigers, The 187
Tim Burton's The Nightmare Before Christmas 64
Time Machine, The 277
Time To Kill, A 135
Tin Cup 91
Tingwell, Charles 105
Titanic 135
To Die For 91
Todd, Cesar 47
Todd, Richard 320, 323
Tom Clancy's Netforce 304
Tombs Of The Blind Dead 216
Tombstone 346
Tomei, Marisa 86, 89
Tomelty, Frances 114
Tomlinson, David 159
Tommy 235
Tomorrow Never Dies 40
Tootsie 91
Top Gun 41
Topol 226, 267
Topor, Roland 210
Tora! Tora! Tora! 328
Torn, Rip 104, 269
Tornatore, Giuseppe 351
Toshiki Sato 53
Toshiro Mifune 151, 316
Total Recall 277
Tourneur, Jacques 194
Towering Inferno, The 136
Towers, Constance 337
Towles, Tom 117
Toy Story 64
Tracey, Spencer 337
Tracy, Spencer 83, 98, 147
Trading Places 92
Train, The 328
Trainspotting 136
Travers, Bill 154, 161

381

Travis, Nancy 292
Travolta, John 17, 24, 88, 168, 177, 227, 233, 282
Trees Lounge 136
Trevor, Claire 171, 346
Trintignant, Jean Louis 351
Tripplehorn, Jeanne 251, 281
Trousdale, Gary 58
True Grit 346
True Lies 41
True Romance 179
Truffaut, Francois 263
Truman Show, The 136
Tsang, Eric 187
Tsui, Elvis 187
Tucci, Stanley 71, 175
Tuchner, Michael 180
Tucker, Anand 117
Tucker, Chris 37, 266
Tucker, Forrest 326, 330
Tudor-Pole, Edward 134
Tune, Tommy 222
Tung Tuanh Tran 80
Turner, Kathleen 28, 37, 45, 92, 100, 237
Turner, Lana 98, 247
Turner, Tina 32, 235
Turney, Michael 161
Turturro, John 98, 104, 109, 130, 175
Tutin, Dorothy 142
Twiggy 222
Twilight 304
Twins 92
Twister 41
Tyler, Liv 261
Tyson, Cathy 297

Ulmer, Edgar G 108
Uncle Buck 92
Underwood, Ron 76, 159
Unforgiven 347
Unger, Deborah 45
Untouchables, The 180
Up! 53
Urban Legend 217
Ure, Mary 328
Ustinov, Peter 150, 151, 268
Usual Suspects, The 137

Vaccaro, Brenda 124
Vadim, Roger 214, 261, 351
Valentine, Anthony 129
Valentino 253
Valli, Alida 199, 205, 215, 303
Valli, Romolo 144
Vallone, Raf 27
Vampira 271
Vampire Bat, The 217
Vampire Circus 217
Vampyros Lesbos 53
Van Cleef, Lee 24, 332, 335, 335, 336
Van Der Ven, Anne 54
Van Dien, Casper 276
Van Dyke, Dick 154, 159
Van Fleet, Jo 110
Van Lee, Ron 182
Van Pallandt, Nina 96, 294
Van Peebles, Mario 176
Van Sant, Gus 91, 110, 116, 300
Van Sloan, Edward 196, 201
Vanel, Charles 353
Vaughan, Vince 300
Vaughn, Robert 284, 339
Vega, Isela 165
Veidt, Conrad 161
Venora, Diane 27, 219

Ventura, Jesse 35
Venus In Furs 54
Verhoeven, Paul 25, 51, 272, 276, 277, 281
Vernon, Howard 189, 260
Vernon, John 21, 68, 341
Vertigo 304
Vesely, Herbert 47
Vidal, Gore 73
Videodrome 217
Vidor, King 151, 152
Vidovic, Ivica 54
Vigne, Daniel 355
Vikings, The 151
Villain 180
Vincent, Jan-Michael 99
Viva 124
Vixen 54
Voight, Jon 14, 20, 33, 124, 168, 170, 241
Volonte, Gian-Maria 330, 333, 335
Von Ryan's Express 328
Von Sydow, Max 19, 34, 81, 198, 254, 265, 267
Von Trier, Lars 101

Wade, Russell 283
Wadleigh, Michael 219
Waggner, George 219
Wagner, Lori 141
Wahlberg, Mark 44
Waise Lee 183
Walcott, Gregory 271
Waldau, Nikolaj 298
Walken, Christopher 16, 22, 58, 98, 172, 173, 177, 179, 188, 287, 320, 336
Walker, Kim 82
Wall Street 137
Wallace, Dee 205, 266, 286
Wallace, Paul 228
Wallace, Vincente 54
Wallach, Eli 145, 149, 169, 335, 339
Wallis, Shani 231
Walsh, J.T. 297
Walsh, Kate 117
Walsh, M Emmet 135, 281, 284
Walsh, Raoul 29
Walt Disney 308
Walters, Charles 230
Walters, Julie 79, 130
Walters, Nancy 222
Walters, Thorley 217
Wanamaker, Sam 167
Wang, George 185
Wang, Wayne 134
Wang Yu 186
Wang Yu, Jimmy 185
War And Peace (1956) 152
War And Peace (1967) 152
War Of The Roses, The 92
War Of The Worlds 277
Ward, Fred 175
Ward, Rachel 77, 179
Ward, Sela 289
Ward, Simon 201
Ward, Vincent 254
Warden, Jack 96, 325
Warner, David 135, 243, 275, 319, 329
Warner Brothers 308
Warren, Jennifer 297
Washbourne, Mona 72
Washington, Denzel 38, 105, 106, 129, 286, 322
Wasson, Craig 283
Waterloo 152
Waters, John 224
Waterston, Sam 120, 244
Watson, Alberta 51

INDEX

Watson, Emily 101, 117
Wayne, John 324, 326, 329, 330, 333, 334, 337, 339, 342, 343, 344, 345, 346
Wayne's World 93
Weathers, Carl 35
Weaver, Fritz 265
Weaver, Sigourney 80, 94, 116, 259, 260, 286
Webb, Alan 79
Webb, Chloe 92, 134
Webber, Robert 66, 88
Weber, Steven 301
Wedding Singer, The 253
Wei, Dick 187
Wei Pai 184
Weir, Peter 107, 136, 138, 321
Welch, Raquel 62, 70, 266
Weld, Tuesday 104
Weller, Peter 126, 272
Welles, Orson 104, 152, 303
Wellman, William 177
Wells, Vernon 32
Wenders, Wim 350
Wennemann, Klaus 318
Wernicke, Otto 353
West Side Story 236
West, Simon 18
Westworld 278
Whale, James 201
Whaley, Frank 109
What Dreams May Come 254
Whateley, Kevin 311
Whatham, Claude 235
What's New Pussycat? 93
Whelan, Tim 161
When Harry Met Sally 254
Where Eagles Dare 328
Whitaker, Forest 80, 106, 134
White, Harriet 216
White Men Can't Jump 93
White Palace 254
White Zombie 218
Whitehouse, Paul 310
Whitelaw, Billie 172
Whitfield, June 309
Whiting, Leonard 250
Whitman, Stuart 162
Whitmore, James 133, 164
Whittaker, Forest 118
Whitton, Margaret 43
Who Framed Roger Rabbit? 64
Whore 54
Who's Afraid Of Virginia Woolf? 137
Wicker Man, The 218
Wicki, Bernhard 324
Widerberg, Bo 352
Widmark, Richard 99, 285, 329
Wiest, Dianne 81, 118, 156, 207, 241
Wilcox, Fred M 267
Wild At Heart 254
Wild Bill 347
Wild Bunch, The 348
Wild, Jack 231
Wilde 138
Wilder, Billy 327
Wilder, Gene 73, 89, 94
Wilkinson, Tom 80
Williams, Edy 44
Williams, Jason 49
Williams, Jo Beth 22, 211
Williams, Lia 46
Williams, Lori 49
Williams, Michael 79
Williams, Michelle 203
Williams, Robin 57, 80, 88, 97, 107, 116, 158, 254

Williams, Treat 229
Williamson, Fred 166, 176
Williamson, Nicol 143
Willis, Bruce 21, 27, 33, 38, 77, 165, 173, 177, 257, 261, 266
Wills, Chill 329
Wilson, Dooley 102
Wilson, Georges 44
Wilson, Hugh 79
Wilson, Mara 159
Wilson, Richard 164
Wilson, Scott 107, 244, 291
Wilson, Stuart 33
Wilton, Penelope 106
Wincer, Simon 156
Wind In The Willows, The 162
Winfrey, Oprah 105
Winger, Debra 247, 252
Wingett, Mark 232
Winner, Michael 46
Winslet, Kate 135
Winstone, Ray 126
Winter, Alex 72
Winters, Shelley 35
Wise, Kirk 58
Wise, Robert 204, 234, 236, 264, 274, 283, 325
Wiseman, Joseph 22
Witches Of Eastwick, The 93
Witchfinder General 218
Withnail And I 94
Witness 138
Witt, Alicia 217
Wizard Of Oz, The 236
Wolf 219
Wolf Man, The 219
Wolfen 219
Wolfit, Donald 140, 148
Wolheim, Louis 315
Women In Love 255
Wong Lung Wei 48
Wong Tao 185
Wong, Victor 147
Woo, John 17, 24, 182, 183, 184, 185
Woo, Teresa 182
Wood, Edward D 271
Wood, Elijah 242, 265
Wood, Natalie 228, 236, 344
Wood, Sam 76
Woods, James 119, 167, 176, 217, 264, 297, 326
Woodward, Edward 218
Woolf, Emily 91
Working Girl 94
WR Mysteries Of The Organism 54
Wray, Fay 60, 209, 217
Wray, John 315
Wright, Jeffrey 98
Wright, Jenny 209
Wright, Robin 243
Wright, Teresa 251
Wuhl, Robert 80
Wuhrer, Kari 14
Wuthering Heights 255
Wyatt Earp 348
Wyler, William 140, 227, 249, 255, 330
Wymark, Patrick 218, 300, 328
Wyngarde, Peter 267
Wynn, Keenan 299
Wynter, Dana 327

X-Files (TV) 313
X-Files Movie, The 278
Xu Jin Jiang 187

Yam, Simon 183, 186

Yankee Doodle Dandy 236
Yasosuke Bando 354
Yates, Peter 284
Year Of The Dragon 180
Yeh, Sally 185
Yellen, Peter 280
Yen, Donnie 186
Yeoh, Michelle 40
Yi, Maria 184
Yitsuko Yoshimura 355
York, Michael 223, 268
York, Susannah 315
You Only Live Twice 278
Young, Alan 277
Young, Burt 29, 103, 120, 132, 176
Young, Diane 50
Young Frankenstein 94
Young, Gig 29, 165
Young Guns 349
Young Guns II 349
Young, Robert 217
Young, Sean 66, 137, 262, 298
Young, Sharon 182
Young, Stephen 325
Young, Terence 22, 40
You've Got Mail 255
Yuen Baio 183, 186
Yuen King Dan 186
Yuen Siu Tien 187

Zane, Billy 135, 324
Zardoz 278
Zeffirelli, Franco 250
Zellweger, Renee 83
Zemeckis, Robert 15, 37, 64, 77, 243, 264
Zerbe, Anthony 34, 270
Zeta-Jones, Catherine 33
Zieff, Howard 88
Ziehm, Howard 49
Zimbalist, Efrem, Jnr 82
Zinnemann, Fred 115, 149, 287, 336
Zombie Flesh Eaters 220
Zucco, George 244
Zucker, David 67, 86
Zucker, Jerry 67, 244
Zulu 152
Zurick, Edward 38
Zwick, Edward 105, 121, 237, 322